THE RIGHTS OF MAN
IN AMERICA

THE RIGHTS OF MAN
IN AMERICA

BY

THEODORE PARKER

EDITED WITH A PREFACE
BY
F. B. SANBORN

NEGRO UNIVERSITIES PRESS
NEW YORK

Originally published in 1911
by American Unitarian Association, Boston

Reprinted 1969 by
Negro Universities Press
A DIVISION OF GREENWOOD PUBLISHING CORP.
NEW YORK

SBN 8371-1723-2

PRINTED IN UNITED STATES OF AMERICA

EDITOR'S PREFACE

In editing this volume in the long series of Theodore Parker's writings, the present writer has some advantage over the editors of previous volumes. With two exceptions, Wentworth Higginson and Rufus Leighton, they had no special acquaintance with the man, Parker; their knowledge of him is derived from books or from hearsay; to some extent from his biographies. But I knew the man personally for six or eight years, and for most of that time was in close and often daily intimacy with him. After years of this intimacy, he selected me, one of the youngest of his hearers and associates, as his literary executor,— an office which circumstances elsewhere explained, forbade me to perform. When, therefore, I have heard him described with cool misunderstanding, or evident prejudice, I have had only to recur to the memory of my long association with him, to correct the false impressions thus conveyed by persons who never knew him. Especially is this true of his relation to the national sin and curse, negro slavery, against which every great and wise American protested by voice or example, and which no truly sagacious fellow-countryman ever defended for any length of time. Many good men apologized for it, some who, like Jefferson, portrayed with searching acuteness its evils and dangers, may afterwards have seemed to excuse it; but only because they could not see the way clearly to its abolition in their day.

With Parker the course of opinion and action, as with Emerson, was the reverse of this. Called, as both

these leaders of opinion were primarily, to other duties in the work of social reform, they were at first
averse to engaging warmly in a political contest.
Both were originally of the party which called itself
" Whig," and of which the leaders were John Quincy
Adams, Henry Clay, Daniel Webster and Abraham
Lincoln; and in Massachusetts this party declared
itself in 1838 (when Parker was a young and obscure
Unitarian pastor), as opposed to negro slavery, and
in favor of its removal by national legislation. This
fact has been forgotten or overlooked in the flood of
subsequent events, and the recession of some eminent
Whigs from the position then officially taken. But in
March, 1852, Henry Wilson, who in 1838 was one of
the younger Whigs, as Parker was, told the story in a
speech in the State Senate (replying to my old friend
Judge Warren), which is worth quoting: —

"In 1838 Judge Warren represented Bristol county
in this Senate. A series of resolutions was reported here
by James C. Alvord, declaring that Congress has (1)
the power to abolish slavery in the territories; (2) the
power to abolish the slave-trade in the District of Columbia, and ought to exercise that power; (3) the power
to abolish the slave-trade between the States, and ought
to exercise it; (4) the power to prevent the admission of
any more slave States, and to abolish slavery in the District, and ought to exercise both powers. Judge Warren himself moved the resolution for emancipation in the
District of Columbia, in the following words,—' That
Congress ought to take measures to effect the abolition
of slavery in the District of Columbia.' These resolutions, pledging Massachusetts and the Whig party to the
agitation of the slavery question were passed by the
unanimous vote of this Senate. Finding the Whig party
committed to the cause of liberty by these resolutions,

EDITOR'S PREFACE

I joined the ranks of that party, and voted with them in the election of 1838."

Wilson was then twenty-six, and Parker twenty-eight, and they voted together as Whigs. In 1852 they were still together as political anti-slavery men; while Warren, Webster, Choate and other party leaders had changed their ground entirely and were supporting the Fugitive Slave Law, and trying to suppress all discussion of slavery as a national sin. Parker, however, does not seem to have preached specifically against negro slavery until 1841, and in 1842 he declined, for special reasons, to join in the excitement occasioned by the effort to send Latimer, a fugitive slave, back into bondage. It was not that he hated slavery less, but that other questions interested him more. His anti-slavery life had four distinct phases,— the general disgust at slavery which most of the Massachusetts Whigs had, from 1838 to 1844,— the special opposition to Texas annexation and the Mexican War, from 1844 to 1850,— the movement against the execution of the Fugitive Slave Law from 1850 to 1855,— and finally, the movement to protect Kansas from the curse of slavery, to render Judge Taney's infamous Dred Scott decision inoperative, and to support John Brown's active warfare against slavery in Missouri and Virginia. The chapters in this volume, and in that edited by Mr. Hosmer, relate to all these phases of the great dispute, but particularly to the last three. Parker regarded the last stage of the fourth phase,— the John Brown warfare,— as the most important of all,— for he did not live to see the outbreak of the Civil War, except as commenced in its preliminary skirmishes in Kansas and Missouri. On all these phases I shall have something to say; having discussed them for years with Parker and his intimate friends, and heard them debated by others at his house in Exeter Place and elsewhere. Before commenting on particular chapters in this volume, a few general remarks should be made to correct false impressions and loose statements concerning Parker's position in the long warfare against slavery of which he predicted the end by emancipation, during the nineteenth century,— one of the few who ventured to make that confident prophecy before 1860.

Theodore Parker was never a disunionist; nor were John Brown, Gerrit Smith, Dr. Howe or the present writer. Their friends sometimes advocated disunion, as Garrison, Wendell Phillips, and for a short time Wentworth Higginson did. In writing to Higginson, who had signed a call for a meeting at Worcester to debate disunion, Parker thus declared himself (January 18, 1857):

"I am glad to see any sign of manhood in the North. But I do not myself desire a dissolution of the Union. The North is 17,000,000 strong, and the South contains 11,000,000, whereof four are slaves and four millions are 'poor whites.' I don't think it quite right for the powerful North to back out of the Union, and leave the 'poor whites' and the slaves to their present condition, with the ghastly consequences which are sure to follow. Men talk a great deal about the 'compromises of the Constitution,' but forget the *guarantees* of the Constitution. 'The United States shall guarantee a republican form of government to every State.' I would perform that obligation before I dissolved the Union. . . . But if you will make dissolution the basis of agitation, I think much good will come of it. I would say, Freedom shall take and keep (1) the land east of Chesapeake Bay; (2) all that is north of the Potomac and the Ohio,

— all that is west of the Mississippi, that is, the entire States of Missouri, Arkansas and Texas, with the part of Louisiana west of the Mississippi. I think the North will not be content with less than this; nay, I am not sure that, in case of actual separation, Virginia and Kentucky would not beg us to let the amputating knife go clear down to North Carolina and Tennessee and cut there; for I think there is too much freedom yet in the northernmost slave States, to consent to be left to perish with the general rot of the slave limbs."

In opposition to the Texas scheme to extend the area of slavery, and to the needless Mexican War, Webster and Parker were for some years side by side. I have seen the manuscript in Webster's own hand, which he wrote for the anti-Texas convention in January, 1845, and of which, in the speech just quoted, Henry Wilson renders this account:

" In the winter of 1845, when the Texas question was pending before Congress, a State convention was called in Faneuil Hall, without party distinction. Mr. Webster united in the convention with William Lloyd Garrison, Edward Quincy, Joshua Leavitt, Mr. Sewall, Charles Allen, John G. Palfrey, Stephen C. Phillips, Charles Francis Adams. Mr. Webster consulted with and assisted Stephen C. Phillips, Charles Allen and Charles Francis Adams, in preparing the address of convention — an address filled with noble sentiments of hostility to slavery domination. The day I left Boston for the Whig convention of 1848, I met in Court Street one of Mr. Webster's friends, who informed me that several of those friends were assembled in Mr. Webster's office and were anxious to see me. I accompanied him to the office where I found various members of the Webster Club, among them Mr. Burlingame and Mr. Webster's son. They wished to know what I and the ' conscience Whigs,' with whom I acted, intended to do. I told them I had written to Mr. Webster, that I could not vote for Mr. Webster if he used his influence directly or indirectly to aid Taylor's nomination. These gentlemen assured me that Mr. Webster had said that he 'would never recommend the people to support for President an ignorant, swearing, frontier colonel'—they assured me ' Mr. Webster was with us.'

"I left the office and went directly to Philadelphia where I found a note from Mr. Webster, giving me ample assurances. Having received assurance from Mr. Webster, I voted for him; although I knew then as now, that his chances were desperate.

"In 1848, Gen. Taylor was nominated as the Whig candidate for President on the 9th of June; on the 28th one of the largest conventions ever assembled in Massachusetts met at Worcester. There and then the organization of the Free-soil party was begun, and their principles were proclaimed. Many of Mr. Webster's friends attended — among them his son. They urged us to speak kindly of Mr. Webster, assuring us that he was with us. The convention expressed confidence in him, and called upon him to lead the friends of freedom. A few days after I called on Mr. Webster at his own request, at his office. He expressed his cordial assent to the principles of the convention, and said if we would make a public sentiment that would sustain public men in being true to the sentiments of the North, we should accomplish everything, for we had always been beaten by the treachery of Northern men."

There is no doubt that the events here related by Mr. Wilson did occur. I remember them well, as they were then reported in the newspapers; and it was believed for months that Webster would not support the nomination of Taylor, which he had declared to be " a nomination not fit to be made." Why he changed his mind may be matter of opinion and dispute; but

those at the time who knew Mr. Webster's habit of receiving money in connection with his political course,
had much reason to believe that it was in the interest
of his pocket and his political ambition that he added
his own example to the long list of what he called
" the treachery of Northern men."

Taylor was elected, but, contrary to the expectation
of his slaveholding supporters, he refused to be a
party to any schemes for disunion. The occasion is
well known, and the words of President Taylor have
been quoted by three persons to whom he uttered them,
— Hamlin of Maine, then a Democrat; Thurlow Weed
of New York, a Whig, and Gen. Pleasonton, an army
officer who had served under Taylor in Mexico.
The last-named called on his chief, then President,
late in June, 1850, when under orders to join the army
in New Mexico. Then followed these remarks by
Taylor:

" I am glad you are going to New Mexico; I want
officers of judgment and experience there. These Southern men in Congress are trying to bring on civil war.
They are now organizing a military force in Texas, for
the purpose of taking possession of New Mexico and annexing it to Texas. I have ordered the troops in New
Mexico to be reinforced, and have directed that no armed
force from Texas be permitted to go into that territory.
Tell Colonel Monroe there that he has my full confidence;
and if he has not force enough to support him," (his
features assuming the firmest expression) " I will be with
you myself. I will be there before those people shall
go into that country, or have a foot of that territory. The
whole business is infamous, and must be put down."

About the same time, Senator Hamlin, having occasion to call on the President, met Stephens, after-

wards vice-president of the Southern Confederacy, and Toombs of Georgia, coming out of the President's room, much excited. Entering himself, he found Taylor pacing up and down, " like an enraged lion in his cage." Still pacing across the room, he said, " Mr. Hamlin, what are you doing in the Senate with that bill? " The senator replied, that the pro-slavery bill was wrong in principle, and that he was doing what he could to defeat it. To which the President instantly rejoined: " Stand firm! don't yield! it means disunion; and I am pained to learn that we have disunion men to contend with. Disunion is treason; and if they try to carry out their schemes while I am President, they shall be dealt with as by law they deserve, and be executed."

As Mr. Hamlin came down the steps of the White House, he met Mr. Weed going in and told him he would find the President much excited. Mr. Weed had just before met Stephens, Toombs and Clingman of North Carolina, coming away from their interview. As he entered the room, Gen. Taylor said to him,— " Did you meet those damned traitors? They came to talk with me about my policy, and when I told them I would approve any constitutional bill Congress might pass, and would execute the laws, they began to threaten a dissolution of the Union."

He further said that he told those disunionists, that, if necessary, he would take command of the Union army in person, and if they were themselves taken in rebellion, he would hang them with less reluctance than he had seen deserters and spies hanged in Mexico. Becoming less agitated, the old soldier told his friend Weed that these traitors presumed on his being a Kentuckian and a slaveholder; that before he looked into the question as chief magistrate he had expressed opinions to his son-in-law, Jefferson Davis, that he was ready to stand with the South in maintaining all the guarantees of the Constitution. But now, having looked carefully into the merits of the long-standing controversy, he had found that the exactions and aims of the South were intolerant and revolutionary. He added that Davis seemed to be the chief conspirator in the scheme which Toombs, Stephens and Clingman (all claiming to be Whigs) had revealed to him. This was more than ten years before Davis became the leader of the rebellion which, in 1850, Taylor had told them he would put down by arms, as Lincoln afterward did.

Where then did Daniel Webster stand in this well-known conspiracy of Davis and the disunionists of 1850? He had, three months before, given in his adhesion to the permanence of slavery, in his famous speech of March 7, and he was soon to become part of the administration of the slavery-protecting Fillmore, who succeeded to the Presidency by the untimely death of Taylor in July. In the same month of 1850 Webster became the Secretary of State under President Fillmore, and lent his aid in that position to the advocates of slavery, while still professing, as he had eloquently declared many times in his earlier career, that he regarded slavery as wrong, and would gladly see it abolished. But while making these professions, largely from the force of habit (as he continued to indulge too freely in the use of ardent spirits, for the same habitual reason), all his influence was given to the support of the slaveholders' policy. Under the administration of which he was the most distinguished and the ablest member, fugitive slaves were captured, kidnapped and returned to slavery from Pennsylvania, Ohio and Massachusetts. He went about the country lecturing in favor of the Compromises of 1850, and denouncing both the abolitionists, and the higher law, which they had declared was sure to prevail, and ought to prevail. Webster denied that there is any law higher than the statutes of men; and he carried on at the same time, through his many friends, an active campaign for the Presidency, but could never secure the confidence of the people sufficiently to warrant them in giving him their highest elective office, the Presidency.

All through the remaining two years of his ever busy life, he spent his energies in maintaining the institution of negro slavery where it already existed,— the same serfdom he had spent the more active years of his life in denouncing. The change of opinion was so marked and so extreme that it is no wonder people were surprised at the betrayal of the mission they had confided to him, and revolted rather than to follow him in his crooked course. At the first opportunity they voted against Webster's friends, and their representatives in the next year, elected Charles Sumner to fill Webster's seat in the Senate. Webster survived this rejection of him by Massachusetts a little more than a year, and died too early to cast his ballot for his lifelong political opponent, Franklin Pierce,— having already abandoned his own Whig party because it did not sufficiently oppose emancipation and favor the extension of negro slavery.

In what Parker said publicly and privately of Webster, and the men who clustered round him and applauded the unhappy and disgraceful last years of his disappointed life, he had the facts all about him, and within his daily observation. He left little to inference, and he withheld from his public utterances much that was privately known to him. He had grown up in admiration of Webster, had often listened to his grander passages of oratory, and seen him manage his cases in court with that mixture of ability and arrogance which had from the first made him noted in his prosecutions, defenses and general practice at the bar. Parker had hoped much from him in the greatest of all his cases, the contest over negro slavery between the North and the South,— between the ideas of Massachusetts and New Hampshire, and the selfish institutions of South Carolina and the later Virginia. Even in 1848, when the presidential election threw Webster for a few months out of relation with his own political party, as had been the case in 1841–43, when a member of Tyler's Cabinet,— Parker, like many anti-slavery men, hoped and trusted that the most powerful oratory in New England would be on the side of freedom, as, up to that time Webster's had been, at least nominally. He had never, as Everett had done in 1826, volunteered a defense of slavery, nor quoted Scripture in its favor; he had resisted strenuously the secessionist movement of Calhoun and Hayne in Carolina, and with full knowledge that behind that frustrated effort lay the determination of the slavemasters to extend and strengthen the area of negro slavery. But in 1849 the temptations of money and power were too much for his feeble moral sense, long weakened by habits of self-indulgence and pecuniary recklessness. He opposed the honest soldierly determination of Taylor as President, to follow Jackson's course in dealing with disunion; he had surrendered to the South, after parleying for months, in his

7th of March speech, and he soon became the most violent denouncer of the practical anti-slavery men, as
well as of the few disunionist abolitionists. Contrary
to his natural character, which was arrogant rather
than crafty, with flashes of generosity which endeared
him to his friends, Webster now stooped to duplicity.
He had consulted (as Henry Wilson says, and as Mr.
Giddings of Ohio wrote to Parker in a letter now in my
possession) "with J. R. Giddings, Thaddeus Ste-
vens, and other anti-slavery members of Congress,
touching his course of action; had given them to understand that he would sustain by speech and vote their
doctrine of opposition to slavery extension and domination, and had received assurances from them that
they would gladly follow his lead." Mr. Giddings
adds, " He even submitted the skeleton of his speech
to the inspection of one or more leaders of that party,
who pronounced it satisfactory." Mr. Giddings was
himself one of the leaders, and spoke from positive
knowledge. Dr. Henry Ingersoll Bowditch, a well-
known Boston physician of high standing, says in his
autobiography:

" At the time of preparing his 7th of March speech,
Webster wrote to his intimate friend, J. T. Stevenson, to
know how far he could go ' in behalf of freedom and be
sustained by the North.' The reply was ' Take the highest ground in behalf of freedom.' When the hour came
for Mr. Webster to speak, Stevenson said to my brother,
J. I. Bowditch, at his office in State Street, ' Oh, how
Webster is giving it now to Southern insolence!' So entirely had Webster deceived and wheedled even his best
friends."

The correspondence with Stevenson was known to
Parker at the time through Miss Hannah Stevenson,

his sister, who was then an inmate of the household at Exeter Place. It was indeed the common talk of Boston, where the speech, in its final half, pledging Webster's support to slave-hunting at the North, shocked and disgusted many of his own friends. The Fugitive Slave Bill, which Mason of Virginia had introduced by way of menace and experiment, rather than with the expectation of passing it, was carried through both houses, largely by Webster's influence, — for he was then Secretary of State under Fillmore, and his successor in the Senate, R. C. Winthrop, voted against the bill. Neither Webster nor Clay voted for it, and twenty-one senators, including Benton of Missouri, abstained from voting. When Horace Greeley, soon after (according to Clay's grandson, in the latest biography of that statesman) remonstrated with his political leader against " the asperities of the Fugitive Slave Law," Clay said he " sincerely regretted them, and would have fought to exclude them, if he had not been absent at Newport when the bill was passed by the Senate."

At first the new slave-hunting law was coldly received in Boston — even by the friends of Webster and the pro-slavery Democrats, like Judge Woodbury and Hallett. The first slave-catchers who appeared in Boston under Mr. Webster's law were two low characters from Macon in Georgia, John Knight and William Hughes,— the first a mechanic or " poor white," and the other the jailer at Macon. They arrived in Boston just about a month after the passage of the bill, which was September 19, 1850. Giving an angry account of his attempt and its failure, Hughes wrote in the Macon *Telegraph* the following December as follows:

EDITOR'S PREFACE

"I reached Boston the 19th day of October. I began operations within ten minutes, as soon as I could find the gentleman to whom I carried letters. I called on Judge Woodbury, who advised me to see Mr. (George) Lunt, U. S. district attorney; whom I should pronounce to be a disgrace to his country, his profession and his office; for he deliberately stated to me as a reason for declining, that he had a recent case, and the excitement was so great that he would not undertake another. . . . My next visit was to Mr. B. F. Hallett, another United States commissioner, and this legal phenomenon replied that the law did not authorize the warrants to be issued, and that it was my duty to arrest the negroes without a warrant, and bring them before him. . . . I may misconstrue his character; some of my friends seem to think Mr. Hallett a happy combination of the knave and fool. . . . My next visit was to Judge (Peleg) Sprague, another judge on the supreme bench. This personage strongly reminded me of the celebrated Dutch judge who would never hear but one side of a case, because the two sides always confused him. Here we had re-enacted the same tortuous, twisting, shuffling, contemptible evasion of a poor pettifogging lawyer, and it makes me wonder by what legerdemain so poor a creature was placed in an honorable and responsible office. I next turned my face on Mr. Curtis, another commissioner, and a worthy Bostonian; who, from a slowness of comprehension or a want of familiarity with his duties, desired time to conquer this abstruse and difficult subject. After great unnecessary delay, those judges and commissioners, who had refused to issue the warrants because they were not the proper persons, did meet and issue them in open court. . . . The judges, in my opinion, soil the ermine with an infamy as deep, as damnable and as durable as ever stained the name of Jeffreys. As for the commissioners, they want only opportunity to become notable and famous Dogberries. . . . Could I have obtained the warrants (which honorable officials would have issued) I think it not only probable, but very certain I could have been more than half way to Georgia before a mob could have interfered. . . . By great secrecy and despatch I could have stolen the negroes from Boston. But I could have stolen them just as well before the ' Slave Bill ' as after,— and probably a little better. This bill was to prevent the necessity of stealing our own property. . . . In Boston the law cannot be executed by the public authorities, and a man must recover his own by stealing,— and that before they can find him out,— or, probably, murder him in open day."

Without approving the language of this Georgian's statement, I must say it was in substance true, so great was the abhorrence of the Bostonians to slave-catching in their free city. This, with a little party-fencing between Woodbury and Hallett, Democrats, and Lunt and Curtis, Webster Whigs, accounts for the reluctance of these four worthies to mix themselves up with a slave case.

Now who were these despised " niggers " whom Hughes and Knight had come a thousand miles to kidnap, under cover of Webster's " Slave Bill "? As it happened, they were parishioners of Theodore Parker, and as it also happens, I knew them some fifteen years after, when they returned to Boston from England, where Parker and his friends had sent them, in order to keep them out of the hands of Mr. Webster's friends in Boston. They were handsome and every way respectable colored persons, largely of white blood,— William and Ellen Craft by name,— who had earned their right to freedom if any Algerian captive or Dartmoor-prisoned New England sailor ever did, by a daring and successful flight. No man or woman with a human heart, who knew their romantic story, ever begrudged them their well-earned liberty; the ignorant and the knavish alone turn slave-hunters for such as these two. Ellen was so nearly white,— her parentage being what my friend Hosmer defines as "an evil out of which good may come,"— that in her journey of four days from Macon to Philadelphia she passed successfully as a young slave-holder traveling North with his body-servant (her husband). William had bought his own freedom over and over, by the wages he had paid his master, who seems to have been a Dr. Robert Collins, and had earned the money for it by working along with the "poor white," John Knight, in a Macon cabinet shop. He was pursuing the same honest calling in a Boston shop, and supporting his family by his labor. I now quote from the Journal of Parker for 1850, which lies before me:

"(Saturday, Oct. 26.) It seems a miserable fellow by the name of Knight came here to Boston from Macon in Georgia, sent out by the former owner of the Crafts. He used to work in the cabinet shop with William, but was dull and imbecile, so that his chief function was to wait upon the rest. There came with him one Mr. Hughes, who is the jailer at Macon. Last Tuesday, the 22nd, Knight called on Craft at his shop, expressed pleasure to see him, etc. Craft asked him if he came on alone. 'Yes, there's nobody with me.' But he wanted William to go round with him, to show him the streets and the curiosities of Boston. No,— William was on his guard,— was 'busy,' 'had work to attend to' and could not go The next day he came again; wanted William to go round the Common with him. No, he could not go then. Told William, 'Perhaps you would like to come to the United States Hotel and see me; your wife might like to

come also, to talk about her mother. If you will write,
I will take the letter home."

All this time Hughes was at the hotel under the
false name of William Hamilton, by which he registered, and was described in the warrant which the four
reluctancies had finally issued. William declined to
call at the hotel, or to write the decoy letter. Knight
then wrote as follows:

"Boston, Oct. 22, 1850, 11 o'clk. P. M.
"Wm. Craft — Sir — I have to leave so Eirley in the
moring that I could not call according to promis, so if
you want me to carry a letter home with me, you must
bring it to the united States Hotel, to morrow, and leave
it in Box 44, or come yourself to morro Eavening after
tea and bring it. let me no if you come yourself by
sending a note to Box 44 U. S. Hotel, so that I may
no whether to wate after tea or not, by the Bearer. If
your wif wants to see me you cold bring her with you
if you come yourself.   JOHN KNIGHT.
"P. S. I shall leave for home eirley a Thursday
moring."

Parker's Journal goes on:

"The lad who brought the letter informed William of
the other person who came with him (Knight), told his
name, etc.
"Finding this failed, Hughes applied to the court and
got a warrant. . . . I saw William Craft this morning about a quarter past eleven. He was at Lewis Hay-
den's (a fugitive from Kentucky), seemed cool and reso-
lute. I told him I thought it no use to put the matter
off, and cut off the dog's tail by inches. If he was to
take the bull by the horns, he had better do it to-day
rather than to-morrow. So he thought. I inspected his
arms, a good revolver with six caps on, a large pistol,

and small ones; a large dirk and a short one. All was right.

"Meeting of the Legal Committee of the Vigilance Committee at half-past twelve. Richard H. Dana, Jr., in the chair. Writs are out against Knight and Hughes, — one for slander against Craft, one for carrying dangerous weapons with intent to commit an assault on Craft. Also a habeas corpus is ready for William in case of need. But I think he has a *non habeas corpus* in his pocket.

"Went out in the afternoon to Brookline, and saw Ellen Craft. She is now at Ellis Gray Loring's. She seems composed, and we assured her that her husband would not be carried off.

"(Monday, Oct. 28.) Went down to the U. S. Hotel at half-past seven to see the slave-hunters. Bowditch breakfasted with them, but they slipped off and we could not catch them again. Heard that Ellen Craft was at the table at Loring's; so went out to Brookline in a coach with Miss Stevenson and (Rev.) John Parkman. Went to Loring's; Ellen not there; to (Samuel) Philbrick's; found her and William. Brought them into town. I wanted Ellen to stay with us till all is safe and slave-hunters crushed. The Vigilance Committee is in permanent session. We met at seven P. M. again. Sent a committee of twelve with Robert E. Apthorp as chairman, to see Spooner, keeper of the U. S. Hotel. He says the slave-hunters are satisfied they cannot arrest Craft or carry him off. (Tuesday, 29th.) (Charles) Sumner and Apthorp have both seen Spooner to-day. He was much impressed by the other committee on Monday night. (Francis) Jackson and (C. F.) Hovey saw him on Sunday night. Lobdell, a baker and treasurer of the hotel, told Jackson he would 'carry out the law if it was to apply to my own daughter.' No doubt; perhaps it does. But suppose it came to his dividends,— *ce serait autre chose.*"

So the campaign went on till on Wednesday afternoon, at 2:30 P. M., the slave-hunters took the New York train at Newton and returned to Georgia. Knight, who was incapable of writing it, signed a statement dated at Macon, November 11, in which he seemed to say:

"Mr. Hughes applied to three separate commissioners, who sent him from one to another. The last one refused till he could get all the judges and commissioners together. In this way the business was deferred until Thursday night (Oct. 24), when the meeting was held. At this our business and the names of the parties for whom the warrant was demanded leaked out. Friday morning Judge Woodbury issued the warrant about nine o'clock, in open court. It was at once known, and the negroes and abolitionists began to assemble about the court-house and to watch us. Every few minutes a negro lawyer would peep into the marshal's office to see what was going on. The excitement was great; nothing was done; marshal said if he could be convinced that Craft was in Cambridge Street, he would go and arrest him; but seemed timid and inclined to back out."

As this marshal was then Charles Devens, afterwards a Civil War general, judge of the State Supreme Court, and member of President Hayes's cabinet, timidity could hardly be alleged of him; but he knew he was in a base business, and was very glad when he got out of it after Webster's death, and had for a successor Watson Freeman, one of whose last official acts was trying to get paid for a night-attempt to kidnap me in my own house at Concord, and carry me to Washington to testify before Senator Mason's committee, in April, 1860. He was as unlucky then as he had been lucky in carrying Antony Burns off from

EDITOR'S PREFACE

Boston in June, 1854,— an achievement instantly followed at the November election by the defeat and disintegration of Webster's Whig party in Massachusetts. Knight, the " poor white," went on:

" Wednesday, Oct. 30, very early, Rev. Theodore Parker came to our room, followed by fifty or sixty persons, greatly excited; said he had suppressed a mob twice,— came as a Christian, a servant of the Lord, and a friend, to request us to leave the city instantly; not to wait for the cars, but to take a carriage; did not think he could suppress the mob any longer. We refused; told him that we should treat the committee with perfect contempt; would leave when the mob dispersed and our convenience suited, but not before. In the evening came to New York, by advice of counsel, in order to get further instructions, and to allow the excitement to die away. During this time Craft and wife were reported to be locked up in the house of a white man, whose name I forget."

(It was, of course, Parker's four-story house in Exeter Place, hardly a good rifle-shot from the hotel where these actors in Webster's fugitive-slave drama were going through the prologue to its six years' performance.)

William Craft's fellow-workman at Macon, exalted by his experiences into a sage forecaster of the next few years in Boston, then delivered himself thus in the Macon newspaper:

" I am convinced that public opinion in Boston is undergoing a change. It is true the abolitionists and negroes are very numerous, and apparently have things very much their own way at present. The business men and men of property with whom I conversed, generally took but little interest in the matter; but said the law

ought to be executed, that they wished to get rid of the
negroes, and that, if it came to a trial of strength, the
negroes and abolitionists would be put down. This,
however, will take time. I believe that Mr. Hughes will
ultimately succeed in getting the negroes."

On November 7, Parker remarried these brave
fugitives, at a boarding house. His record says:

"Married William and Ellen Craft; they are fugitive
slaves; their history is well known; they have long been
married. But their marriage lacks the solemnity of law;
so yesterday they got a certificate, and this day I married
them. I told him his duty was to protect the life, liberty
and limbs of his wife, at all manly hazards; that he was
to do it though it dug his own grave, and the graves of
a thousand men. Still I counseled mildness and Christian feelings, but by all means liberty. After the marriage I put a short dagger in his hands, as a symbol
of one kind of work, and a Bible as a symbol of another
sort of work. I gave him the Bible with the record of
his marriage. At half-past two P. M. this day, they are
to go to Portland (by rail) and at night take a steamer
for St. Johns, then a steamer for Windsor, stages to
Halifax, and then the steamer for England. So I am
obliged to send my parishioners to *that* country for freedom, whence our fathers fled for it."

Parker never saw Ellen Craft again until the summer of 1859, when, passing through England on his
way to meet Sumner in Paris, he and his family were
called upon by her in London, where they were receiving the calls and hospitalities of John Bright, of Mar-
tineau, of Frances Power Cobbe, of Thoreau's admirer, Thomas Cholmondeley, and hosts of friends,
old and new. No visit gave him greater pleasure than
hers; and he noticed, as I did, six or eight years later,

when the Crafts returned to Boston, that a few years of freedom had done more for the education and civilization of their race than two centuries of " civilizing " slavery.

The next fugitive slave case in Boston was more provoking to Webster and his slave-hunting friends, there and in Washington; but not a whit more successful. A poor fellow named Shadrach was laid hold of the next winter by Marshal Devens, about February 15, shut up for safe-keeping in the court-house in Court Square, and was about to be delivered over to the slave-catchers by George T. Curtis, the slave-law commissioner, when a few negroes moved a sudden stay of proceedings, and Shadrach found himself that night at my neighbor Bigelow's in Concord, on his way to Leominster, and thence to Canada. That part of his story is told in the Life of Dr. Howe by Mrs. Richards; he was aided with carriages and drivers by some white friends; but the actual rescue is related by Dr. Bowditch, in a manner I have never heard disputed. He says:

" The news came to a poor, but quiet, industrious negro, working for my friend John L. Emmons, that the boy who had grown up under his own eye at Norfolk, Va., and who, like himself, had fled from slavery, had been arrested, and was then before Commissioner Curtis. The hour, as he told me, had come: he was doomed to rescue his friend or die. Accordingly, being faithful in all things, he said to his master that he felt he must go and see if the story was true. Emmons bade him Godspeed, and the truth was soon proved by sight; he saw his friend seated between two officers. He returned and said to his master, ' Farewell,— you may never see me again,' and returned to the court-house. He found a number around the door; they were laughing and jeering, and his heart sank within him. 'My friends,' said he, 'this is not the time for laughing or talking, but for acting; will you follow me and rescue him?' 'Wait a little,' said they. 'So it has always been with you; now is the time. Let us go.' Finally he succeeded in getting two or three to promise to follow; yet they had no plans. They had, however, a leader who was quiet and calm and full of faith; unarmed, he felt that he was to lose his life or rescue his friend; the means would come as he wanted them. At length the court was adjourned till Monday, and the slave remanded to the custody of the deputy marshal, Pat Riley. The company was about departing; one of the lawyers was leaving, when the door was suddenly burst open, and in rushed the negroes in numbers, our friend taking the lead. Riley seized him and two more fell upon him. They wrestled together; the negro was victorious, and seeing the marshal's sword lying in a chair, he drew it, and, beckoning to the prisoner said, 'Fly, this moment!' The poor wretch stood motionless, his knees quivering. 'Depart,— go this way,' motioning with the sword, and keeping off the officers with it. 'Give me my sword,' said the marshal. 'Stand off!' said our hero, again waving off his antagonists. Others having come to the rescue, Shadrach was dragged into liberty by his victorious friends. Our poor hero was the last to leave the room, and finally got his young friend down into Court Square. Then leaving him in the care of friends, he quietly entered a neighboring shop, laid the sword on the counter, and asked the man to let it remain until called for by its owner. Then he followed the crowd, saw Shadrach safely out of town, and quickly returned to work as if nothing had happened. I saw the man this evening. We hired a cab, and now he is out of reach of the tools of the diabolical Fugitive Slave Law."

This view of the case was naturally not that taken by Pat Riley, by George Lunt, the district attorney,

nor entirely by Charles Devens. Riley appealed to
the public through the newspapers, and blamed the
city mayor and city marshal for not bringing the police to his aid, when he was vanquished by his own
sword. The *Boston Courier*, quoting Riley, went on
to say:

" The rescue was at a time when more than forty city
policemen were assembled in Marshal Tukey's office, not
a hundred paces from the scene of riot. That Mr. Riley
did all that he could to execute the law, nobody will deny.
His defense, when attacked by the mob, was as able as
his circumscribed means would permit. Had the rioters
who assembled near the court-house been driven away
by the chief of police, this outrage upon the laws would
not have been perpetrated on Saturday."

President Fillmore and his secretary, Webster, took
care that Marshal Tukey was in his duty at the next
slave-catching, in the following April,— that of
Thomas Sims, sufficiently described in the copious text
of Parker; and they called in United States soldiers
to force the odious statute upon the freemen of Massachusetts. By force and in contempt of constitutional law, Sims was carried away into slavery on
April 19, 1851. The next week, the election of
Charles Sumner, which had been delayed for three
months by the friends of slavery, was completed, and
he was sent to take Webster's place in the Senate at
Washington, with more than Webster's influence, and
by a life tenure; for he died in that office thirty-three
years afterward, and there witnessed and helped bring
about the complete abolition of negro slavery. In this
election, and in the support of Sumner so long as
Parker lived, the Boston preacher had great influence; and it was his friends and Sumner's friends who
emancipated the slave.

EDITOR'S PREFACE

Parker's sermon on Webster, though violently attacked by that statesman's personal and political friends, was approved in its substance by the more impartial among his contemporaries. Perhaps the most significant among the comments which it called forth at the time (the late autumn of 1852) were the letter of Senator Seward in that year (Dec. 27, 1852) and that of an older Whig, James Kent, the son of Chancellor Kent, six years later. Mr. Seward said:

" Webster never rose to the moral majesty of Milton or Burke,— lacking the moral quality suited to his intellectual greatness. . . . While he was for ' Union and Liberty,' he was for Union more than for Liberty. So he was a statesman for Britain rather than for our country; for the past rather than for our own times. Beyond all doubt, his great infirmity was *timidity*. His great offense was not his surrender of the Wilmot Proviso, nor even his supporting the Fugitive Slave Law, but his attempt to suppress and silence debate and speech on slavery; yet his greatest offense was timidity. I give you my sincere thanks for the copy of your sermon on the death of Webster. I am sure that all the world will agree that it is executed with a masterly force, and with a severe study of truth and justice."

Judge Kent was more specific in his comment on the sermon,— all the more noteworthy because he was, like Webster in his youth, a member of the old Federal party of Napoleon's time, and, like Webster, soon joined, or naturally adopted the creed of that Hamiltonian party. But before quoting his searching analysis of Webster's character and abilities, I will give the statement of Dr. J. G. Palfrey, eminent as clergyman, congressman and historian, on receiving (March 21, 1853) Parker's Webster sermon:

EDITOR'S PREFACE

"I have taken time to read your masterly discourse on Mr. Webster, and have read it with new admiration of your powers of analysis, of expression and illustration; of your freedom in exhibiting a morbid anatomy, and your generous feeling for what was lovable and pitiable in your subject. You, with others of your time, are incorporating a new era in biography. It will assume a vastly more beneficent function than heretofore. It will be made immensely to serve the cause of humanity, by enforcing upon the weak and wicked great a restraining sense of the doom which an earthly futurity is to pronounce."

Judge Kent, of Fishkill, N. Y., to whom Parker was introduced in 1858, by their common friend, Joseph Lyman (like Kent the son of an old Federalist) wrote to him a few weeks later (Sept. 21, 1858) thus:

"I left Fishkill this morning in the train with your volume containing the Webster discourse. I was enchained by it, buried in it,— insensible to the jarrings and the shrieking of the engine; lost to everything but the magic power of the orator. It is a wonderful oration. Daniel Webster never in life produced a speech comparable to it in depth of thought, richness of imagery and eloquence of expression. I write under the fresh influence of the eloquence, but with perfect sincerity. In some respects Webster's fame will be indebted to you for this very speech. You will give to future times a more impressive view of this extraordinary man than his works will convey. But do you not overestimate his mental powers? His writings are, after all, pretty dull reading. When you call him the greatest orator who has spoken the English tongue, do you not go too far? Is he superior to Burke, from whom he took several of his happiest rhetorical figures? Indeed, is not Burke superior to Webster in everything except in mere logical reasoning? Webster was not a *great* lawyer. Some of his arguments, especially on constitutional questions, are very fine. But

of black-letter law he knew little, and he despised it;
and from the constitution of his mind he did not pursue,
and perhaps was scarcely able to follow the subtile threads
of thought which lawyers like Charles Austin and Har-
grave delighted in.

"Where in all his speeches was a great philosophic
thought exhibited? What truth of universal application
has he declared? What great sophistry has he unveiled?
What discovery in politics or morals has he made? His
style is singularly clear, vigorous and impressive; but
what expressions of his have become incorporated in the
common language? I have sometimes thought that his
immense personal influence was to be ascribed to his face
and figure; for there was truth in the saying of Charles
Fox concerning Thurlow, that 'he must be an impostor,
since nobody could be so wise as Thurlow looked.'"

These were the queries and opinions of a good lawyer, contemporary with Webster, though twenty years
younger; but one a little outside the circle in which
Webster dazzled and was adored.

In revising the Webster sermon (which I heard)
for the final edition, Parker took great pains, and
seldom made a mistake in fact. The true statement
(questioned by some) that in 1815 "Webster sought
the office of attorney-general of New Hampshire"
rested with Parker on the authority of Judge C. E.
Potter of Manchester, N. H., one of the best anti-
quaries of his time, who wrote the fact to Parker, and
his letter is before me. John Taylor Gilman of Exeter was then governor of New Hampshire, and was
to be succeeded by a Democrat, William Plumer of
Epping. Judge Potter wrote (March 28, 1853):

"Mr. Webster was an applicant for the office of attorney-general in 1815, after he discovered that the Feder-

alists were in a minority in New Hampshire, and that he could not be continued in Congress. The appointment was made December 15, 1815: Mr. Webster was an applicant and Gov. Gilman intended that he should be appointed. The three Democrats in the council (which numbers five) were determined he should not be appointed, — his anti-war course in Congress having embittered the Democrats against him. On the day named, Gov. Gilman nominated Mr. Webster, and was supported by the two Federalists in the council,— the three Democrats opposing and defeating the nomination. The afternoon of the same day, Gen. Pierce of Hillsborough, father of our President, proposed George Sullivan (son of Gen. John Sullivan) for the office, was supported by the other two Democrats, and Gov. Gilman confirmed the nomination. Mr. Webster thus defeated, and seeing his political fate was sealed in New Hampshire, forthwith determined to remove to Boston, and did so the following year, 1816."

These are the recorded facts in the case, which never rested on gossip, but on the well-known course of politics in the State. It was the son of the old Revolutionary soldier, afterwards Governor Pierce, whom Webster was favoring for the Presidency at the time of his death in 1852. It was not true, however, that he "continued as congressman."

Up to the position finally taken by Mr. Webster, Parker had been an admirer of his genius, and generally a supporter of his national policy, though regretting his well-known laxity of morals, and his occasional lapses from political morality in his public career. But when Webster coöperated with the disunionists of the South, Mason of Virginia, Davis of Mississippi, Stephens and Toombs of Georgia, and their associates, in passing the Fugitive Slave Bill of September, 1850, Parker, who had previously confined

his attacks on slavery to sermons and speeches, became (in 1850) an active protector of his parishioners
and others, who were subject to kidnapping under
that infamous legislation, enforced as it soon was by
some of the basest and meanest of the Bostonian population, as well as by others of higher social standing.
As we have seen, he brought William and Ellen Craft,
courageous fugitives from Southern slavery, to his
own house and sheltered them from the slave-hunters,
whom he also persuaded to leave Boston. In the next
important case, that of Shadrach, Parker took part to
the extent of writing, as I suppose, the "Proclamation" against Caphart, who had caused Shadrach's
arrest, and in other ways he had opposed the execution
of Webster's law in Massachusetts. The facts concerning the Crafts (whom I knew after their return
from England to emancipated America) are set forth
in this and a preceding volume; but since the inter-
esting facts in the Shadrach case are not so well
known, I have made them the subject of one of the sections of this volume.

The whole history of Parker's connection with the
revolt against the Fugitive Slave Bill and the repeal
of the Missouri Compromise (for the express purpose
of introducing slavery into Kansas and Colorado),
will be found in the extracts made from Parker's un-
spoken but published "Defense" against the monstrous and futile indictment of him and others in 1854;
an action and an extraordinary sequence of events,
which the uprising of the North against the Kansas-
Nebraska Act prevented from being as injurious to
the opponents of Webster and of his pro-slavery measures as it had been judicially determined in advance
those arrests and indictments should be. The judicial

history of the dismal period from the autumn of 1850 to the decision of Taney in 1857, finds one of its best chapters in Parker's book.

In reading the anti-slavery sermons and speeches of Parker, if they are read with an open mind, and not through the spectacles of old prejudice, which some of the present survivors cannot lay aside, one is struck with the profound political philosophy they disclose, and with the prognostication, based on induction and insight, which appears here and there, especially in the later years, and after he had ceased to publish much. The late Dr. William T. Harris, an early disciple of Parker in German philosophy and in politics, said to me in the last conversation I had with him, in September, 1909, " I regard Theodore Parker as the most profound political philosopher America has yet had; he went to the root of the matter, and reasoned, as few of our statesmen did, from first principles." In this respect, although with slower steps, Abraham Lincoln followed him, and Harris added that apparently Lincoln was much influenced in his anti-slavery views by what he read of Parker in sermons and speeches, with which his partner Herndon supplied him, as well as reading to him the letters he received from Parker in the years 1854–58. The " house divided against itself " came out in Parker's published words, long before Lincoln adopted that strong figure and gave it universal currency.

I have often had occasion to think that persons of my own and later times who write and speak so glibly about Parker, have never read him carefully, and have no conception of the depth of principle and the vast collection of contemporary facts on which he based

his inductions and predictions. No American of his
time had a wider correspondence, or intercourse with
a more varied circle of acquaintances than Theodore
Parker, as I have reason to know from the many volumes of his correspondence long in my hands by the
bequest of Mrs. Parker, and from which I have drawn
in editing this volume. Few historical students have
seen these volumes, or have any clear idea of their
contents. Those portions printed by Weiss in his
two-volume Life, give some conception of this mass,
but a very imperfect one. Many of the letters never
came into his hands, and he did not always understand
the connection of those which he printed. The same
is true to some extent of Parker's journals, all now in
my possession.

An effort is sometimes made by persons (as Lowell
said) "mole-blind to the soul's make and style," to
place Webster and Abraham Lincoln on the same platform as to slavery. Nothing could be further from
the fact. Clay was the admiration of young Lincoln,
but he had even a greater aversion to negro slavery
than Clay had. Lincoln was the most humble of great
men; Webster the most arrogant; Lincoln the most un-
selfish, Webster the most self-indulgent. Lincoln was
always meditating on justice and the moral sanctions;
Webster seems to have had no general principles, and
to have rated law above justice. There was in fact
much congeniality of sentiment between Lincoln and
Parker, and their political philosophy was much the
same. Parker stated his principles with more method,
but Lincoln arrived at the same results by a concise
logic of his own. He was for years an eager reader
of Parker's sermons and speeches, furnished to him by
his law-partner, Herndon, whose correspondence with

EDITOR'S PREFACE

Parker has this year been published in Iowa by Rev. Joseph Newton, to whom I made over the manuscripts early in 1909. Of Lincoln, after reading his speeches in the Douglas debate of 1858, and some earlier speeches of 1856, Parker had high hopes as a leader of anti-slavery opinion; and in 1860 preferred him to Seward, whom he had long favored as a presidential candidate. Had Parker lived a year longer, he would have voted for Lincoln, and would have commended his courageous policy, as he had in 1858, when Lincoln and his friends, Trumbull and Herndon, held Illinois in the Republican party, instead of turning it over to Senator Douglas, as Seward, Greeley and Henry Wilson eagerly advocated. On this point the Parker-Herndon correspondence is very illuminating.

The anxiety of Lincoln on the subject of the increasing spread of slavery, from 1854 to 1859, is marked, and in sharp contrast to the subservience of Webster in 1850–52 to the plans of the slaveholders. Both were lovers of the Union; but with Lincoln the controlling wish was for a Union without chattel slavery; with Webster the wish was for Union first and liberty afterwards, if at all. He had deserted his early position, and seems to have despaired of seeing slavery abolished; while Lincoln, and more strongly Parker, foresaw that it must go down before the spirit of the nineteenth century, which, Parker declared, would witness the emancipation of the slaves that Lincoln effected. The disastrous self-destruction of Webster's reputation, which Parker more than once characterized as it deserved, was more philosophically censured by Emerson, who, like Parker, but even more intimately, had been bred in the admiration of that man's attitude and eloquence. Thoreau said of John

Brown, " He could not be tried by his peers,— for
they did not exist." But in all the attributes of intellect and in the more subtile charms of oratory, Emerson was the peer of Webster; and what was his verdict? He said at New York, March 7, 1854, when
the evil fruits of Webster's betrayal of his trust were
glaringly manifest in the movement to repeal the Missouri Compromise:

" Four years ago to-night, on one of those high critical
moments in history when great issues are determined,
when the powers of right and wrong are mustered for
conflict, and it lies with one man to give a casting vote,—
Mr. Webster, most unexpectedly, threw his whole weight
on the side of slavery, and caused by his personal and
official authority the passage of the Fugitive Slave Bill.
It is remarked of the Americans that they value dexterity
too much and honor too little. Whether this defect be
national or not, it is the defect and calamity of Mr.
Webster. He decided for slavery; and that when the
aspect of that institution was no longer doubtful,— no
longer feeble and apologetic, and proposing soon to end
itself,— but strong, aggressive, and threatening an il-
limitable increase. Here was the question; Are you for
man and for the good of man, or are you for the hurt
and harm of man? It was the question whether the
negro shall be, as the Indians were in Spanish America,
a piece of money; whether this system, which is a kind
of factory for converting men into monkeys, shall be up-
held and enlarged. And Mr. Webster and the country
went for the application to these poor men of quadruped
law. . . . Angry parties went from bad to worse,
and the decision of Webster was accompanied with
everything offensive to freedom and good morals. He
did as immoral men usually do; made very low bows to
the Christian Church, and went through all the Sunday
decorums; but when allusion was made to the question

of duty and the sanctions of morality, he very frankly spoke, at Albany, of ' some higher law, something existing somewhere between here and the Third Heaven,— I do not know where.' And this wretched atheism found some laughter in the company."

Such were the terms of just indignation in which Emerson, like Parker, spoke of the hurtful closing years of Webster's life. But in his private journal he wrote down the stinging epigram, only made public since Emerson's death,—

Why did all manly powers in Webster fail?
He wrote on Nature's noblest brow, ' For Sale.'

Not wholly unlike this analysis of Webster by Emerson was the judgment of Calhoun upon him in 1832: " Mr. Webster will never be President. He lacks the qualifications of a leader; he has no faith in his own convictions; he can never be the head of a party. Superior in intellect to Mr. Clay, he lacks Clay's moral courage and his strong convictions. Hence Clay will always be the head of the party, and Webster will follow."

This age, at the end of a century from his birth, is still too near Theodore Parker, this great scholar and brave champion of every good cause, to appreciate him rightly. The men of his own time knew him or misconceived him; he was intensely loved and virulently hated; but the men of genius in each age know and describe their contemporaries better than the next generation or two usually can. Of all his contemporaries, Emerson, who knew him intimately for a quarter-century, at his death passed the best judgment upon Parker, which time will only confirm, when the loves and hates of threescore years have died away:

EDITOR'S PREFACE

" 'Tis plain to me that he has achieved a historic immortality here; that he has so woven himself into the history of Boston in these few years, that he can never be left out of your annals. It will not be in the Acts of city councils, nor of obsequious mayors; nor in the State-house the proclamations of governors, with their failing virtue,— failing them at critical moments,— that coming generations will study what really befell; but in the plain lessons of Theodore Parker in this Music Hall, in Faneuil Hall, or in legislative committee-rooms, that the true temper and authentic record of these days will be read. The next generation will care little for the chances of elections that govern governors now; it will care little for fine gentlemen who behaved shabbily; but it will read very intelligently in his rough story, fortified with exact anecdotes, precise with names and dates, what part was taken by each actor; who threw himself into the cause of humanity and came to the rescue of civilization at a hard pinch, and who blocked its course.

" His ministry fell on a political crisis; on the years when Southern slavery broke over its old banks, made new and vast pretensions, and wrung from the weakness or treachery of Northern people fatal concessions in the Fugitive Slave Bill and the repeal of the Missouri Compromise. Two days, bitter in the memory of Boston, the days of the rendition of Sims and of Burns, made the occasion of his most remarkable discourses. He kept nothing back. In terrible earnest he denounced the public crime, and meted out to every official, high and low, his due portion. It was his great service to freedom. He took away the reproach of silent consent that would otherwise have lain against the indignant minority, by uttering, in the hour and place wherein these outrages were done, the stern protest.

" Ah, my brave brother! it seems as if, in a frivolous age, our loss were immense, and your place cannot be supplied. But you will already be consoled in the trans-

EDITOR'S PREFACE

fer of your genius, knowing well that the nature of the world will affirm to all men, in all times, that which for twenty-five years you valiantly spoke; that the winds of Italy murmur the same truth over your grave,— the winds of America over these bereaved streets; that the sea which bore your mourners home affirms it, the stars in their courses, and the inspirations of youth; whilst the polished and pleasant traitors to human rights, with perverted learning and disgraced graces, rot and are forgotten with their double tongue, saying all that is sordid for the corruption of man."

F. B. SANBORN.

Volume XI. of this edition, entitled The Slave Power, contains eleven of the earlier addresses of Theodore Parker on anti-slavery themes.

Five later addresses on anti-slavery themes by Theodore Parker, with notes by Mr. Sanborn, will be found in the last volume (XIV.) of this edition of his works, entitled Miscellanies. The addresses bear the following titles: "A New Lesson for the Day," "The Aspect of Slavery in America," "The Effect of Slavery on the American People," "Parker's Indictment and the Fugitive Slave Cases." "The John Brown Campaign."

CONTENTS

		PAGE
I.	THE MEXICAN WAR.	1
II.	THE ADMINISTRATION OF PRESIDENT POLK	48
III.	THE STATE OF THE NATION	92
IV.	THE LIKE AND THE DIFFERENT	182
V.	THE FUGITIVE SLAVE LAW	143
VI.	AN ANTI-SLAVERY ADDRESS	153
VII.	THE PROGRESS OF AMERICA	196
VIII.	THE NEW CRIME AGAINST HUMANITY	250
IX.	THE RIGHTS OF MAN IN AMERICA	333
X.	THE PRESENT ASPECT OF THE ANTI-SLAVERY ENTERPRISE	397
XI.	THE PRESENT CRISIS IN AMERICAN AFFAIRS	430

I

THE MEXICAN WAR

1848

Soon after the commencement of the war against Mexico, I said something respecting it in this place. But while I was printing the sermon, I was advised to hasten the compositors in their work, or the war would be over before the sermon was out. The advice was like a good deal of the counsel that is given to a man who thinks for himself, and honestly speaks what he unavoidably thinks. It is now more than two years since the war began; I have hoped to live long enough to see it ended, and hoped to say a word about it when over. A month ago, this day, the 25th of May, the treaty of peace, so much talked of, was ratified by the Mexican Congress. A few days ago, it was officially announced by telegraph, to your collector in Boston, that the war with Mexico was at an end.

There are two things about this war quite remarkable. The first is, the manner of its commencement. It was begun illegally, without the action of the constitutional authorities; begun by the command of the President of the United States, who ordered the American army into a territory which the Mexicans claimed as their own. The President says, " It is ours; " but the Mexicans also claimed it, and were in possession thereof until forcibly expelled. This is a plain case; and, as I have elsewhere treated at length of this matter,* I will not dwell upon it again, except to mention

* In the Massachusetts *Quarterly Review,* Vol. I., Art. I. See also the paper on the administration of Mr. Polk, in Vol. III., Art. VIII.

a single fact but recently divulged.   It is well known
that Mr. Polk claimed the territory west of the Nueces
and east of the Rio Grande, as forming a part of
Texas, and therefore as forming part of the United
States after the annexation of Texas.   He contends
that Mexico began the war by attacking the American
army while in that territory and near the Rio Grande.
But, from the correspondence laid before the American
Senate, in its secret session for considering the treaty,
it now appears that on the 10th of November, 1845,
Mr. Polk instructed Mr. Slidell to offer a relinquish-
ment of American claims against Mexico, amounting
to $5,000,000 or $6,000,000 for the sake of having the
Rio Grande as the western boundary of Texas; yes,
for that very territory which he says was ours without paying a cent.   When it was conquered, a military government was established there, as in other
places in Mexico.

The other remarkable thing about the war is, the
manner of its conclusion.   The treaty of peace which
has just been ratified by the Mexican authorities, and
which puts an end to the war, was negotiated by a man
who had no more legal authority than any one of us
has to do it.   Mr. Polk made the war, without consulting Congress, and that body adopted the war by
a vote almost unanimous.   Mr. Nicholas P. Trist made
the treaty, without consulting the President; yes, even
after the President had ordered him to return home.
As the Congress adopted Mr. Polk's war, so Mr. Polk
adopted Mr. Trist's treaty; and the war illegally begun
is brought informally to a close.   Mr. Polk is now in
the President's chair, seated on the throne of the
Union, although he made the war; and Mr. Trist, it is
said, is under arrest for making the treaty.

When the war began, there was a good deal of talk about it here; talk against it. But, as things often go in Boston, it ended in talk. The newsboys made money out of the war. Political parties were true to their wonted principles, or their wonted prejudices. The friends of the party in power could see no informality in the beginning of hostilities; no injustice in the war itself; not even an impolicy. They were offended if an obscure man preached against it of a Sunday. The political opponents of the party in power talked against the war, as a matter of course; but, when the elections came, supported the men that made it with unusual alacrity — their deeds serving as commentary upon their words, and making further remark thereon, in this place, quite superfluous. Many men — who, whatever other parts of Scripture they may forget, never cease to remember that " money answereth all things,"— diligently set themselves to make money out of the war and the new turn it gave to national affairs. Others thought that " glory " was a good thing, and so engaged in the war itself, hoping to return, in due time, all glittering with its honors.

So what with the one political party that really praised the war, and the other who affected to oppose it, and with the commercial party, who looked only for a market — this for merchandise, and that for " patriotism "— the friends of peace, who seriously and heartily opposed the war, were very few in number. True, the " sober second thought " of the people has somewhat increased their number; but they are still few, mostly obscure men.

Now peace has come, nobody talks much about it; the newsboys have scarce made a cent by the news. They fired cannons, a hundred guns on the Common,

for joy at the victory of Monterey; at Philadelphia,
Baltimore, Washington, New York, men illuminated
their houses in honor of the battle of Buena Vista, I
think it was; the custom-house was officially illuminated at Boston for that occasion. But we hear
of no cannons to welcome the peace. Thus far, it
does not seem that a single candle has been burnt in
rejoicing for that. The newspapers are full of talk,
as usual; flags are flying in the streets; the air is a
little noisy with hurrahs; but it is all talk about the
conventions at Baltimore and Philadelphia; hurrahs
for Taylor and Cass. Nobody talks of the peace.
Flags enough flap in the wind, with the names of rival
candidates; but nowhere do the stripes and stars bear
" Peace " as their motto. The peace now secured is
purchased with such conditions imposed on Mexico,
that while every one will be glad of it, no man that
loves justice can be proud of it. Very little is said
about the treaty. The distinguished senator from
Massachusetts did himself honor, it seems to me, in
voting against it on the ground that it enabled us to
plunder Mexico of her land. But the treaty contains
some things highly honorable to the character of the
nation, of which we may well enough be proud, if
ever of anything. I refer to the twenty-second and
twenty-third articles, which provide for arbitration
between the nations, if future difficulties should occur;
and to the pains taken, in case of actual hostilities,
for the security of all unarmed persons, for the protection of private property, and for the humane treatment of all prisoners taken in war. These ideas, and
the language of these articles, are copied from the
celebrated treaty between the United States and Prussia, the treaty of 1785. It is scarcely needful to

add that they were then introduced by that great
and good man, Benjamin Franklin, one of the nego-
tiators of the treaty. They made a new epoch in
diplomacy, and introduced a principle previously unknown in the law of nations. The insertion of these
articles in the new treaty is, perhaps, the only thing
connected with the war which an American can look
upon with satisfaction. Yet this fact excites no attention.

Mr. Trist introduced these articles without having instructions to do so; the honor, therefore, is
wholly due to him. There were some in the Senate
who opposed them.

Still, while so little notice is taken of this matter,
in public and private, it may be worth while for a
minister, on Sunday, to say a word about the peace;
and, now the war is over, to look back upon it, to
see what it has cost, in money and in men, and what
we have got by it; what its consequences have been,
thus far, and are likely to be for the future; what
new dangers and duties come from this cause inter-
polated into our nation. We have been long promised " indemnity for the past, and security for the
future; " let us see what we are to be indemnified for,
and what secured against. The natural justice of
the war I will not look at now.

First, then, of the cost of the war. Money is the
first thing with a good many men; the only thing
with some, and an important thing with all. It is a little difficult to determine the actual cost of the war, thus
far — even its direct cost — for the bills are not all
in the hands of government; and then, as a matter
of political party-craft, the government, of course,
is unwilling to let the full cost become known be-

fore the next election is over. So it is to be expected that the government will keep the facts from the people as long as possible. Most governments would do the same. But truth has a right of way everywhere, and will recover it at last, spite of the adverse possession of a political party. The indirect cost of the war must be still more difficult to come at, and will long remain a matter of calculation, in which it is impossible to reach certainty. We do not know yet the entire cost of the Florida War, or the late war with England; the complete cost of the Revolutionary War must forever be unknown.

It is natural for most men to exaggerate what favors their argument; but when I cannot obtain the exact figures, I will come a good deal within the probable amount. The military and naval appropriations for the year ending in June, 1847, were $40,-865,155.96; for the next year, $31,377,679.92; the sum asked for the present year, till next June, $42,-224,000; making a whole of $114,466,835.88. It is true that all this appropriation is not for the Mexican War, but it is also true that this sum does not include all the appropriations for the war. Estimating the sums already paid by the government, the private claims presented, and to be presented, the $15,000,000 to be paid Mexico as purchase-money for the territory we take from her, the $5,000,000 or $6,000,000 to be paid our own citizens for their claims against her,— I think I am a good deal within the mark when I say the war will have cost $150,000,-000 before the soldiers are at home, discharged, and out of the pay of the State. In this sum I do not include the bounty lands to be given to the soldiers and officers, nor the pensions to be paid them, their widows and orphans, for years to come. I will estimate that at $50,000,000 more, making a whole of $200,000,000 which has been paid or must be. This is the direct cost to the Federal Government, and of course does not include the sums paid by individual States, or bestowed by private generosity, to feed and clothe the volunteers before they were mustered into service. This may seem extravagant; but, fifty years hence, when party spirit no longer blinds men's eyes, and when the whole is a matter of history, I think it will be thought moderate, and be found a good deal within the actual and direct cost. Some of this cost will appear as a public debt. Part of this war debt is funded already, part not yet funded. When the outstanding demands are all settled, and the treasury notes redeemed, there will probably be a war debt of not less than $125,000,000. But, not to exaggerate, let us call it only $100,000,000.

It will, perhaps, be said, Part of this money, all that is paid in pensions, is a charity, and therefore no loss. But it is a charity paid to men who, except for the war, would have needed no such aid; and, therefore, a waste. Of the actual cost of the war, some three or four millions have been spent in extravagant prices for hiring or purchasing ships, in buying provisions and various things needed by the army, and supplied by political favorites at exorbitant rates. This is the only portion of the cost which is not a sheer waste; here the money has only changed hands: nothing has been destroyed, except the honesty of the parties concerned in such transactions. If a farmer hires men to help him till the soil, the men earn their subsistence and their wages, and leave, besides, a profit to their employer; when the season is over, he has his crops and his improvements as the return for their pay and subsistence. But for all that the soldier has consumed, for his wages, his clothes, his food and drink, the fighting tools he has worn out, and the ammunition he has expended, there is no available return to show; all that is a clear waste. The beef is eaten up, the cloth worn away, the powder is burnt, and what is there to show for it all? Nothing but the " glory." You sent out sound men, and they come back, many of them, sick and maimed; some of them are slain.

The indirect pecuniary cost of the war is caused, first, by diverting some 150,000 men, engaged in the war directly or remotely, from the works of productive industry, to the labors of war, which produce nothing; and, secondly, by disturbing the regular business of the country, first, by the withdrawal of men from their natural work; then, by withdrawing large quantities of money from the active capital of the nation; and, finally, by the general uncertainty which it causes all over the land, thus hindering men from undertaking or prosecuting successfully their various productive enterprises. If 150,000 men earn on the average but $200 apiece, that alone amounts to $30,000,000. The withdrawal of such an amount of labor from the common industry of the country must be seriously felt. At any rate, the nation has earned $30,000,000 less than it would have done if these men had kept about their common work.

But the diversion of capital from its natural and pacific direction is a greater evil in this case. America is rich, but her wealth consists mainly in land, in houses, cattle, ships, and various things needed for human comfort and industry. In money, we are poor. The amount of money is small in proportion to the actual wealth of the nation, and also in proportion to its activity, which is indicated by the business of the nation. In actual wealth, the free States of America are probably the richest people in the world; but in money we are poorer than many other nations. This is plain enough, though, perhaps not very well known, and is shown by the fact that interest, in European States, is from two to four per cent. a year, and in America from six to nine. The active capital of America is small. Now in this war a national debt has accumulated, which probably is or will soon be $100,000,000 or $125,000,000. All this great sum of money has, of course, been taken from the active capital of the country, and there has been so much less for the use of the farmer, the manufacturer, and the merchant. But for this war, these 150,000 men and these $100,000,000 would have been devoted to productive industry; and the result would have been shown by the increase of our annual earnings, in increased wealth and comfort.

Then war produced uncertainty, and that distrust amongst men. Therefore many were hindered from undertaking new works, and others found their old enterprises ruined at once. In this way there has been a great loss, which cannot be accurately estimated. I think no man, familiar with American industry, would rate this indirect loss lower than $100,000,000; some, perhaps, at twice as much; but to avoid all possibility of exaggeration, let us call it half the smallest of these sums, or $50,000,000, as the complete pecuniary cost of the Mexican War, direct and indirect.

What have we got to show for all this money? We have a large tract of territory, containing, in all, both east and west of the Rio Grande, I am told. between 700,000 and 800,000 square miles. Accounts differ as to its value. But it appears, from the recent correspondence of Mr. Slidell, that in 1845 the President offered Mexico, in money, $25,000,000 for that territory, which we now acquire under this new treaty. Suppose it is worth more, suppose it is worth twice as much, or all the indirect cost of the war ($50,000,-000), then the $200,000,000 are thrown away.

Now, for this last sum, we could have built a sufficient railroad across the Isthmus of Panama, and another across the continent, from the Mississippi to the Pacific. If such a road with its suitable equipment cost $100,000 a mile, and the distance should amount to 2,000 miles, then the $200,000,000 would just pay the bills. That would have been the greatest national work of productive industry in the world. In comparison with it, the Lake Mœris and the Pyramids of Egypt, and the Wall of China, seem but the works of a child. It might be a work to be proud of till the world ends; one, too, which would advance the industry, the welfare, and general civilization of mankind to a great degree, diminishing the distance round the globe; saving millions of property and many lives each year; besides furnishing, it is thought, a handsome income from the original outlay. But, perhaps, that would not be the best use which might be made of the money; perhaps it would not have been wise to undertake that work. At any rate, two Pacific railroads would be better than one Mexican War. We are seldom aware of the cost of war. If a single regiment of dragoons cost only $700,000 a year, which is a good deal less than the actual cost, that is considerably more than the cost of twelve colleges like Harvard University, with its schools for theology, law, and medicine; its scientific school, observatory, and all. We are, taken as a whole, a very ignorant people; and while we waste our school-money and school-time, must continue so.

A great man, who towers far above the common heads, full of creative thought, of the ideas which move the world, able to organize that thought into institutions, laws, practical works; a man of a million, a million-minded man, at the head of a nation, putting his thought into them; ruling not barely by virtue of his position, but by the intellectual and moral power to fill it; ruling not over men's heads, but in their minds and hearts, and leading them to new fields of toil, increasing their numbers, wealth, intelligence, comfort, morals, piety — such a man is a noble sight; a Charlemagne, or a Genghis Khan, a Moses leading his nation up from Egyptian bondage to freedom and the promised land. How have the eyes of the world been fixed on Washington! In darker days than ours, when all was violence, it is easy to excuse such men if they were warriors also, and made, for the time, their nation but a camp. There have been ages when the most lasting ink was human blood. In our day, when war is the exception, and that commonly needless, such a man, so getting the start of the majestic world, were a far grander sight. And with such a man at the head of this nation, a great man at the head of a free nation, able and energetic, and enterprising as we are, what were too much to hope? As it is, we have wasted our money, and got the honor of fighting such a war.

Let me next speak of the direct cost of the war in men. In April, 1846, the entire army of the United States consisted of 7,244 men; the naval force of about 7,500. We presented the gratifying spectacle of a nation of 20,000,000 strong, with a sea-coast of 3,000 or 4,000 miles, and only 7,000 or 8,000 soldiers, and as many armed men on the sea, or less than 15,-000 in all! Few things were more grateful to an American than this thought, that his country was so nearly free from the terrible curse of a standing army. At that time the standing army of France was about 480,000 men; that of Russia nearly 800,000. Most of the officers in the American army and navy, and most of the rank and file, had probably entered the service with no expectation of ever shedding the blood of men. The navy and army were looked on as instruments of peace; as much so as the police of a city.

The first of last January there was, in Mexico, an American army of 23,695 regular soldiers, and a little more than 50,000 volunteers, the number cannot now be exactly determined, making an army of invasion of about 75,000 men. The naval forces, also, had been increased to 10,000. Estimating all the men engaged in the service of the army and navy; in making weapons of war and ammunition; in preparing food and clothing; in transporting those things and the soldiers from place to place, by land or sea, and in performing the various other works incident to military operations, it is within bounds to say that there were 80,000 or 90,000 men engaged indirectly in the works of war. But not to exaggerate, it is safe to say that 150,000 men were directly or indirectly engaged in the Mexican War. This estimate

will seem moderate, when you remember that there
were about 5,000 teamsters connected with the army
in Mexico.

Here, then, were 150,000 men whose attention and
toil were diverted from the great business of productive
industry to merely military operations, or preparations for them. Of course, all the labor of these men
was of no direct value to the human race. The food
and clothing and labor of a man who earns nothing
by productive work of hand or head, is food, clothing, and labor thrown away — labor in vain. There
is nothing to show for the things he has consumed.
So all the work spent in preparing ammunition and
weapons of war is labor thrown away, an absolute
loss, as much as if it had been spent in making
earthen pitchers and then in dashing them to pieces.
A country is the richer for every serviceable plough
and spade made in it, and the world the richer; they
are to be used in productive work, and when worn
out, there is the improved soil and the crops that
have been gathered, to show for the wear and tear of
the tools. So a country is the richer for every industrious shoemaker and blacksmith it contains; for
his time and toil go to increase the sum of human
comfort, creating actual wealth. The world also is
better off, and becomes better through their influence.
But a country is the poorer for every soldier it maintains, and the world poorer, as he adds nothing to
the actual wealth of mankind; so is it the poorer for
each sword and cannon made within its borders, and
the world poorer, for these instruments cannot be
used in any productive work, only for works of destruction.

So much for the labor of these 150,000 men; labor

wasted in vain. Let us now look at the cost of life.
It is not possible to ascertain the exact loss suffered
up to this time, in killed, deceased by ordinary diseases, and in wounded; for some die before they are
mustered into the service of the United States, and
parts of the army are so far distant from the seat of
government that their recent losses are still unknown.
I rely for information on the last report of the Secretary of War, read before the Senate, April 10,
1848, and recently printed. That gives the losses of
parts of the army up to December last; other accounts
are made up only till October, or till August. Recent losses will of course swell the amount of destruction. According to that report, on the American
side there had been killed in battle, or died of wounds
received therein, 1,689 persons; there had died of
diseases and accidents, 6,173; 3,743 have been wounded
in battle, who were not known to be dead at the date
of the report.

This does not include the deaths in the navy, nor
the destruction of men connected with the army in
various ways, as furnishing supplies and the like. Considering the sickness and accidents that have happened in the present year, and others which may
be expected before the troops reach home, I may
set down the total number of deaths on the American
side, caused by the war, at 15,000, and the number
of wounded men at 4,000. Suppose the army on the
average to have consisted of 50,000 men for two
years, this gives a mortality of fifteen per cent. each
year, which is an enormous loss even for times of war,
and one seldom equaled in modern warfare.

Now, most of the men who have thus died or been
maimed were in the prime of life, able-bodied and

hearty men. Had they remained at home in the works
of peace, it is not likely that more than 500 of the
number would have died. So then 14,500 lives may
be set down at once to the account of the war. The
wounded men are of course to thank the war, and
that alone, for their smart, and the lifelong agony
which they are called on to endure.

Such is the American loss. The loss of the Mexicans we cannot now determine. But they have been
many times more numerous than the Americans; have
been badly armed, badly commanded, badly trained,
and besides, have been beaten in every battle; their
number seemed often the cause of their ruin, making
them confident before battle, and hindering their retreat after they were beaten. Still more, they have
been ill provided with surgeons and nurses to care for
the wounded, and were destitute of medicines. They
must have lost in battle five or six times more than
we have done, and have had a proportionate number
of wounded. To "lie like a military bulletin" is a
European proverb; and it is not necessary to trust
reports which tell of 600 or 900 Mexicans left dead
on the ground, while the Americans lost but five or six.
But when we remember that only twelve Americans
were killed during the bombardment of Vera Cruz,
which lasted five days; that the citadel contained more
than 5,000 soldiers and over 400 pieces of cannon,
we may easily believe the Mexican losses, on the whole,
have been 10,000 men killed and perished of their
wounds. Their loss by sickness would probably be
smaller than our own, for the Mexicans were in their
native climate, though often ill-furnished with clothes,
with shelter, and provisions; so I will put down their
loss by ordinary diseases at only 5,000, making a

total of 15,000 deaths. Suppose their number of wounded was four times as great as our own, or 20,-000; I should not be surprised if this were only half the number.

Put all together, and we have in total Americans and Mexicans, 24,000 men wounded, more or less, and the greater part maimed for life; and we have 30,-000 men killed on the field of battle, or perished by the slow torture of their wounds, or deceased of diseases caused by extraordinary exposure; 24,000 men maimed; 30,000 dead!

You all remember the bill which so hastily passed Congress in May, 1846, and authorized the war previously begun. You perhaps have not forgot the preamble, " Whereas war exists by the act of Mexico." Well, that bill authorized the waste of $200,000,000 of American treasure, money enough to have built a railroad across the Isthmus of Panama, and another to connect the Mississippi and the Pacific Ocean; it demanded the disturbance of industry and commerce all over the land, caused by withdrawing $100,000,000 from peaceful investments, and diverting 150,000 Americans from their productive and peaceful works; it demanded a loss yet greater of the treasure of Mexicans; it commanded the maiming of 24,000 men for life, and the death of 30,000 men in the prime and vigor of manhood. Yet such was the state of feeling, I will not say of thought, in the Congress, that out of both houses only sixteen men voted against it. If a prophet had stood there he might have said to the representative of Boston, " You have just voted for the wasting of 200,000,000 of the very dollars you were sent there to represent; for the maiming of 24,000 men and the killing of 30,000 more — part by disease, part by the sword, part by the slow and awful lingerings of a wounded frame! Sir, that is the English of your vote." Suppose the prophet, before the votes were taken, could have gone round and told each member of Congress, " If there comes a war, you will perish in it; " perhaps the vote would have been a little different.   It is easy to vote away blood, if it is not your own!

Such is the cost of the war in money and in men. Yet it has not been a very cruel war. It has been conducted with as much gentleness as a war of invasion can be. There is no agreeable way of butchering men. You cannot make it a pastime. The Americans have always been a brave people; they were never cruel. They always treated their prisoners kindly — in the Revolutionary War, in the late war with England. True, they have seized the Mexican ports, taken military possession of the custom-houses, and collected such duties as they saw fit; true, they sometimes made the army of invasion self-subsisting, and to that end have levied contributions on the towns they have taken; true, they have seized provisions which were private property, snatching them out of the hands of men who needed them; true, they have robbed the rich and the poor; true, they have burned and bombarded towns, have murdered men and violated women. All this must of course take place in any war. There will be the general murder and robbery committed on account of the nation, and the particular murder and robbery on account of the special individual. This also is to be expected. You cannot set a town on fire and burn down just half of it, making the flames stop exactly where you will. You cannot take the most idle, ignorant, drunken, and vicious men out of the low population in our cities and large towns, get them drunk enough or foolish enough to enlist, train them to violence, theft, robbery, murder, and then stop the man from exercising his rage or lust on his own private account. If it is hard to make a dog understand that he must kill a hare for his master, but never for himself, it is not much easier to teach a volunteer that it is a duty, a distinction, and a glory to rob and murder the Mexican people for the nation's sake, but a wrong, a shame, and a crime to rob or murder a single Mexican for his own sake. There have been instances of wanton cruelty, occasioned by private licentiousness and individual barbarity. Of these I shall take no further notice, but come to such as have been commanded by the American authorities, and which were the official acts of the nation.

One was the capture of Tabasco. Tabasco is a small town several hundred miles from the theater of war, situated on a river about eighty miles from the sea, in the midst of a fertile province. The army did not need it, nor the navy. It did not lie in the way of the American operations; its possession would be wholly useless. But one Sunday afternoon, while the streets were full of men, women, and children, engaged in their Sunday business, a part of the naval force of America swept by; the streets running at right angles with the river were enfiladed by the hostile cannon, and men, women, and children, unarmed and unresisting, were mowed down by the merciless shot. The city was taken, but soon abandoned, for its possession was of no use. The killing of those men, women, and children was as much a piece of murder as it would be to come and shoot us to-day, and in this house. No valid excuse has been given for this cold-blooded massacre; none can be given. It was not battle, but wanton butchery. None but a Pequod Indian could excuse it. The theological newspapers in New England thought it a wicked thing in Dr. Palfrey to write a letter on Sunday, though he hoped thereby to help end the war. How many of them had any fault to find with this national butchery on the Lord's day? Fighting is bad enough any day; fighting for mere pay, or glory, or the love of fighting, is a wicked thing; but to fight on that day when the whole Christian world kneels to pray in the name of the Peacemaker; to butcher men and women and children, when they are coming home from church, with prayer-books in their hands, seems an aggravation even of murder; a cowardly murder, which a Hessian would have been ashamed of. " But, 'twas a famous victory."

One other instance, of at least apparent wantonness, took place at the bombardment of Vera Cruz. After the siege had gone on for awhile, the foreign consuls in the town, " moved," as they say, " by the feeling of humanity excited in their hearts by the frightful results of the bombardment of the city," requested that the women and children might be allowed to leave the city, and not stay to be shot. The American general refused; they must stay and be shot.

Perhaps you have not an adequate conception of the effect produced by bombarding a town. Let me interest you a little in the details thereof. Vera Cruz is about as large as Boston was in 1810; it contains about 30,000 inhabitants. In addition, it is protected by a castle, the celebrated fortress of St. Juan d'Ulloa, furnished with more than 5,000 soldiers and over 400 cannons. Imagine to yourself Boston as it was forty

years ago, invested with a fleet on one side and an
army of 15,000 men on the land, both raining cannon-
balls and bomb-shells upon your houses; shattering
them to fragments, exploding in your streets, churches,
houses, cellars, mingling men, women, and children in
one promiscuous murder.   Suppose this to continue
five days and nights; imagine the condition of the city;
the ruins, the flames; the dead, the wounded, the widows, the orphans; think of the fears of the men anticipating the city would be sacked by a merciless soldiery;
think of the women!   Thus you will have a faint notion of the picture of Vera Cruz at the end of March,
1847.   Do you know the meaning of the name of
the city?   Vera Cruz is the True Cross.   " See how
these Christians love one another."   The Americans
are followers of the Prince of Peace; they have more
missionaries amongst the " heathen " than any other
nation, and the President, in his last message, says,
" No country has been so much favored, or should
acknowledge with deeper reverence the manifestations
of the Divine protection."   The Americans were fighting Mexico to dismember her territory, to plunder her
soil, and plant thereon the institution of slavery, " the
necessary background of freedom."

Few of us have ever seen a battle, and without that
none can have a complete notion of the ferocious passions which it excites.   Let me help your fancy a little
by relating an anecdote which seems to be very well au-
thenticated, and requires but little external testimony
to render it credible.   At any rate, it was abundantly
believed a year ago; but times change, and what was
then believed all round may now be " the most im-
probable thing in the world."   At the battle of Buena
Vista, a Kentucky regiment began to stagger under

the heavy charge of the Mexicans. The American commander-in-chief turned to one who stood near him, and exclaimed, "By God, this will not do. This is not the way for Kentuckians to behave when called on to make good a battle. It will not answer, sir." So the general clenched his fist, knit his brows, and set his teeth hard together. However, the Kentuckians presently formed in good order and gave a deadly fire, which altered the battle. Then the old general broke out with a loud hurrah. "Hurrah for old Kentuck," he exclaimed, rising in his stirrups; "that's the way to do it. Give 'em hell, damn 'em," and tears of exultation rolled down his cheeks as he said it. You find the name of this general at the head of most of the Whig newspapers in the United States. He is one of the most popular candidates for the Presidency. Cannons were fired for him, a hundred guns, on Boston Common, not long ago, in honor of his nomination for the highest office in the gift of a free and Christian people. Soon we shall probably have clerical certificates, setting forth, to the people of the North, that he is an exemplary Christian. You know how Faneuil Hall, the old "Cradle of Liberty," rang with "Hurrah for Taylor," but a few days ago. The seven wise men of Greece were famous in their day; but now nothing is known of them except a single pungent aphorism from each, "Know thyself," and the like. The time may come when our great men shall have suffered this same reduction, descending, all their robes of glory having vanished save a single thread. Then shall Franklin be known only as having said, "Don't give too much for the whistle;" Patrick Henry for his "Give me liberty or give me death;" Washington for his "In peace prepare for war;" Jefferson for his

" All men are created equal; " and General Taylor
shall be known only by his attributes " rough and
ready," and for his aphorism, " Give 'em hell, damn
'em." Yet he does not seem to be a ferocious man,
but generous and kindly, it is said, and strongly opposed to this particular war, whose " natural justice "
it seems he looked at, and which he thought was wicked
at the beginning, though, on that account, he was none
the less ready to fight it.

One thing more I must mention in speaking of the
cost of men. According to the report quoted just
now, 4,966 American soldiers had deserted in Mexico.
Some of them had joined the Mexican army. When
the American commissioners, who were sent to secure
the ratification of the treaty, went to Queretaro, they
found there a body of 200 American soldiers, and
800 more were at no great distance, mustered into
the Mexican service. These men, it seems, had served
out their time in the American camp, and notwithstanding they had, as the President says in his message, " covered themselves with imperishable honors,"
by fighting men who never injured them, they were
willing to go and seek a yet thicker mantle of this imperishable honor, by fighting against their own country! Why should they not? If it were right to kill
Mexicans for a few dollars a month, why was it not
also right to kill Americans, especially when it pays
the most? Perhaps it is not an American habit to inquire into the justice of a war, only into the profit
which it may bring. If the Mexicans pay best, in
money, these 1,000 soldiers made a good speculation.
No doubt in Mexico military glory is at a premium,
though it could hardly command a greater price just
now than in America, where, however. the supply
seems equal to the demand.

The numerous desertions and the readiness with which the soldiers joined the " foe," show plainly the moral character of the men, and the degree of " patriotism " and " humanity " which animated them in going to war. You know the severity of military discipline; the terrible beatings men are subjected to before they can become perfect in the soldier's art; the horrible and revolting punishments imposed on them for drunkenness, though little pains were taken to keep the temptation from their eyes, and for disobedience of general orders. You have read enough of this in the newspapers. The officers of the volunteers, I am told, have generally been men of little education, men of strong passions and bad habits; many of them abandoned men, who belonged to the refuse of society. Such men run into an army as the wash of the street runs into the sewers. When such a man gets clothed with a little authority, in time of peace, you know what use he makes of it; but when he covers himself with the " imperishable honors " of his official coat, gets an epaulet on his shoulder, a sword by his side, a commission in his pocket, and visions of " glory " in his head, you may easily judge how he will use his authority, or may read in the newspapers how he has used it. When there are brutal soldiers, commanded by brutal captains, it is to be supposed that much brutality is to be suffered.

Now, desertion is a great offense in a soldier; in this army it is one of the most common; for nearly ten per cent. of the American army has deserted in Mexico, not to mention the desertions before the army reached that country. It is related that forty-eight men were hanged at once for desertion; not hanged as you judicially murder men in time of peace, privately, as if ashamed of the deed, in the corner of a jail, and by a contrivance which shortens the agony, and makes death humane as possible. These forty-eight men were hanged slowly; put to death with painful procrastinations, their agony wilfully prolonged, and death embittered by needless ferocity. But that is not all: it is related, that these men were doomed to be thus murdered on the day when the battle of Churubusco took place. These men, awaiting their death, were told they should not suffer till the American flag should wave its stripes over the hostile walls. So they were kept in suspense an hour, and then slowly hanged one by one. You know the name of the officer on whom this barbarity rests: it was Colonel Harney, a man whose reputation was black enough and base enough before. His previous deeds, however, require no mention here. But this man is now a general, and so on the high road to the Presidency, whenever it shall please our Southern masters to say the word. Some accounts say there were more than forty-eight who thus were hanged. I only give the number of those whose names lie printed before me as I write. Perhaps the number was less; it is impossible to obtain exact information in respect to the matter, for the government has not yet published an account of the punishments inflicted in this war. The information can only be obtained by a " resolution " of either house of Congress, and so is not likely to be had before the election. But at the same time with the execution, other deserters were scourged with fifty lashes each, branded with a letter D, a perpetual mark of infamy on their cheek, compelled to wear an iron yoke, weighing eight pounds, about their neck. Six men were made to dig the grave of their companions, and were then flogged with two hundred lashes each.

I wish this hanging of forty-eight men could have taken place in State Street, and the respectable citizens of Boston, who like this war, had been made to look on and see it all; that they had seen those poor culprits bid farewell to father, mother, wife, or child, looking wistfully for the hour which was to end their torment, and then, one by one, have seen them slowly hanged to death; that your representative, ye men of Boston, had put on all the halters! He did help put them on; that infamous vote — I speak not of the motive, it may have been as honorable as the vote itself was infamous — doomed these eight and forty men to be thus murdered.

Yes, I wish all this killing of the 2,000 Americans on the field of battle, and the 10,000 Mexicans; all this slashing of the bodies of 24,000 wounded men; all the agony of the other 18,000, that have died of disease, could have taken place in some spot where the President of the United States and his Cabinet, where all the Congress who voted for the war, with the Baltimore conventions of '44 and '48, and the Whig convention of Philadelphia, and the controlling men of both political parties, who care nothing for this bloodshed and misery they have idly caused, could have stood and seen it all; and then that the voice of the whole nation had come up to them and said, " This is your work, not ours. Certainly we will not shed our blood, nor our brothers' blood, to get never so much slave territory. It was bad enough to fight in the cause of freedom. In the cause of slavery — God forgive us for that! We have trusted you thus far, but please God we never will trust you again."

Let us now look at the effect of this war on the morals of the nation. The Revolutionary War was the contest for a great idea. If there were ever a just war it was that — a contest for national existence. Yet it brought out many of the worst qualities of human nature on both sides, as well as some of the best. It helped make a Washington, it is true, but a Benedict Arnold likewise. A war with a powerful nation, terrible as it must be, yet develops the energy of the people, promotes self-denial, and helps the growth of some qualities of a high order. It had this effect in England from 1798 to 1815. True, England for that time became a despotism, but the self-consciousness of the nation, its self-denial and energy, were amazingly stimulated; the moral effect of that series of wars was doubtless far better than of the infamous contest which she has kept up against Ireland for many years. Let us give even war its due: when a great boy fights with an equal, it may develop his animal courage and strength — for he gets as bad as he gives; but when he only beats a little boy that cannot pay back his blows, it is cowardly as well as cruel, and doubly debasing to the conqueror. Mexico was no match for America. We all knew that very well before the war began. When a nation numbering 8,000,000 or 9,000,000 of people can be successfully invaded by an army of 75,000 men, two-thirds of them volunteers, raw and undisciplined; when the invaders with less than 15,000 can march two hundred miles into the very heart of the hostile country, and with less than 6,000 can take and hold the capital of the nation, a city of 100,000 or 200,000 inhabitants, and dictate a peace, taking as much territory as they will — it is hardly fair to dignify such

operations with the name of war. The little good
which a long contest with an equal might produce in
the conqueror, is wholly lost. Had Mexico been a
strong nation, we should never have had this conflict. A few years ago, when General Cass wanted a
war with England, " an old-fashioned war," and declared it " unavoidable," all the men of property trembled. The Northern men thought of their mills and
their ships; they thought how Boston and New York
would look after a war with our sturdy old father over
the sea; they thought we should lose many millions of
dollars and gain nothing. The men of the South, who
have no mills and no ships, and no large cities to be
destroyed, thought of their " peculiar institutions; "
they thought of a servile war; they thought what
might become of their slaves if a nation which gave
$100,000,000 to emancipate her bondmen should send a
large army with a few black soldiers from Jamaica;
should offer money, arms, and freedom to all who
would leave their masters and claim their inalienable
rights. They knew the Southern towns would be burnt
to ashes, and the whole South from Virginia to the
Gulf, would be swept with fire; and they said, " Don't."
The North said so, and the South; they feared such a
war with such a foe. Everybody knows the effect
which this fear had on Southern politicians in the beginning of this century, and how gladly they made
peace with England soon as she was at liberty to turn
her fleet and her army against the most vulnerable
part of the nation. I am not blind to the wickedness
of England more than ignorant of the good things she
has done and is doing; a paradise for the rich and
strong, she is still a purgatory for the wise and the
good, and the hell of the poor and the weak. I have

no fondness for war anywhere, and believe it needless
and wanton in this age of the world — surely needless
and wicked between Father England and Daughter
America; but I do solemnly believe that the moral effect of such an old-fashioned war as Mr. Cass in 1845
thought unavoidable, would have been better than that
of this Mexican War. It would have ended slavery;
ended it in blood, no doubt, the worst thing to blot out
an evil with; but ended it, and for ever. God grant
it may yet have a more peaceful termination. We
should have lost millions of property and thousands
of men, and then, when peace came, we should know
what it was worth; and as the burnt child dreads the
fire, no future President, or Congress, or convention,
or party, would talk much in favor of war for some
years to come.

The moral effect of this war is thoroughly bad. It
was unjust in the beginning. Mexico did not pay her
debts; but though the United States, in 1783, acknowledged the British claims against ourselves, they were
not paid till 1803; our claims against England, for her
depredations in 1793, were not paid till 1804; our
claims against France, for her depredations in
1806–13, were not paid us till 1834. The fact that
Mexico refused to receive the resident minister whom
the United States sent to settle the disputes, when a
commissioner was expected — this was no ground of
war. We have lately seen a British ambassador ordered to leave Spain within eight-and-forty hours, and
yet the English Minister of Foreign Affairs, Lord Pal-
merston — no new hand at diplomacy — declares that
this does not interrupt the concord of the two nations!
We treated Mexico contemptuously before hostilities
began; and when she sent troops into a territory which

she had always possessed, though Texas had claimed it, we declared that that was an act of war, and ourselves sent an army to invade her soil, to capture her cities, and seize her territory. It has been a war of plunder, undertaken for the purpose of seizing Mexican territory, and extending over it that dismal curse which blackens, impoverishes, and barbarizes half the Union now, and swiftly corrupts the other half. It was not enough to have Louisiana a slave territory; not enough to make that institution perpetual in Florida; not enough to extend this blight over Texas — we must have yet more slave soil, one day to be carved into slave States, to bind the Southern yoke yet more securely on the Northern neck; to corrupt yet more the politics, literature, and morals of the North. The war was unjust at its beginning; mean in its motives, a war without honorable cause; a war for plunder; a quarrel between a great boy and a little puny weakling who could not walk alone, and could hardly stand. We have treated Mexico as the three Northern powers treated Poland in the last century — stooped to conquer. Nay, our contest has been like the English seizure of Ireland. All the justice was on one side, the force, skill, and wealth, on the other.

I know men say the war has shown us that Americans could fight. Could fight? Almost every male beast will fight, the more brutal the better. The long war of the Revolution, when Connecticut, for seven years, kept 5,000 men in the field, showed that Americans could fight; Bunker Hill and Lexington showed that they could fight, even without previous discipline. If such valor be a merit, I am ready to believe that the Americans, in a great cause like that of Mexico, to resist wicked invasion, would fight as men never fought before. A republic like our own, where every free man feels an interest in the welfare of the nation, is full of the elements that make soldiers. Is that a praise? Most men think so, but it is the smallest honor of a nation. Of all glories, military glory, at its best estate, seems the poorest.

Men tell us it shows the strength of the nation, and some writers quote the opinions of European kings who, when hearing of the battles of Monterey, Buena Vista, and Vera Cruz, became convinced that we were a " great people." Remembering the character of these kings, one can easily believe that such was their judgment, and will not sigh many times at their fate, but will hope to see the day when the last king, who can estimate a nation's strength only by its battles, has passed on to impotence and oblivion. The power of America — do we need proof of that? I see it in the streets of Boston and New York; in Lowell and in Lawrence; I see it in our mills and our ships; I read it in those letters of iron written all over the North, where he may read that runs; I see it in the unconquered energy which tames the forest, the rivers, and the ocean; in the school-houses which lift their modest roof in every village of the North; in the churches that rise all over the freeman's land: would God that they rose higher, pointing down to man and to human duties, and up to God and immortal life! I see the strength of America in that tide of population which spreads over the prairies of the West, and, beating on the Rocky Mountains, dashes its peaceful spray to the very shores of the Pacific sea. Had we taken 150,000 men and $200,000,000, and built two railroads across the continent, that would have been a worthy sign of the nation's strength. Perhaps those kings could not see it; but sensible men could see it and be glad. This waste of treasure and this waste of blood is only a proof of weakness. War is a transient weakness of the nation, but slavery a permanent imbecility.

What falsehood has this war produced in the executive and legislative power; in both parties, Whigs and Democrats! I always thought that here in Massachusetts the Whigs were the most to blame; they tried to put the disgrace of the war on the others, while the Democratic party coolly faced the wickedness. Did far-sighted men know that there would be a war on Mexico, or else on the tariff or the currency, and prefer the first as the least evil?

See to what the war has driven two of the most famous men of the nation: one wished to " capture or slay a Mexican; " the other could encourage the volunteers to fight a war which he had denounced as needless, " a war of pretexts," and place the men of Monterey before the men of Bunker Hill; each could invest a son in that unholy cause. You know the rest: the fathers ate sour grapes, and the children's teeth were set on edge. When a man goes on board an emigrant ship, reeking with filth and fever, not for gain, not for " glory," but in brotherly love, catches the contagion, and dies a martyr to his heroic benevolence, men speak of it in corners, and it is soon forgot; there is no parade in the streets; society takes little pains to do honor to the man. How rarely is a pension given to his widow or his child; only once in the whole land, and then but a small sum. But when a volunteer officer — for of the humbler and more excusable men that fall we take no heed, war may mow that crop of " vulgar deaths " with what scythe he will — falls or dies in the quarrel which he had no concern in, falls in a broil between the two nations, your newspapers extol the man, and with martial pomp, " sonorous metal blowing martial sounds," with all the honors of the most honored dead, you lay away his body in the tomb. Thus is it that the nation teaches these little ones that it is better to kill than to make alive.

I know there are men in the army, honorable and high-minded men, Christian men, who dislike war in general, and this war in special; but such is their view of official duty, that they obeyed the summons of battle, though with pain and reluctance. They knew not how to avoid obedience. I am willing to believe there are many such. But with volunteers, who, of their own accord, came forth to enlist, men not blinded by ignorance, not driven by poverty to the field, but only by hope of reward — what shall be said of them? Much may be said to excuse the rank and file, ignorant men, many of them in want — but for the leaders, what can be said? Had I a brother who, in the day of the nation's extremity, came forward with a good conscience, and periled his life on the battle-field, and lost it " in the sacred cause of God and his country," I would honor the man, and when his dust came home, I would lay it away with his fathers'; with sorrow indeed, but with thankfulness of heart that, for conscience' sake, he was ready even to die. But had I a brother who, merely for his pay, or hope of fame, had voluntarily gone down to fight innocent men, to plunder their territory, and lost his life in that felonious essay — in sorrow and in silence, and in secrecy, would I lay down his body in the grave; I would not court display, nor mark it with a single stone.

See how this war has affected public opinion. How many of your newspapers have shown its true atrocity?

how many of the pulpits? Yet, if any one is appointed to tell of public wrongs, it is the minister of religion. The governor of Massachusetts is an officer of a Christian church; a man distinguished for many excellencies, some of them by no means common: it is said he is opposed to the war in private, and thinks it wicked; but no man has lent himself as a readier tool to promote it. The Christian and the man seem lost in the office, in the governor! What a lesson of falseness does all this teach to that large class of persons who look no higher than the example of eminent men for their instruction. You know what complaints have been made by the highest authority in the nation, because a few men dared to speak against the war. It was " affording aid and comfort to the enemy." If the war party had been stronger, and feared no public opinion, we should have had men hanged for treason, because they spoke of this national iniquity! Nothing would have been easier. A " gag law " is not wholly unknown in America.

If you will take all the theft, all the assaults, all the cases of arson, ever committed in time of peace in the United States, since the settlement of Jamestown in 1608, and add to them all the cases of violence offered to woman, with all the murders, they will not amount to half the wrongs committed in this war for the plunder of Mexico. Yet the cry has been, and still is, " You must not say a word against it; if you do, you ' afford aid and comfort to the enemy.' " Not tell the nation that she is doing wrong? What a miserable saying is that; let it come from what high authority it may, it is a miserable saying. Make the case your own. Suppose the United States were invaded by a nation ten times abler for war than we are, with a cause no more just, intentions equally bad; invaded for the purpose of dismembering our territory and making our own New England the soil of slaves; would you be still? would you stand and look on tamely while the hostile hosts, strangers in language, manners, and religion, crossed your rivers, seized your ports, burnt your towns? No, surely not. Though the men of New England would not be able to resist with most celestial love, they would contend with most manly vigor; and I should rather see every house swept clean off the land, and the ground sheeted with our own dead; rather see every man, woman, and child in the land slain, than see them tamely submit to such a wrong. And so would you. No; sacred as life is, and dear as it is, better let it be trodden out by the hoof of war, rather than yield tamely to a wrong. But while you were doing your utmost to repel such formidable injustice, if in the midst of your invaders, men rose up and said, " America is in the right, and, brothers, you are wrong; you should not thus kill men to steal their land: shame on you! " how should you feel towards such? Nay, in the struggle with England, when our fathers periled everything but honor, and fought for the inalienable rights of man, you all remember, how in England herself there stood up noble men, and with a voice that was heard above the roar of the populace, and an authority higher than the majesty of the throne, they said, " You do a wrong; you may ravage, but you cannot conquer. If I were an American, while a foreign troop remained in my land, I would never lay down my arms; no, never, never, never! "

But I wander a little from my theme, the effect of the war on the morals of the nation. Here are 50,000

or 75,000 men trained to kill. Hereafter they will be
of little service in any good work. Many of them
were the offscouring of the people at first. Now,
these men have tasted the idleness, the intemperance,
the debauchery of a camp; tasted of its riot, tasted of
its blood! They will come home before long, hirelings
of murder. What will their influence be as fathers,
husbands? The nation taught them to fight and plunder the Mexicans for the nation's sake; the governor
of Massachusetts called on them in the name of " patriotism " and " humanity " to enlist for that work:
but if, with no justice on our side, it is humane and
patriotic to fight and plunder the Mexicans on the
nation's account, why not for the soldier to fight and
plunder an American on his own account? Aye, why
not? — that is a distinction too nice for common
minds; by far too nice for mine.

See the effect on the nation. We have just plundered Mexico; taken a piece of her territory larger
than the thirteen states which fought the Revolution,
a hundred times as large as Massachusetts; we have
burnt her cities, have butchered her men, have been
victorious in every contest. The Mexicans were as unprotected women; we, armed men. See how the lust
of conquest will increase. Soon it will be the ambition of the next President to extend the " area of freedom " a little further south; the lust of conquest will
increase. Soon we must have Yucatan, Central America, all of Mexico, Cuba, Porto Rico, Hayti, Jamaica
— all the islands of the Gulf. Many men would
gladly, I doubt not, extend the " area of freedom " so
as to include the free blacks of those islands. We
have long looked with jealous eyes on West Indian
emancipation — hoping the scheme would not succeed.

How pleasant it would be to re-establish slavery in Hayti and Jamaica, in all the islands whence the gold of England or the ideas of France have driven it out. If the South wants this, would the North object? The possession of the West Indies would bring much money to New England, and what is the value of freedom compared to coffee and sugar and cotton?

I must say one word of the effect this war has had on political parties. By the parties I mean the leaders thereof, the men that control the parties. The effect on the Democratic party, on the majority of Congress, on the most prominent men of the nation, has been mentioned before. It has shut their eyes to truth and justice; it has filled their mouths with injustice and falsehood. It has made one man " available " for the Presidency who was only known before as a sagacious general, that fought against the Indians in Florida, and acquired a certain reputation by the use of bloodhounds, a reputation which was rather unenviable, even in America. The battles in northern Mexico made him conspicuous, and now he is seized on as an engine to thrust one corrupt party out of power, and to lift in another party, I will not say less corrupt, I wish I could; it were difficult to think it more so. This latter party has been conspicuous for its opposition to a military man as ruler of a free people; recently it has been smitten with sudden admiration for military men, and military success, and tells the people, without a blush, that a military man fresh from a fight which he disapproved of, is most likely to restore peace, " because most familiar with the evils of war! " In Massachusetts the prevalent political party, as such, for some years, seems to have had no moral principle; however, it had a prejudice

in favor of decency: now it has thrown that overboard,
and has not even its respectability left. What are its
" resolutions? " Some men knew what they were
worth long ago; now all men can see what they are
worth.

The cost of the war in money and men I have tried
to calculate, but the effect on the morals of the people,
on the press, the pulpit, and the parties, and through
them on the rising generation, it is impossible to tell.
I have only faintly sketched the outline of that. The
effect of the war on Mexico herself, we can dimly see
in the distance. The Government of the United States
has wilfully, wantonly broken the peace of the continent. The Revolutionary War was unavoidable; but
for this invasion there is no excuse. That God, whose
providence watches over the falling nation as the falling sparrow, and whose comprehensive plans are now
advanced by the righteousness and now by the wrath
of man; He who stilleth the waves of the sea and the
tumult of the people, will turn all this wickedness to
account in the history of man — of that I have no
doubt. But that is no excuse for American crime. A
greater good lay within our grasp, and we spurned it
away.

Well, before long the soldiers will come back, such
as shall ever come — the regulars and volunteers, the
husbands of the women whom your charity fed last
winter, housed and clad and warmed. They will come
back. Come, New England, with your posterity of
States, go forth to meet your sons returning all " covered with imperishable honors." Come, men, to meet
your fathers, brothers. Come, women, to your husbands and your lovers; come. But what! is that the
body of men who a year or two ago went forth so full

of valor and of rum? Are these rags the imperishable honors that cover them? Here is not half the
whole. Where is the wealth they hoped from the spoil
of churches? But the men — "Where is my husband?" says one; "And my son?" says another.
"They fell at Jalapa, one, and one at Cerro Gordo ;
but they fell covered with imperishable honor, for
'twas a famous victory." "Where is my lover?"
screams a woman whom anguish makes respectable,
spite of her filth and ignorance ; —"And our father,
where is he?" scream a troop of half-starved children,
staring through their dirt and rags. "One died of
the vomit at Vera Cruz. Your father, little ones, we
scourged the naked man to death at Mixcoac."

But that troop which is left, who are in the arms of
wife and child, they are the best sermon against war;
this has lost an arm and that a leg ; half are maimed
in battle or sickened with the fever; all polluted with
the drunkenness, idleness, debauchery, lust, and murder of a camp. Strip off this man's coat, and count
the stripes welted into his flesh, stripes laid on
by demagogues that love the people —"the dear
people!" See how affectionately the war-makers
branded the "dear soldiers" with a letter D, with a
red-hot iron, in the cheek. The flesh will quiver as
the irons burn ; no matter: it is only for love of the
people that all this is done, and we are all of us covered with imperishable honors! D stands for deserter
— aye, and for demagogue — yes, and for demon too.
Many a man shall come home with but half of himself,
half his body, less than half his soul.

> "Alas! the mother that him bare,
> If she could stand in presence there,
> In that wan cheek and wasted air,
>   She would not know her child."

" Better," you say, " for us better, and for themselves better by far, if they had left that remnant
of a body in the common ditch where the soldier finds
his ' bed of honor; ' better have fed therewith the vul-
tures of a foreign soil than thus come back." No;
better come back, and live here, mutilated, scourged,
branded, a cripple, a pauper, a drunkard, and a felon;
better darken the windows of the jail, and blot the gallows with unusual shame, to teach us all that such is
war, and such the results of every " famous victory,"
such the imperishable honors that it brings, and how
the war-makers love the men they rule!

O Christian America! O New England, child of
the Puritans! Cradled in the wilderness, thy swad-
dling garments stained with martyrs' blood, hearing
in thy youth the war-whoop of the savage and thy
mother's sweet and soul-composing hymn:

> " Hush, my child, lie still and slumber,
>   Holy angels guard thy bed;
> Heavenly blessings, without number,
>   Rest upon thine infant head."

Come, New England, take the old banners of thy
conquering host, the standards borne at Monterey,
Palo Alto, Buena Vista, Vera Cruz, the " glorious
stripes and stars " that waved over the walls of Churubusco, Contreras, Puebla, Mexico herself, flags black-
ened with battle and stiffened with blood, pierced by
the lances and torn with the shot; bring them into thy
churches, hang them up over altar and pulpit, and let
little children, clad in white raiment and crowned with
flowers, come and chant their lessons for the day.

" Blessed are the pure in heart, for they shall see
God.

" Blessed are the peacemakers, for they shall be called the children of God."

Then let the priest say, " Righteousness exalteth a nation, but sin is a reproach unto any people. Blessed is the Lord my strength, which teacheth my hands to war, and my fingers to fight. Happy is that people that is in such a case. Yea, happy is that people whose God is the Lord, and Jesus Christ their Saviour."

Then let the soldiers who lost their limbs and the women who lost their husbands and their lovers in the strife, and the men — wiser than the children of light — who made money out of the war: let all the people, like people and like priest, say, " Amen."

But suppose these men were to come back to Boston on a day when, in civil style, as having never sinned yourself, and never left a man in ignorance and want to be goaded into crime, you were about to hang three men — one for murder, one for robbery with the armed hand, and one for burning down a house. Suppose, after the fashion of " the good old times," you were to hang those men in public, and lead them in long procession through your streets, and while you were welcoming these returned soldiers and taking their officers to feast in the " Cradle of Liberty," they should meet the sheriff's procession escorting those culprits to the gallows. Suppose the warriors should ask, " Why, what is that? " What would you say? Why, this: " These men, they broke the law of God, by violence, by fire and blood, and we shall hang them for the public good, and especially for the example, to teach the ignorant, the low, and the weak." Suppose those three felons, the halters round their neck, should ask also, " Why, what is that? " You would say, "They are the soldiers just come back from war. For two long years they have been hard at work, burning cities, plundering a nation, and butchering whole armies of men. Sometimes they killed a thousand in a day. By their help, the nation has stolen seven hundred thousand square miles of land!" Suppose the culprits ask, "Where will you hang so many?" "Hang them!" is the answer, "we shall only hang you. It is written in our Bible that one murder makes a villain, millions a hero. We shall feast these men full of bread and wine; shall take their leader, a rough man and a ready, one who by perpetual robbery holds a hundred slaves and more, and make him a king over all the land. But as you only burnt, robbed, and murdered on so small a scale, and without the command of the President or the Congress, we shall hang you by the neck. Our governor ordered these men to go and burn and rob and kill; now he orders you to be hanged, and you must not ask any more questions, for the hour is already come."

To make the whole more perfect — suppose a native of Loo-Choo, converted to Christianity by your missionaries in his native land, had come hither to have "the way of God" "expounded unto him more perfectly," that he might see how these Christians love one another. Suppose he should be witness to a scene like this!

To men who know the facts of war, the wickedness of this particular invasion and its wide-extending consequences, I fear that my words will seem poor and cold and tame. I have purposely mastered my emotion, telling only my thought. I have uttered no denunciation against the men who caused this destruction of treasure, this massacre of men, this awful

degradation of the moral sense.   The respectable men
of Boston —" the men of property and standing "
all over the State, the men that commonly control the
politics of New England — tell you that they dislike
the war.   But they re-elect the men who made it.   Has
a single man in all New England lost his seat in any
office because he favored the war?   Not a man.   Have
you ever known a Northern merchant who would not
let his ship for the war, because the war was wicked
and he a Christian?   Have you ever known a Northern manufacturer who would not sell a kernel of powder, nor a cannon-ball, nor a coat, nor a shirt for the
war?   Have you ever known a capitalist, a man who
lives by letting money, refuse to lend money for the
war because the war was wicked?   Not a merchant,
not a manufacturer, not a capitalist.   A little money
— it can buy up whole hosts of men.   Virginia sells
her negroes; what does New England sell?   There was
once a man in Boston, a rich man too, not a very
great man, only a good one who loved his country, and
there was another poor man here, in the times that
tried men's souls; but there was not money enough in
all England, not enough promise of honors, to make
Hancock and Adams false to their sense of right.   Is
our soil degenerate, and have we lost the breed of
noble men?

No, I have not denounced the men who directly
made the war, or indirectly egged the people on.   Pardon me, thou prostrate Mexico, robbed of more than
half thy soil, that America may have more slaves; thy
cities burned, thy children slain, the streets of thy capital trodden by the alien foot, but still smoking with
thy children's blood; pardon me if I seem to have forgotten thee!   And you, ye butchered Americans, slain

by the vomito, the gallows, and the sword; you, ye maimed and mutilated men, who shall never again join hands in prayer, never kneel to God once more upon the limbs He made you; you, ye widows, orphans of these butchered men, far off in that more sunny South, here in our own fair land; pardon me that I seem to forget your wrongs! And thou, my Country, my own, my loved, my native land, thou child of great ideas and mother of many a noble son, dishonored now, thy treasure wasted, thy children killed or else made murderers, thy peaceful glory gone, thy government made to pimp and pander for lust of crime; forgive me that I seem over-gentle to the men who did and do the damning deed which wastes thy treasure, spills thy blood, and stains thine honor's sacred fold! And you, ye sons of men everywhere, thou child of God, mankind, whose latest, fairest hope is planted here in this New World,— forgive me if I seem gentle to thy enemies, and to forget the crime that so dishonors man, and makes this ground a slaughter-yard of men — slain, too, in furtherance of the basest wish! I have no words to tell the pity that I feel for them that did the deed. I only say, " Father, forgive them, for they know full well the sin they do! "

A sectarian church could censure a general for holding his candle in a Catholic cathedral; it was " a candle to the pope; " yet never dared to blame the war. While we loaded a ship of war with corn, and sent off the Macedonian to Cork, freighted by private bounty to feed the starving Irishman, the State sent her ships to Vera Cruz, in a cause most unholy, to bombard, to smite, and to kill. Father! forgive the State; forgive the Church. It was an ignorant State. It was a silent Church — a poor, dumb dog, that dared not bark at the wolf who prowls about the fold, but only at the lamb.

Yet ye leaders of the land, know this,— that the blood of thirty thousand men cries out of the ground against you. Be it your folly or your crime, still cries the voice, " Where is thy brother? " That thirty thousand — in the name of humanity I ask, " Where are they? " In the name of justice I answer, " You slew them! "

It was not the people who made this war. They have often enough done a foolish thing. But it was not they who did this wrong. It was they who led the people; it was demagogues that did it. Whig demagogues and demagogues of the Democrats; men that flatter the ignorance, the folly, or the sin of the people, that they might satisfy their own base purposes. In May, 1846, if the facts of the case could have been stated to the voters, and the question put to the whole mass of the people, " Shall we go down and fight Mexico, spending two hundred millions of dollars, maiming four-and-twenty thousand men, and butchering thirty thousand; shall we rob her of half her territory? "— the lowest and most miserable part of the nation would have said as they did say, " Yes; " the demagogues of the nation would have said as they did say, " Yes; " perhaps a majority of the men of the South would have said so, for the humanity of the nation lies not there; but if it had been brought to the great mass of the people at the North,— whose industry and skill so increase the national wealth, whose intelligence and morals have given the nation its character abroad,— then they, the great majority of the land, would have said, " No. We will have no war! If we want more land, we will buy it in the open mar-

ket, and pay for it honestly. But we are not thieves,
nor murderers, thank God, and will not butcher a nation to make a slave-field out of her soil." The people
would not have made this war.

Well, we have got a new territory, enough to make
one hundred States of the size of Massachusetts. That
is not all. We have beaten the armies of Mexico, destroyed the little strength she had left, the little self-
respect, else she would not so have yielded and given
up half her soil for a few miserable dollars. Soon
we shall take the rest of her possessions. How can
Mexico hold them now — weakened, humiliated, divided worse than ever within herself. Before many
years, all of this northern continent will doubtless be
in the hands of the Anglo-Saxon race. That of itself
is not a thing to mourn at. Could we have extended
our empire there by trade, by the Christian arts of
peace, it would be a blessing to us and to Mexico; a
blessing to the world. But we have done it in the
worst way, by fraud and blood; for the worst purpose,
to steal soil and convert the cities of men into the
shambles for human flesh; have done it at the bidding
of men whose counsels long have been a scourge and
a curse — at the bidding of slaveholders. They it is
that rule the land, fill the offices, buy up the North
with the crumbs that fall from their political table,
make the laws, declare hostilities, and leave the North
to pay the bill. Shall we ever waken out of our
sleep? shall we ever remember the duties we owe to the
world and to God, who put us here on this new continent? Let us not despair.

Soon we shall have all the southern part of the continent, perhaps half the islands of the Gulf. One
thing remains to do — that is, with the new soil we

have taken, to extend order, peace, education, religion;
to keep it from the blight, the crime, and the sin of
slavery. That is for the nation to do; for the North
to do. God knows the South will never do it. Is
there manliness enough left in the North to do that?
Has the soil forgot its wonted faith, and borne a different race of men from those who struggled eight
long years for freedom? Do we forget our sires, forget our God? In the day when the monarchs of Europe are shaken from their thrones; when the Russian
and the Turk abolish slavery; when cowardly Naples
awakes from her centuries of sleep, and will have freedom; when France prays to become a republic, and in
her agony sweats great drops of blood; while the
Tories of the world look on and mock and wag their
heads; and while the Angel of Hope descends with
trusting words to comfort her,— shall America extend
slavery? butcher a nation to get soil to make a field
for slaves? I know how easily the South can buy of-
fice-hunters; Whig or Democrat, the price is still the
same. The same golden eagle blinds the eyes of each.
But can she buy the people of the North? Is honesty gone, and honor gone, your love of country gone,
religion gone, and nothing manly left — not even
shame? Then let us perish; let the Union perish!
No; let that stand firm, and let the Northern men
themselves be slaves; and let us go to our masters and
say, "You are very few, we are very many; we have
the wealth, the numbers, the intelligence, the religion
of the land, but you have the power; do not be hard
upon us; pray give us a little something, some humble
offices; or if not these, at least a tariff, and we will be
content."

Slavery has already been the blight of this nation,

the curse of the North and the curse of the South.   It has hindered commerce, manufactures, agriculture. It confounds your politics.   It has silenced your ablest men.   It has muzzled the pulpit, and stifled the better life out of the press.   It has robbed three million men of what is dearer than life; it has kept back the welfare of seventeen millions more.   You ask, O Americans, where is the harmony of the Union?   It was broken by slavery.   Where is the treasure we have wasted?   It was squandered by slavery.   Where are the men we sent to Mexico?   They were murdered by slavery; and now the slave power comes forward to put her new minions, her thirteenth President, upon the nation's neck!   Will the North say " Yes "?

But there is a Providence which rules the world — a plan in His affairs.   Shall all this war, this aggression of the slave power, be for nothing?   Surely not. Let it teach us two things: Everlasting hostility to slavery; everlasting love of justice and of its eternal right.   Then, dear as we may pay for it, it may be worth what it has cost — the money and the men.   I call on you, ye men — fathers, brothers, husbands, sons — to learn this lesson, and, when duty calls, to show that you know it — know it by heart and at your fingers' ends!   And you, ye women — mothers, sisters, daughters, wives — I call on you to teach this lesson to your children, and let them know that such a war is sin, and slavery sin, and, while you teach them to hate both, teach them to be men, and do the duties of noble, Christian, and manly men!   Behind injustice there is ruin, and above man there is the everlasting God.

II

THE ADMINISTRATION OF PRESIDENT POLK

1849

The administration of Mr. Polk took place at an important period in the affairs of the nation; it is connected with some of the most remarkable events which have happened in America since the adoption of the Constitution — events which will deeply and long affect the welfare of the people. The time has not yet come when the public, or any person, can fully appreciate the causes then put or kept in action. But the administration was so remarkable, the events connected with it so new in our history, and so important, that it seems worth while to pause a moment and study this chapter in American politics, with such light as we now possess. It becomes the more important to do this just as a new Congress is about to assemble, while the government is connected with a new President not very well tried in political affairs. In judging the contemporary events of our country it would be ridiculous in us to pretend the same coolness and impartiality which it is easy to have in studying the politics of times a thousand years gone by; still, we think we have no prejudice against Mr. Polk or his administration, or in favor thereof; certainly we do not look through the partisan eyes of a Democrat, a Whig or a Free-soiler, but are ready to praise or blame an idea, a measure, or an act, on its own account, without asking what political family it belongs to.

The materials for the history of this administration

are abundant and accessible.   We make no pretensions
to a knowledge of the secrets of either party; they
would be of small value if known.   The volumes of
private and confidential letters of some New York
politicians, of which so much talk was made a few
years ago, contain much matter for gossip, some even
for scandal, little for history, and for political philosophy nothing at all.   We neither seek nor welcome
information from such quarters.   In politics, as in all
science, the common and obvious facts are of the
greatest value.   With the secret history of the Baltimore Convention, of the Congress, or the Cabinet, we
have nothing to do, only with their public acts.   Our
information will be drawn chiefly from public documents.

Politicians are as honest as the majority of men
would be, exposed to the same temptations, under the
same circumstances.   The misdeeds of other men are
done on a small scale or in an obscure way, while the
private character of a politician becomes public, his
deeds appear before the sun.   If the transactions of
State Street and Wall Street were public as the acts
of Congress, men would not think more highly, perhaps, of mercantile honor than now of political integrity.   A little acquaintance with political doings
shows that while each party is, consciously or blindly,
led forward by its idea, and so helps or hinders the
progress of mankind, under similar circumstances, the
one has about as much patriotism and political honesty as the other.   In point of deeds the party that
has been long in power is certainly more corrupt than
the opposite party, who are limited by their position to
longings and intentions.   So the apples which have
long been exposed for sale in a huckster's basket get

bruised with the huckster's attempts to show only their fair sides, and with frequent handling by the public, and begin to rot sooner than other apples from the same branch, but kept out of sight in the barrel, which otherwise resemble them " as much as one apple is like another." The party that is full and the party that is hungry seldom differ much in their political honesty.

In estimating the administration of men like Jefferson and Jackson, men of decided thoughts or decided deeds, the personal character and opinions of the President are important elements to be considered. But Mr. Polk was remarkable neither for thought nor action ; he had no virtues or vices to distinguish him from the common run of politicians, who swim with the party tide, up or down, in or out, as it may be. His character seems to have had no weight in the public scale, and does not appear to have given the balance a cast to either side. He might follow a multitude, in front or rear — he could not lead. God never gave him " the precious gift " of leading. For his office, no qualities marked him more than a thousand other men in the land. Like Mr. Harrison and Mr. Tyler, he was indebted for the Presidency to " the accident of an accident." So the god Apis was selected from other bullocks for some qualities known only to the priests ; though to laical eyes he was nothing but a common stot, distinguished by no mark and likelihood ; soon as selected he became a god, and had the homage of his worshipers. The nomination of the Apis might be one " not fit to be made," but when clerically made it always had the laic confirmation, and no Apis was ever found too brute to receive worship.

It was said in 1848, that it was not of much consequence who was President if he were only a Whig ; it

did not require much ability to fill the office; much acquaintance with the philosophy of politics, nor even
much knowledge of the facts of politics; nay, not any
eminence of character.   Mr. Polk was not the first or
the last attempt to demonstrate this by experiment.

His private life was marred by no unusual blemish,
and set off by no remarkable beauty.   He kept the
Ten Commandments very much as other men; was
sober, temperate, modest in his deportment; what seems
latterly rather unusual for a President, he did not
swear profanely.   On his death-bed he " professed
justifying faith in the Lord Jesus Christ," " relying
alone for salvation on the great doctrine of atone-
ment," and " received the ordinance of baptism; " thus
he secured that good name in the churches, not yet
accorded to Franklin and Washington.   Estimating
him by the ordinary standard about him (the true way
to judge such a man), he has been set down as an exemplary man, using his opportunities with common
fidelity.   Some official acts of his were purely official.
His friends, since his death, claim but little for him.
Eulogies are not supposed to limit themselves to telling the truth, or to extend themselves to telling the
whole truth.   Still they are a good test of public opinion.   Burr got none; General Jackson had many;
those on Mr. Polk were chiefly official, and their tem-
perature, for official panegyrics, was uncommonly low,
plainly intimating that little could be made of such a
subject.   Mr. Polk was hardly susceptible of rhetorical
treatment after death.   While in power he could
easily be praised.   Excepting some of the eminent
leaders, almost any prominent man in the Democratic
party, if made President under such circumstances,
would have done very much as Mr. Polk did; would

have been merely a portion of the party machine.
Last year the Whigs said, also, it was not very important what the personal opinions of the President
were.

After eliminating these elements, the matter becomes
quite simple: we have only to deal with the ideas of
the administration,— the measures proposed as an
expression thereof,— and the acts in which these ideas
took a concrete form. These, of course, will be complicated with the adverse ideas and measures of the
other party. Such is the theme before us.

However, it is necessary to look a moment at the
state of the nation when Mr. Polk came to power. In
our foreign relations all was serene except in the English and Mexican quarter. In the one the weather
seemed a little uncertain; in the other there were decided indications of a storm.

In 1842, Mr. Webster, for a short time dignifying
the office of Secretary of State, had performed the
most valuable public service he has yet rendered his
country. He had negotiated the treaty of Washington by which the north-eastern boundary was settled.
That was a very important matter, and Mr. Webster
deserves the lasting gratitude of both nations for the
industry, courtesy, and justice with which he managed that complicated, difficult, and vexatious affair.
He is often celebrated as the defender of the Constitution, but his services in that work, when looked at with
impartial eyes, diminish a good deal, and perhaps will
not be much spoken of when a few years have dispelled
the mists which hang over all contemporary greatness.
It was a real dignity and honor to negotiate the treaty.
Certainly there were few men, perhaps not another in
the nation, who could have done it. We do not mean

to say that a board of civil engineers, or three good,
honest men could not as well settle questions in themselves more difficult.   But such was the state of feeling
in England and America, that none but a distinguished politician could be trusted with the matter,
and none possessed the requisite qualities in so eminent
a degree as Mr. Webster.

There still remained another affair to be settled
with England: we refer to the boundaries of Oregon.
That question was purposely made difficult by small
politicians who exasperated the public on both sides
of the water.   The cry was raised " Oregon or fight; "
" The whole of Oregon or none; " " 54, 40." The
legislature of Maine went a little further north, and
shouted " 54, 49."   Some men, whose names are by
no means forgotten, made a great outcry, and egged
the ignorant headlong towards dangerous measures,
threatening " war with England; " men who, like
frogs in the spring just escaping from their winter
of obscurity, for their own purposes, made a great deal
of noise with very little sense.   The intrinsic difficulty
of the case was very small.   England made large pretensions; so did we; both desiring a wide margin of
oscillation before they settled down on a permanent
boundary.   But England was pacific, though firm, and
not foolish enough to wish to fight with one whose
peace was so profitable.   A war between England and
America is, on each side, a quarrel with a good cus-
tomer.   That is the mercantile aspect of the case.
An administration which should seek honestly to settle
the Oregon question would find no difficulty; had Mr.
Webster remained a year more in the Cabinet, we doubt
not this affair, also, would have been amicably settled.

Affairs certainly looked threatening in the neighborhood of Mexico; there were troubles past, present, and to come. Americans had excited the revolution in Texas; fought her battles, and fomented her intrigues. Texas had just been annexed, or, as the phrase originally was, *re*-annexed. Texas and Mexico had been long at war; though not actively fighting at the time of annexation, the war was not ended. We took Texas with a defective title, subject to the claims of Mexico. If she did not prosecute those claims it was because she was too feeble, not that she had relinquished them. That was not all — we had insulted Mexico and deeply injured her; not by accident, but with our eyes open, and of set purpose. We had wronged Mexico deeply, and then added new insults to old injuries. What made our conduct worse, we were powerful and Mexico defenseless. The motive which lay at the bottom of all makes this accumulated baseness still more detestable; it was done to establish a bulwark for American slavery.

To this origin of the Mexican War we will now add a few words respecting the scheme of annexation. In 1803, Mr. Jefferson purchased Louisiana of France, a vast territory west of the Mississippi, for $15,000,000. He thought he transgressed the Constitution in doing so, and expected an " act of indemnity " by the people, to justify the deed. The Senate thought otherwise. Slavery was already established in Louisiana. In 1812, the present State of Louisiana was admitted to the Union with a constitution authorizing slavery. In 1820, a new State was formed from what had been the more northern portion of Louisiana. Should it be a slave State, or free? The South, " on principle," favored slavery; the North, " on princi-

ple," opposed it. But both parties laid aside their
" principles " and made a compromise, such as Mr.
Clay and Mr. Clayton so much admire. Slavery was
allowed only south of Mason and Dixon's line, 36° 40′
of north latitude. This was the famous Missouri
Compromise. But only a small part of Missouri lay
south of the line. All the new territory, therefore,
could make only two slave States, Louisiana and Arkansas. In 1836, Arkansas was admitted into the
Union. Florida territory alone remained to be made
into slave States. Thus the territorial extension of
the slave power was at an end, while vast regions were
left into which the stream of Northern enterprise continually poured itself. The North rapidly increased
in numbers, in wealth, and in the political power which
wealth and numbers give ; the rapid rise of new States
was to the South a fearful proof of this.

The North has always been eminently industrial,
particularly eminent in the higher modes of industry,
work that demands the intelligent head. The South
has always been deficient in industry, especially in the
higher modes of industry. The North has an abundance of skilled labor; the South chiefly brute labor.
This industrial condition of the South is to be ascribed
to the institution of slavery, though perhaps something must be allowed for the climate, and for the inferior character and motives of the original colonists
who settled that part of the country. But while the
North is industrial, the South is political; the North
sends its ablest men to trade, the South to politics.
The race for public welfare and political power was
to be run by those two competitors, " not without dust
and heat." After the Revolution, the opposite characteristics of the North and South appeared more

prominently than before. The North increased rapidly in numbers, and outpeopled the South. The Revolution itself showed the comparative military power of the " Southern chivalry " and the hardy industry of the North. After the adoption of the Federal Constitution, the North increased with still greater rapidity, and began to show a decided superiority to the South. This is partly the result of the industry of the North; but in part the result of our navigation laws, which gave American bottoms a great national privilege. Most of the ships belonged, as they still do, to the North; they were the fruits of her industry. Did the Constitution guarantee slavery to the South, it *protected the ships of the North.* The South got a political advantage, and the North a commercial privilege, whose value in dollars has been greater than that of all the slaves in the United States. In all contests about money, the North carries it over the South; in all contests for immediate political power the South over the North.

Some thirty years later, the nation changed its policy. It had taken pains to encourage commerce, and had a revenue tariff. Now it took pains to restrict trade, and established a protective tariff; so the North engaged in manufactures to a greater degree than before. The South could not do this: the slaves were too ignorant, and must remain so as long as they are slaves, otherwise they could not be kept together in the large masses which manufacturing purposes require; the whites were too indolent and too proud. The South continued to increase constantly in numbers and in wealth, but compared with the North, she did not increase. It soon became plain that the political center of gravity was traveling northwards continu-

ally, and with such swiftness that the South before long
would lose the monopoly of the government, which she
had long enjoyed by reason of her political character,
and which the North cared little for so long as money
could be made without it.   The prosperity of the
North rests on an industrial basis, that of the South
on a political basis.

So the South must contrive to outweigh the North.
How?   Not by industry, which creates wealth directly,
and indirectly multiplies men, but by politics.   The
North works after its kind, and is satisfied with the
possession of commerce and manufactures; the South,
after its kind, rejoices in slavery, and thinks to outwit
the laws of nature by a little juggling in politics.   Behold the results.   To balance the North, the South
must have new slave States to give her power in the
Federal Government.   New territory must be got to
make them of.

Texas lay there conveniently near.   It had once
been a part of Louisiana, as far west as the Nueces.
In 1819, James Long went from Natchez in Louisiana
to Nacogdoches in Texas, and, on the 23rd of June,
declared the independence of the republic of Texas.
About two years later, Mr. Austin and his colony
went thither from Mississippi, carrying their slaves
with them.   In 1826, another insurrection took place,
under Benjamin W. Edwards, and another declaration
of independence followed.   At that time the American
Government did not interfere nor much covet the territory.   Texas was a convenient neighbor, and not a
dangerous one; slaveholders could migrate thither with
their slaves.   But in 1824, the Mexicans forbade the
introduction of slaves, and declared all free as soon
as they were born; Mexico refused to surrender up fugi-

tive slaves. In 1827, Texas and Coahuila were united into one State with a constitution which allowed no new slaves, born or brought thither, and in 1829 Mexico emancipated all her slaves.

As Mexico made advances toward emancipation, the American Government began to covet Texas. In 1827, under the administration of Mr. Adams, an attempt was made to purchase Texas, $1,000,000 were offered. In 1829, Mr. Benton desired " the *retrocession*." His reasons are instructive: — we have now " a non-slaveholding empire in juxtaposition with the slaveholding Southwest ; " and " five or six new slaveholding States may be added to the Union." Yes, " nine States as large as Kentucky." A Charleston newspaper desired it because " it would have a favorable influence on the future destinies of the South, by increasing the votes of the slaveholding States in the United States Senate. In 1829, in a Virginia convention, Judge Upshur said the annexation of Texas " would raise the price of slaves, and be of great advantage to the slaveholders of that State ; " in 1832, Mr. Gholson, in the Virginia legislature, thought " it would raise the price of slaves fifty per cent. at least." To sharpen the public appetite for Texas, in 1829 the cry was raised that " England wanted Texas ; British merchants had offered to loan Mexico $5,000,000 if she would place Texas under British protection." This trick was frequently resorted to, but the apprehension was groundless. The same year, the first of Gen. Jackson's administration, our minister offered $5,000,-000 for Texas ; the offer was rejected. He then offered a loan of $10,000,000, taking Texas as collateral security ; that, also, was rejected. He tried also, but in vain, to obtain a treaty for the surrender of fugitive slaves.

By 1840, the State of Texas had made large grants of land to various persons, some of which had been bought up by Americans. So in addition to the general desire of the slaveholders, the owners of Texan lands had a special motive to stimulate them. Joint-stock companies were formed in the United States; there were the " Galveston Bay and Texas Company; " the " Arkansas and Texas Company; " the " Rio Grande Company." These had their headquarters at New York. Then there was the " Union Land Company," and the " Trinity Land Company," and others. In Mississippi and Arkansas, attempts were publicly made to excite the people of Texas to revolt. In 1830, candidates for Congress in Mississippi were publicly catechised as to their opinion of annexation. The same year Samuel Houston got up his expedition to wrest Texas from Mexico. In 1832, Mexico was obliged to withdraw her troops from Texas, to suppress disturbances in other quarters; emigrants continually went with their slaves from the United States. In 1833, Texas organized as a separate State; Mexico refused her assent, and sent troops which were repulsed. Texan agents traversed the United States, addressing public meetings, enlisting troops, and despatching military supplies to the revolted province. On the 2nd of March, 1836, the insurgents issued their declaration of independence, and fifteen days after adopted a constitution establishing perpetual slavery. Of the fifty-seven signers to this declaration, fifty were emigrants from the slave States, and only three Mexicans by birth. The constitution prohibited the importation of slaves *except from the United States;* but every negro in Texas, or who might come there, was declared a slave!

During the war between Mexico and Texas, the American Government took little or no pains to prevent our citizens from aiding the Texans; vessels were openly fitted out in our harbors, and sent to war on a friendly power, yet the Secretary of State had the hardihood to say that the President (General Jackson) "took all the measures in his power to prevent it;" Mr. Van Buren said the same thing. Yet he allowed the brigadier-general of the Texan army publicly to advertise for volunteers for that army, in North Carolina, and to enlist soldiers. The Mexican minister protested; it was all in vain. The President sent General Gaines with an army to lie on the Texan frontier, ready to further the designs of our citizens against Mexico. He was ordered to advance as far as Nacogdoches, if needful, and Mr. Forsyth told the Mexican minister "our troops might, if necessary, be sent into the heart of Mexico." Our government tried to force Mexico into a war with us. American troops were on the soil of Mexico; her minister complained, and requested that they might be withdrawn, the answer is "No." Two days after (Oct. 15th, 1836), the Mexican minister demands his passports and goes home.

Mexico was too feeble to fight. Neither our infraction of a treaty, nor the insults added to that injury, could provoke her to a war. Other measures were to be tried; the American Government got up its "claims" on Mexico — fifteen in number.

On the 1st of March, 1837, the Senate acknowledged the independence of Texas; a minister was sent and one was received. In August, 1837, General Hunt, the Texan minister, proposed annexation. Mr. Van Buren was then President: he has been called " the

Northern man with Southern principles," though he
deserves the title rather less than some others not so
stigmatized.   The offer of annexation was declined:
Mexico was still at war with Texas; the legislatures of
New York, Pennsylvania, and all the New England
States had protested against annexation.   In regard
to Texas Van Buren did not " follow in the steps of his
illustrious predecessor."   During his administration
little was done to promote annexation, nothing by the
government.   The third non-slaveholding President
did not desire to extend the area of bondage.

In 1841, the Whigs came into power with the shout
of " Tippecanoe and Tyler too ; " as Mackay, an English traveler, has said, " Log cabins with their songs
and speeches, their orgies on bacon and hard cider,
had more to do with the election of General Harrison,
. . . than had less exceptionable means."   The
Whigs then gave the Democrats an opportunity, much
needed, to turn themselves out of office.   The nomination of Mr. Tyler for the Vice-Presidency was characteristic of the party.   What followed would once
have been regarded as " judicial," a " direct interven-
tion of God " to punish an artifice.   Mr. Tyler, becoming President, was true to his former character
and conduct.   He set about the work of annexation
in good earnest.   Commodore Jones was sent with a
fleet to lie on the western shore of Mexico — to be
ready in case of any outbreak with America.   His
conduct shows the expectation and design of our government.   Mr. Upshur, Tyler's Secretary of State, is
a good exponent of the policy of the administration.
In Sept., 1843, he says " few calamities could befall
this country [the United Sates] more to be deplored
than the establishment of a predominant British in-

fluence [of which there was not the least danger], and the *abolition of domestic slavery in Texas!*" General Lamar, once president of Texas, had written to his friends in Georgia that without annexation " *the anti-slavery party in Texas will acquire the ascendency . . . and may abolish slavery. . . . The majority of the people of Texas are not owners of slaves.*"

In October, 1843, Mr. Upshur took the initiative and proposed annexation to the Texans; he told them, (16th Jan., 1844), that without annexation "they cannot maintain that institution [slavery] ten years; probably not half that time." If Texas is not annexed, he says again, "the people of the Southern States will not run the hazard of subjecting their slave property to the control of a population who are anxious to abolish slavery." Mr. Upshur was not so crafty as Mr. Murphy, his agent at Texas, who said, "Take this position on the side of the Constitution and the laws, and the civil, political, and religious liberties of the people of Texas secured thereby (saying nothing about abolition), and all the world will be with you;" say "nothing which can offend even our fanatical brethren of the North; let the United States espouse at once the cause of civil, political, and religious liberty in this hemisphere." A treaty was made, but " our fanatical brethren of the North " were offended, and on the 8th of June, 1844, the Senate rejected it by a vote of 35 to 16.

" The immediate annexation of Texas " was now the favorite measure of the slave power. They had little fear but that, in the next presidential term, they could repeal the tariff of '42, but felt doubtful of the success of annexation. Mr. Upshur feared New England; had he lived at Boston, and known the influences then controlling New England, he would have seen there was no reason for fear. A presidential election was at hand; the Democratic convention was to meet at Baltimore in May. Mr. Van Buren was the most prominent candidate of the party. Most of the delegates to the convention had been instructed to support him. But he was a Northern man; while President he had *not* favored annexation; he had lately written a public letter (April 20, 1844), and plainly declared himself hostile to annexation. Mr. Ritchie, " the senior field-marshal of Van Buren's party," forsook and opposed his old friend. Mr. Cross, of Arkansas, " would not vote under any circumstances for a man opposed to the annexation of Texas; " Van Buren was " not the proper person for the party to rally around in the coming struggle; " " nine out of ten of our friends think so." The Tyler committee wrote on their card, as for Van Buren, " Texas has destroyed him; " " the last, best, and wisest counsel of Andrew Jackson was — the annexation of Texas."

The convention assembled; Van Buren got more than a majority, but could not get two-thirds. Candidates were numerous, Cass, Calhoun, Buchanan, Tyler, Tecumseh-Johnson; some even thought it best to take again Andrew Jackson, gallant " Old Ironsides "; Commodore Stewart was talked of. When the political tide ebbs clean out of the harbor, strange things appear on the bottom, only seen on such occasions. Men thought it very surprising that such a man should be spoken of — certainly it had no precedent, and he no political experience. Now the nomination would not be at all surprising or irregular. The Commodore's letter looks silly enough now. But who knows,

if only elected, that he would not have been as great
a man as Mr. Polk, nay, as Tyler, or Taylor? He
was for " immediate annexation," and would " throw
ourselves on the justice of our cause before God and
the nations." Valiant Commodore! he might have
been as great a man as Mr. Polk, had the tide of nomination served in his favor.

After all the mountainous labor of the Baltimore
Convention, there came forth Polk; Mr. James K. Polk.
Men wondered. " Who the devil *is* James — K ——
Polk? " said many Democrats; and when told, they
thought it was " a nomination not fit to be made."
None of them proved it, by facts and arguments, quite
so faithfully as the distinguished author of that phrase
did on a recent occasion at Marshfield; they left that
for Mr. Polk to do (not by logic, but by experiment),
and he did — in due time. Mr. Van Buren was " sincerely desirous " for the success of the nominees. The
Whigs were pretty firmly united in support of Mr.
Clay, " Harry of the West," and " that same old
coon," as he has publicly called himself. He was not,
publicly, much opposed to annexation, nor much in
favor of it, and in respect to that was a pretty good
index of his party. Yet some Whigs were seriously
and conscientiously opposed to the annexation of
Texas as a slave territory; so were a few Democrats,
who constituted the moral element of the party. Both
of these minorities have since reported their presence
in the politics of the land, indications of something
yet future. It was a rash movement of the Democratic party, this changing their leader and their line
on the very brink of battle, under the guns of their
opponent, already put in battery and ready to fire;
but they were confident in their strength, and so well

drilled that they only needed the word of command to perform any political evolution or revolution.

It is curious to look back.   On the 3rd of March, 1843, twenty-one members of Congress solemnly declared that " annexation would be identical with dissolution; would be an attempt to eternize an institution and a power of a nature so unjust . . .   as . . . *not only to result in a dissolution of the Union, . . .   but fully to justify it.*" Five of the twenty-one were from Massachusetts.   The protest of March 3rd was not very distinctly remembered at a later date by every one of the signers thereof.

At the other extreme was South Carolina.   This is a very remarkable State, and her doings — we mean the doings of her lips — deserve a special notice.   Before the Baltimore Convention of 1844 it was necessary for that State to speak out, her trumpet giving no uncertain sound.   So, on the 15th of May, the people of Charleston, who had " forborne to give any public declaration of . . .   opinions and wishes, . . .   and patiently waited," at length and solemnly " resolved " that annexation is " an American and national measure, antagonistic to foreign interference and domestic abolitionism; " " if the treaty for the recovery (!) of Texas be defeated because of the increase it will give to the slaveholding States, it will be the denial of a vital right to them."

Even after the convention the danger of the patriarchal institution is so great that there must be a Southern convention.   The *South Carolinian,* of May 30th, said, annexation is " a question not of party, but of country, and to the South one of absolute self-preservation; " " under the subtle encroachments of our old enemy of Britain, aided by the traitorous abolitionists at home, . . . her doom is sealed if she does not arise in her might . . . and effect a union with Texas; " " England once firmly seated in Texas, there is an end of all power or safety for the South, which would soon be made another San Domingo." A convention of slave States was to be called " to take into consideration the question of annexing Texas to the Union, if *the Union will accept it;* or if the Union *will not accept it,* then of *annexing Texas to the Southern States.*" The convention was to offer the Union this " alternative: " " either to *admit Texas into the Union,* or to proceed *peaceably and calmly to arrange the terms of a dissolution of the Union.*" A meeting in the Williamsburg district declared, quite " in the Ercles " dialect of that region, that " the doom of the South is sealed and the dirge of our fair Republic will ere long be sung by liberty's last minstrel, if she does not arise in her might and effect a union with Texas."

An " unsuspected nullifier " of 1832 came out to assure the people that " the political Moses [to wit, Mr. Moses-Calhoun] is neither lost nor dead, but he is ready to follow the pillar of cloud by day, or fire by night." " True, there is a Joshua [Mr. Joshua Polk], full of the spirit of wisdom, for that Moses has laid his hands on him; " but " there is still no prophet in Israel like Moses." But somehow it seemed Moses had been so long talking with *his* Lord, that the Baltimore Convention,— could not steadfastly look upon the face of *this* Moses and make him their President; and so, the people of South Carolina wot not what would become of him, nor even of themselves without Texas. A writer in the *Charleston Mercury* asked, " What is the remedy for the evils which afflict the South? " and is thus replied to by a far-sighted man in the same journal: " I answer, unreservedly, *Resistance — combined Southern resistance, if you can procure it; if not, then State resistance.*"

The *Mercury* exclaimed, " Two thousand eight hundred and thirty-two men, with arms in their hands, in the drill-field, have expressed their decided determination to sustain the measure." This was the thing — " combined Southern resistance if it could be had; if not, then State resistance "— the resistance of South Carolina. In the times of nullification in 1832, the great oath of Andrew Jackson laid South Carolinian valor low in the dust; to accomplish that in 1844 it took only the common swearing of John Tyler. The only aggressive act committed by the petulant little commonwealth, spite of the resolutions of its forty-third regiment, of the " decided determination " of the " two thousand eight hundred and thirty-two men with arms in their hands," was the expulsion of an unarmed gentleman, Samuel Hoar, on the 5th of December, who had been sent from Massachusetts to look after her own citizens. Thus was " abolition " repelled. There are noble elements in that State, and some noble men. If ever it becomes a democracy and not an oligarchy, if the majority ever rule there, we shall see very different things, and South Carolina will not be a proverb in the nation.

Mr. Polk was elected. In January, 1845, a joint resolution for annexation passed the House of Representatives, by a vote of 120 to 98, and soon after the Whig Senate by a majority of two votes; it was signed by the President on the 1st of March. So the work of annexation was completed before Mr. Polk came into power, though by no means without his aid.

If this could have been done justly, without extending slavery, few men at the North would have had cause to complain. We do not blame the Texans for desiring independence, or achieving it; we find no fault with extending the area of freedom over the whole world. We cannot think that Mexico had just cause of war in the bare act of annexation. But when we remember that America colonized Texas for the sake of wresting it from Mexico, who would not sell it; that Americans got up the Texan revolution, and fought it through, and did all this for the sake of getting nine slave States as large as Kentucky; that this was done secretly, fraudulently, with a lie on the lips of the government — we must say the deed itself was a base deed, and the motive base and miserable.

In 1845, such was the state of foreign affairs. In all that concerned domestic welfare, the nation was never so well off before. There had been a considerable period of remarkable prosperity. It must be a very bad government which, in four years, can seriously injure a nation like this, where so little depends on the central power. Mr. Tyler appealed to the judgment of posterity for his vindication; but certainly no party was sorry when he went out of office.

During the year ending June 30th, 1845, the imports of the United States amounted in value to $117,254,564; the exports to $114,646,606. The national revenue was $29,769,133; the expenditures $29,968,207. There was a balance in the treasury of $7,658,306. The amount of public debt on the 1st of October, was $17,075,445.

The distinctive measures proposed for Mr. Polk were:

1. " The separation of the money of government from banking institutions."

2. " A tariff for revenue."

3. " The re-occupation of Oregon."

These measures were seldom submitted to a scientific and careful examination. They were abundantly discussed in Congress and out of Congress, but almost wholly in the spirit of party. Some of them were finally carried by a mere party vote; measures, too, on which the welfare of the nation was thought to depend. As we look over the speeches made in reference to the tariff or the subtreasury, we find ability enough; now and then a knowledge of the subject in hand, though that is far enough from common,— but fairness which is willing to see good in the measures of a political opponent we almost never find.

In his first message (Dec. 2nd, 1845), Mr. Polk recommended the establishment of a " constitutional treasury . . . as a secure depository for the public money, without any power to make loans or discounts, or to issue any paper whatever as a currency or circulation." In conformity with this suggestion, a bill was reported with a proviso called " the specie clause "— that all payments to or from the government should be made in gold or silver. This bill passed the House by a vote of 123 to 64, the Senate by 28 to 24, and went into operation on the 1st of January, 1847, though the government did not pay specie till the 1st of April following. Before the end of the year Mr. Polk could say with truth (Message, Dec. 8th, 1846), " that the amount of gold and silver coin in circulation in the country is greater than ever before." The banks were kept from inflating the currency. The measure has proved itself a wise one. Its good effect in retaining

coin in the country and thus preventing a suspension
of specie payment by the banks during the commercial
crisis of 1847–1849, was felt throughout the land,
and is now extensively acknowledged. The administration deserves the gratitude of the people for this
measure. But what Whig journal will venture to do
justice to the subtreasury!

Mr. Polk also recommended a " tariff for revenue ; "
Mr. Walker, the Secretary of the Treasury, presented
his scheme of such a tariff. In due time a bill was
reported. There was no impartial discussion of the
subject in Congress, or in the newspapers. We doubt
that there is a single political or commercial journal
in the United States, which would open its columns
to a free and full discussion of the subject on the
merits of the case. Political economy can hardly be
considered an exact science as yet ; but American politicians, even the most eminent, with here and there an
exception, seem ignorant of the conclusions which may
be regarded as established. Very few of them seem
to study political economy — even to learn the facts
on which it is based, still less to learn the natural laws
on which the material prosperity of the nation depends. It is a tiresome work to instruct a great nation, and mankind seldom loves its school-masters in
their lifetime, while it requires little effort to swim with
the tide. In 1827, the citizens of Boston " assembled to take into consideration the proposed increase
of duties ; " their committee made a long and very able
report adverse to that increase, and very justly say : —

" The success or failure of the candidates for the Presidency,
may be of great moment to the country, and still greater to
those partisans whose political fortunes are depending on that
event; but to the nation at large, the evil or the good which
may arise out of the choice of the one or the rejection of the

other, can only be of temporary and limited importance, compared with the wise and just disposition of a question on which our whole foreign and domestic policy turns, and which may, in its consequences, affect the stability and happiness of the Union for ages to come."

In 1789, a moderate protective duty was established, on all imported articles; in 1816, a high protective tariff was for the first time established. Mr. Clay and Mr. Calhoun were its most important advocates. The tariff was raised in 1818 and in 1822, and was made much higher in 1824. Mr. Webster opposed it with his peculiar ability, in a speech not yet forgotten. In 1828, a very high tariff was established by what has been called the " Bill of Abominations." In 1832–3, the tariff relaxed a little, to avert a civil war. Mr. Clay got his celebrated " compromise act " established. The compromise lasted about nine years, till 1842. The tariff of 1842 was passed under the administration of Mr. Tyler. Mr. Webster admitted it had " its imperfections."

Mr. Polk came into power with the idea of a revenue tariff in his mind. The bill passed the House of Representatives by a vote of 114 to 95, 1 Whig and 113 Democrats voting on that side; 71 Whigs, 18 Democrats, and 6 " native Americans " voting on the opposite side. It passed the Senate by the casting vote of the Vice-President, who was pledged to the measure before his election. A law of this magnitude has seldom passed any modern legislature with such imperfect discussion. In the Senate only a single man, Mr. Lewis, spoke in defense of the bill. Certainly the conduct of the friends of the bill was eminently unjust, and the bill itself was carried, not by its merits, but by the power of the party; not by force of mind, but force of numbers.

Mr. Webster made a learned, and in many respects a very able, speech, though he weakened his rhetoric with a little extravagance, unusual with him,— against the new tariff — against its general principles, and its particular details.   He said, in the Senate:

"The Treasury cannot, in my opinion, be supplied at the ratio which has been stated, and is expected, by any possible, I will say passible, augmentation of importations." "Why, the effect of this bill is to diminish freights, and to affect the navigating interests of the United States most seriously, most deeply; and therefore it is, that all the ship-owners of the United States, without an exception, so far as we hear from them, oppose the bill.   It is said to be in favor of free trade and against monopoly.   But every man connected with trade is against it; and this leads me to ask, and I ask with earnestness, and hope to receive an answer, at whose request, at whose recommendation, for the promotion of what interest, is this measure introduced? Is it for the importing merchants?   They all reject it, to a man. Is it for the owners of the navigation of the country?   They remonstrate against it.   The whole internal industry of the country opposes it.   The shipping interest opposes it.   The importing interest opposes it.   Who is it that calls for it, or proposes it?   Who asks for it?   Who?   Has there been one single petition presented in its favor from any quarter of the country? Has a single individual in the United States come up here and told you that his interest would be protected, promoted, and advanced, by the passage of a measure like this?   Sir, there is an imperative unity of the public voice the other way, altogether the other way.   And when we are told that the public requires this, and that the people require it, we are to understand by the public, certain political men, who have adopted the shibboleth of party, for the public; and certain persons who have symbols, ensigns, and party flags, for the people; and that is all."

Before the passage of the bill, Mr. Webster presented in the Senate a memorial " signed by every importer of dry goods in the city of Boston," against it.

Has the tariff of 1846 failed to produce a revenue? has it drained the specie out of the country? has it led to a great extension of paper money? has it produced the confusion occasioned by the tariffs of '16, of '28, of '42? Has it impoverished the nation? The answer is all about us! Still, by adopting the *ad valorem* instead of *specific* duties, an opportunity has been left for fraudulent invoices, and great fraud has been committed, doing a wrong to the government, and still more to the fair and honorable merchant.

The " re-occupation of Oregon " was recommended in Mr. Polk's first message. Our title to the whole of Oregon territory was " asserted, and, as is believed, maintained, by irrefragable facts and arguments; " our " claims could not be abandoned without a sacrifice of both national honor and interests," and " no compromise which the United States ought to accept could be effected." He recommended that we should give the British notice of our intention to terminate the period of joint occupancy, as the treaty of 1818 allowed either party to do. Mr. Polk, on other occasions, showed himself rather raw in diplomatic affairs; it would seem that he knew little of the matter in hand when he wrote the sentences above. They show him as a mere servant of his party, not as a great statesman, able to mediate between two mighty nations, and distribute justice with an even hand.

A great deal of discussion took place. The *Union* — the organ of the government at Washington — contended for " the whole of Oregon or none." But the *Charleston Mercury* was all at once afflicted with a conscience, and could distinguish between " claims " and " rights." We shall presently see the reason of the difference. In the Senate, Mr. Sevier, of Arkansas, said that " war will come; " Mr. Breese, of Illinois, would not have the government " grant any position to Great Britain upon any spot whatever of

Oregon." Mr. Allen, of Ohio, said the " American Government could not recede short of 54, 40." Mr. Hannegan, of Indiana, thought that " the abandonment or surrender of any portion of . . . Oregon would be an abandonment of the power, character, and best interests of the American people." Mr. Cass thought war, " an old-fashioned war," was " almost inevitable; " Great Britain " might be willing to submit the question to arbitration, but the crowned heads whom she would propose as arbitrators would not be impartial, for they would cherish anti-republican feelings." He would negotiate, as Mr. Webster very justly said, with the avowed predetermination to take nothing less than the whole of the territory in dispute. In the House of Representatives, John Quincy Adams went in for the territory on religious grounds, and claimed the whole of Oregon on the strength of the first chapter of Genesis. His conduct and his counsels on this occasion can hardly be called less than rash.

The South was not anxious to obtain the whole of Oregon. Mr. Calhoun was singularly moderate in his desire for re-occupation; nice about questions of title and boundary, and desirous of keeping the peace. The reason is obvious. Mr. Hannegan said well, " If it [Oregon] was good for the production of sugar and cotton, it would not have encountered the objection it has done." " I dreaded, on the part of those who were so strenuously in favor of the annexation of Texas at the Baltimore Convention,— I dreaded, on their part, Punic faith." Poor, deluded Mr. Hannegan! he found it. After Texas was secured, they who hunted after Oregon were left to beat the bush alone; nay, were hindered.

" Here," says he, " we are told that we must be careful and
not come in collision with Great Britain about a disputed
boundary! But if it were with feeble Mexico that we were
about to come into collision, we would then hear no such cau-
tions. There was a question of disputed boundary between this
country and Mexico, and those who have a right to know something of the history of that boundary told us that our rights
extended only to the Nueces. How did we find the friends of
Texas moving on that occasion? Did they halt for a moment
at the Nueces? No, sir; at a single bound they cross the
Nueces, and their war-horses prance upon the banks of the
Rio del Norte. There was no negotiation then — we took the
whole; but when Oregon is concerned, it is all right and proper
to give away an empire, if England wills it."

In the House, Mr. Winthrop suggested that, " in
arbitration, reference was not necessarily to crowned
heads," but the matter might be left to " a commission
of able and dispassionate citizens, either from the two
countries   .   .   .   or the world at large." Mr. Benton was moderate and wise; his speeches on the Oregon
question did much to calm the public mind and prepare for a peaceful settlement of the difficulty. The
conduct of Mr. Webster was worthy of the great man
who had negotiated the treaty of Washington. He
said in the beginning, " Let our arguments be fair; let
us settle the question reasonably."

Congress resolved to terminate the joint occupancy.
The British Government was willing to settle the business by arbitration or direct negotiation. America
prefers the latter. Britain sends over her proposition
to settle on the 49th degree as a general basis. Mr.
Polk referred the whole matter to the Senate, and
asked their advice. He had not changed his opinion.
If the Senate did not take the responsibility and advise him to accept the British proposal, he should feel
it his duty to reject the offer. Thus the responsibility
was thrown upon the Senate. The proposal was ac-

cepted, a treaty was speedily made, and the only remaining cause of contention with England put to rest for ever. The conduct of Mr. Polk, in making such pretensions, and holding out such boasts, on such a subject, was not merely rash, weak, and foolish; it was far worse than that. But for the unexpected prudence of a few men in the Senate, and the aversion of the South to acquire free territory, he would have lit the flames of war anew, and done a harm to mankind which no services he could render would ever atone for.

On the 4th of July, 1845, Texas accepted the contract of annexation, and on the 22nd of December, two hundred and twenty-five years after the landing of the Pilgrims on Plymouth Rock, the Senate of the United States passed upon the matter finally, and the work was done. However, previous to this event, Mr. Polk had proposed to renew our diplomatic relations with Mexico, which had been broken off. Mexico consented to receive " a commissioner . . . with full powers to settle the present dispute." America sent Mr. Slidell as a permanent minister plenipotentiary. He was refused *pro causa*. The instructions given to Mr. Slidell have not, we think, been *officially* published, though they were requested by the House. However, a document purporting to contain those instructions was published *un*officially. From that it appears that he was instructed to purchase New Mexico and California; he was allowed to offer $25,000,000 and the American claims on Mexico, amounting, by his estimate, to $8,187,684. Thus the whole territory of New Mexico and California was thought to be worth $33,187,684.

Soon after the accession of Mr. Polk to office, Gen-

eral Taylor was ordered to Texas with an army. On
the 15th of June, he was advised by the Secretary of
War, Mr. Marcy: "The point of your ultimate des-
tination is the western portion of Texas, where you
will select and occupy, on or near the Rio Grande del
Norte, such a site as . . . will be best adapted to
repel invasion. You will limit yourself to the defense
of the territory, unless Mexico shall declare war
against the United States." General Taylor took possession on the Nueces at Corpus Christi, "the most
western point ever occupied by Texas," but nearly two
hundred miles east of the Rio Grande. August 6th,
Mr. Marcy writes: —

"Orders have already been issued to send ten thousand
muskets and a thousand rifles into Texas."

August 23rd,

"Should Mexico assemble a large body of troops on the Rio
Grande, and cross it with a considerable force, such a movement would be regarded as an invasion of the United States."

August 30th,

"An *attempt* to cross, . . . with such a force, will be
considered in the same light. . . . Mexico having thus commenced hostilities, you may . . . cross the Rio Grande, disperse or capture the forces," etc.

He was authorized to draw militia from five States
— Alabama, Mississippi, Louisiana, Kentucky, and
Tennessee. Still General Taylor remained at Corpus
Christi, not undertaking to commit an act of war by
marching into the territory of Mexico. On the 13th
of July, 1846, he was ordered to advance and occupy . . . positions on or near the east bank of
the Rio Grande. Accordingly General Taylor
marches from the Nueces to the Rio Grande, finding no

Texans or Americans on his way — only " small armed parties of Mexicans," who appeared " desirous to avoid us." He takes his position on the left bank of the Rio Grande, and plants his guns — four eighteen-pounders — so as to " bear directly upon the public square of Matamoras, and within good range for demolishing the town." Behold General Taylor nearly two hundred miles within the territory of Mexico, by the command of Mr. Polk — in a district, to use the words of Mr. Trist in his letter to Mr. Buchanan, which " just as certainly constituted a part of Tamaulipas, and not of Texas, . . . as it is certain that the counties of Acomac and Northampton do now constitute a part of the State of Virginia and not of Maryland." An interview took place between the American general, Worth, and General Vega on the part of Mexico. General Vega remarked that " we " felt indignant at seeing the American flag placed on the Rio Grande, in a portion of the Mexican territory. General Worth replied, " that was a matter of taste; notwithstanding there it would remain." On the 12th of April, the Mexican general, Ampudia, very justly said, " Your government . . . has not only insulted, but exasperated the Mexican nation, bearing its conquering banner to the left bank of the Rio Grande del Norte."

It was plain that America had committed an act of war; still the Mexicans did not commence hostilities. On the 12th of April, Ampudia summoned the American general to " withdraw within twenty-four hours; " he answered the same day that he " should not retrograde." On the 17th he blockaded the mouth of the Rio Grande, thus cutting off supplies from Matamoras, and wrote home that " it will at any rate compel the

Mexicans either to withdraw their army from Matamoras, where it cannot be subsisted, or to assume the
offensive on this side of the river." Still there was
no fighting. But on the 23rd of April, General Taylor thus writes:

"With a view to check the depredations of small parties of
Mexicans on this side of the river, Lieutenants Dobbins, 3rd
infantry, and Porter, 4th infantry, were authorized by me, a
few days since, to scour the country for some miles, with a
select party of men, and capture or destroy any such parties
that they might meet. It appears that they separated, and that
Lieutenant Porter, at the head of his own detachment, surprised
a Mexican camp, drove away the men, and took possession of
their horses. Soon afterwards there fell a heavy rain, and, at
a moment when the party seem to have been quite unprepared
for an attack, they were fired upon from the thicket. In attempting to return it, the muskets missed fire, and the party
dispersed in the thicket."

It is plain that America not only committed the first
act of war, by invading the territory of Mexico, but
actually first commenced hostilities. It is true the
president of Mexico, on the 18th of April, had said:
"From this day begins our defensive war, and every
part of our territory attacked or invaded shall be defended." On the 24th he issued his proclamation declaring that "hostilities have been commenced by the
United States, in making new conquests upon our territories within the boundaries of Tamaulipas and New
Leon. I have not the right to declare war." The
same day General Arista informed General Taylor that
he considered hostilities commenced, and should prosecute them. It was on that very day that the two parties "became engaged."

General Taylor's letters reached Washington on
Saturday, May 9th; on Monday, Mr. Polk sent a message to Congress and declared that —

"War exists, and notwithstanding all our efforts to avoid it, exists by the act of Mexico;" "the Mexican government have at last invaded our territory, and shed the blood of our fellow-citizens on our own soil;" "we have been exerting our best efforts to propitiate her good will;" "we have tried every effort at reconciliation." "The cup of forbearance had been exhausted even before the recent information from the frontier of the Del Norte. But now Mexico has passed the boundary of the United States, has invaded our territory, and shed American blood upon the American soil."

Documents accompanied the message. Mr. Winthrop proposed they should be read. No. In a very short time a bill passed the House placing the army and navy at the President's disposal, authorizing him to raise 50,000 volunteers, and putting in his hands $10,000,000, for the purpose of enabling him to "prosecute said war to a speedy and successful termination." In the Senate, the same bill passed the next day. The preamble was in these memorable words: "Whereas, by the act of the Republic of Mexico, war exists between that government and the United States." In the House, fourteen voted against the bill, and two in the Senate.* Six of the sixteen were from Massachusetts, two were from other parts of New England, and five from Ohio, one of her daughter States.

The history of the war is well known. It was conducted with great vigor; on the whole, with great military skill, and with as much humanity as could be expected. War at best is prolonged cruelty. Still we

---

* Here are the names. In the Senate,— *Thomas Clayton*, Delaware; *John Davis*, Massachusetts. In the House,— *John Quincy Adams*, *George Ashmun*, *Joseph Grinnell*, *Charles Hudson*, *Daniel P. King*, of Massachusetts; *Henry P. Cranston*, Rhode Island; *Luther Severance*, Maine; *Erastus D. Culver*, New York; *John Strahan*, Pennsylvania; *Columbus Delano*, *Joseph M. Root*, *Daniel R. Tilden*, *Joseph Vance*, *Joshua R. Giddings*, Ohio.

have read of no war conducted with less inhumanity than this. Some acts of wantonness were certainly committed. The capture of Tabasco is an example. The conduct of the volunteers was often base and revolting. General Taylor was furnished with a proclamation, to distribute in Mexico, designed to foment discord, to promote hostility between the rich and poor. Their leaders were called " tyrants," and " their real purpose " was " to proclaim and establish a monarchy." Colonel Stevenson was told to make the people " feel that we come as deliverers; their rights of person, property, and religion must be respected and sustained." General Kearney proclaimed: " It is the wish and intention of the United States to provide for New Mexico a free government,— similar to those in the United States." " We shall want from you," says General Taylor's proclamation, " nothing but food for our army, and for this you shall always be paid in cash the full value." But on the 9th of July, General Taylor was told in a confidential letter: —

" You will also readily comprehend that in a country so divided into races, classes, and parties, as Mexico is, and with so many local divisions among departments, and personal divisions among individuals, there must be great room for operating on the minds and feelings of large portions of the inhabitants, and inducing them to wish success to an invasion which has no desire to injure their country; and which, in overthrowing their oppressors, may benefit themselves. Between the Spaniards, who monopolize the wealth and power of the country, and the mixed Indian race, who bear its burdens, there must be jealousy and animosity. The same feelings must exist between the lower and higher orders of the clergy; the latter of whom have the dignities and the revenues while the former have poverty and labor. . . . In all this field of division — in all these elements of social, political, personal, and local discord — there must be openings to reach the interests, passions, or principles of some of the parties, and thereby to conciliate their good will, and make them co-operate with us in bringing about an honorable and speedy peace.

"Availing yourself of divisions which you may find existing among the Mexican people — to which allusion has been made — it will be your policy to encourage the separate departments or States, and especially those which you may invade and occupy, to declare their independence of the central government of Mexico, and either to become our allies, or to assume, as it is understood Yucatan has done, a neutral attitude in the existing war between the United States and Mexico."

The war once begun, it was to be prosecuted to a " successful termination; " that is, to the dismemberment of Mexico. Captain Sloat lands at Monterey, on the Pacific coast of Mexico, on the 7th of July, 1846, issues his proclamation, and declares that, " henceforward California will be a portion of the United States, . . . and the same protection will be extended as to the other States of the Union." Commodore Stockton sets up his " Ebenezer " at Ciudad de los Angeles on the 17th of August, 1846, and says, " I, Robert F. Stockton, . . . do hereby make known to all men, . . . do now declare Upper and Lower California to be a territory of the United States, under the name of the territory of California." Here is annexation without the least delay; swift enough to satify even South Carolina.

One pleasant thing we find in looking through the disagreeable and often hypocritical documents connected with the Mexican War, the instructions sent by Secretary Bancroft to Commodore Conner, July 11th, 1845: —

" This is, perhaps, the largest fleet that ever sailed under the American flag; and while it is sufficient, in case of war, to win glory for yourself, your associates, and the country, you will win still higher glory if, by the judicious management of your force, you contribute to the continuance of peace."

In his second annual message, Dec. 8th, 1846, Mr. Polk said, " The war has not been waged with a view to conquest; but having been commenced by Mexico it has been carried into the enemy's country, and will be vigorously prosecuted there, with a view to obtain an honorable peace, and thereby secure an ample indemnity for the expenses of the war." But in the message of Dec. 7th, 1847, he says: " As Mexico refuses all indemnity, we should adopt measures to indemnify ourselves, by appropriating permanently a portion of her territory." " New Mexico and California were taken possession of by our forces; I am satisfied that they should never be surrendered to Mexico." Some one said to General Pillow, " I thought the object of your movement in this war was a treaty of peace." " True," (replied General Pillow) " that is the object of the *war;* but the object of *this campaign* was to *capture the capital,* and *then* make peace; " again, " *this* army has not come to conquer *a peace;* it has come to conquer the country; we will make them *dine* and *sup* on the *horrors of war.*" The statements of Mr. Polk require no comment. We do not wish to apply to them the only word in the English tongue which describes them. The President made the war, and Mr. Nicholas P. Trist, a secretary in the Department of State, made the peace. As the war was begun by Mr. Polk without legal authority, so the treaty was made without legal authority. The Senate confirmed it.

One or two things in the correspondence of Mr. Trist are too remarkable to pass by. June 2nd, 1847, he writes to Secretary Buchanan, speaking of a certain boundary:

" It includes a vast and rich country, with many inhabitants. It is too much to take. The population is mostly as dark as our mulattoes, and nominally free, and would be actually so under our government. The North would oppose taking it lest slavery should be established there; and the South lest its colored population should be received as citizens, and protect their runaway slaves."

Again September 4:

" Among the points which came under discussion was the exclusion of slavery from all territory which should pass from Mexico. I was told that if it were proposed to the people of the United States to part with a portion of their territory, in order that the Inquisition should be therein established, the proposal could not excite stronger feelings of abhorrence than those awakened in Mexico by the prospect of the introduction of slavery in any territory parted with by her. Our conversation on this topic was perfectly frank, and no less friendly; and the more effective upon their minds, inasmuch as I was enabled to say with perfect security, that although their impressions respecting the practical fact of slavery, as it existed in the United States, were, I had no doubt, entirely erroneous; yet there was probably no difference between my individual views and sentiments on slavery, considered in itself, and those which they entertained. I concluded by assuring them that the bare *mention* of the subject in any treaty to which the United States were a party, was an absolute impossibility; that no President of the United States would dare to present any such treaty to the Senate; and that if it were in their power to offer me the whole territory described in our project, increased tenfold in value, and, in addition to that, covered a foot thick all over with pure gold, upon the single condition that slavery should be excluded therefrom, I could not entertain the offer for a moment, nor think even of communicating it to Washington."

America had Mexico entirely at her mercy, and wanted " indemnity for the past, and security for the future," — indemnity for the cost of the war. She took California and New Mexico. The portion of the territory west of the Rio Grande, according to Mr. Walker's statement, amounts to 526,078 square miles, or 336,689,920 acres; (Texas, within its "assumed limits," contains 325,529 square miles, or 208,-332,800 acres.)   For this the United States were to pay Mexico $15,000,000, and abandon all the celebrated claims which Mr. Slidell estimated at $8,187,-684, paying to our citizens, however, not more than $3,250,000.   Taking the smallest sum — the United States pays Mexico for the territory $18,250,000, and throws in the cost of the war.   Certainly, we must be in great want of land to refuse to pay more than our " claims " and $25,000,000, and then actually pay the claims and $15,000,000, flinging in all the cost of the war, and the loss of life.

If England had one of her victims as completely at her feet as Mexico lay helpless at ours, she would have demanded all the public property of Mexico, a complete " indemnity for the cost of the war," and a commercial treaty highly disadvantageous to Mexico, and highly profitable to England.   Why was Mr. Polk so moderate?   Had the administration become moral, and though careless of the natural justice of the war, careful about justice in the settlement?   No,— there were a few men in the land hostile to the war; some because it was war, some because it was a wicked war.   These men, few in number, obscure in position, often hated, and sometimes persecuted, reproached by the President as affording " aid and comfort to the enemy," being on the side of the Eternal Justice, had it on their side.   The moral portion of both political parties — likewise a small portion, and an obscure, not numbering a single eminent name — opposed the war, and the government trembled.   The pretensions of the South, her arrogance, her cunning, awakened at last the tardy North.   Men began to talk of the Wilmot Proviso; of restricting slavery. True, some men fired by the instinct for office cried "Be still," and others fired with the instinct for gold, repeated the cry. Those who had the instinct for justice would not be still; no, nor will not; never. The slaveholders themselves began to tremble — and hence the easy conditions on which Mexico was let off.

The whole direct cost of the war is a tax of $10 on each person in the United States, bond or free, old or newly born, rich or poor; like all other taxes, it is ultimately to be paid by the labor of the country, by the men who work with their hands, chiefly by poor men. The twenty-million-headed nation, blindly led by guides not blind, little thought of this when they shouted at each famous victory, and denounced humble men who both considered the natural justice of the war, and counted its cost.

Mr. Polk found the nation with a debt of $17,075,445; he left it with a debt of $64,938,401. That was the debt on the 4th of March, 1849.

Mr. Polk refused his signature to three bills passed by Congress; one making "appropriations for the improvement of certain harbors and rivers," one for the ascertainment and satisfaction of "claims of American citizens" on France before the 31st of July, 1801, a third "for continuing certain works in the territory of Wisconsin, and for other purposes." It is a little remarkable to find a man who commenced war upon Mexico by invading her territory, seized with such scruples about violating the Constitution while paying an honest debt. The Constitution which can be violated to promote slavery, can easily afford an excuse for the neglect of justice.

Mr. Polk has gone to the Judge of all men, who is

also their Father. The hurrah of the multitude and the applause of an irresponsible party are of no more value than the water which a Methodist minister sprinkled on the head of the dying man. His wealth became nothing; his power and his fame went back to those that gave; at the grave's mouth his friends (and he had friends) forsook him; and the monarch of the nation, the master of negro slaves, the author of a war, was alone with his God. Not a slave in the whole wide world would have taken his place. But God sees not as man. Here let us leave him, not without pity for his earthly history — not without love for a brother man whose weakness, not his wickedness, wrought for our nation such shame and woe. He proved by experiment that his was " a nomination not fit to be made; " not fit to be confirmed after the convention had made it; he demonstrated by experiment the folly of putting a little man into a great man's place; the folly of taking the mere creature of a party to be the President of a nation. It was not the first time this had been done, nor the last.

Yet such is the structure of government and society in America, such the character of the people, so young, so free, so fresh, and strong — that not even such an administration as Mr. Polk's can permanently impede the nation's march. Cattle and corn were never more abundant. Foreigners came here in great numbers, 220,483 in the year 1848. Our total increase must have been considerably more than half a million a year. Not long ago men sneered at America — a republic could not hold its own, or only with men like Washington at its head. But in 1848, when the nations of Europe were convulsed with revolutions, whose immediate failure is now the joy of the enemies of man-

kind, west of the ocean not less than east thereof —
America stood firm, though her nominal guide was only
James K. Polk. Ours is the most complicated government in the world, but it resembles the complica-
tion of the human body, not that of a fancy watch.
Our increase in wealth was greater far than our proportionate growth of numbers. When trade is free,
and labor free, and institutions free for all men, there
is no danger that men will multiply faster than bread to
fill their mouths. This is God's world and not the
devil's.

We are a new people in a new world; flexible still,
and ready to take the impress of a great idea. Shame
on us that we choose such leaders; men with no noble
gifts of leadership, no lofty ideas, no humane aims;
men that defile the continent with brother's blood most
wickedly poured out! The President of the Democrats
showed himself the ally of the autocrats of the East.

The good things of Mr. Polk's administration we
have spoken of and duly honored; the abomination
thereof — whence came that? From the same source
out of which so much evil has already come: from
slavery. A nation, like a man, is amenable to the law
of God; suffers for its sin, and must suffer till it ends
the sin. In the North, national unity of action is
preserved with little sacrifice of individual variety of
action; the union of the people and the freedom of
the person are carefully kept secure. Hence each
man has as much freedom as he can have in the present state of physical, moral, and social science. But
in the South it is not so; there, in a population of
7,334,431 persons, there are 2,486,326 slaves; so if
the average amount of freedom in the North be represented by *one*, in the South it will be but about two-

thirds; it is doubtful that the inhabitants of any part of Europe, except Russia and Turkey, have less. Think you, O reader, while we thus trample on the rights of millions of men, we shall not suffer for the crime? No! God forbid that we should not suffer!

There are two things the nation has to fear — two modes of irresponsible power. One is the power of party; one the power of gold. Mr. Polk was the creature of a party; his ideas were party ideas, his measures party measures, his acts party acts, himself a party man. A party can make a President, as a heathen his idol, out of anything; no material is too vulgar; but a party cannot make a great man out of all the little ones which can be scented out by the keenest convention which ever met. The Democratic party made Mr. Polk; sustained him; but no huzzas could make him a great man, a just man, or a fair man. No king is more tyrannical than a party when it has the power; no despot more irresponsible. The Democrats and Whigs are proof of this. One has noble instincts and some noble ideas — so had the other once; but consider the conduct of the Baltimore Convention in 1844; their conduct for five years after. Consider the convention of Philadelphia in 1848, and the subsequent conduct of the Whigs! This irresponsible power of party has long been controlled by the South.

The irresponsible power of gold appears in two forms, as it is held by individuals or corporations. The power of gold, when vast sums are amassed by a single individual who owns more property than five counties of Massachusetts, is certainly dangerous, and of an evil tendency. But yet as the individual is transient, it is not presently alarming; a wise law, unwelcome often to the rich man, limits his control to a few years. His children may be fathers of poor men. But when vast sums are held by a corporation, permanent in itself, though composed of fleeting elements, this power, which no statute of mortmain here holds in check, becomes alarming as well as dangerous. This power of gold belongs to the North, and is likewise irresponsible. Sometimes the two help balance, and counteract one another. It was so in the administration of Jackson and Van Buren. Jackson set the power of party to smite the power of gold. Even Mr. Polk did so in two remarkable instances. But this is not always to be expected; the two are natural allies. The feudalism of birth, depending on a Caucasian descent, and the feudalism of gold, depending on its dollars, are of the same family, only settled in different parts of the land; they are true yoke-fellows. The slaveocracy of the South, and the plutocracy of the North, are born of the same mother. Now, for the first time for many years, they have stricken hands; but the Northern power of gold at the Philadelphia convention was subjugated by the Southern power of party, and lent itself a willing tool. Together they have selected the man of their choice, confessedly ignorant of politics, of small ability, and red with war; placed him on the throne of the nation. The slaveocracy and the plutocracy each gave him its counsel. By his experiment he is to demonstrate his fitness, his impotence, or his crime. He is on trial before the nation. It is not ours to judge, still less to prejudge him. Let General Taylor be weighed in an even balance. We wish there might be a more honorable tale to tell of the first mere military chief the nation ever chose. There are great problems before the nation, involving the welfare of millions of men. We pause, with hope and fear, for the Whigs to solve them as they can under the administration of Taylor and Fillmore.

III

THE STATE OF THE NATION

1850

Righteousness exalteth a nation: but sin is a reproach to any people. — Proverbs xiv. 34.

We come together to-day, by the governor's proclamation, to give thanks to God for our welfare, not merely for our happiness as individuals or as families, but for our welfare as a people. How can we better improve this opportunity, than by looking a little into the condition of the people? And accordingly I invite your attention to a sermon of the State of this Nation. I shall try to speak of the condition of the nation itself, then of the causes of that condition, and, in the third place, of the dangers that threaten, or are alleged to threaten, the nation.

First, of our condition. Look about you in Boston. Here are a hundred and forty thousand souls, living in peace and in comparative prosperity. I think, without doing injustice to the other side of the water, there is no city in the Old World, of this population, with so much intelligence, activity, morality, order, comfort, and general welfare, and, at the same time, with so little of the opposite of all these. I know the faults of Boston, and I would not disguise them; the poverty, unnatural poverty, which shivers in the cellar; the unnatural wealth which bloats in the parlor; the sin which is hid in the corners of the jail; and the more dangerous sin which sets up Christianity for a pretense; the sophistry which lightens in the newspapers, and thunders in the pulpit — I know all these things, and do not pretend to disguise them; and still I think no city of the Old World, of the same population, has so much which good men prize, and so little which good men deplore.

See the increase of material wealth; the buildings for trade and for homes; the shops and ships. This year Boston will add to her possessions some ten or twenty millions of dollars, honestly and earnestly got. Observe the neatness of the streets, the industry of the inhabitants, their activity of mind, the orderliness of the people, the signs of comfort. Then consider the charities of Boston; those limited to our own border, and those which extend further, those beautiful charities which encompass the earth with their sweet influence. Look at the schools, a monument of which the city may well be proud, in spite of their defects.

But Boston, though we proudly call it the Athens of America, is not the pleasantest thing in New England to look at; it is the part of Massachusetts which I like the least to look at, spite of its excellence. Look further, at the whole of Massachusetts, and you see a fairer spectacle. There is less wealth at Provincetown, in proportion to the numbers, but there is less want; there is more comfort; property is more evenly and equally distributed there than here, and the welfare of a country never so much depends upon the amount of its wealth, as on the mode in which its wealth is distributed. In the State, there are about one hundred and fifty thousand families — some nine hundred and seventy-five thousand persons, living with a degree of comfort, which, I think, is not anywhere enjoyed by such a population in the Old World. They are mainly industrious, sober, intelligent, and moral. Everything thrives; agriculture, manufactures, commerce. " The carpenter encourages the goldsmith; he that smites the anvil, him that smootheth with the hammer." Look at the farms, where intelligent labor wins bread and beauty both, out of the sterile soil and climate not over-indulgent. Behold the shops all over the State; the small shops where the shoemaker holds his work in his lap, and draws his thread by his own strong muscles; and the large shops where machines, animate with human intelligence, hold, with iron grasp, their costlier work in their lap, and spin out the delicate staple of Sea Island cotton. Look at all this; it is a pleasant sight. Look at our hundreds of villages, by river, mountain, and sea; behold the comfortable homes, the people well fed, well clad, well instructed. Look at the school-houses, the colleges of the people; at the higher seminaries of learning; at the poor man's real college further back in the interior, where the mechanic's and farmer's son gets his education, often a poor one, still something to be proud of. Look at the churches, where, every Sunday, the best words of Hebrew and of Christian saints are read out of this Book, and all men are asked, once in the week, to remember they have a Father in heaven, a faith to swear by, and a heaven to live for, and a conscience to keep. I know the fault of these churches. I am not in the habit of excusing them; still I know their excellence, and I will not be the last man to acknowledge that. Look at the roads of earth and iron which join villages together, and make the State a whole. Follow the fisherman from his rocky harbor at Cape Ann; follow the mariner in his voyage round the world of waters; see the industry, the intelligence, and the comfort of the people. I think Massachusetts is a State to be thankful for. There are faults in her institutions and in her laws, that need change very much. In her form of society, in her schools, in her colleges, there is much which clamors loudly for alteration — very much in her churches to be Christianized. These changes are going quietly forward, and will in time be brought about.

I love to look on this State, its material prosperity, its increase in riches, its intelligence and industry, and the beautiful results that are seen all about us to-day. I love to look on the face of the people, in halls and churches, in markets and factories; to think of our great ideas; of the institutions which have come of them; of our schools and colleges, and all the institutions for making men wiser and better; to think of the noble men we have in the midst of us, in every walk of life, who eat an honest bread, who love mankind, and love God, who have consciences they mean to keep, and souls which they intend to save.

The great business of society is not merely to have farms, and ships, and shops — the greater shops and the less — but to have men; men that are conscious of their manhood, self-respectful, earnest men, that have a faith in the living God. I do not think we have many men of genius. We have very few that I call great men; I wish there were more; but we have an intelligent, an industrious, and noble people here in Massachusetts, which we may be proud of.

Let us go a step further. New England is like Massachusetts in the main, with local differences only. All the North is like New England in the main; this portion is better in one thing; that portion worse in another thing. Our ideas are their ideas; our institutions are the same. Some of the Northern States have institutions better than we. They have added to our experience. In revising their constitutions and laws, or in making new ones, they go beyond us, they introduce new improvements, and those new improvements will give those States the same advantage over us, which a new mill, with new and superior machinery, has over an old mill, with old and inferior machinery. By and by we shall see the result, and take counsel from it, I trust.

All over the North we find the same industry and thrift, and similar intelligence. Here attention is turned to agriculture, there to mining; but there is a similar progress and zeal for improvement. Attention is bestowed on schools and colleges, on academies and churches. There is the same abundance of material comfort. Population advances rapidly, prosperity in a greater ratio. Everywhere new swarms pour forth from the old hive, and settle in some convenient nook, far off in the West. So the frontier of civilization every year goes forward, further from the ocean. Fifty years ago it was on the Ohio; then on the Mississippi; then on the upper Missouri; presently its barrier will be the Rocky Mountains, and soon it will pass beyond that bar, and the tide of the Atlantic will sweep over to the Pacific — yea, it is already there! The universal Yankee freights his schooner at Bangor, at New Bedford, and at Boston, with bricks, timber, frame-houses, and other " notions," and by and by drops his anchor in the smooth Pacific, in the Bay of St. Francis. We shall see there, ere long, the sentiments of New England, the ideas of New England, the institutions of New England; the school-house, the meeting-house, the court-house, the town-house. There will be the same industry, thrift, intel-

ligence, morality, and religion, and the idle ground
that has hitherto borne nothing but gold, will bear
upon its breast a republic of men more precious than
the gold of Ophir, or the rubies of the East.

Here I wish I could stop. But this is not all. The
North is not the whole nation; New England is not
the only type of people. There are other States
differing widely from this. In the Southern States
you find a soil more fertile under skies more genial.
Through what beautiful rivers the Alleghenies pour
their tribute to the sea! What streams beautify the
land in Georgia, Alabama, Louisiana, and Mississippi!
There genial skies rain beauty on the soil. Nature is
wanton of her gifts. There rice, cotton, and sugar
grow; there the olive, the orange, the fig, all find a
home. The soil teems with luxuriance. But there is
not the same wealth, nor the same comfort. Only
the ground is rich. You witness not a similar thrift.
Strange is it, but in 1840 the single State of New
York alone earned over four million dollars more
than the six States of North and South Carolina,
Georgia, Alabama, Louisiana, and Mississippi! The
annual earnings of little Massachusetts, with her seven
thousand eight hundred square miles, are nine million dollars more than the earnings of all Florida,
Georgia, and South Carolina! The little county of
Essex, with ninety-five thousand souls in 1840, earned
more than the large State of South Carolina, with
five hundred and ninety-five thousand.

In those States we miss the activity, intelligence, and
enterprise of the North. You do not find the little
humble school-house at every corner; the frequent
meeting-house does not point its taper finger to the
sky. Villages do not adorn the margin of the moun-

tain stream, and sea; shops do not ring with industry; roads of earth and iron are poorer and less common. Temperance, morality, comfort are not there as here. In the slave States, in 1840, there were not quite three hundred and two thousand youths and maidens in all the schools, academies, and colleges of the South; but in 1840, in the free States of the North there were more than two million two hundred and twelve thousand in such institutions! Little Rhode Island has five thousand more girls and boys at school than large South Carolina. The State of Ohio alone has more than seventeen thousand children at school beyond what the whole fifteen slave States can boast. The permanent literature of the nation all comes from the North; your historians are from that quarter — your Sparkses, your Bancrofts, your Hildreths, and Prescotts, and Ticknors; the poets are from the same quarter — your Whittiers and Longfellows, and Lowells, and Bryants; the men of literature and religion — your Channings, and Irvings, and Emersons — are from the same quarter! Preaching — it is everywhere, and sermons are as thick almost as autumnal leaves; but who ever heard of a great or famous clergyman in a Southern State? of a great and famous sermon that rang through the nation from that quarter? No man. Your Edwards of old time, and your Beechers, old and young, your Channing and Buckminster, and the rest, names which throng to every man's lips — all are from the North Nature has done enough for the South, God's cup of blessing runs over — and yet you see the result! But there has been no pestilence at the South more than at the North; no earthquake has torn the ground beneath their feet; no war has come to disturb them more than us. The government has never laid a withering hand on their commerce, their agriculture, their schools and colleges, their literature and their church.

Still, letting alone the South and the North as such, not considering either exclusively, we are one nation. What is a nation? It is one of the great parties in the world. It is a sectional party, having geographical limits; with a party organization, party opinions, party mottoes, party machinery, party leaders, and party followers; with some capital city for its party headquarters. There has been an Assyrian party, a British, a Persian, an Egyptian, and a Roman party; there is now a Chinese party, and a Russian, a Turkish, a French, and an English party; these are also called nations. We belong to the American party, and that includes the North as well as the South; and so all are brothers of the same party, differing amongst ourselves — but from other nations in this, that we are the American party, and not the Russian nor the English.

We ought to look at the whole American party, the North and South, to see the total condition of the people. Now at this moment there is no lack of cattle and corn and cloth in the United States, North or South, only they are differently distributed in the different parts of the land. But still there is a great excitement. Men think the nation is in danger, and for many years there has not been so great an outcry and alarm amongst the politicians. The cry is raised, " The Union is in danger! " and if the Union falls, we are led to suppose that everything falls. There will be no more Thanksgiving Days; there will be anarchy and civil war, and the ruin of the American people! It is curious to see this material plenty, on the one side, and this political alarm and confusion on the other.

Let me now come to the next point, and consider the causes of our present condition. This will involve a consideration of the cause of our prosperity and of our alarm.

1. First, there are some causes which depend on God entirely; such as the nature of the country, soil, climate, and the like; its minerals, and natural productions; its seas and harbors, mountains and rivers. In respect to these natural advantages, the country is abundantly favored, but the North less so than the South. Tennessee, Virginia, and Alabama, certainly have the advantage over Maine, New Hampshire, and Ohio. That I pass by; a cause which depends wholly on God.

2. Then again, this is a wide and new country. We have room to spread. We have not to contend against old institutions, established a thousand years ago; and that is one very great advantage. I make no doubt that in crossing the ocean, our fathers helped forward the civilization of the world at least a thousand years; I mean to say, it would have taken mankind a thousand years longer to reach the condition we have attained in New England, if the attempt had of necessity been made on the soil of the Old World and in the face of its institutions.

3. Then, as a third thing, much depends on the peculiar national character. Well, the freemen in the North and South are chiefly from the same race, this indomitable Caucasian stock; mainly from the same composite stock, the tribe produced by the mingling of Saxon, Danish, and Norman blood. That makes the present English nation, and the American also.

This is a very powerful tribe of men, possessing some very noble traits of character; active and creative in all the arts of peace; industrious as a nation never was before; enterprising, practical; fond of liberty, fond also of law, capable of organizing themselves into great masses, and acting with a complete concert and unity of action. In these respects, I think this tribe, which I will call the English tribe, is equal to any race of men in the world that has been or is; perhaps superior to any race that has been developed hitherto. But in what relates to the higher reason and imagination, to the affections and to the soul, I think this tribe is not so eminent as some others have been. North and South, the people are alike of Anglo-Norman descent.

4. Another cause of our prosperity, which depends a great deal on ourselves, is this — the absence of war and of armies. In France, with a population of less than forty millions, half a million are constantly under arms. The same state of things prevails substantially in Austria, Prussia, and in all the German States. Here in America, with a population of twenty millions, there is not one in a thousand that is a soldier or marine. In time of peace, I think we waste vast sums in military preparations, as we did in actual war not long since. Still, when I compare this nation with others, I think we have cause to felicitate ourselves on the absence of military power.

5. Again, much depends on the past history of the race; and here there is a wide difference between the different parts of the country. New England was settled by a religious colony. I will not say that all the men who came here from 1620 to 1650 were moved by religious motives; but the controlling men were brought

here by these motives, and no other. Many who cared
less for religious ideas, came for the sake of a great
moral idea, for the sake of obtaining a greater degree
of civil freedom than they had at home. Now the
Pilgrims and the Puritans are only a little way behind
us. The stiff ruff, the peaked beard, the " Prophesy-
ing Book " are only six or seven generations behind the
youngest of us. The character of the Puritans has
given to New England much of its present character
and condition. They founded schools and colleges;
they trained up their children in a stern discipline
which we shall not forget for two centuries to come.
The remembrance of their trials, their heroism, and
their piety affects our preaching to-day, and our politics also. The difference between New England and
New York, from 1750 to 1790, is the difference between the sons of the religious colony and the sons
of the worldly colony. You know something of New
York politics before the Revolution, and also since
the Revolution; the difference between New York and
New England politics at that time, is the difference
between the sons of religious men and the sons of men
who cared very much less for religion.

Just now, when I said that all the North is like New
England, I meant substantially so. The West is our
own daughter. New England has helped people the
western part of the State of New York; and the best
elements of New England character mingling with
others, its good qualities will appear in the politics of
that mighty State.

The South, in the main, had a very different origin
from the North. I think few if any persons settled
there for religion's sake; or for the sake of freedom
in the State. It was not a moral idea which sent men

to Virginia, Georgia, and Carolina. " Men do not gather grapes of thorns." The difference of the seed will appear in the difference of the crop. In the character of the people of the North and South, it appears at this day. The North is not to be praised, nor the South to be blamed for this; they could not help it: but certainly it is an advantage to be descended from a race of industrious, moral and religious men; to have been brought up under their training, to have inherited their ideas and institutions,— and this is a circumstance which we make quite too little account of. I pass by that.

6. There are other causes which depend on ourselves entirely. Much depends on the political and social organization of the people. There is no denying that government has a great influence on the character of the people; on the character of every man. The difference between the development of England and the development of Spain at this day, is mainly the result of different forms of government; for three centuries ago the Spaniards were as noble a race as the English.

A government is carried on by two agencies: the first is public opinion, and the next is public law,— the fundamental law which is the Constitution, and the subsidiary laws which carry out the ideas of the Constitution. In a government like this, public opinion always precedes the laws, overrides them, takes the place of laws when there are none, and hinders their execution when they do not correspond to public opinion. Thus the public opinion of South Carolina demands that a free colored seaman from the North shall be shut up in jail at his employer's cost. The public opinion of Charleston is stronger than the public law of the United States on that point, stronger than the Constitution, and nobody dares execute the laws of the United States in that matter. These two things should always be looked at, to understand the causes of a nation's condition — the public opinion, as well as the public law. Let me know the opinions of the men between twenty-five and thirty-five years of age, and I know what the laws will be.

Now in public opinion and in the laws of the United States, there are two distinct political ideas. I shall call one the democratic, and the other the despotic idea. Neither is wholly sectional; both chiefly so. Each is composed of several simpler ideas. Each has enacted laws, and established institutions. This is the democratic idea; that all men are endowed by their Creator with certain natural rights, which only the possessor can alienate; that all men are equal in these rights; that amongst them is the right to life, liberty, and the pursuit of happiness; that the business of the government is to preserve for every man all of these rights until he alienates them.

This democratic idea is founded in human nature, and comes from the nature of God who made human nature. To carry it out politically is to execute justice, which is the will of God. This idea, in its realization, leads to a democracy, a government of all, for all, by all. Such a government aims to give every man all his natural rights; it desires to have political power in all hands, property in all hands, wisdom in all heads, goodness in all hearts, religion in all souls. I mean the religion that makes a man self-respectful, earnest, and faithful to the Infinite God, that disposes him to give all men their rights, and to claim his own rights at all times; the religion which is piety within you, and goodness in the manifestation. Such a government has laws, and the aim thereof is to give justice to all men; it has officers to execute these laws, for the sake of justice. Such a government founds schools for all; looks after those most who are most in need; defends and protects the feeblest as well as the richest and most powerful. The State is for the individual, and for all the individuals, and so it reverences justice, where the rights of all, and the interests of all, exactly balance. It demands free speech; everything is open to examination, discussion, " agitation," if you will. Thought is to be free, speech to be free, work to be free, and worship to be free. Such is the democratic idea, and such the State which it attempts to found.

The despotic idea is just the opposite: That all men are *not* endowed by their Creator with certain natural rights which only the possessor can alienate, but that one man has a natural right to overcome and make use of some other men for his advantage and their hurt; that all men are *not* equal in their rights; that all men have *not* a natural right to life, liberty, and the pursuit of happiness; that government is *not* instituted to preserve these natural rights for all.

This idea is founded on the excess of human passions, and it represents the compromise between a man's idleness and his appetite. It is not based on facts eternal in human nature, but on facts transient in human nature. It does not aim to do justice to all, but injustice to some; to take from one man what he ought not to lose, and give to another what he ought not to get.

This leads to aristocracy in various forms, to the government of all by means of a part and for the sake of a part. In this state of things political power must be in few hands; property in few hands; wisdom in few heads; goodness in few hearts, and religion in few souls. I mean the religion which leads a man to respect himself and his fellow-men; to be earnest, and to trust in the Infinite God; to demand his rights of other men and to give their rights to them.

Neither the democratic nor the despotic idea is fully made real anywhere in the world. There is no perfect democracy, nor perfect aristocracy. There are democrats in every actual aristocracy; despots in every actual democracy. But in the Northern States the democratic idea prevails extensively and chiefly, and we have made attempts at establishing a democratic government. In the Southern States the despotic idea prevails extensively and chiefly, and they have made attempts to establish an aristocratic government. In an aristocracy there are two classes: the people to be governed, and the governing class, the nobility which is to govern. This nobility may be movable, and depend on wealth; or immovable, and depend on birth. In the Southern States the nobility is immovable, and depends on color.

In 1840, in the North there were ten million free men, and in the South five million free men and three million slaves. Three-eighths of the population have no human rights at all — privileges as cattle, not rights as men. There the slave is protected by law, as your horse and your ox, but has few more human rights.

Here, now, is the great cause of the difference in the condition of the North and South; of the difference in the material results, represented by towns and villages, by farms and factories, ships and shops. Here is the cause of the difference in schools, colleges, churches, and in the literature; the cause of the difference in men. The South, with its despotic idea, dishonors labor, but wishes to compromise between its idleness and its appetite, and so kidnaps men to do its work. The North, with its democratic idea, honors labor; does not compromise between its idleness and its appetite, but lays its bones to the work to satisfy its appetite; instead of kidnapping a man who can run away, it kidnaps the elements, subdues them to its command, and makes them do its work. It does not kidnap a freeman, but catches the winds, and chains them to its will. It lays hands on fire and water, and breeds a new giant, which " courses land and ocean without rest," or serves while it stands and waits, driving the mills of the land. It kidnaps the Connecticut and the Merrimac; does not send slave-ships to Africa, but engineers to New Hampshire; and it requires no fugitive slave law to keep the earth and sea from escaping, or the rivers of New England from running up hill.

This is not quite all. I have just now tried to hint at the causes of the difference in the condition of the people, North and South. Now let me show the cause of the agitation and alarm. We begin with a sentiment; that spreads to an idea; the idea grows to an act, to an institution; then it has done its work.

Men seek to spread their sentiments and ideas. The democratic idea tries to spread; the despotic idea tries to spread. For a long time the nation held these two ideas in its bosom, not fully conscious of either of them. Both came here in a state of infancy, so to say, with our fathers; the democratic idea very dimly understood; the despotic idea not fully carried out, yet it did a great mischief in the State and Church. In the Declaration of Independence, writ by a young man, only the democratic idea appears, and that idea never got so distinctly stated before. But mark you, and see the confusion in men's minds. That democratic idea was thus distinctly stated by a man who was a slaveholder almost all his life; and unless public rumor has been unusually false, he has left some of his own offspring under the influence of the despotic and not the democratic idea; slaves and not free men.

In the Constitution of the United States these two ideas appear. It was thought for a long time they were not incompatible; it was thought the great American party might recognize both, and a compromise was made between the two. It was thought each might go about its own work and let the other alone; that the hawk and the hen might dwell happily together in the same coop, each lay her own eggs, and rear her own brood, and neither put a claw upon the other.

In the meantime each founded institutions after its kind; in the Northern States, democratic institutions; in the Southern, aristocratic. What once lay latent in the mind of the nation has now become patent. The thinking part of the nation sees the difference between the two. Some men are beginning to see that the two are completely incompatible, and cannot be good friends. Others are asking us to shut our eyes and not see it, and they think that so long as our eyes are shut, all things will go on peacefully. Such is the wisdom of the ostrich.

At first the trouble coming from this source was a very little cloud, far away on the horizon, not bigger than a man's hand. It seemed so in 1804, when the brave senator from Massachusetts, a Hartford Convention Federalist, a name that calls the blood to some rather pale cheeks now-a-days, proposed to alter the Constitution of the United States, and cut off the North from all responsibility for slavery. It was a little cloud not bigger than a man's hand; now it is a great cloud which covers the whole hemisphere of heaven, and threatens to shut out the day.

In the last session of Congress, ten months long, the great matter was the contest between the two ideas. All the newspapers rang with the battle. Even the pulpits now and then alluded to it; forgetting their " decency, that they must preach ' only religion,' which has not the least to do with politics and the welfare of the State."

Each idea has its allies, and it is worth while to run our eye over the armies and see what they amount to. The idea of despotism has for its allies: —

1. The slaveholders of the South with their dependents; and the servile class who take their ideas from the prominent men about them. This servile class is more numerous at the South than even at the North.

2. It has almost all the distinguished politicians of the North and South; the distinguished great politicians in the Congress of the nation, and the distinguished little politicians in the Congresses of the several States.

3. It has likewise the greater portion of the wealthy and educated men in many large towns of the North; with their dependents and the servile men who take their opinions from the prominent class about them. And here, I am sorry to say, I must reckon the greater portion of the prominent and wealthy clergy, the clergy in the large cities. Once this class of men were masters of the rich and educated; and very terrible masters they were in Madrid and in Rome. Now their successors are doing penance for those old sins. " It is a long lane," they say, " which has no turn," and the clerical has had a very short and complete turn.

When I say the majority of the clergy in prominent situations in the large cities are to be numbered among the allies of the despotic idea, and are a part of the great pro-slavery army, I know there are some noble and honorable exceptions, men who do not fear the face of gold, but reverence the face of God.

Then on the side of the democratic idea there are: —

1. The great mass of the people at the North; farmers, mechanics, and the humbler clergy. This does not appear so at first sight, because these men have not much confidence in themselves, and require to be shaken many times before they are thoroughly waked up.

2. Beside that, there are a few politicians at the North who are on this side; some distinguished ones in Congress, some less distinguished ones in the various legislatures of the North.

3. Next there are men, North and South, who look at the great causes of the welfare of nations, and make up their minds historically, from the facts of human history, against despotism. Then there are such as study the great principles of justice and truth, and judge from human nature, and decide against despotism. And then such as look at the law of God, and believe Christianity is sense and not nonsense; that Christianity is the ideal for earnest men, not a pretense for a frivolous hypocrite. Some of these men are at the South; the greater number are in the North; and here again you see the difference between the son of the planter and the son of the Puritan.

Here are the allies, the threefold armies of despotism on the one side, and of democracy on the other.

Now it is not possible for these two ideas to continue to live in peace. For a long time each knew not the other, and they were quiet. The men who clearly knew the despotic idea, thought, in 1787, it would die " of a rapid consumption: " they said so; but the culture of cotton has healed its deadly wound, at least for the present. After the brief state of quiet, there came a state of armed neutrality. They were hostile, but under bonds to keep the peace. Now the neutrality is over; attempts are made to compromise, to compose the difficulty. Various peace measures were introduced to the Senate last summer; but they all turned out war measures, every one of them. Now there is a trial of strength between the two. Which shall recede? which be extended? Freedom or slavery? That is the question; refuse to look at it as we will,— refrain or refrain not from " political agitation," that is the question.

In the last Congress it is plain the democratic idea was beaten. Congress said to California, " You may come in, and you need not keep slaves unless you please." It said, " You shall not bring slaves to Washington for sale, you may do that at Norfolk, Alexandria, and Georgetown, it is just as well, and this ' will pacify the North.' " Utah and New Mexico were left open to slavery, and fifty thousand or seventy thousand square miles and ten million dollars were given to Texas lest she should " dissolve the Union," — without money or men! To crown all, the Fugitive Slave Bill became a law.

I think it is very plain that the democratic idea was defeated, and it is easy to see why. The three powers which are the allies of the despotic idea, were ready, and could act in concert — the Southern slaveholders, the leading politicians, the rich and educated men of the Northern cities, with their appendages and servile adherents.   But since then, the conduct of the people in the North, and especially in this State, shows that the nation has not gone that way yet.   I think the nation never will; that the idea of freedom will never be turned back in this blessed North.   I feel sure it will at last overcome the idea of slavery.

I come to this conclusion, firstly, from the character of the tribe: this Anglo-Norman-Saxon tribe loves law, deliberation, order, method; it is the most methodical race that ever lived.   But it loves liberty, and while it loves law, it loves law chiefly because it keeps liberty; and without that it would trample law under foot.

See the conduct of England.   She spent one hundred millions of dollars in the attempt to wipe slavery from the West Indies.   She keeps a fleet on the coast of Africa to put down the slave-trade there — where we also have, I think, a sloop-of-war.   She has just concluded a treaty with Brazil for the suppression of the slave-trade in that country, one of her greatest achievements in that work for many years.

See how the sons of the Puritans, as soon as they came to a consciousness of what the despotic idea was, took their charters and wiped slavery clean out, first from Massachusetts, and then from the other States, one after another.   See how every Northern State, in revising its constitution, or in making a new one, declares all men are created equal, that all have the right to life, liberty, and the pursuit of happiness.

Then the religion of the North demands the same thing.   Professors may try to prove that the Old Testament establishes slavery; that the New Testament justifies the existence of slavery; that Paul's epistle to Philemon was nothing more than another fugitive slave law, that Paul himself sent back a runaway; but it does not touch the religion of the North. We know better. We say if the Old Testament does that and the New Testament, so much the worse for them both. We say, " Let us look and see if Paul was so benighted," and we can judge for ourselves that the professor was mistaken more than the apostle.

Again, the spirit of the age, which is the public opinion of the nations, is against slavery. It has broken down in England, France, Italy, and Spain; it cannot stand long against civilization and good sense; against the political economy and the religious economy of the civilized world. The genius of freedom stands there, year out, year in, and hurls firebrands into the owl's nest of the prince of darkness, continually,— and is all this with no effect?

Besides that, it is against the law of God. That guides this universe, treating with even-handed justice the great geographical parties, Austrian, Roman, British, or American, with the same justice wherewith it dispenses its blessings to the little local factions that divide the village for a day; marshaling mankind forward in its mighty progress towards wisdom, freedom, goodness towards men, and piety towards God.

Of the final issue I have no doubt; but no man can tell what shall come to pass in the meantime. We see that political parties in the State are snapped asunder: whether the national party shall not be broken up, no man can say. In 1750, on the 28th day of November, no man in Old England or New England could tell what 1780 would bring forth. No man, North or South, can tell to-day what 1880 will bring to pass. He must be a bold man who declares to the nation that no new political machinery shall be introduced, in the next thirty years, to our national mill. We know not what a day shall bring forth, but we know that God is on the side of right and justice, and that they will prevail so long as God is God.

Now, then, to let alone details, and generalize into one all the causes of our condition, this is the result: We have found welfare just so far as we have followed the democratic idea, and enacted justice into law. We have lost welfare just so far as we have followed the despotic idea, and made iniquity into a statute. So far as we have reaffirmed the ordinance of nature and re-enacted the will of God, we have succeeded. So far as we have refused to do that, we have failed. Of old it was written, " Righteousness exalteth a nation: but sin is a reproach to any people."

And now a word of our dangers. There seems no danger from abroad; from any foreign State, unless we begin the quarrel; none from famine. The real danger, in one word, is this — That we shall try to enact injustice into a law, and with the force of the nation to make iniquity obeyed.

See some of the special forms of injustice which threaten us, or are already here. I shall put them into the form of ideas.

1. One, common among politicians, is,— That the State is for a portion of the people, not the whole. Thus it has been declared that the Constitution of the United States did not recognize the three million slaves as citizens, or extend to them any right which it guarantees to other men. It would be a sad thing for the State to declare there was a single child in the whole land to whom it owed no protection. What, then, if it attempts to take three millions from under its shield? In obedience to this false idea, the counsel has been

given, that we must abstain from all " political agitation " of the most important matter before the people. We must leave that to our masters, for the State is for them, it is not for you and me. They must say whether we shall " agitate " and " discuss " these things or not. The politicians are our masters, and may lay their fingers on our lips when they will.

2. The next false idea is,— That government is chiefly for the protection of property. This has long been the idea on which some men legislated, but on the 19th day of this month, the distinguished Secretary of State,* in a speech at New York, used these words: " The great object of government is the protection of property at home and respect and renown abroad." You see what the policy must be where the government is for the protection of the hat, and only takes care of the head so far as it serves to wear a hat. Here the man is the accident, and the dollar is the substance for which the man is to be protected. I think a notion very much like this prevails extensively in the great cities of America, North and South. I think the chief politicians of the two parties are agreed in this — that government is for the protection of property, and everything else is subsidiary. With many persons politics are a part of their business; the State House and the custom-house are only valued for their relation to trade. This idea is fatal to a good government.

Think of this, that " the great object of government is the protection of property." Tell that to Samuel Adams, and John Hancock, and Washington, and the older Winthrops, and the Bradfords and Carvers! Why! it seems as if the buried majesty of Mas-

* Daniel Webster.

sachusetts would start out of the ground, and with its
Bible in its hand say — This is false!

3. The third false idea is this — That you are
morally bound to obey the statute, let it be never so
plainly wrong and opposed to your conscience.   This
is the most dangerous of all the false ideas yet named.
Ambitious men, in an act of passion, make iniquity
into a law, and then demand that you and I, in our
act of prayer, shall submit to it and make it our daily
life; that we shall not try to repeal and discuss and
agitate it!   This false idea lies at the basis of every
despot's throne, the idea that men can make right
wrong, and wrong right.   It has come to be taught in
New England, to be taught in our churches — though
seldom there, to their honor be it spoken, except in
the churches of commerce in large towns — that if
wrong is law, you and I must do what it demands,
though conscience declares it is treason against man
and treason against God.   The worst doctrines of
Hobbes and Filmer are thus revived.

I have sometimes been amazed at the talk of men
who call on us to keep the Fugitive Slave Law, one of
the most odious laws in a world of odious laws — a law
not fit to be made or kept.   I have been amazed that
they should dare to tell us the law of God, writ on the
heavens and our hearts, never demanded we should
disobey the laws of men!   Well, suppose it were so.
Then it was old Daniel's duty at Darius's command
to give up his prayer; but he prayed three times a day,
with his windows up.   Then it was John's and Peter's
duty to forbear to preach of Christianity; but they
said, " Whether it be right in the sight of God to
hearken unto you more than unto God, judge ye."
Then it was the duty of Amram and Jochebed to take

up their new-born Moses and cast him into the Nile; for
the law of King Pharaoh, commanding it, was " constitutional," and " political agitation " was discounte-
nanced as much in Goshen as in Boston. But Daniel
did not obey; John and Peter did not fail to preach
Christianity; and Amram and Jochebed refused " passive obedience " to the king's decree! I think it will
take a strong man all this winter to reverse the judgment which the world has passed on these three cases.

However, there is another ancient case, mentioned
in the Bible, in which the laws commanded one thing and
conscience just the opposite. Here is the record of
the law:—" Now both the chief priests and the Pharisees had given a commandment, that if any one knew
where he [Jesus] were, he should show it, that they
might take him." Of course, it became the official and
legal business of each disciple who knew where Christ
was, to make it known to the authorities. No doubt
James and John could leave all and follow him, with
others of the people who knew not the law of Moses,
and were accursed; nay, the women, Martha and Mary,
could minister unto him of their substance, could wash
his feet with tears, and wipe them with the hairs of
their head. They did it gladly, of their own free will,
and took pleasure therein, I make no doubt. There
was no merit in that —" Any man can perform an
agreeable duty." But there was found one disciple
who could " perform a disagreeable duty." He went,
perhaps " with alacrity," and betrayed his Saviour to
the marshal of the district of Jerusalem, who was called
a centurion. Had he no affection for Jesus? No
doubt; but he could conquer his prejudices, while Mary
and John could not.

Judas Iscariot has rather a bad name in the Chris-

tian world: he is called " the son of perdition," in the
New Testament, and his conduct is reckoned a " transgression ; " nay, it is said the devil " entered into him,"
to cause this hideous sin.   But all this it seems was
a mistake; certainly, if we are to believe our republican lawyers and statesmen, Iscariot only fulfilled his
" constitutional obligations."   It was only " on that
point," of betraying his Saviour, that the constitutional
law required him to have anything to do with Jesus.
He took his thirty pieces of silver — about fifteen dollars ; a Yankee is to do it for ten, having fewer prejudices to conquer — it was his legal fee, for value received.   True, the Christians thought it was " the
wages of iniquity," and even the Pharisees — who commonly made the commandment of God of none effect
by their traditions — dared not defile the temple with
this " price of blood ; " but it was honest money.   It
was as honest a fee as any American commissioner or
deputy will ever get for a similar service.   How mistaken we are !   Judas Iscariot is not a traitor; he was
a great patriot; he conquered his prejudices, performed a disagreeable duty as an officer of " high morals and high principle ; " he kept the law and the Constitution, and did all he could to " save the Union ; "
nay, he was a saint, " not a whit behind the very chief-
est apostles."   " The law of God never commands us
to disobey the law of man."   *Sancte Iscariote, ora pro
nobis!*

It is a little strange to hear this talk in Boston, and
hear the doctrine of passive obedience to a law which
sets Christianity at defiance, taught here in the face of
the Adamses, and Hancock, and Washington!   It is
amazing to hear this talk, respecting such a law,
amongst merchants.   Do they keep the usury laws?

I never heard of but one money-lender who kept them,* and he has been a long time dead, and I think he left no kith nor kin! The temperance law,— is that kept? The fifteen gallon law,— were men so very passive in their obedience to that, that they could not even " agitate? " yet it violated no law of God — was not unchristian. When the government interferes with the rumsellers' property, the law must be trod under foot; but when the law insists that a man shall be made a slave, I must give up conscience in my act of prayer, and stoop to the vile law men have made in their act of passion!

It is curious to hear men talk of law and order in Boston, when the other day one or two hundred smooth-faced boys, and youths beardless as girls, could disturb a meeting of three or four thousand men, for two hours long; and the chief of the police and the mayor of the city stood and looked on, when a single word from their lips might have stilled the tumult and given honest men a hearing.†

Talk of keeping the Fugitive Slave Law! Come, come, we know better. Men in New England know better than this. We know that we ought not to keep a wicked law, and that it must not be kept when the law of God forbids!

But the effect of a law which men cannot keep without violating conscience, is always demoralizing. There are men who know no higher law than the statute of the State. When good men cannot keep a law that is base, some bad ones will say, " Let us keep no law at all,"— then where does the blame lie? On him that enacts the outrageous law.

* The late Mr. John Parker.
† At a meeting in Faneuil Hall to welcome Mr. George Thompson, Nov. 15, 1850.

The idea that a statute of man frees us from obligation to the law of God, is a dreadful thing. When that becomes the deliberate conviction of the great mass of the people, North or South, then I shall despair of human nature; then I shall despair of justice, and despair of God. But this time will never come.

One of the most awful spectacles I ever saw, was this: A vast multitude attempting, at an orator's suggestion, to howl down the " higher law; " and when he said, " Will you have this to rule over you? " they answered, " Never! " and treated the " higher law " to a laugh and a howl! It was done in Faneuil Hall; * under the eyes of the three Adamses, Hancock, and Washington; and the howl rang round the venerable arches of that hall! I could not but ask, " Why do the heathen rage, and the people imagine a vain thing? the rulers of the earth set themselves, and kings take counsel against the Lord and say, ' Let us break his bands asunder, and cast off his yoke from us.' " Then I could not but remember that it was written, " He that sitteth in the heavens shall laugh; the Lord shall have them in derision. He taketh up the isles as a very little thing, and the inhabitants of the earth are as grasshoppers before him." Howl down the law of God at a magistrate's command! Do this in Boston! Let us remember this — but with charity.

Men say there is danger of disunion, of our losing fealty for the Constitution. I do not believe it yet! Suppose it be so. The Constitution is the machinery of the national mill; and suppose we agree to take it out and put in new; we might get worse,— very true, but we might get better. There have been some mod-

* At the " Union meeting," two days before the delivery of this sermon.

ern improvements; we might introduce them to the State as well as the mill. But I do not believe there is this danger. I do not believe the people of Massachusetts think so. I think they are strongly attached to the Union yet, and if they thought the Union was in peril — this day, and everything the nation prizes was likely to be destroyed,— we should not have had a meeting of a few thousands in Faneuil Hall, but the people would have filled up the city of Worcester with a hundred thousand men, if need be; and they would have come with the cartridge-box at their side, and the firelock on their shoulder. That is the way the people of Massachusetts would assemble if they thought there was real danger.

I do not believe the South will withdraw from the Union, with five million free men, and three million slaves. I think Massachusetts would be no loser, I think the North would be no loser; but I doubt if the North will yet allow them to go, or is so disposed. Do you think the South is so mad as to wish it?

But I think I know of one cause which may dissolve the Union — one which ought to dissolve it, if put in action: that is, a serious attempt to execute the Fugitive Slave Law, here and in all the North. I mean an attempt to recover and take back all the fugitive slaves in the North, and to punish, with fine and imprisonment, all who aid or conceal them. The South has browbeat us again and again. She has smitten us on the one cheek with " Protection," and we have turned the other, kissing the rod; she has smitten that with " Free Trade." She has imprisoned our citizens; driven off, with scorn and loathing, our officers sent to ask constitutional justice. She has spit upon us. Let her come to take back the fugitives — and trust me, she " will wake up the lion."

In my humble opinion, this law is a wedge — sharp at one end, but wide at the other — put in between the lower planks of our Ship of State. If it be driven home, we go to pieces. But I have no thought that that will be done quite yet. I believe the great politicians, who threaten to drive it through the gaping seams of our argosy, will think twice before they strike again. Nay, that they will soon be very glad to bury the wedge " where the tide ebbs and flows four times a day." I do not expect this of their courage, but of their fears; not of their justice — I am too old for that — but of their concern for property, which it is the " great object of government " to protect.

I know how some men talk in public, and how they act at home. I heard a man the other day, at Faneuil Hall, declare the law must be kept, and denounce, not very gently, all who preached or prayed against it, as enemies of " all law." But that was all talk, for this very man, on that very day, had violated the law; had furnished the golden wheels on which fugitives rode out of the reach of the arms which the marshal would have been sorry to lift. I could tell things more surprising — but it is not wise just now!

I do not believe there is more than one of the New England men who publicly helped the law into being, but would violate its provisions; conceal a fugitive; share his loaf with a runaway; furnish him golden wings to fly with. Nay, I think it would be difficult to find a magistrate in New England, willing to take the public odium of doing the official duty.* I believe it is not possible to find a regular jury, who will

* Subsequent events have shown the folly of this statement. Clergymen, it is said, are wont to err, by overrating the moral principle of men. (T. P., 1851.)

punish a man for harboring a slave, for helping his escape, or fine a marshal or commissioner for being a little slow to catch a slave.*   Men will talk loud in public meetings, but they have some conscience after all, at home.   And though they howl down the higher law in a crowd, yet conscience will make cowards of them all, when they come to lay hands on a Christian man, more innocent than they, and send him into slavery for ever!   One of the commissioners of Boston talked loud and long, last Tuesday, in favor of keeping the law.   When he read his litany against the law of God, and asked if men would keep the "higher law," and got "Never" as the welcome, and "Amen" for response — it seemed as if the law might be kept, at least by that commissioner, and such as gave the responses to his creed.   But slave-hunting Mr. Hughes, who came here for two of our fellow-worshipers,† in his Georgia newspaper, tells a different story. Here it is, from the *Georgia Telegraph*, of last Friday.   "I called at eleven o'clock at night, at his [the commissioner's] residence, and stated to him my business, and asked him for a warrant, saying that if I could get a warrant, I could have the negroes [William and Ellen Craft] arrested.   He said the law did not authorize a warrant to be issued: that it was my duty to go and arrest the negro without a warrant, and bring him before him!"

This is more than I expected.   "Is Saul among the prophets?"   The men who tell us that the law must be kept, God willing, or against His will —

* Recent experiments fortunately confirm this, and, spite of all the unjust efforts to pack a jury, none has yet been found to punish a man for such a "crime."

† Mr. William Craft, and Mrs. Ellen Craft.

there are Puritan fathers behind them also; Bibles
in their houses; a Christ crucified, whom they think
of; and a God even in their world, who slumbers not,
neither is weary, and is as little a respecter of parch-
ments as of persons! They know there is a people,
as well as politicians, a posterity not yet assembled,
and they would not like to have certain words writ on
their tombstone. "Traitor to the rights of mankind,"
is no pleasant epitaph. They, too, remember there is
a day after to-day; aye, a forever; and, "Inasmuch as
ye have not done it unto one of the least of these my
brethren, ye have not done it unto me," is a sentence
they would not like to hear at the day of judgment.*

Much danger is feared from the "political agitation" of this matter. Great principles have never been
discussed without great passions, and will not be, for
some time, I suppose. But men fear to have this despotic idea become a subject of discussion. Last
spring, Mr. Webster said here in Boston, "We shall
not see the legislation of the country proceed in the old
harmonious way, until the discussion in Congress and
out of Congress, upon the subject [of slavery], shall
be in some manner suppressed. Take that truth home
with you!" We have lately been told that political
agitation on the subject must be stopped. So it seems
this law, like that which Daniel would not keep, is
one that may not be changed, and must not be
talked of.

Now there are three modes in which attempts may
be made to stop the agitation.

1. By sending

---

* This also appears to have been a mistake. Still I let the
passage stand.

"——— troops, with guns and banners,
Cut short our speeches and our necks,
And break our heads to mend our manners."

That is the Austrian way, which has not yet been tried here, and will not be.

2. By sending lecturers throughout the land, to stir up the people to be quiet, and agitate them till they are still; to make them sign the pledge of total abstinence from the discussion of this subject. That is not likely to effect the object.

3. For the friends of silence to keep their own counsel — and this seems as little likely to be tried, as the others to succeed.

Strange is it to ask us to forbear to talk on a subject which involves the welfare of twenty million men! As well ask a man in a fever not to be heated, and a consumptive person not to cough, to pine away and turn pale. Miserable counselors are ye all, who give such advice! But we have seen lately the lion of the Democrats, and the lamb of the Whigs, lie down together, joined by this opinion, so gentle and so loving, all at once, that a little child could lead them, and so " fulfil the sure prophetic word." Yes, we have seen the Herod of one party, and the Pilate of the other, made friends for the sake of crucifying the freedom of mankind.

But there is one way in which, I would modestly hint, that we might stop all this talk " in Congress and out of Congress; " that is, to " discuss " the matter till we had got at the truth, and the whole truth; then to " agitate " politically, till we had enacted justice into law, and carried it out all over the North, and all over the South. After that there would be no more discussion about the Fugitive Slave Bill, than about the

Boston Port Bill; no more agitation about American slavery, than there is about the condition of the people of Babylon before the flood. I think there is no other way in which we are likely to get rid of this discussion.

Such is our condition, such its causes, such our dangers. Now, for the lesson, look a moment elsewhere. Look at continental Europe, at Rome, Austria, Prussia, and the German States — at France. How uncertain is every government! France — the stablest of them all! Remember the revolution which two years ago shook those States so terribly, when all the royalty of France was wheeled out of Paris in a street cab. Why are those States so tottering? Whence those revolutions? They tried to make iniquity their law, and would not give over the attempt! Why are the armies of France five hundred thousand strong, though the nation is at peace with all the world? Because they tried to make injustice law! Why do the Austrian and German monarchs fear an earthquake of the people? Because they tread the people down with wicked laws! Whence came the crushing debts of France, Austria, England? From the same cause: from the injustice of men who made mischief by law!

It is not for men long to hinder the march of human freedom. I have no fear for that, ultimately,— none at all, simply for this reason, that I believe in the Infinite God. You may make your statutes; an appeal always lies to the higher law, and decisions adverse to that get set aside in the ages. Your statutes cannot hold Him. You may gather all the dried grass and all the straw in both continents; you may braid it into ropes to bind down the sea; while it is calm, you

may laugh, and say, " Lo, I have chained the ocean!"
and howl down the law of Him who holds the universe
as a rosebud in His hand — its every ocean but a drop
of dew. " How the waters suppress their agitation,"
you may say. But when the winds blow their trum-
pets, the sea rises in its strength, snaps asunder the
bonds that had confined his mighty limbs, and the
world is littered with the idle hay! Stop the human
race in its development and march to freedom? As
well might the boys of Boston, some lustrous night,
mounting the steeples of this town, call on the stars
to stay their course! Gently, but irresistibly, the
Greater and the Lesser Bear move round the pole;
Orion, in his mighty mail, comes up the sky; the Bull,
the Ram, the Heavenly Twins, the Crab, the Lion, the
Maid, the Scales, and all that shining company, pursue their march all night, and the new day discovers
the idle urchins in their lofty places, all tired, and
sleepy, and ashamed.

It is not possible to suppress the idea of freedom,
or for ever hold down its institutions. But it is possible to destroy a State; a political party with geographical bounds may easily be rent asunder. It is
not impossible to shiver this American Union. But
how? What clove asunder the great British party,
one nation once in America and England? Did not
our fathers love their fatherland? Aye. They called
it home, and were loyal with abundant fealty; there
was no lack of piety for home. It was the attempt to
make old English injustice New England law! Who
did it,— the British people? Never. Their hand did
no such sacrilege! It was the merchants of London,
with the Navigation Act; the politicians of Westminster with the Stamp Act; the Tories of America,

who did not die without issue, that for office and its gold would keep a king's unjust commands. It was they, who drove our fathers into disunion against their will. Is here no lesson? We love law, all of us love it; but a true man loves it only as the safeguard of the rights of man. If it destroys these rights, he spurns it with his feet. Is here no lesson? Look further, then.

Do you know how empires find their end? Yes, the great States eat up the little. As with fish, so with nations. Aye, but how do the great States come to an end? By their own injustice, and no other cause. They would make unrighteousness their law, and God wills not that it be so. Thus they fall; thus they die. Look at these ancient States, the queenliest queens of earth. There is Rome, the widow of two civilizations, — the pagan and the Catholic. They both had her, and unto both she bore daughters and fair sons. But, the Niobe of nations, she boasted that her children were holier and more fair than all the pure ideas of justice, truth, and love, the offspring of the eternal God. And now she sits there, transformed into stone, amid the ruins of her children's bones. At midnight I have heard the owl hoot in the Coliseum and the Forum, giving voice to desolation; and at midday I have seen the fox in the palace where Augustus gathered the wealth, the wit, the beauty, and the wisdom of a conquered world; and the fox and the owl interpreted to me the voice of many ages, which came to tell this age, that though hand joined in hand, the wicked shall not prosper.

Come with me, my friends, a moment more, pass over this Golgotha of human history, treading reverent as you go, for our feet are on our mothers' grave, and our shoes defile our fathers' hallowed bones. Let us not talk of them; go further on, look and pass by. Come with me into the Inferno of the nations, with such poor guidance as my lamp can lend. Let us disquiet and bring up the awful shadows of empires buried long ago, and learn a lesson from the tomb.

Come, old Assyria, with the Ninevitish dove upon thy emerald crown! What laid thee low? "I fell by own injustice. Thereby Nineveh and Babylon came, with me, also, to the ground."

Oh, queenly Persia, flame of the nations, wherefore art thou so fallen, who troddest the people under thee, bridgedst the Hellespont with ships, and pouredst thy temple-wasting millions on the western world? "Because I trod the people under me, and bridged the Hellespont with ships, and poured my temple-wasting millions on the western world. I fell by own misdeeds."

Thou muse-like, Grecian queen, fairest of all thy classic sisterhood of States, enchanting yet the world with thy sweet witchery, speaking in art, and most seductive song; why liest thou there with beauteous yet dishonored brow, reposing on thy broken harp? "I scorned the law of God; banished and poisoned wisest, justest men; I loved the loveliness of flesh, embalmed it in the Parian stone; I loved the loveliness of thought, and treasured that in more than Parian speech. But the beauty of justice, the loveliness of love, I trod them down to earth! Lo, therefore, have I become as those Barbarian States — as one of them!"

Oh, manly and majestic Rome, thy sevenfold mural crown, all broken at thy feet, why art thou here? It was not injustice brought thee low; for thy great book of law is prefaced with these words, Justice is the unchanging, everlasting will to give each man his right! "It was not the saint's ideal: it was the hypocrite's pretense! I made iniquity my law. I trod the nations under me. Their wealth gilded my palaces,— where thou mayst see the fox and hear the owl,— it fed my courtiers and my courtesans. Wicked men were my cabinet-counselors, the flatterer breathed his poison in my ear. Millions of bondmen wet the soil with tears and blood. Do you not hear it crying yet to God? Lo, here have I my recompense, tormented with such downfall as you see! Go back and tell the new-born child, who sitteth on the Alleghanies, laying his either hand upon a tributary sea, a crown of thirty stars about his youthful brow — tell him that there are rights which States must keep, or they shall suffer wrongs! Tell him there is a God who keeps the black man and the white, and hurls to earth the loftiest realm that breaks His just, eternal law! Warn the young Empire that he come not down dim and dishonored to my shameful tomb! Tell him that justice is the unchanging, everlasting will to give each man his right. I knew it, broke it, and am lost. Bid him to know it, keep it, and be safe!"

"God save the Commonwealth!" proclaims the governor. God will do His part,— doubt not of that. But you and I must help Him save the State. What can we do? Next Sunday I will ask you for your charity; to-day I ask a greater gift, more than the abundance of the rich, or the poor widow's long-remembered mite. I ask you for your justice. Give that to your native land. Do you not love your country? I know you do. Here are our homes and the graves of our fathers; the bones of our mothers are under the sod. The memory of past deeds is fresh

with us; many a farmer's and mechanic's son inherits
from his sires some cup of manna gathered in the
wilderness, and kept in memory of our exodus; some
stones from the Jordan, which our fathers passed over
sorely bested and hunted after; some Aaron's rod,
green and blossoming with fragrant memories of the
day of small things, when the Lord led us — and all
these attach us to our land, our native land. We love
the great ideas of the North, the institutions which
they founded, the righteous laws, the schools, the
churches, too — do we not love all these? Aye. I
know well you do. Then by all these, and more than
all, by the dear love of God, let us swear that we will
keep the justice of the Eternal Law. Then are we
all safe. We know not what a day may bring forth,
but we know that eternity will bring everlasting peace.
High in the heavens, the pole-star of the world, shines
justice; placed within us, as our guide thereto, is conscience. Let us be faithful to that —

> " Which though it trembles as it lowly lies,
>   Points to the light that changes not in heaven."

IV

THE LIKE AND THE DIFFERENT
1851

A few months ago, the Right Honorable W. E. Gladstone, member of the British Parliament for Oxford, published " Two Letters to the Earl of Aberdeen on the State Prosecutions of the Neapolitan Government." Mr. Gladstone appears to be one of the most conservative Commoners in England; and he writes to one of the most conservative of the Lords. The letters have filled England with amazement. The work was published last July, and it is now the twenty-fourth of October while I write; but ten editions have already been exhausted in England, and the eleventh has had time to travel three thousand miles, and find its way to my desk.

Mr. Gladstone makes some disclosures which have astonished the simplicity of Father England. He accuses the government of Naples, in its treatment of those accused of political offenses, of " an outrage upon religion, upon civilization, upon humanity, and upon decency." What is more, he abundantly substantiates his accusation by details so horrible, that he thinks they will not be credited by his countrymen; for the actual wickedness of the Neapolitan Government surpasses all that Englishmen had thought it possible for malice to invent or tyranny to inflict.

He says: " It is not mere imperfection, not ambition in low quarters, not occasional severity, that I am about to describe; it is an incessant, systematic, deliberate violation of the law by the power appointed to

132

watch over and maintain it. It is such violation of human and written law as this, carried on for the purpose of violating every other law, unwritten and eternal, human or divine." "It is the awful profanation of public religion, by its notorious alliance, in the governing powers, with the violation of every moral law, under the stimulant of fear and vengeance." "The effect of all this is total inversion of all the moral and social ideas. Law, instead of being respected, is odious. Force, and not affection, is the foundation of government. The governing power is clothed with all the vices for its attributes."

Mr. Gladstone thinks there are not less than twenty thousand prisoners for political offenses, locked up in jail; between four and five hundred were to be tried for their lives on the 15th of May. Of one hundred and forty deputies who formed the Legislative Assembly in 1849, seventy-six had been arrested, or had fled into exile. The law of Naples requires that "personal liberty shall be inviolable, except under a warrant from a court of justice, authorized for the purpose." But in defiance of this law, "the government watches and dogs the people; pays domiciliary visits very unceremoniously at night; ransacks houses; seizes papers; imprisons men by the score — by the hundred — by the thousand — without any warrant whatever, sometimes without any written authority at all, or anything beyond the word of a policeman."

After the illegal arrest, the trial is long delayed,— sometimes more than two years. "Every effort is made to concoct a charge, by the perversion and partial production of real evidence; and, this failing, the resort is to perjury and forgery. The miserable creatures, to be found in most communities, who are ready to sell the liberty and life of fellow-subjects for gain, and throw their own souls into the bargain, are deliberately employed by the executive power to depose, according to their instructions, against the men whom it is thought desirable to ruin." If the defendant has counter-evidence, he is not allowed to produce it in court.

Here are matters of fact of a more particular nature. The filth of the prisons is beastly. The doctors never visit the prisoners. Three or four hundred prisoners " all slept in a long, low, vaulted room, having no light except from a single and very moderate-sized grating at one end." From December 7th, 1850, to February 3rd, 1851, Signor Pironte, a gentleman who had been a judge, was shut up in a cell " about eight feet square, below the level of the ground, with no light except a grating at the top of the wall, out of which he could not see." This was in the city of Naples.

Signor Carlo Poerio, formerly a minister of the Court, was illegally arrested, thrown into jail, and kept for seven or eight months in total ignorance of the offense charged against him. At length he was accused of belonging to a party which did not exist. He was tried by a special court. The only evidence against him was that of a hired and worthless informer of the government; even that was inconsistent, contradictory, and of no value. Of course, Signor Poerio was found guilty. He was sentenced to twenty-four years imprisonment in irons. He and sixteen others were confined in the Bagno of Niseda, in a cell about thirteen feet by ten, and ten feet high. When the beds were let down for these seventeen men, there was no space between them. The prisoners were chained in pairs, with irons that weigh about thirty-three pounds to each man. The chains are never taken off. The food is bread, and a soup so nauseous that only famine can force it down the throat.

To justify itself, the government has published a " Philosophical Catechism for the Use of Schools," which teaches the theory which the authorities practise. It declares that the prince is not bound to keep the constitution when it " impugns the right of sovereignty " of himself. " Whenever the people may have proposed a condition which impairs the sovereignty [the arbitrary power of the king], and when the prince may have promised to observe it, that proposal is an absurdity, that promise is null." " It is the business of the sovereign " " to decide when the promise is null." This catechism, which seeks to justify the perjury of a monarch, and announces the theory of crime, is published by authority, and in the name of " the Most Holy and Almighty God, the Trinity in Unity."

The disclosures in Mr. Gladstone's letters filled England with horror. Even Naples fears the public opinion of Europe, and the Neapolitan Government became alarmed. Some attempts have been made by its officials, to deny the facts. The British thought them too bad to be true. Yet the government of Naples is not wholly inaccessible to mercy. For Mr. Morris, the American minister at Naples, becoming interested in a young man, Signor Domenico Nostromarina, confined in the island of Capri for some alleged political offense, asked his pardon of the king, and it was granted.

The American Declaration of Independence announces as self-evident, that all men are created

equal, and with certain inalienable rights, and amongst
them the right to life, liberty, and the pursuit of happiness; and the design of government is to secure those
rights.   The Constitution of Massachusetts provides
that " every person has a right to be secure from all
unreasonable searches and seizures of his person," and
" all warrants therefore are contrary to this right,
if the cause or foundation of them be not previously
supported by oath or affirmation."   But, in September, 1851, more than fifty persons were seized by the
creatures of the city government of Boston, with no
warrant, not for the purpose of a trial, and were
publicly exhibited, by the marshal of the city, to the
mob who came to stare at them.

In April, 1851, an officer in the pay of the city of
Boston, with no warrant, seized Thomas Sims, then
an inhabitant of that city, on a false pretense, by
night, and brought him before a subaltern officer
of the general government of the United States.   He
was confined in a court-house belonging to one of
the counties of Massachusetts, which was, for the
time, converted into a jail for his detention, contrary
to the law of the State.   Officers acting under the
laws of Massachusetts, and subject to its penalties,
aided in kidnapping and detaining this unfortunate
man, though the law of Massachusetts forbids such
conduct on their part.

At the request of Mr. Sims, I visited him in his
place of confinement, where he was guarded by about
a dozen men who were in the same room with him.
One of them had a drawn sword in his hand.

After what was called a trial, before a single man,
and he a creature of the government, who was to be
paid twice as much for deciding against his prisoner

as for him, a trial conducted without " due form of law," Mr. Sims was sentenced to bondage for his natural life. Yet he was accused of no offense, except that of escaping from those who had stolen him from himself, and claimed his labor and his limbs as theirs. When he was to be carried off, and delivered to his tormentors, fifteen hundred citizens of Boston volunteered to conduct the victim of illegal tyranny out of the State, and deliver him up to the men who had taken him at first. A brigade of soldiers, since called " The Sims Brigade," was called out at the expense of the city, and by direction of its magistrates, and kept under arms day and night, to aid in violating the laws of Massachusetts, and profaning the laws of God. Their headquarters were in what was once called the " Cradle of Liberty," in Faneuil Hall.

The court-house was surrounded by chains for several days, and guarded by mercenaries of the city, hired for the purpose, and armed with bludgeons. I counted forty-four of these men on guard at the same time. They molested and turned back men who had business in the court-house, but admitted any " gentleman from the South." The judges of the State courts stooped and crouched down, and crawled under the chain, to go, emblematically, to their places.

A portion of the city police, armed with swords, was drilled one day in a public square, and the movements of the awkward squad were a little ridiculous to such as had never seen British clowns under a drill sergeant. One of the by-standers laughed, and the chief police officer on the station threatened to lock him up in a jail if he laughed again.

The mayor of the city rose, soberly, and with two

or three hundred of the police of the city, armed with bludgeons and swords, in the darkest hour of the night, took their victim, weeping, out of his jail. Some benevolent men furnished him with clothes for his voyage. He was then conducted by this crew of kidnappers through the principal street of the city to a vessel waiting to receive him. As he went aboard, he burst into tears, and exclaimed, " This is Massachusetts liberty! " Several of the inhabitants of the city attended their victim to Savannah, in Georgia, whence he had fled away. There they were honored with a public entertainment given by the citizens of that place.

Their victim was conducted to jail, and severely flogged. He was not allowed to see his mother, or any other relative. It was afterwards related that his master, still keeping him in jail, ordered him to be tortured every day with a certain number of lashes on his bare back, but once offered to remit a part of the torture on condition that he should ask pardon for running away: he refused, and took the blows. But one day, the jail-doctor, finding the man feeble and daily failing, told the master his slave was too unwell to bear that torture. The master said, " Damn him, give him the lashes if he dies! " and the lashes fell.

Mr. Sims was a smart, dashing young fellow, of some one or two and twenty years. He had a wife at Savannah (handsome, and nearly white), not belonging to his master, it is said. After his escape to Boston, he informed her of his hiding-place. She was the concubine of a white man, and told him her husband's secret. He informed the master, and at his direction, with some witnesses hired for the pur-

pose, came to Boston in search of the runaway. By
the illegal measures of the city government of Boston,
the slave-hunter secured his object and returned home.
In Boston, a dealer in goods for the Southern market, a rich man, entertained the slave-hunter and his
crew while there, took them to ride in a coach, and
gave them a costly supper at one of the principal
hotels in the city.

The last legal effort to save the man from the terrible punishment which the Bostonians were desirous of
inflicting upon him, was made by a distinguished
citizen of this State, before the circuit judge. I shall
not now tell all I know about the matter here; but
when the judge decided against his victim, and thus
cut off his last hope, the sentence was received by the
rich and mercantile audience that crowded the court-
house with applause and the clapping of hands.
Leading citizens of Boston rejoiced at the transaction
and its result. Some of them publicly mocked at all
efforts made in behalf of the unfortunate man who
had been kidnapped. The commercial and political
newspapers of the city gave expression to the common joy, that an inhabitant of Boston had, for the
first time for many years, and at the expense of the
city, been doomed to eternal bondage by the authorities of the place. It was thought trade would improve; and it is now stated that Boston has had more
Southern " patronage " since the kidnapping of Sims,
than in any previous six months since the adoption
of the Constitution.

The leading clergy of the town were also deeply delighted at the success of this kidnapping; several of
them, in their pulpit services, expressed their approbation of the deed, and gave God thanks, in their

public prayers, that the Fugitive Slave Law had been executed in Boston. One of them, the most prominent clergyman in the city, declared, in private, that if a fugitive should seek shelter of him, " I would drive him away from my own door." Another had previously declared, in public, that he would send his own mother into slavery to keep the law. At a subsequent period, the President of the United States, in his visit to Boston, congratulated the authorities of the State on this execution of his law.

The laws of Massachusetts are flagrantly violated in Boston; especially the usury laws and the license law. At this moment there are, probably, at least a thousand places in the city where liquor is publicly sold in violation of the law. It is notorious that even the banks daily violate the usury law. These are matters of continual occurrence. But, last spring, a citizen of Boston was assassinated, in broad daylight, in Haymarket Square. The assassin was well known, but he has not been arrested. The city government has, as yet, offered no public reward for his apprehension. It is rumored that the man was murdered by one whom he had complained of for violating the license law.

The Fugitive Slave Law drove into exile about four or five hundred inhabitants of Boston in less than a year. They had committed no crime, except to believe themselves the owners of their own bodies, and act on that belief. Several Unitarian clergymen have been driven from their parishes in consequence of opposing that law. It has been proclaimed by the most eminent politicians of the nation, that there is no law higher than the statutes of Congress. Prominent clergymen assent to the doctrine. Thus the negation

of God is made the first principle of politics. In a
certain town, in Massachusetts, the names of all anti-
slavery men are rejected from the list of jurors. Some
of the leading commercial newspapers of Boston advise men not to employ such as are opposed to the
Fugitive Slave Law.

Many clergymen declare that slavery is a Christian
institution; some of great eminence,— as men estimate clerical eminence,— have undertaken to support
and justify it out of the Bible. Several wealthy citizens of Boston are known to own slaves at this moment; they buy them and sell them. There is one who
has made a large fortune by selling rum on the coast
of Africa, and thence carrying slaves to America. In
Boston it is respectable to buy and sell men,— the
slave-hunter, the kidnapper, is an " honorable man," —
even the defender of kidnapping and slave-hunting is
respected and beloved, while the philanthropist, who
liberates bondmen, is held in abhorrence. The blacks
are driven from the public schools by a law of the
city. There is a church in which colored men are not
allowed to buy a pew. They are not permitted to
enter the schools of theology or of medicine. They
are shut out from our colleges. In some places they
are not allowed to be buried with white men. An
Episcopal church, in New York, holds a cemetery on
this condition, that " they shall not suffer any colored
person to be buried in any part of the same." A
Presbyterian church advertised that in its grave-yard,
" neither negroes nor executed felons " should ever be
buried there. No sect opposes slavery; no prominent
sectarian. The popular religion of New England
teaches that it is Christian to buy slaves, sell slaves,
and make slaves. " Slavery, as it exists, at the pres-

ent day," says an eminent divine, " is agreeable to the order of Divine Providence."

One of the newspapers in Boston, on the 10th of October, 1851, speaking of the abolitionists and liberty party men, says: " Such traitors should every one be *garroted* " — strangled to death. Another, of the same date, says that Mr. Webster's " wonderful labors in behalf of the Constitution " " have vindicated his claim to the highest title yet bestowed upon man." The Church and the State alike teach that though the law of God may be binding on him, it is of no validity before an Act of Congress.

America is a republic; and Millard Fillmore is by accident President of the United States. Naples is a monarchy; and Ferdinand is " by the grace of God " King. Such is the different; reader, behold the like!

V

THE FUGITIVE SLAVE LAW *
1851

The subject of debate was " The Duty of Ministers under the Fugitive Slave Law." This had been brought up, by Rev. Mr. May of Syracuse, at a business meeting of the American Unitarian Association, and was refused a hearing. It was again brought forward at the meeting of the Ministerial Conference on Wednesday. The Conference adjourned to Thursday morning, at nine o'clock.

On Tuesday and Wednesday afternoons, a good deal was done to prevent the matter from being discussed at all; and done, as it seemed to me, in a disingenuous and unfair manner. And on Thursday morning much time was consumed in mere trifles, apparently with the intention of wearing away the few hours which would otherwise be occupied in discussing the matter at issue, before the Conference. At length the question was reached, and the debate began.

Several persons spoke. Mr. Pierpont made a speech, able and characteristic, in which he declared that the Fugitive Slave Bill lacked all the essentials of a law; that it had no claim to obedience; and that it could not be administered with a pure heart or unsullied ermine.

Several others made addresses. Rev. Mr. Osgood of New York defended his ministerial predecessor, Rev. Dr. Dewey — making two points.

1. Dr. Dewey's conduct had been misrepresented; he had never said that he would send his own *mother*

* Speech delivered at a Ministerial Conference in Boston.

into slavery to preserve the Union; it was only his *son*, or *brother*. [Mr. Parker remarked that the principle was the same in all three cases, there was only a diversity of measure.]

2. Dr. Dewey's motives had been misrepresented. He had conversed with Dr. Dewey; and Dr. Dewey felt very bad; was much afflicted — even to weeping, at the misrepresentations made of him. He had not been understood. Dr. Dewey met Dr. Furness in the street, [Dr. Furness had most manfully preached against the Fugitive Slave Act, and thereby drawn upon himself much odium in Philadelphia, and the indignation of some of his clerical brethren elsewhere,] and said, " Brother Furness — you have taken the easy road to duty. It is for me to take the hard and difficult way! I wish it could be otherwise. But I feared the dissolution of the Union! " etc., etc.

Mr. Osgood then proceeded to censure " one of this Conference " [Mr. Parker] for the manner in which he had preached on this matter of the Fugitive Slave Law. " It was very bad; it was unjust! " etc.

Rev. Dr. Gannett spoke at some length.

1. He said the brethren had laughed, and shown an indecorum that was painful; it was unpardonable. [The chairman, Rev. Dr. Farley, of Brooklyn, N. Y., thought otherwise.]

2. He criticized severely the statement of Rev. Mr. Pierpont that the Fugitive Slave Law " could not be administered with a pure heart or unsullied ermine." [Mr. Pierpont affirmed it anew, and briefly defended the statement. Mr. Gannett still appeared dissatisfied.] His parishioner, Mr. George T. Curtis, had the most honorable motives for attempting to execute the law.

3. He (Dr. Gannett) was in a minority, and the majority had no right to think that he was not as honest in his opinion as the rest.

4. Here Dr. Gannett made two points in defense of the Fugitive Slave Bill, of making and obeying it.

(1.) If we did not obey it the disobedience would lead to the violation of *all law*. There were two things — law without liberty; and liberty without law. Law without liberty was only despotism; liberty without law only license. Law without liberty was the better of the two. If we began by disobeying any one law, we should come to violating all laws.

(2) We must obey it to preserve the Union: without the Fugitive Slave Law, the Union would have been dissolved; if it were not obeyed it would also be dissolved, and then he did not know what would become of the cause of human freedom and human rights.

Then Rev. George E. Ellis of Charlestown spoke. He would not have the Conference pass any resolutions; he stood on the first principles of Congregationalism — that the minister was not responsible to his brothers, but to himself and his God. So the brethren have no right to come here and discuss and condemn the opinions or the conduct of a fellow-minister. We cannot bind one another; we have no right to criticize and condemn.

Next he declared his hatred of the Fugitive Slave Bill. If we must either keep it or lose the Union, he said, " Perish the Union." He had always said so, and preached so.

After Mr. Ellis, Mr. Parker spoke as follows:

MR. CHAIRMAN AND GENTLEMEN — I am one of those that laughed with the rest, and incurred the displeasure of Dr. Gannett. It was not from lightness, however; I think no one will accuse me of that. I am earnest enough; so much so as to be grim. Still it is natural even for a grim man to laugh sometimes; and in times like these I am glad we can laugh.

I am glad my friend, Mr. Ellis, said the brethren had no right here to criticize and condemn the opinions of one of their members; but I wish he and they had come to this opinion ten years ago. I should have been a gainer by it; for this is the first time for nine years that I have attended this Conference without hearing something which seemed said with the intention of insulting me. I will not say I should have been in general a happier man if Mr. Ellis's advice had been followed; nay, if he had always followed it himself; but I should have sat with a little more comfort in this body if they had thought I was not responsible to them for my opinions.

I am glad also to hear Dr. Gannett say we have no right to attribute improper motives to any one who differs from us in opinion. It was rather gratuitous, however; no man has done it here to-day. But it is true, no man has a right thus to " judge another." But I will remind Dr. Gannett that, a few years ago, he and I differed in opinion on a certain matter of considerable importance, and after clearly expressing our difference, I said, " Well, there is an honest difference of opinion between us," and he said, " Not an *honest* difference of opinion, Brother Parker," for he called me " brother " then, and not " Mr." as since, and now, when he has publicly said he cannot take my hand *fraternally*. Still there was an honest difference of opinion on his part as well as mine.

Mr. Osgood apologizes for Dr. Dewey; — that is, he defends his motives. I am glad he does not undertake to defend his conduct, only to deny that he [Dr. Dewey] uttered the words alleged. But I am sorry to say that I cannot agree with Mr. Osgood in his defense. I do not believe a word of it to be true: I have evidence enough that he said so.

Mr. Gannett in demanding obedience to the Fugitive Slave Law made two points, namely; if it be not obeyed, first, we shall violate all human laws; and next, there will be a dissolution of the Union.

Let me say a word of each. But first let me say that I attribute no unmanly motive to Mr. Gannett. I thought him honest when he denied that I was; I think him honest now. I know him to be conscientious, laborious, and self-denying. I think he would sacrifice himself for another's good. I wish he could now sink through the floor for two or three minutes, that I might say of him absent yet more of honorable praise, which I will not insult him with or address to him while before my face. Let me only say this, that if there be any men in this Conference who honor and esteem Dr. Gannett, I trust I am second to none of them. But I do not share his opinions nor partake of his fears. His arguments for obeying the Fugitive Slave Law (*ab inconvenienti*) I think are of no value.

If we do not obey this law, he says, we shall disobey all laws. It is not so. There is not a country in the world where there is more respect for human laws than in New England; nowhere more than in Massachusetts. Even if a law is unpopular, it is not popular to disobey it. Our courts of justice are popular bodies, nowhere are judges more respected than in New England. No officer, constable or sheriff, hangman or jail-keeper, is unpopular on account of his office. Nay, it is popular to inform against your neighbor when he violates the law of the land. This is not so in any other country of the Christian world; but the informer is infamous everywhere else.

Why are we thus loyal to law? First, because we make the laws ourselves, and for ourselves; and next, because the laws actually represent the conscience of the people, and help them keep the laws of God. The value of human laws is only this — to conserve the great eternal law of God; to enable us to keep that; to hinder us from disobeying that. So long as laws do this we should obey them: New England will be loyal to such laws.

But the Fugitive Slave Law is one which contradicts the acknowledged precepts of the Christian religion, universally acknowledged. It violates the noblest instincts of humanity; it asks us to trample on the law of God. It commands what nature, religion, and God alike forbid; it forbids what nature, religion, and God alike command. It tends to defeat the object of all just human law; it tends to annihilate the observance of the law of God. So faithful to God, to religion, to human nature, and in the name of law itself, we protest against this particular statute, and trample it under our feet.

Who is it that oppose the Fugitive Slave Law? Men that have always been on the side of " law and order," and do not violate the statutes of men for their own advantage. This disobedience to the Fugitive Slave Law is one of the strongest guarantees for the observance of any *just* law. You cannot trust a people who will keep law; *because it is law;* nor need we distrust a people that will only keep a law when it is just. The Fugitive Slave Law itself, if obeyed, will

do more to overturn the power of human law, than all
disobedience to it — the most complete.

Then as to dissolution of the Union. I [have]
thought if any State wished to go, she had a natural
right to do so. But what States wished to go? Certainly not New England: by no means. Massachusetts has always been attached to the Union, — has
made sacrifices for it. In 1775, if she had said,
" There shall be no Revolution," there would have been
none. But she furnished nearly half the soldiers for
the war, and more than half of the money. In '87,
if Massachusetts had said, " Let there be no Union ! "
there would have been none. It was with difficulty
that Massachusetts assented to the Constitution. But
that once formed, she has adhered to it; faithfully adhered to the Union. When has Massachusetts
failed in allegiance to it? No man can say. There
is no danger of a dissolution of the Union; the men
who make the cry know that it is vain and deceit-
ful. You cannot drive us asunder — just yet.

But suppose that was the alternative: that we must
have the Fugitive Slave Law, or dissolution. Which
were the worst; which comes nearest to the law of
God which we all are to keep? It is very plain. Now
for the first time since '87, many men of Massachusetts
calculate the value of the Union. What is it worth?
Is it worth so much to us as conscience; so much as
freedom; so much as allegiance to the law of God?
let any man lay his hand on his heart and say, " I
will sacrifice all these for the union of the thirty
States! For my own part, I would rather see my
own house burnt to the ground, and my family thrown,
one by one, amid the blazing rafters of my own roof,
and I myself be thrown in last of all, rather than

have a single fugitive slave sent back as Thomas Sims was sent back. Nay, I should rather see this Union " dissolved " till there was not a territory so large as the county of Suffolk! Let us lose everything but fidelity to God.

Mr. Osgood reflects on me for my sermons; they are poor enough. You know it if you try to read such as are in print. I know it better than you. But I am not going to speak honeyed words and prophesy smooth things in times like these, and say, " Peace! peace! when there is no peace! "

A little while ago we were told we must not preach on this matter of slavery, because it was " an abstraction; " then because the North was " all right on that subject; " and then because we had " nothing to do with it," we " must go to Charleston or New Orleans to see it." But now it is a most concrete thing. We see what public opinion is on the matter of slavery; what it is in Boston; nay, what it is with members of this Conference. It favors slavery and this wicked law! We need not go to Charleston and New Orleans to see slavery; our own court-house was a barracoon; our officers of this city were slave-hunters, and members of Unitarian churches in Boston are kidnappers.

I have in my church black men, fugitive slaves. They are the crown of my apostleship, the seal of my ministry. It becomes me to look after their bodies in order to " save their souls." This law has brought us into the most intimate connection with the sin of slavery. I have been obliged to take my own parishioners into my house to keep them out of the clutches of the kidnapper. Yes, gentlemen, I have been obliged to do that; and then to keep my doors guarded by day as well as by night. Yes, I have had to arm myself. I have written my sermons with a pistol in my desk,— loaded, a cap on the nipple, and ready for action. Yea, with a drawn sword within reach of my right hand. This I have done in Boston; in the middle of the nineteenth century; been obliged to do it to defend the [innocent] members of my own church, women as well as men!

You know that I do not like fighting. I am no non-resistant, " that nonsense* never went down with me." But it is no small matter which will compel me to shed human blood. But what could I do? I was born in the little town where the fight and bloodshed of the Revolution began. The bones of the men who first fell in that war are covered by the monument at Lexington, it is " sacred to liberty and the rights of mankind; " those men fell " in the sacred cause of God and their country." This is the first inscription that I ever read. These men were my kindred. My grandfather drew the first sword in the Revolution; my fathers fired the first shot; the blood which flowed there was kindred to this which courses in my veins to-day. Besides that, when I write in my library at home, on the one side of me is the Bible which my fathers prayed over, their morning and evening prayer, for nearly a hundred years. On the other side there hangs the firelock my grandfather fought with in the old French war, which he carried at the taking of Quebec, which he zealously used at the battle of Lexington, and beside it is another, a trophy of that war, the first gun taken in the Revolution, taken also by my grandfather.

* Mr. May of Syracuse afterwards objected to the word *nonsense* as applied to non-resistance. The phrase was quoted from another member of the Conference, whose eye caught mine while speaking, and suggested his own language.

With these things before me, these symbols; with these memories in me, when a parishioner, a fugitive from slavery, a woman, pursued by the kidnappers, came to my house, what could I do less than take her in and defend her to the last? But who sought her life — or liberty? A parishioner of my brother Gannett came to kidnap a member of my church; Mr. Gannett preaches a sermon to justify the Fugitive Slave Law, demanding that it should be obeyed; yes, calling on his church members to kidnap mine, and sell them into bondage forever.

Yet all this while Mr. Gannett calls himself a " Christian," and me an " infidel;" his doctrine is " Christianity," mine only " infidelity," " deism, at the best!"

O my brothers, I am not afraid of men, I can offend them. I care nothing for their hate, or their esteem. I am not very careful of my reputation. But I should not dare to violate the eternal law of God. You have called me " infidel." Surely I differ widely enough from you in my theology. But there is one thing I cannot fail to trust; that is the Infinite God, Father of the white man, Father also of the white man's slave. I should not dare violate His laws, come what may come; — should you? Nay, I can love nothing so well as I love my God.

VI

AN ANTI-SLAVERY ADDRESS *
1854

LADIES AND GENTLEMEN,— I shall ask your attention this evening to some few thoughts on the present condition of the United States in respect to slavery. After all that has been said by wise, powerful, and eloquent men, in this city, this week, perhaps I shall have scarce anything to present that is new.

As you look on the general aspect of America to-day, its main features are not less than sublime, while they are likewise beautiful exceedingly. The full breadth of the continent is ours, from sea to sea, from the Great Lakes to the great Gulf. There are three million square miles, with every variety of climate, and soil, and mineral; great rivers, a static force, inclined planes for travel reaching from New Orleans to the Falls of St. Anthony, from the mouth of the St. Lawrence to Chicago; smaller rivers, a dynamic force, turning the many thousand mills of the industrious North. There is a coast most richly indented, to aid the spread of civilization. The United States has more than twelve thousand miles of shore line on the continent; more than nine thousand on its islands; more than twenty-four thousand miles of river navigation. Here is the material groundwork for a great State — not an empire, but a commonwealth. The world has not such another.

There are twenty-four millions of men; fifteen and a half millions with Anglo-Saxon blood in their veins — strong, real Anglo-Saxon blood; eight millions and

* Address delivered before the New York Anti-Slavery Society.

a half more of other families and races, just enough to temper the Anglo-Saxon blood, to furnish a new composite tribe, far better, I trust, than the old. What a human basis for a State to be erected on this material groundwork!

On the eastern slopes of the continent, where the high lands which reach from the Katahdin mountain in Maine to the end of the Appalachians in Georgia— on the Atlantic slopes, where the land pitches down to the sea from the 48th to the 28th parallel, there are fifteen States, a million square miles communicating with the ocean. In the South, rivers bear to the sea rice, cotton, tobacco, and the products of half-tropic agriculture; in the North, smaller streams toil all day, and sometimes all night, working wood, iron, cotton, and wool into forms of use and beauty, while iron roads carry to the sea the productions of temperate agriculture, mining and manufactures.

On the western slope, where the rivers flow down to the Pacific Ocean from the 49th to the 32nd parallel, is a great country, almost eight hundred thousand square miles in extent. There, too, the Anglo-Saxon has gone; in the South, the gold-hunter gathers the precious metals, while the farmer, the miner, and the woodman gather far more precious products in the North.

In the great basin between the Cordilleras of the West and the Alleghanies, where the Mississippi drains half the continent to the Mediterranean of the New World, there also the Anglo-Saxon has occupied the ground — twelve hundred thousand square miles; in the south to rear cotton, rice, and sugar; in the north to raise cattle and cereal grasses, for beast and for man.

What a spectacle it is! A nation not eighty years old and still in its cradle, and yet grown so great. Two hundred and fifty years ago, there was not an Anglo-Saxon on all this continent. Now there is an Anglo-Saxon commonwealth twenty-four millions strong. Rich as it is in numbers, there are not yet eight men to the square mile.

All this is a republic; it is a democracy. There is no born priest to stand betwixt the nation and its God; no pope to entail his nephews on the Church; no bishop claiming divine right to rule over the people and stand betwixt them and the Infinite. There is no king, no born king, to ride on the nation's neck. There are noble-men, but none noble-born to usurp the land, to monopolize the government and keep the community from the bosom of the earth. The people is priest, and makes its own religion out of God's revelation in man's nature and history. The people is its own king to rule itself; its own noble to occupy the earth. The people make the laws and choose their own magistrates. Industry is free; travel is free; religion is free; speech is free; there are no shackles on the press. The nation rests on industry, not on war. It is formed of agriculturists, traders, sailors, miners — not a nation of soldiers. The army numbers ten thousand — one soldier for every twenty-four thousand men. The people are at peace; no nation invades us. The government is firmly fixed and popular. A nation loving liberty, loves likewise law; and when it gets a point of liberty, it fences it all round with law as high up as the hands reach. We annually welcome four hundred thousand immigrants who flee from the despotism of the Old World.

The country is rich — after England, the richest

on earth in cultivated lands, roads, houses, mills. Four million tons of shipping sail under the American flag. This year we shall build half a million tons more, which, at forty dollars a ton, is worth twenty millions of dollars. That is the ship crop. Then, the corn crop is seven hundred millions of bushels — Indian corn. What a harvest of coal, copper, iron, lead, of wheat, cotton, sugar, rice, is produced!

Over all and above all these there rises the great American political idea, a " self-evident truth "— which cannot be proved — it needs no proof; it is anterior to demonstration; namely, that every man is endowed by his Creator with certain inalienable rights, and in these rights all men are equal; and on these the government is to rest, deriving its sole sanction from the governed's consent.

Higher yet above this material groundwork, this human foundation, this accumulation of numbers, of riches, of industry — as the cross on the top of a tall, wide dome, whose lantern is the great American political idea — as the cross that surmounts it rises the American religious idea — one God; Christianity the true religion; and the worship of God by love; inwardly it is piety, love to God; outwardly love to man — morality, benevolence, philanthropy.

What a spectacle to the eyes of the Scandinavian, the German, the Dutchman, the Irishman, as they view America from afar! What a contrast it seems to Europe. There liberty is ideal, it is a dream; here it is organic, an institution; one of the establishments of the land.

That, ladies and gentlemen, is the aspect which America presents to the oppressed victims of European despotism in Church and in State. Far off on the

other side of the Atlantic, among the Apennines, on
the plains of Germany, and in the Slavonian lands, I
have met men to whom America seemed as this fair-
proportioned edifice that I have thus sketched out before your eyes. But when they come nearer, behold half
the land is black with slavery. In 1850, out of more
than two hundred and forty hundred thousand Americans (24,000,000), thirty-two hundred thousand
(3,200,000) were slaves — more than an eighth of the
population counted as cattle; not as citizens at all.
They are only human material, not yet wrought into
citizens — nay, not counted *human*. They are cattle,
property; not counted men, but animals and no more.
Manhood must not be extended to them. Listen while
I read to you from a Southern print. It was recommended by the governor of Alabama that the legislature should pass a law prohibiting the separation of
families; whereupon the *Richmond Inquirer* discourses
thus: —

" This recommendation strikes us as being most unwise and
impolitic. If slaves are property, *then should they be at the
absolute disposal of the master,* or be subject only to such
legal provisions as are designed for the protection of life and
limb. If the relation of master and slave be infringed for one
purpose, it would be difficult to fix any limit to the encroach-
ment."

They are property, no more, and must be treated as
such, and not as men.

Slavery is on the Atlantic slopes of the continent.
There are one million six hundred thousand (1,600,-
000) slaves between the Alleghany range and the Atlantic coast. Slavery is in the central basin. There
are a million and a half of slaves on the land drained
by the Mississippi. Spite of law and constitution,
slavery has gone to the Pacific slopes, travelling with

the goldhunter into California. The State whose capital county " in three years committed over twelve hundred murders " has very appropriately legalized slavery for a limited time. I suppose it is only preliminary to legalizing it for a time limited only by the Eternal God. In the very capital of the Christian democracy there are four thousand purchased men. In the Senate-house, a few years ago, a Mississippi senator belched out his imprecations against that one New Hampshire senator who has never yet been found false to humanity. Mr. Foote was a freeman, a citizen, and a " Democrat ; " and while, in the halls of Congress, he was threatening to hang John P. Hale on the tallest pine tree in Mississippi, there toiled in a stable, whose loft he slept in by night, one of that senator's own brothers. The son of Mr. Foote's father was a slave in the capital of the United States, while his half-brother — by the father's side — threatened to hang on the tallest pine in Mississippi the only senator that New Hampshire sent to Washington who dared be true to truth and free for freedom.

But a few years ago, Mr. Hope H. Slatter had his negro market in the capital of the United States ; one of the greatest slave-dealers in America. He was a member also, it is said, of a " Christian church." The slave-pen is a singular institution for a democratic metropolis, and the slave-trader a peculiar ornament for the Christian church in the capital of a democracy. He grew rich, went to Baltimore, had a fine house, and once entertained a " President of the United States " in his mansion. The slave-trader and the Democratic President met together — Slatter and Polk ! fit guest and fitting host !

In all the three million square miles of American

land there is no inch of free soil, from the St. John's
to the Rio Gila, from Madawasca to San Diego. The
star-spangled banner floats from Vancouver Island
by Nootka Sound to Key West, on the south of Florida, and all the way the flag of our Union is the standard of slavery. In all the soil that our fathers fought
to make free from English tyranny, there is not an
inch where the black man is free, save the five thousand
miles that Daniel Webster surrendered to Lord Ash-
burton by the treaty of 1842. The symbol of the
Union is a fetter. The President should be sworn on
the auction block of a slave-trader. The New Hampshire President, in his inaugural, declared, publicly,
his allegiance to the slave power — not to the power
of Northern mechanics, free farmers, free manufac-
turers, free men; but allegiance to the slave power; he
swears special protection to no property but " property " in slaves; specific allegiance to no law but the
Fugitive Slave Bill; devotion to no right but the slaveholder's " right " to his property in man.

The Supreme Court of the United States is a slave
court; a majority of the Senate and of the House of
Representatives the same. It has been so this forty
years. The majority of the House of Representatives are obedient to the lords of the lash; a majority
of Northern politicians, especially of that denomination which is called " dough-faces," are only overseers
for the owner of the slave. Mr. Douglas is a great
overseer; Mr. Everett is a little overseer, very little.

The nation offers a homestead out of its public
land; it is only to the *white* man. What would you
say if the emperor of Russia offered land only to
nobles; the pope only to priests; Queen Victoria only
to lords? Each male settler in Utah, it seems, is to

have four hundred and eighty acres of land if he is not married, and a hundred and sixty more, I believe, according to one proposition, for every wife that he has got. But if he has the complexion of the only children that Madison left behind him, he can have no land at all.

Even a Boston school-house is shut against the black man's children. The arm of the city government slams the door in every colored boy's face. His father helps pay for the public school; the son and daughter must not come in.

In the slave States, it is a crime to teach the slave to read and write. Out of four millions of children of America at school in 1850, there were twenty-six thousand that were colored. There were more than four hundred thousand free colored persons, and there were more than two hundred and fourteen thousand thereof under the age of twenty; of these, there were at school only twenty-six thousand — *one child in nine!* Out of three and a quarter millions of slaves, there *was not one at school.* It is *a crime by the statute in every slave State to teach a slave to spell " God."* He may be a Christian; he must not write " Christ." He must worship the Bible; he must not read it! It is a crime even in a Sunday School to teach a child the great letters which spell out " Holy Bible." I knew a minister, he was a Connecticut man, too, who went off from New Orleans because he did not dare to stay; and he did not dare to stay because he tried to teach the slave to read in his Sunday School. He went back to Connecticut, whence he will, perhaps, go as missionary to China or Turkey, and find none to hinder his Christian work.

At the North, the black man is shut out of the

meeting-house. In heaven, according to the theology of America, he may sit down with the just made perfect, his sins washed white " in the blood of the Lamb; " but when he comes to a certain Baptist church in Boston, he cannot own a pew. And there are few churches where he can sit in a pew. The rich and the poor are there; the one Lord is the Maker of them all; but the Church thinks He did not make the black as well as the white. Nay; he is turned out of the omnibus, out of the burial ground. There is a burial ground in this State, and in the deed that confers the land it is stipulated that no colored person or convict can ever be buried there. He is turned out of the graveyard, where the great mother of our bodies gathers our dust when the sods of the valley are sweet to the soul. Nowhere but in the jail and on the gallows has the black man equal rights with the white in our American legislation!

The American press — it is generally the foe of the slave, the advocate of bondage.

In Virginia, it is felony to deny the master's right to own his slave. There is an old law, re-enacted in the revision of the Virginia statute, which inflicts a punishment of not more than one year's confinement on any one guilty of that offense. It was proposed in the Virginia legislature, last winter, that if a man had conscientious objections to holding slaves, he should not be allowed to sit on any jury where the matter of a man's freedom was in question. Nor is that all. There is a law in Virginia, it is said, that when a man has three-quarters white blood in his veins, he may recover his freedom in virtue of that fact. It is well known that at least half the slaves in Virginia are half white and one-quarter of them three-quarters white.

XIII—11

Accordingly, it was proposed in one of their newspapers that that old law should be repealed, and another substituted, providing that no man should recover his freedom in consequence of his complexion, unless he had more than nine-tenths white blood in his veins.

The slave has no rights; the ideas of the Declaration of Independence are repudiated; he is not "endowed by his Creator" with "certain inalienable rights" to "life, liberty, and the pursuit of happiness." Accomplished Mr. Agassiz comes all the way from Switzerland to teach us the science which God has stored up in the ground under our feet — the perennial Old Testament — or in the frames of our bodies, this living New Testament of Almighty God in man; and he tells us this: "*The Mandingo and the Guinea negro*" together "*do not differ more from the orang outang than the Malay or white man differs from the negro.*" So, according to Mr. Agassiz, the negro is a sort of arithmetic mean proportional between a man and a monkey. The upright form, the power of speech, the religious faculty, permanence of affection, self-denial, power to master the earth, and smelt iron ore, as the African has done, and is doing still, every year, do not distinguish the black man from the *orang outang*.

> "O star-eyed science! hast *thou* wandered there,
> To waft us home the message of despair?"

Mr. Agassiz is an able man, of large genius, industry that never surrenders, and was a bold champion of freedom on his own Swiss hills. He comes to America; he is subdued to the temper of our atmosphere; and, from a great man of science, he becomes the

Swiss of slavery. Southern journals rejoice at the confirmation of their opinion. Listen to what a Southern editor says. I am quoting now from one of the most powerful Southern journals, printed at the capital of Virginia, the *Richmond Examiner;* and the words which I read were written by the American *chargé d'affaires* at Turin. He says: " The foundation and right of negro slavery is in its utility and the fitness of things; *it is the same right by which we hold property in domestic animals.*" The negro is " *the connecting link between the human and brute creation.*" " The negro is not the white man. Not with more safety do we assert *that a horse is not a hog.* Hay is good for horses — but not for hogs; liberty is good for *white men,* but not for *negroes.*" " *A law rendering perpetual the relation between a negro and his master is no wrong, but a right.*"

Then, in reply to some writer in the *Tribune,* who had asked, " Have they no souls? " he says, " They may have souls for aught I know to the contrary; so *may horses and hogs.*" Then, when somebody quotes the Bible in behalf of the rights of men, he answers: " The Bible has been vouchsafed to mankind for the purpose of keeping us out of hell-fire and getting us into heaven *by the mysteries of faith and the inner life;* not to teach us a government political economy," etc.

The American Church repudiates the Christian religion when it comes to speak about the African. It does not apply the Golden Rule to the slave. The " *servants* " of the New Testament, in the slave language, were " slaves," and the American Church commands them to be obedient to their masters. There must be no *marriage* — the affectional and passional

union of one man and one woman for life — only
transient concubinage. Marriage is inconsistent with
slavery, and the slave wedlock in the American Church
is not a sacrament. " Manifest destiny " is the cry of
politicians, and that demands slavery: " the will of
God " is the cry of the priests, and it demands the
same thing. I am not speaking of *ministers of Christianity;* they are very different sort of men, and preach
a very different creed from that — only of the ministers in the churches of commerce. According
to the popular theology of all Christendom, Jesus
Christ came on earth to seek and to save that which
is lost. The good physician does not go among
the whole, but among the sick. If he were to
come here to seek to relieve the slave, the leading
men in American denominations would tell him he came
before he was called; he ran before he was sent — that
it was no mission from God to break a single American
fetter, nor to let the oppressed go free. Is not the
" Constitution " above " conscience," and the Fugitive
Slave Bill more holy than the Bible? the commissioner
of more authority than Christ?

> " O Faith of Christians, hast thou wandered there
>   To waft us home the message of despair?
>   Then bind the palm *thy sage's brow to suit,*
>   *Of blasted leaf and death-distilling fruit."*

Such is the aspect of America when the immigrant
comes near and looks the nation in the face. What a
spectacle that is to put alongside of the other! Europe repudiates bondage — Scandinavia, Holland,
France, England. Since Britain emancipated her
slaves, the present Emperor of Russia has set free over
seven million of slaves that belonged to his own private domain, and established more than *four thousand*

schools, free for those seven millions of emancipated slaves; and did he not fear an outbreak in a country where " revolution is endemic," he would set free the other five-and-thirty millions that occupy his soil to-day. And when he extends his territory, he never extends the area of bondage, only the area of what in Russia is freedom.

What a spectacle! A country reaching from sea to sea, from the gulf of tropic heat to Lake Superior's arctic cold, and not an inch of free soil all the way! Three millions of square miles, and not a foot where a fugitive from slavery can be safe! A democracy, and every eighth man bought and sold!

It is the richest nation in the world, after England; yet, we are so poor that every eighth man is unable to say that he owns the smallest finger on his feeblest hand. So poor are we amid our riches, that every eighth woman is to such an extent a pauper that she does not own the baby she has borne into the world, nor even the baby that she bears under her bosom! Maternity is put up at public vendue, and the auctioneer says, " So much for the mother and so much for the hopes and expectations of another life that is to be born ! "

America calls herself " the best educated nation in the world," and yet, in fifteen democratic States, it is a felony by statute to teach a child to know the three letters that spell " God." What a spectacle is that!

Nor is that all; but able men, well-educated and well-endowed, come forward to teach us that slavery is not only no evil, but is right as a principle, and is divine — is a part of the divine revelation which the great God miraculously made to man. What a spectacle!

Four hundred thousand immigrants come here openly every year, and a thousand fugitives flee off by night, escaping from American despotism. They go by the underground railroad, shut up in boxes smaller than a coffin, or, as lately happened, riding through the storms of ocean in the fore-chains of a packet ship, wet by every dash of the sea, and frozen by the winter's wind. Far off in the South the spirit of freedom came in the Northern blast to the poor man, and said to him, " It is better to enter into freedom halt and maimed rather than, having two hands and two feet, to continue in bondage for ever; " and he puts himself in the fore-chains of a packet ship, and, half frozen, with the loss of two of his limbs, he gets to the North, and thanks God that he has got one hand and one foot to enter into freedom with. Alas! he is carried back, halt and maimed, to die; then he goes from bondage to that other Commonwealth where even the American slave is free from his master, and Democrats " cease from troubling."

America translates the Bible — I am glad of it, and would give my mite thereto — into a hundred and forty-seven different tongues, and sends missionaries all over the world; and here at home are three and a quarter millions of American men who have no Bible, whose only missionary is the overseer.

In the Hall of Independence, Judge Kane and Judge Grier hold their court. Two great official kidnappers of the Middle States hold their slave-court in the very building where the Declaration of Independence was decreed, was signed, and thence published to the world. What a spectacle it is! We thought, a little while ago, that Judge Jeffreys was an historical fiction; that Scroggs was impossible. We did not think such a thing could exist. Jeffreys is repeated in Philadelphia; Scroggs is brought back to life in various Northern towns. What a spectacle is that for the Swiss, the German, and the Scandinavian who come here!

Do these immigrants love American slavery? The German, the Swiss, the Scandinavian hate it. I am sorry to say there is one class of men that come here who love it; it is the class most of all sinned against at home. When the Irishman comes to America, he takes ground against the African. I know there are exceptions, and I would go far to honor them; but the Irish, as a body, oppose the emancipation of the blacks as a body. Every sect that comes from abroad numbers friends of freedom — except the Catholic. Those who call themselves infidels from Germany do not range on the slaveholder's side. I have known some men who take the ghastly and dreadful name of atheists; but they said, " there is a law higher than the slaveholder's statute." But do you know a Catholic priest that is opposed to slavery? I wish I did. There are good things in the Catholic faith — the Protestants have not wholly outgrown it — not yet. I wish I could hear of a single Catholic priest of any eminence who ever cared anything for the freedom of the most oppressed men that are here in America. I have heard of none.

Look a little closer. The great interests prized most in America are commerce and politics. The great cities are the headquarters of these, too. Agriculture and the mechanic arts, they are spread abroad all over the country. Commerce and politics predominate in the cities. New York is the great metropolis of commerce; Washington of politics. What have been the views of American commerce in respect to freedom? It has been against it, I am sorry to say so.

In Europe commerce is the ally of freedom, and has been, so far back that the memory of man runs not to the contrary. In America, the great commercial centers, ever since the Revolution, have been hostile to freedom. In Massachusetts we have a few rich men friendly to freedom — they are very few; the greater part of even Massachusetts capital goes towards bondage — not towards freedom. In general, the great men of commerce are hostile to it. They want first money, next money, and money last of all; fairly if we can get it — if not, unfairly. Hence the commercial cities are the headquarters of slavery; all the mercantile capitals execute the Fugitive Slave Bill — Philadelphia, New York, Boston, Buffalo, Cincinnati — only small towns repudiate man-stealing. The Northern capitalists lend money and take slaves as collateral; they are good security: you can realize on it any day. The Northern merchant takes slaves into his ships as merchandise. It pays very well. If you take them on a foreign voyage, it is "piracy;" but taken coastwise, the domestic slave trade is a legal traffic. In 1852, a ship called the "Edward Everett" made two voyages from Baltimore to New Orleans, and each time it carried slaves, once twenty, once twelve.

A sea captain in Massachusetts told a story to a commissioner sent to look after the Indians, which I will tell you. He commanded a small brig, which plied between Carolina and the Gulf States. "One day, at Charleston," said he, "a man came and brought to me an old negro slave. He was very old, and had fought in the Revolution, and been very distinguished for bravery and other soldierly qualities. If he had not been a negro, he would have become a captain at least, perhaps a colonel. But, in his old age, his master found no use for him, and said he could not afford to keep him. He asked me to take the revolutionary soldier and carry him South and sell him. I carried him," said the man, " to Mobile, and I tried to get as good and kind a master for him as I could, for I didn't like to sell a man that had fought for his country. *I sold the old revolutionary soldier for a hundred dollars* to a citizen of Mobile, who raised poultry, and he set him to attend a hen-coop." I suppose the South Carolina master drew the pension till the soldier died. " Why did you do such a thing? " said my friend, who was an anti-slavery man. " If I didn't do it," he replied, " I never could get a bale of cotton, nor a box of sugar, nor anything to carry from or to any Southern port."

In politics, almost all leading men have been servants of slavery. Three " major prophets " of the American Republic have gone home to render their account, where the servant is free from his master and " the wicked cease from troubling," and the " weary are at rest." Clay, Calhoun, Webster; they were all prophets of slavery against freedom. No men of high political standing and influence have ever lived in this century who were sunk so deep in the mire of slavery as they during the last twenty years. No political footprints have sunk so deep into the soil — their tracks run towards bondage. Where they marched slavery followed.

Our Presidents must all be pro-slavery men. John Quincy Adams even, the only American thus far who inherited a great name and left it greater, as President, did nothing against slavery that has yet come to

light; said nothing against it that has yet come to
light. The brave old man, in his latter days, stirred
up the nobler nature that was in him, and amply re-
paid for the sins of omission. But the other Presidents, a long line of them — Jackson, Van Buren,
Harrison (they are growing smaller and smaller), Tyler, Polk, Taylor (who was a brave, earnest man, and
had a great deal of good in him — and now they begin
to grow very rapidly small), Fillmore, Pierce — can
you find a single breath of freedom in these men? Not
one. The last slave President, though his cradle was
rocked in New Hampshire, is Texan in his latitude.
He swears allegiance to slavery in his inaugural address.

Is there a breath of freedom in the great Federal
officers — secretaries, judges? Ask the Cabinet; ask
the Supreme Court; the Federal officers; they are, almost without exception, servants of slavery. Out of
forty thousand government officers to-day, I think
thirty-seven thousand are strongly pro-slavery; and
of the three thousand who I think are at heart anti-
slavery, we have yet to listen long before we shall hear
the first anti-slavery lisp. I have been listening ever
since the 4th of March, 1853, and have not heard a
word yet. In the English Cabinet there are various
opinions on important matters; in America, they " are
a unit," a unit of bondage. In Russia, a revolutionary man sometimes holds a high post and does great
service; in America, none but the servant of slavery
is fit for the political functions of democracy. I believe, in the United States, there is not a single editor
holding a government office who says anything against
the Nebraska Bill. They do not dare. Did a Whig
office-holder oppose the Fugitive Slave Bill or its en-

forcement? I never heard of one. The day of office, like the day of bondage, "takes off half a man's manhood," and the other half it hides! A little while ago, an anti-slavery man in Massachusetts carried a remonstrance against the Nebraska Bill, signed by almost every voter in his town, to the postmaster, and asked him, "Will you sign it?" "No, I shan't," said he. "Why not?" Before he answered, one of his neighbors said, "Well, I would not sign it if I was he." "Why not?" said the man. "Because if he did, he would be turned out of office in twenty-four hours; the next telegraph would do the business for him." "Well," said my friend, "if I held an office on that condition, I would get the biggest brass dog-collar I could find and put it around my neck, and have my owner's name on it, in great, large letters, so that everybody might see whose dog I was."

In the individual States, I think there is not a single anti-slavery government. I believe Vermont is the only State that has an anti-slavery Supreme Court; and that is the only State which has not much concern in commerce or manufactures. It is a State of farmers.

For a long time the American Government has been controlled by slavery. There is an old story told by the Hebrew rabbis, that before the flood there was an enormous giant, called Gog. After the flood had got into full tide of successful experiment, and everybody was drowned except those taken into the ark, Gog came striding along after Noah, feeling his way with a cane as long as a mast of the "Great Republic." The waters had only just come up to his girdle. It was then over the hill tops, and was still rising — raining night and day. The giant hailed the Patriarch.

Noah put his head out of the window and said, "Who is there?" "It is I," said Gog. "Take us in; it is wet outside!" "No," said Noah, "you're too big; no room. Besides, you're a bad character. You would be a very dangerous passenger, and would make trouble in the ark; I shall not take you;" and he clapped to the window. "Go to thunder," said Gog: "I will ride after all;" and he strode after him, wading through the waters and keeping out of the deep holes, and *mounting on the top of the ark*, with one leg over the larboard and the other over the starboard side, steered it just as he pleased, and made it rough weather inside. Now, in making the Constitution, we did not care to take in slavery in express terms. It looked ugly. So it got on the top astride, and it steers us just where it pleases.

The slave power controls the President, and fills all the offices. Out of the twelve elected Presidents, four have been from the North, and the last of them might just as well have been taken by lot at the South anywhere. Mr. Pierce, I just now said, was Texan in his latitude. His conscience is Texan; only his cradle was New Hampshire. Of the nine judges of the Supreme Court, five are from the slave States — the chief justice from the slave States. A part of the Cabinet are from the North — I forget how many; it makes no difference; they are all of the same Southern complexion; and the man that was taken from the farthest north, Caleb Cushing, I think is most Southern in his slavery proclivities.

The nation fluctuates in its policy. Now it is for internal improvements: then it is against them. Now it is for a bank; then a bank is unconstitutional. Now it is for free-trade; then for protection; then for

free-trade again — protection is altogether unconstitutional. Mr. Calhoun turns clear round. When the
North went for free-trade and grew rich by that, Calhoun did not like it, and wanted protection. He
thought the South would grow rich by it. And when
the North grew rich under protection, he turned round
to free-trade again. Now the nation is for giving
away the public lands. Sixteen millions of acres of
" swamp lands " are given, within seven years, to
States. Twenty-five millions of the public lands are
given away gratuitously to soldiers — six millions in
a single year. Forty-seven millions of the public
lands to seventeen States for schools, colleges, etc.
Forty-seven thousand acres for deaf and dumb
asylums. And look; just now it changes its policy,
and Mr. Pierce is opposed to granting any land —
it is not constitutional — to Miss Dix, to make the
insane sober, and bring them to their right minds.
He may have a private reason for keeping the people
in a state of craziness, for aught I know.

The public policy changes in these matters. It
never changes in respect to slavery. Be the Whigs in
power, slavery is Whig; be the Democrats, it is Democratic. At first, slavery was an exceptional measure,
and men tried to apologize for it and excuse it. Now
it is a normal principle, and the institution must be
defended and enlarged.

Commercial men must be moved, I suppose, by commercial arguments. Look, then, at this statement of
facts.

Slavery is unprofitable for the people. America is
poorer for slavery. I am speaking in the great focus
of American commerce * — the third city for popula-

* New York City.

tion and riches in the Christian world. Let me, therefore, talk about dollars. America, I say, is poorer for slavery. If the three and a quarter millions of slaves were freemen, how much richer would she be? There is no State in the Union but it is poorer for slavery. It is a bad tool to work with. The educated freeman is the best working-power in the world.

Compare the North with the South, and see what a difference in riches, comfort, education. See the superiority of the North. But the South started with every advantage of nature — soil, climate, everything. To make the case plainer, let me take two great States, Virginia and New York. Compare them together.

In geographical position Virginia has every advantage over New York. Almost everything that will grow in the Union will grow somewhere in Virginia, save sugar. The largest ships can sail up the Potomac a hundred miles, as far as Alexandria. The Rappahannock, York, James, are all navigable rivers. The Ohio flanks Virginia more than three hundred miles. There is sixty miles of navigation on the Kanawha. New York has a single navigable stream with not a hundred and fifty miles of navigation, from Troy to the ocean. Virginia has the best harbor on the Atlantic coast, and several smaller ones. Your State has but a single maritime port. Virginia abounds in water-power for mills. I stood once on the steps of the Capitol at Washington, and within six miles of me, under my eyes, there was a water-power greater than that which turns the mills of Lawrence, Lowell, and Manchester, all put together. In 1836 it did not turn a wheel; now, I am told, it drives a grist mill. No State is so rich in water-power. The Alleghenies are a great watershed, and at the eaves the

streams rush forward as if impatient to turn mills.
New York has got very little water-power of this sort.
Virginia is full of minerals — coal, iron, lead, copper, salt. Her agricultural resources are immense.
What timber clothes her mountains! what a soil for
Indian corn, wheat, tobacco, rice! even cotton grows
in the southern part. Washington said the central
counties of Virginia were the best land in the United
States. Daniel Webster, reporting to Virginians of
his European tour, said he saw no lands in Europe
so good as the valley of the Shenandoah. Virginia
is rich in mountain pastures favorable to sheep and
horned cattle. Nature gives Virginia everything that
can be asked of nature. What a position for agriculture, manufactures, mining, commerce! Norfolk is a
hundred miles nearer Chicago than New York is, but
she has no intercourse with Chicago. It is three hundred miles nearer the mouth of the Ohio; but if
a Norfolk man wants to go to St. Louis, I believe his
quickest way lies through New York. It is not a
day's sail farther from Liverpool; it is nearer to the
Mediterranean and South American points. But what
is Norfolk, with her 23,000 tons of shipping and her
14,000 population? What is Richmond, with her 27,-
000 men — 10,000 of them slaves? Nay, what is Virginia itself, the very oldest State? Let me cipher
out some numerical details.

In 1790 she had 748,000 inhabitants; now she has
1,421,000. She has not doubled in sixty years. In
1790 New York had 340,000; now she has 3,048,000.
She has multiplied her population almost ten times.
In Virginia, in 1850, there were only 452,000 more
freemen than sixty years before; in New York, there
were 2,724,000 *more freemen than there were in* 1790.

There are only 165,000 dwellings in Virginia; 463,-
000 in New York. Then the Virginia farms were
worth $216,000,000, yours $554,000,000; Virginia is
wholly agricultural, while you are also manufacturing
and commercial. Her farm tools were worth $7,000,-
000; yours $22,000,000. Her cattle $33,000,000;
yours $73,000,000. The orchard products of Virginia
were worth $177,000; of New York $1,762,000. Virginia had 478 miles of railroad; you had 1,826 miles.
She had 74,000 tons of shipping; you had 942,000.
The value of her cotton factories was not two millions; the value of yours was four and a quarter millions. She produced $841,000 worth of woolen goods;
you produced $7,030,000. Her furnaces produced
two millions and a half; yours produced eight millions.
Her tanneries $894,000; yours $9,804,000. All of
her manufactures together were not worth $9,000,000;
those of the *city of New York* alone have an annual
value of $105,000,000. Her attendance at school
was 109,000; yours 693,000.

But there is one thing in which Virginia is far in
advance of you. Of native Virginians, over twenty
years old, who could not read the name of " Christ"
nor the word " God " — free white people who cannot spell " democrat " — there were 87,383. That
is, out of every five hundred free white persons, there
were *one hundred and five* that could not spell
" Pierce." In New York there are 30,670 — no more;
so that, out of five hundred persons, there are *six*
that cannot read and write. Virginia is advancing
rapidly upon you in this respect. In 1840 she had
only 58,787 adults that could not read and write;
now 28,596 more. So, you see, she is advancing.

Virginia has 87 newspapers: New York 428. The

Virginia newspaper circulation is 89,000; New York newspaper circulation is 1,622,000. The *Tribune* — and I think it is the best paper there is in the world — has an aggregate circulation of 110,000; 20,000 more than all the newspapers of Virginia! Virginia prints every year 9,000,000 of copies of newspapers all told. New York prints 115,000,000. The New York *Tribune* prints 15,000,000 — more than the whole State of Virginia put together. Such is the state of things counted in the gross, but I think the New York quality is as much better as the quantity is more.

Virginia has 88,000 books in libraries not private. New York 1,760,000; a little more than twenty times as much. Virginia exports $3,500,000; New York $53,000,000. Virginia imports $426,000; New York $111,000,000. But in one article of export she is in advance of you — she sends to the man-markets of the South about $10,000,000 or $12,000,000 worth of her children every year; *exports slaves!* The value of all the property real and personal in the State of Virginia, *including* slaves, is $430,701,882; of New York $1,080,000,000, without estimating the value of the men who own it. Virginia has got 472,528 slaves. I will estimate them at less than the market value — at $400 each; they come to $189,000,000. I subtract the value of the working people of Virginia, and she is worth not quite $242,000,000. Now, the State of New York might buy up all the property of Virginia, including the slaves, and still have $649,000,000 left; might buy up all the real and personal property of Virginia, except the working-men, and have $838,000,-000 left. The North appropriates the rivers, the mines, the harbors, the forests, fire and water — the South kidnaps men. Behold the commercial result.

Virginia is a great State — very great! You don't
know how great it is. I will read it to you presently.
Things are great and small by comparison. I am
quoting again from the *Richmond Examiner* (March
24th, 1854.) "Virginia in this confederacy is the
impersonation of the well-born, well-educated, well-
bred aristocrat" [*well-born*, while the children of
Jefferson and the only *children* of Madison are a
"connecting link between the human and brute creation;" *well-educated*, with 21 per cent. of her white
adults unable to read the vote they cast against the inalienable rights of men; *well-bred*, when her great
product for exportation is — the *children of her own
loins!* Slavery is a "patriarchal institution;" the
Democratic Abrahams of Virginia do not offer up
their Isaacs to the Lord; that would be a *sacrifice;*
they only *sell them.* So]; "she looks down from her
elevated pedestal upon her *parvenu,* ignorant, men-
dacious Yankee vilifiers, as coldly and calmly as a
marble statue; occasionally she condescends to recognize the existence of her adversaries at the very moment when she crushes them. But she does it without anger, and with no more hatred of them than
the gardener feels towards the insects which he finds
it necessary occasionally to destroy." "She feels that
she is the sword and buckler of the South — that it
is her influence which has so frequently defeated and
driven back in dismay the abolition party when flushed
by temporary victory. Brave, calm and determined,
wise in times of excitement, *always true to the slave
power,* never rash or indiscreet, the waves of Northern fanaticism burst harmless at her feet; the contempt
for her Northern revilers is the result of her consciousness of her influence in the political world. *She makes*

and unmakes Presidents; she dictates her terms to the Northern Democracy, and they obey her.   She selects from among the faithful of the North a man upon whom she can rely, and she makes him President." [This latter is true! The opinion of Richmond is of more might than the opinion of New York. Slavery, the political Gog on the outside, steers the ark of commercial Noah, and makes it rough or smooth weather inside, just as he likes.]

" In the early days of the Republic, the superior sagacity of her statesmen enabled them to rivet so firmly the shackles of the slave, *that the abolitionists will never be able to unloose them.*"

" A wide and impassible gulf separates the noble, proud, glorious Old Dominion from her Northern traducers ; the mastiff does not willingly assail the skunk ! "
" When Virginia takes the field, she crushes the whole abolition party ; her slaughter is wholesale, and a hundred thousand abolitionists are cut down when she issues her commands ! "

Again (April 4th, 1854), " A hundred Southern gentlemen, armed with riding-whips, could chase an army of invading abolitionists into the Atlantic."

In reference to the project at the North of sending Northern abolitionists along with the Northern slave-breeders to Nebraska, to put freedom into the soil before slavery gets there, the *Examiner* says —" *Why, a hundred wild, lank, half-horse, half-alligator Missouri and Arkansas emigrants would, if so disposed, chase out of Nebraska and Kansas all the abolitionists* who have figured for the last twenty years at anti-slavery meetings."

I say slavery is not profitable for the nation nor for a State, but it is profitable for *slave-owners*.   You will see why. If the Northern capitalist owned the weavers and spinners at Lowell and Lawrence, New England would be poorer, and the working-men would not be so well off, or so well educated; but Undershot and Overshot, Turbine Brothers, Spindle and Co., would be richer, and would get larger dividends. Land monopoly in England enfeebles the island, but enriches the aristocracy. How poor, ill-fed, and ill-clad were the French peasants before the Revolution; how costly was the *chateau* of the noble. Monopoly was bad for the people; profitable for the rich men. How poor are the people in Italy; how rich the cardinals and the pope! Oppression enriches the oppressor; it makes poorer the downtrodden. Piracy is very costly to the merchant and to mankind; but it enriches the pirate. Slavery impoverishes Virginia, but it enriches the master. It gives him money — commercial power — office — political power. The slave-holder is drawn in his triumphal chariot by two chattels: one, the poor black man, whom he " owns legally "; the other is the poor white man, whom he owns morally, and harnesses to his chariot. Hence these American lords of the lash cleave to this institution — they love it. To the slaveholders, slavery is money and power!

Now the South, weak in numbers, feeble in respect to money, has continually directed the politics of America just as she would. Her ignorance and poverty were more efficacious than the Northern riches and education. She is in earnest for slavery; the North not *in earnest for freedom! only earnest for money.* So long as the Federal Government grinds the axes of the Northern merchant, he cares little whether the stone is turned by the free man's labor or the slave's. Hence, *the great centers of Northern commerce* and manu-

factures are also the *great centers of pro-slavery* politics.   Philadelphia, New York, Boston, Buffalo, Cincinnati, they all liked the Fugitive Slave Bill; all took
pains to seize the fugitive who fled to a Northern altar
for freedom; nay, the most conspicuous clergymen in
those cities became apostles of kidnapping; their
churches were of commerce, not Christianity.   The
North yielded to that last most insolent demand.   Under the influence of that excitement she chose the present administration, the present Congress.   Now see
the result!   Whig and Democrat meet on the same
platform at Baltimore.   It was the platform of slavery.   Both candidates gave in their allegiance to the
same measure — Scott and Pierce — it was the measure which compromised the first principles of the American Independence — they were sworn on the Fugitive
Slave Bill.   Whig and Democrat knew no " higher
law," only the statute of slaveholders.   Conscience
bent down before the Constitution.   What sort of a
government can you expect from such conduct?   What
representatives?   Just what you have got.   Sow the
wind, will you? then reap the whirlwind.   Mr. Pierce
said in his inaugural, " I believe that involuntary servitude is recognized by the Constitution; " " that it
stands like any other admitted right.   I hold that the
compromise measures (*i. e.*, the Fugitive Slave Bill)
are strictly constitutional, and *to be unhesitatingly
carried into effect.*"   The laws to secure the master's
right to capture a man in the free States " should be
respected and obeyed, *not with a reluctance* encouraged by abstract opinions as to their propriety in a
different state of society, *but cheerfully* and according
to the decision of the tribunal to which their exposition
belongs."   These   words   were   *historical* — reminis-

cences of the time when " *no higher law* " was the watchword of the American State and the American Church; they were *prophetic* — ominous of what we see to-day.

I. Here is the Gadsden Treaty which has been negotiated. How bad it is I cannot say; only this. If I am rightly informed, a tract of 39,000,000 acres, larger than all Virginia, is " re-annexed " to the slave soil which the " flag of our Union " already waves over. The whole thing, when it is fairly understood by the public, I think will be seen to be a more iniquitous matter than this Nebraska wickedness.

II. Then comes the Nebraska Bill, yet to be consummated. While we are sitting here in cold debate, it may be the measure has passed. From the beginning I have never had any doubts that it would pass; if it could not be put through this session — as I thought it would — I felt sure that before this Congress goes out of office, Nebraska would be slave soil. You see what a majority there was in the Senate; you see what a majority there is in the House. I know there is an opposition — and most brilliantly conducted, too, by the few faithful men; but see this: the administration has yet three years to run. There is an annual income of sixty millions of dollars. There are forty thousand offices to be disposed of — four thousand very valuable. And do you think that a Democratic administration, with that amount of offices, of money and time, cannot buy up Northern doughfaces enough to carry any measure it pleases? I know better. Once I thought that Texas could not be annexed. It was done. I learned wisdom from that. I have taken my counsel of my fears. I have not seen any barrier on which the North would rally that we have come to yet. There are some things behind us. John Randolph said, years ago, " We will drive you from pillar to post, back, back, back." He has been as good as his word. We have been driven " back, back, back." But we cannot be driven much farther. There is a spot where we shall stop. I am afraid we have not come to it yet. I will say no more about it just now — because, not many weeks ago, I stood here and said a great deal. You have listened to me when I was feeble and hollow-voiced; I will not tax your patience now, for in this, as in a celebrated feast of old, they have " kept the good wine until now! " (alluding to Garrison and Phillips, who were to follow).

If the Nebraska Bill *is* defeated, I shall rejoice that iniquity is foiled once more. But if it become a law — there are some things which seem probable.

1. On the 4th of March, 1856, the Democrats will have *leave to withdraw* from office.

2. Every Northern man who has taken a prominent stand in behalf of slavery will be politically ruined. You know what befell the Northern politicians who voted for the Missouri Compromise; a similar fate hangs over the men who enslave Nebraska. Already, Mr. Everett is, theologically speaking, among the lost; and, of all the three thousand New England ministers whose petition he dared not present, not one will ever pray for his political salvation.

Pause with me and drop a tear over the ruin of Edward Everett, a man of large talents and commensurate industry, very learned, the most scholarly man, perhaps, in the country, with a persuasive beauty of speech only equaled by this American (Mr. Phillips), who surpasses him; he has had a long career of public service, public honor — clergyman, professor, editor, representative, governor, ambassador, president of Harvard College, alike the ornament as the auxiliary of many a learned society — he yet comes to such an end.

> "This is the state of man: to-day, he puts forth
> The tender leaves of hope; to-morrow, blossoms,
> And bears his blushing honors thick upon him;
> The third day comes a frost, *Nebraska's* frost;
> And, when he thinks, good easy man, full surely,
> His greatness is a-ripening, nips his root,
> And then he falls ———."

> "O, how wretched
> Is that poor man that hangs on *public* favors!
> There is betwixt that smile *he* would aspire to,
> That sweet aspect of *voters,* and their ruin,
> More pangs and fears than wars or women have;
> And when he falls, he falls like Lucifer,
> Never to hope again!"

Mr. Douglas also is finished; the success of his measure is his own defeat. Mr. Pierce has three short years to serve; then there will be one more ex-President — ranking with Tyler and Fillmore. Mr. Seward need not agitate,

> ———"Let it work,
> For 'tis the sport to have the engineer
> Hoist with his own petard."

III. The next thing is the enslavement of Cuba. That is a very serious matter. It has been desired a long time. Lopez, a Spanish filibuster, undertook it and was legally put to death. I am not an advocate for the *garrote,* but I think, all things taken into consideration, that he did not meet with a very inadequate mode of death: and I believe that is the general opinion, not only in Cuba, but in the United States. But Young America is not content with that. Mr. Dean,

a little while ago, in the House, proposed to repeal the
neutrality laws — to set filibusterism on its legs again :
You remember the President's message about the
" Black Warrior "— how black-warrior like it was ;
and then comes the " unanimous resolution " of the
Louisiana legislature asking the United States to interfere and declare war, in case Cuba should undertake
to emancipate her slaves.   Senator Slidell's speech is
still tingling in our ears, asking the government to repeal the neutrality laws and allow every pirate who
pleases, to land in Cuba and burn and destroy.   You
know Mr. Soulé's conduct in Madrid.   It is rumored
that he has been authorized to offer $250,000,000 for
Cuba.   The sum is enormous ; but, when you consider
the character of *this* administration and the inaugural
of President Pierce, the unscrupulous abuse made of
public money, I do not think it is a very extraordinary
supposition.

But this matter of getting possession of Cuba is
something dangerous as well as difficult.   There are
three conceivable ways of getting it : one is by buying,
and that I take it is wholly out of the question.   If
I am rightly informed, there is a certain Spanish debt
owing to Englishmen, and that Cuba is somehow
pledged as a sort of collateral security for the Spanish
bonds.   I take it for granted that Cuba is not to be
bought for many years without the interference of
England, and depend upon it England will not allow it
to be sold *for the establishment of slavery;* for I think
it is pretty well understood by politicians that there is
a regular agreement entered into between Spain on
one side and England on the other, that at a certain
period within twenty-five years every slave in Cuba
shall be set free.   I believe this is known to men some-

what versed in the secret history of the two cabinets of England and of Spain. England has the same wish for land which fires our Anglo-Saxon blood. She has islands in the West Indies; the Morro in Cuba is only 100 miles from Jamaica. If we get Cuba for slavery, we shall next want the British West Indies for the same institution. Cuba filled with filibusters would be a dangerous neighbor.

Then there are two other ways: one is by filibusterism, and that Mr. Slidell and Mr. Dean want to try; the other is by open war. Now, filibusterism will lead to open war, so I will consider only this issue.

I know that Americans will fight more desperately, perhaps, on land or sea, than any other people. But fighting is an ugly business, especially with such antagonists as we shall have in this case. It is a matter well understood that the captain-general of Cuba has a paper in his possession authorizing him discretionally to free the slaves and put arms in their hands whenever it is thought necessary. It is rather difficult to get at the exact statistics of Cuba. There has been no census since 1842, I think, when the population was estimated at a million. I will reckon it now at 1,300,000 — 700,000 blacks, and 600,000 whites. Of the 700,000 blacks, half a million are slaves and *200,000 free men*. Now, a black free man in Cuba is a very different person from the black free man in the United States. He has rights. He is not turned out of the omnibus nor the meeting house nor the graveyard. He is respected by the law; he respects himself, and is a formidable person; let the blacks be furnished with arms, they are formidable foes. And remember there are mountain fastnesses in the center of the island; that it is as defensible as San Domingo;

and it has a very unhealthy climate for Northern men. The Spaniard would have great allies. The vomito is there; typhoid, dysentery, yellow fever — the worst of all — is there. A Northern army even of filibusters would fight against the most dreadful odds. " The Lord from on high," as the old Hebrew would say, would fight against the Northern men; the pestilence that swept off Sennacherib's host would not respect the filibuster.

That is not all. What sort of a navy has Spain? *One hundred and seventy-nine* ships of war! They are small mostly, but they carry over 1,400 cannon and 24,000 men — 15,000 marines and 9,000 sailors. The United States has *seventy-five* ships of war; 2,200 cannon, 14,000 men — large ships, heavy cannon. That is not all. Spaniards fight desperately. A Spanish armada I would not be very much afraid of; but Spain will issue letters of marque, and a Portuguese or Spanish pirate is rather an uncomfortable being to meet. Our commerce is spread all over the seas; there is no mercantile marine so unprotected as ours. Our ships do not carry muskets, still less cannon, since pirates have been swept off the sea. Let Spain issue letters of marque, England winking at it, and Algerine pirates from out the Barbary States of Africa and other pirates from the Brazilian, Mexican, and the West Indian ports, would prowl about the coast of the Mediterranean and over all the bosom of the Atlantic; and then where would be our commerce? The South has nothing to fear from that. She has got no shipping. Yes, Norfolk has 23,000 tons. The South is not afraid. The North has nearly four million tons of shipping. But touch the commerce of a Northern man and you touch his heart.

England has conceded to us as a measure just what we asked. We have always declared " free ships make free goods." England said " enemies' goods make enemies' ships." Now she has not affirmed our principle; she has assented to our measure. That is all you can expect her to do. But, if we repeal our neutrality laws and seek to get Cuba in order to establish slavery there, endangering the interests of England, and the freedom of her colored citizens, depend upon it England will not suffer this to be done without herself interfering. If she is so deeply immersed in European wars that she cannot interfere directly, she will indirectly. But I have not thought that England and France are to be much engaged in a European war. I suppose the intention of the American Cabinet is to seize Cuba as soon as the British and Russians are fairly fighting, thinking that England will not interfere. But in " this war of elder sons " which now goes on for the dismemberment of Turkey, it is not so clear that England will be so deeply engaged that she cannot attend to her domestic affairs, or the interest of her West Indies. I think these powers are going to divide Turkey between them, but I do not believe they are going to do much fighting there. If we are bent on seizing Cuba, a long and ruinous fight is a thing that ought to enter into men's calculations. Now, let such a naval warfare take place, and how will your insurance stock look in New York, Philadelphia, and Boston? How will your merchants look when reports come one after another that your ships are carried in as prizes by Spain, or sunk on the ocean after they have been plundered? I speak in the great commercial metropolis of America. I wish these things to be seriously considered by Northern men.

Though I would not fear a naval war, let the Northern men look out for their own ships.   But here is a matter which the South might think of.   In case of foreign war, the North will not be the battle-field.   An invading army would attack the South.   Who would defend it — the local militia, the " chivalry " of South Carolina, the " gentlemen " of Virginia, who are to slaughter 100,000 abolitionists in a day?   Let an army set foot on Southern soil, with a few *black regiments;* let the commander offer *freedom to all the slaves and put arms in their hands;* let him ask them to *burn houses and butcher men;* and there would be a state of things not quite so pleasant for gentlemen of the South to look at.   " They that laughed at the groveling worm and trod on him may cry and howl when they see the stoop of the flying and fiery-mouthed dragon! "   Now, there is only one opinion about the valor of President Pierce.   Like the sword of Hudibras, it cut into itself,

> ———" for lack
> Of other stuff to hew and hack."

But would he like to stand with such a fire in his rear?   Set a house on fire by hot shot, and you don't know how much of it will burn down.

IV. Well, if Nebraska is made a slave territory, as I suppose it will be, the next thing is the possession of Cuba.   Then the war against Spain will come, as I think, inevitably.   But even if we don't get Cuba, slavery must be extended to other parts of the Union. This may be done *judicially* by the Supreme Court — one of the powerful agents to destroy local self-government and legalize centralization; or *legislatively* by Congress.   Already slavery is established in Califor-

nia.   An attempt, you know, was made to establish it
in Illinois.   Senator Toombs, the other day, boasted
to John P. Hale, that it would "not be long before
the slaveholder will sit down at the foot of Bunker
Hill monument with his slaves."   You and I may live
to see it — at least to see the attempt made.   A writer
in a prominent Southern journal, the *Charleston Courier*
(of March 16, 1854), declares that "domestic slavery is a constitutional institution, and cannot be
prohibited in a territory by either territorial or con-
gressional legislation.   It is recognized by the Constitution as an existing and lawful institution . . .
and by the recognition of slavery *eo nomine* in the
District of Columbia, under the constitutional provision
for the acquisition of and exclusive legislation over
such a capitoline district; and by that clause also
which declares that the citizens of each State shall be
entitled to all the privileges and immunities of citizens
in the several States."   "The citizens of any State
. . . cannot be constitutionally denied the equal
right . . . of sojourning or settling . . .
with their man-servants and maid-servants . . .
in any portion of the widespread Canaan which the
Lord their God hath given them, there to dwell unmolested in person or property."   Admirable exposition
of the Constitution!   The free black man must be shut
up in jail if he goes from Boston in a ship to Charleston, but the slaveholder may bring his slaves to Massachusetts and dwell there *unmolested with his property in men.*   South Carolina has a white population
of 274,567 persons, considerably less than half the
population of this city.   But, if South Carolina says
to the State of New York, with three million men in it,
Let us bring our slaves to New York, what will the

" Hards," and the " Softs," and the " Silver Greys "
answer? Gentlemen, we shall hear what we shall hear.
I fear not an office-holder of any note would oppose
the measure. It might be carried with the present
Supreme Court, or Congress, I make no doubt.

But this is not the end. After the Gadsden Treaty,
the enslavement of Nebraska, the extension of slavery
to the free States, the seizure of Cuba, with other
islands — San Domingo, etc.,— there is one step more
— THE RE-ESTABLISHMENT OF THE AFRICAN SLAVE-
TRADE.

A recent number of the *Southern Standard* thus develops the thought: " With firmness and judgment
we can open up the African slave emigration again to
people the whole region of the tropics. We can
boldly defend this upon the most enlarged system of
philanthropy. It is far better for the wild races of
Africa themselves." " The good old Las Casas, in
1519, was the first to advise Spain to import Africans
to her colonies. . . . Experience has shown his
scheme was founded in wise and Christian philanthropy. . . . The time is coming when we will
boldly defend this emigration [kidnapping men in Africa and selling them in the Christian Republic] before the world. The hypocritical cant and whining
morality of the latter-day saints will die away before
the majesty of commerce. . . . We have too long
been governed by psalm-singing schoolmasters from
the North. . . . The folly commenced in our
own government uniting with Great Britain to declare slave-importing piracy." . . . " A general
rupture in Europe would force upon us the undisputed sway of the Gulf of Mexico and the West Indies. . . . With Cuba and San Domingo, we could

control the . . . power of the world. Our true
policy is to look to Brazil as the next great slave
power. . . . A treaty of commerce and alliance
with Brazil will give us the control over the Gulf of
Mexico and its border countries, together with the
islands; and the consequence of this will place African
slavery beyond the reach of fanaticism at home or
abroad. These two great slave powers . . .
ought to guard and strengthen their mutual interests.
. . . We can not only preserve domestic servitude,
but we can defy the power of the world." . . .
" The time will come that all the islands and regions
suited to African slavery, between us and Brazil, will
fall under the control of these two powers. . . .
In a few years there will be no investment for the $200,-
000,000 . . . so profitable . . . as the development . . . of the tropical regions " [that is,
as the African slave-trade]. . . . " If the slaveholding race in these States are but true to themselves,
they have a great destiny before them."

Now, gentlemen and ladies, who is to blame that
things have come to such a pass as this? The South
and the North; but the North much more than the
South,— very much more. Gentlemen, we let Gog get
upon the ark; we took *pay* for his passage. Our most
prominent men in Church and State have sworn allegiance to Gog. But this is not always to last; there
is a day after to-day — a *forever* behind each to-day.

The North ought to have fought slavery at the
adoption of the Constitution, and at every step since;
after the battle was lost then, we should have resisted each successive step of the slave power. But we
have yielded — yielded continually. We made no
fight over the annexation of slave territory, the ad-

mission of slave States. We should have rent the
Union into the primitive townships sooner than consent to the Fugitive Slave Bill. But as we failed to
fight manfully then, I never thought the North would
rally on the Missouri Compromise line. I rejoice at
the display of indignation I witness here and elsewhere. For once New York appears more moral than
Boston. I thank you for it. A meeting is called in
the Park to-morrow. It is high time.— I doubt
that the North will yet rally and defend the line drawn
in 1820. But there are two lines of defense where
the nation will pause, I think — the *occupation of
Cuba*, with its war so destructive to Northern ships;
and the *restoration of the African slave-trade*. The
slave-breeding States, Maryland, Virginia, Kentucky,
Tennessee, Missouri, will oppose that; for, if the Gulf
States, and the future tropical territories can import
Africans at $100 a head, depend upon it, that will spoil
the market for the slave-breeders of America. And,
gentlemen, if Virginia cannot sell her own children,
how will this " well-born, well-educated, well-bred aristocrat " look down on the poor and ignorant Yankee!
No, gentlemen, this iniquity is not to last for ever.
A certain amount of force will compress a cubic foot
of water into nine-tenths of its natural size; but the
weight of the whole earth cannot make it any smaller.
Even the North is not infinitely compressible. When
atom touches atom, you may take off the screws.

Things cannot continue long in this condition.
Every triumph of slavery is a day's march towards its
ruin. There is no higher law, is there? " He taketh
the wise in their own craftiness, the council of the
wicked is carried "— aye, but *it is carried headlong.*

Only see what a change has been coming over our

spirit just now. Three years ago, Isaiah Rynders and Hiram Ketchum domineered over New York; and those gentlemen who are to follow me, and whom you are impatient to hear, were mobbed down in the city of New York, two years ago; they could not find a hall that would be leased to them for money or love, and had to adjourn to Syracuse to hold their convention. Look at this assembly now.

A little while ago all the leading clergymen were in favor of the Fugitive Slave Bill; now three thousand of New England ministers remonstrate against Nebraska. They know there is a fire in their rear, and, in theological language, it is a fire that " is not quenched." It goeth not out by day, and there is no night there. The clergymen stand between eternal torment on one side and the little giant of slavery on the other. They do not go back! Two thousand English clergymen once became non-conformists in a single day. Three thousand New England ministers remonstrated against the enslavement of Nebraska. Now is the time to push and be active, call meetings, bring out men of all parties, all forms of religion, agitate, agitate, agitate. Make a fire in the rear of the government and the representatives. The South is weak — only united. The North is strong in money, in men, in education, in the justice of our great cause — only not united for freedom. Only be faithful to ourselves, and slavery will come down, not slowly, as I thought once, but when the people of the North say it, it will come down with a great crash.

Then, when we are free from this plague-spot of slavery — the curse to our industry, our education, our politics, and our religion — we shall increase more rapidly in number and still more abundantly be rich.

The South will be as the North — active, intelligent — Virginia rich as New York, the Carolinas as active as Massachusetts. Then, by peaceful purchase, the Anglo-Saxon may acquire the rest of this North American continent. The Spaniards will make nothing of it. Nay, we may honorably go farther South, and possess the Atlantic and Pacific slopes of the Northern continent, extending the area of freedom at every step. We may carry thither the Anglo-Saxon vigor and enterprise, the old love of liberty, the love also of law; the best institutions of the present age — ecclesiastical, political, social, domestic. Then what a nation we shall one day become. America, the mother of a thousand Anglo-Saxon States, tropic and temperate, on both sides of the equator, may behold the Mississippi and the Amazon uniting their waters, the drainage of two vast continents in the Mediterranean of the western world; may count her children at last by hundreds of millions — and among them all behold no tyrant and no slave! What a spectacle — the Anglo-Saxon family occupying a whole hemisphere, with industry, freedom, religion. The fulfilment of this vision is our province; we are the involuntary instruments of God. Shall America scorn the mission God sends her on? Then let us all perish, and may Russia teach justice to mankind.

VII

THE PROGRESS OF AMERICA
1854

At this day there are two great tribes of men in Christendom, which seem to have a promising future before them — the Slavonic and the Anglo-Saxon. Both are comparatively new. For the last three hundred years each has been continually advancing in numbers, riches, and territory; in industrial and military power. To judge from present appearances, it seems probable that a hundred years hence there will be only two great national forces in the Christian world — the Slavonic and the Anglo-Saxon.

The Anglo-Saxon tribe is composite, and the mingling so recent, that we can still easily distinguish the main ingredients of the mixture. There are, first, the Saxons and Angles from North Germany; next, the Scandinavians from Denmark and Sweden; and, finally, the Normans, or Romanized Scandinavians, from France.

This tribe is now divided into two great political branches, namely, the Anglo-Saxon Briton, and the Anglo-Saxon American; but both are substantially the same people, though with different antecedents and surroundings. The same fundamental characteristics belong to the Briton and the American.

Three hundred years ago, the Anglo-Saxons were scarce three millions in number; they did not own the whole of Great Britain. Now there are thirty or forty millions of men with Anglo-Saxon blood in their veins. They possess the British Islands; Heligoland,

196

Gibraltar, Malta, and the Ionian Isles; St. Helena, South Africa, much of East and West Africa; enormous territories in India, continually increasing; the whole of Australia; almost all of North America, and I know not how many islands scattered about the Atlantic and Pacific seas. Their geographical spread covers at least one-sixth part of the habitable globe; their power controls about one-fifth of the inhabitants of the earth. It is the richest of all the families of mankind. The Anglo-Saxon leads the commerce and the most important manufactures of the world. He owns seven-eighths of the shipping of Christendom, and half that of the human race. He avails himself of the latest discoveries in practical science, and applies them to the creation of comforts and luxuries. Iron is his favorite metal; and about two-thirds of the annual iron crop of the earth is harvested on Anglo-Saxon soil. Cotton, wheat, and the potato, are his favorite plants.

The political institutions of the Anglo-Saxon secure national unity of action for the State, and individual variety of action for each citizen, to a greater degree than other nations have thought possible. In all Christendom, there is scarce any freedom of the press except on Anglo-Saxon soil. Ours is the only tongue in which liberty can speak. Anglo-Saxon Britain is the asylum of exiled patriots, or exiled despots. The royal and patrician wrecks of the revolutionary storms of continental Europe, in the last century and in this, were driven to her hospitable shore. Kossuth, Mazzini, Victor Hugo, and Comte, relics of the last revolution, are washed to the same coast. America is the asylum of exiled nations, who flee to her arms, four hundred thousand in a year, and find shelter.

The Slavonians fight with diplomacy and the sword, the Anglo-Saxon with diplomacy and the dollar. He is the Roman of productive industry, of commerce, as the Romans were Anglo-Saxons of destructive conquest, of war. The Slavonian nations, from the accident of their geographical position, or from their ethnological peculiarity of nature, invade and conquer lands more civilized than their own. They have the diplomatic skill to control nations of superior intellectual and moral development. The Anglo-Saxon is too clumsy for foreign politics; when he meddles with the affairs of other civilized people, he is often deceived. Russia outwits England continually in the political game now playing for the control of Europe. The Anglo-Saxon, more invasive than the Slavonian, prefers new and wild lands to old and well-cultivated territories; so he conquers America, and tills its virgin soil: seizes on Africa,— the dry nurse of lions and of savage men,— and founds a new empire in Australia. If he invades Asia, it is in the parts not Christian. His rule is a curse to countries full of old civilization; I take it that England has been a blight to India, and will be to China, if she sets there her conquering foot. The Anglo-Saxon is less pliable than the Romans, a less indulgent master to conquered men; with more plastic power to organize and mold, he has a less comprehensive imagination, limits himself to a smaller number of forms, and so hews off and casts away what suits him not. Austria conquers Lombardy, France Algiers, Russia, Poland, to the benefit of the conquered party, it seems. Can any one show that the British rule has been a benefit to India? The Russians make nothing of their American territory. But what civilization blooms out of the savage ground wherever the Saxon plants his foot!

I must say a word of the leading peculiarities of this tribe.

1. There is a strong love of individual freedom. This belongs to the Anglo-Saxons in common with all the Teutonic family. But with them it seems eminently powerful. Circumstances have favored its development. They care much for freedom, little for equality.

2. Connected with this, is a love of law and order, which continually shows itself on both sides of the ocean. Fast as we gain freedom, we secure it by law and constitution, trusting little to the caprice of magistrates.

3. Then there is a great federative power — a tendency to form combinations of persons, or of communities and states — special partnerships on a small scale for mercantile business; on a large scale, like the American Union, or the Hanse towns, for the political business of a nation.

4. The Anglo-Saxons have eminent practical power to organize things into a mill, or men into a State, and then to administer the organization. This power is one which contributes greatly to both their commercial and political success. But this tribe is also most eminently material in its aims and means; it loves riches, works for riches, fights for riches. It is not warlike, as some other nations, who love war for its own sake, though a hard fighter when put to it.

5. We are the most aggressive, invasive, and exclusive people on the earth. The history of the Anglo-Saxon, for the last three hundred years, has been one of continual aggression, invasion, and extermination.

I cannot now stop to dwell on these traits of our

tribal anthropology, but must yet say a word touching this national exclusiveness and tendency to exterminate.

Austria and Russia never treated a conquered nation so cruelly as England has treated Ireland. Not many years ago, four-fifths of the population of the island were Catholics, a tenth Anglican churchmen. All offices were in the hands of the little minority. Two-thirds of the Irish House of Commons were nominees of the Protestant gentry; the Catholic members must take the declaration against transubstantiation. Papists were forbidden to vote in elections of members to the Irish Parliament. They suffered " under a universal, unmitigated, indispensable, exceptionless disqualification." " In the courts of law, they could not gain a place on the bench, nor act as a barrister, attorney, or solicitor, nor be employed even as a hired clerk, nor sit on a grand jury, nor serve as a sheriff, nor hold even the lowest civil office of trust and profit; nor have any privilege in a town corporation; nor be a freeman of such corporation; nor vote at a vestry." * A Catholic could not marry a Protestant: the priest who should celebrate such a marriage was to be hanged. He could not be " a guardian to any child, nor educate his own child, if its mother were a Protestant," or the child declared in favor of Protestantism. " No Papist might instruct a Protestant. Papists could not supply their want by academies and schools of their own; for a Catholic to teach, even in a private family, or as usher to a Protestant, was a felony, punishable by imprisonment, exile, or death." " To be educated in any foreign Catholic school was

* Bancroft, *History of United States*, vol. v. p. 66, *et seq.*

an unalterable and perpetual outlawry." " The child sent abroad for education, no matter of how tender an age, or himself how innocent, could never after sue in law or equity, or be guardian, executor, or administrator, or receive any legacy or deed of gift; he forfeited all his goods and chattels, and forfeited for his life all his lands; " whoever sent him incurred the same penalties.

The Catholic clergy could not be taught at home or abroad: they " were registered and kept, like prisoners at large, within prescribed limits." " All papists exercising ecclesiastical jurisdiction; all monks, friars, and regular priests, and all priests not actually in parishes, and to be registered, were banished from Ireland under pain of transportation; and, on a return, of being hanged and quartered." " The Catholic priest abjuring his religion, received a pension of thirty, and afterwards of forty pounds." " No nonconforming Catholic could buy land, or receive it by descent, devise, or settlement; or lend money on it as security; or hold an interest in it through a Protestant trustee; or take a lease of ground for more than thirty-one years. If under such a lease he brought his farm to produce more than one-third beyond the rent, the first Protestant discoverer might sue for the lease before known Protestants, making the defendant answer all interrogations on oath; so that the Catholic farmer dared not drain his fields, nor inclose them, nor build solid houses on them." " Even if a Catholic owned a horse worth more than five pounds, any Protestant might take it away," on payment of that sum. " To the native Irish, the English oligarchy appeared as men of a different race and creed, who had acquired the island by force of arms, rapine, and

chicane, and derived revenues from it by the employment of extortionate underlings or overseers." *

The same disposition to invade and exterminate
showed itself on this side of the ocean.

In America, the Frenchman and the Spaniard came
in contact with the red man; they converted him to
what they called Christianity, and then associated with
him on equal terms. The pale-face and the red-skin
hunted in company; they fished from the same canoe
in the Bay of Fundy and Lake Superior; they lodged
in the same tent, slept on the same bear-skin; nay, they
knelt together before the same God, who was " no
respecter of persons," and had made of one blood all
nations of men! The white man married the Indian's
daughter; the red man wooed and won the pale child
of the Caucasian. This took place in Canada, and
in Mexico, in Peru, and Ecuador. In Brazil, the
negro graduates at the college; he becomes a general
in the army. But the Anglo-Saxon disdains to mingle his proud blood in wedlock with the " inferior
races of men." He puts away the savage — black,
yellow, red. In New England, the Puritan converted
the Indians to Christianity, as far as they could accept the theology of John Calvin; but made a careful
separation between white and red, " my people and
thy people." They must dwell in separate villages,
worship in separate houses; they must not intermarry.
The general court of Massachusetts once forbade all
extra-matrimonial connection of white and red, on
pain of death! The Anglo-Saxon has carefully
sought to exterminate the savages from his territory.
The Briton does so in Africa, in Van Diemen's Land,
in New Zealand, in New Holland — wherever he meets

* Bancroft, *ubi sup.* p. 67, *et seq.*

them. The American does the same in the western world. In New England the Puritan found the wild woods, the wild beasts, and the wild men; he undertook to eradicate them all, and has succeeded best with the wild men. There are more bears than Indians in New England. The United States pursues the same destructive policy. In two hundred years more there will be few Indians left between the Lake of the Woods and the Gulf of Mexico, between the Atlantic and Pacific Oceans.

Yet the Anglo-Saxons are not cruel; they are simply destructive. The Dutch, in New York, perpetrated the most wanton cruelties: the savages themselves shuddered at the white man's atrocity: " Our gods would be offended at such things," said they; " the white man's God must be different! " The cruelties of the French, and, still more, of the Spaniards in Mexico, in the West Indies, and South America, are too terrible to repeat, but too well known to need relating. The Spaniard put men to death with refinements of cruelty, luxuriating in destructiveness. The Anglo-Saxon simply shot down his foe, offered a reward for homicide, so much for a scalp, but tolerated no needless cruelty. If the problem is to destroy a race of men with the least expenditure of destructive force on one side, and the least suffering on the other, the Anglo-Saxon, Briton, or American, is the fittest instrument to be found on the whole globe.

So much for the Anglo-Saxon character in general. It is well to know the anthropology of the stock before attempting to appreciate the character of the special people. America has the general characteristics of this powerful tribe, but modified by her peculiar geographical and historical position. Our fathers emigrated from their home in a time of great ferment, and brought with them ideas which could not then be organized into institutions at home. This was obviously the case with the theological ideas of the Puritans, who, with their descendants, have given to America most of what is new and peculiar in her institutions. Still more, the early settlers of the North brought with them sentiments not ripened yet, which, in due time, developed themselves into ideas, and then into institutions.

At first, necessity, or love of change, drove the wanderers to the wilderness; they had no thought of separating from England. The fugitive Pilgrims in the Mayflower, who subscribed the compact, which so many Americans erroneously regard as the " seed-corn of the republican tree, under which millions of her men now stand," called themselves " loyal subjects of our dread sovereign, King James," undertaking to plant a colony " for the glory of God, and advancement of the Christian faith and honor of our king and country." In due time, as the colonists developed themselves in one, and the English at home in a different direction, there came to be a great diversity of ideas, and an opposition of interests. When mutuality of ideas and of interests, as the indispensable condition of national unity of action, failed, the colony fell off from its parent: the separation was unavoidable. Before many years, we doubt not, Australia will thus separate from the mother country, to the advantage of both parties.

In America, two generations of men have passed away since the last battle of the Revolution. The hostility of that contest is only a matter of history to the mass of Britons or Americans, not of daily consciousness; and as this disturbing force is withdrawn, the two nations see and feel more distinctly their points of agreement, and become conscious that they are both but one people.

The transfer of the colonists of England to the western world was an event of great importance to mankind; they found a virgin continent, on which to set up and organize their ideas, and develop their faculties. They had no enemies but the wilderness and its savage occupants. I doubt not that, if the emigrant had remained at home, it would have taken a thousand years to attain the same general development now reached by the free States of North America. The settlers carried with them the best ideas and the best institutions of their native land — the arts and sciences of England, the forms of a representative government, the trial by jury, the common law, the ideas of Christianity, and the traditions of the human race. In the woods, far from help, they were forced to become self-reliant and thrifty men. It is instructive to see what has come of the experiment. It is but two hundred and forty-six years since the settlement of Jamestown — not two hundred and thirty-four years since the Pilgrims landed at Plymouth; what a development since that time — of numbers, of riches, of material and spiritual power!

In the ninth century, Korb Flokki, a half-mythical person, " let loose his three crows," it is said, seeking land to the west and north of the Orkneys, and went to Iceland. In the tenth century, Gunnbjiorn, and Eirek the Red, discovered Greenland, an " ugly and right hateful country," as Paul Egede calls it. In the eleventh century, Leife, son of Eirek, with Tyrker the Southerner, discovered Vinland, some part of North America, but whether Newfoundland, Nova Scotia, or New England, I shall leave others to determine. It is not yet four hundred years since Columbus first dropped his anchor at San Salvador, and Cabot discovered the continent of America, and cruised along its shores from Hudson's Bay to Florida, seeking for a passage to the East Indies. In 1608 the first permanent British settlement was made in America, at Jamestown; in 1620 the Pilgrims began their far-famed experiment at Plymouth. What a change from 1608 to 1854! It is not in my power to determine the number of immigrants before the Revolution. There was a great variety of nationalities — Dutch in New York, Germans in Pennsylvania and Georgia, Swedes and Finns in Delaware, Scotch in New England and North Carolina, Swiss in Georgia; Acadians from Nova Scotia; and Huguenots from France.

America has now a stable form of government. Her pyramid is not yet high. It is only humble powers that she develops, no great creative spirit here as yet enchants men with the wonders of literature and art — but her foundation is wide and deeply laid. It is now easy to see the conditions and the causes of her success. The conditions are, the new continent, a virgin soil to receive the seed of liberty; the causes were, first, the character of the tribe, and next, the liberal institutions founded thereby.

The rapid increase of America in most of the elements of national power, is a remarkable fact in the history of mankind.

Look at the increase of numbers. In 1689, the entire population of the English colonies, exclusive of the Indians, amounted to about 200,000. Twen-

ty-five years later there were 434,000, now 24,000,-
000.*

The present population of the United States con-

* *Table of Population in 1715.*

Colonies.	Whites.	Negroes.	Total.
New Hampshire	9,500	150	9,650
Massachusetts	94,000	2,000	96,000
Rhode Island	8,500	500	9,000
Connecticut	46,000	1,500	47,500
New York	27,000	4,000	31,000
New Jersey	21,000	1,500	22,500
Pennsylvania and Delaware	43,300	2,500	45,800
Maryland	40,700	9,500	50,200
Virginia	72,000	23,000	95,000
North Carolina	7,500	3,700	11,200
South Carolina	6,250	10,500	16,750
	375,750	58,850	134,600

In 1754, another return was made to the Board of Trade, in
the following:

Table of Population in 1754.

Whites.	Blacks.	Total.
1,192,896	292,738	1,485,634

We will now give the population at seven successive periods,
as indicated by the returns of the official census of the United
States.

Table of Population from 1790 to 1850.

Years.	Whites.	Free Colored.	Slaves.	Total.
1790	3,172,464	59,466	697,897	3,929,827
1800	4,304,489	108,395	893,041	5,305,925
1810	5,862,004	186,446	1,191,364	7,239,814
1820	7,872,711	238,197	1,543,688	9,654,596
1830	10,537,378	319,599	2,009,043	12,866,020
1840	14,189,555	386,348	2,487,355	17,069,453
1850	19,630,738	428,661	3,198,324	23,257,723

sists of the following ingredients. The numbers are conjectural and approximate:

Table of Nationality.

White Immigrants since 1790, and their white descendants	4,350,934
Africans, and their descendants	3,626,585
White Immigrants previous to 1790, and their white descendants	15,279,804

This does not include the Indians living within the territories and States of the Union. These facts show that a remarkable mingling of families of the Cau-

---

The following is the official report of immigration from 1790 to 1850. Much of it is conjectural and approximate.

Table of Immigration from 1790 to 1850.

From 1790 to 1800	120,000
From 1810 to 1820	114,000
From 1820 to 1830	203,979
From 1830 to 1840	778,500
From 1840 to 1850	1,542,840
	2,759,329

The immigrants are thus conjecturally distributed among the nations of the earth. The estimate is a rough one.

Table of Nationality.

Celtic — Irish (one-half)	1,350,000
Teutonic — Germans, Danes, Swedes, etc. (one-fourth)	675,000
Miscellaneous — All other nations	734,329

The following statement exhibits the nationality of the immigration to the United States for the calendar year, 1851 (Dec. 31, 1850, to Dec. 31, 1851):—

Nationality of Immigrants in 1851.

From Great Britain and Ireland	264,222
From Germany	72,283
From France	20,107
Of these there were Males	245,017
Of these there were Females	163,745
Of these there were Unknown	66

casian stock is taking place. The exact statistics
would disclose a yet more remarkable mingling of the
Caucasian and the Ethiopian races going on. The
Africans are rapidly " bleaching " under the influence of democratic chemistry. If only one-tenth of
the colored population has Caucasian blood in its veins,
then there are 362,698 descendants of this " amalga-
mation "; but if you estimate these *hybrids* as one in
five, which is not at all excessive, we have then 725,-
397.

The thirty-one States now organized have a surface of 1,485,870 square miles, while the total area
of the United States, so far as I have information,
on the 17th of May, 1853, was 3,220,000 square miles.
In the States, on an average, there are not sixteen
persons to the square mile; in the whole territory,
not eight to a mile. Massachusetts, the most densely
peopled State, has more than one hundred and twenty-
six to the mile, while Texas has but eighty-nine men
for a hundred miles of land, more than eight hundred acres to each human soul.

In 1840, there were ten States, whose united populations exceeded 4,000,000, which yet had no town
with 10,000 inhabitants.*

Table of Immigration for the first four months of 1853.

From the British Islands	15,023
From the French Ports	8,768
From the German Ports	3,511
From the Belgian and Dutch	2,747
From the Spanish, Portuguese, and Italian	135

* The following table shows the occupation of 4,798,870 persons in 1840, ascertained by the census: —

Table of Occupation.

Engaged in Mining	15,211
Engaged in Agriculture	3,719,951

Look next at the products of industry in the United States.*

The contrast between the Spanish and the Anglo-Saxon settlements in America is amazing. A hun-

Engaged in Commerce	117,607
Engaged in Manufactures	791,749
Engaged in Navigation (Ocean)	56,021
Engaged in Navigation (Inland Waters)	33,076
Engaged in Learned Professions	65,255

* I take these results of the census of 1840, as deduced by Professor Tucker, in his admirable book, *Progress of the United States in Population and Wealth in Fifty Years.* New York, 1843. 1 vol. 8vo.

Value of Annual Products of Industry, 1840.

Agriculture	$654,387,597
Manufactures	236,836,224
Commerce	79,721,086
Mining	42,358,761
The Forest	16,835,060
The Ocean	11,996,108

Total $1,063,134,736

In 1850, the iron-crop in the United States amounted to 564,755 tons. The ship-crop was 1360 vessels, with a measurement of 272,218 tons. The increase of American shipping is worth notice, and is shown in the following:

Table of American Tonnage from 1815 to 1850.

Years.	Tons.
1815	1,368,127
1820	1,280,165
1825	1,423,110
1830	1,181,986
1835	1,824,939
1840	2,180,763
1845	2,417,001
1850	3,535,454

The tonnage is still on the increase. In 1851 it amounted to 3,772,439, and at this moment must be considerably more than 4,000,000. The first ship built in New England was the " Blessing

dred years ago, Spain, the discoverer of America, had undisputed sway over all South America, except Brazil and the Guianas. All Mexico was hers — all Central America, California unbounded on the north, extending indefinitely, Louisiana, Florida, Cuba, Porto Rico, and part of Hayti. She ruled a population of twenty million men. Now Cuba trembles in her faltering hand; all the rest has dropped from the arms of that feeble mother of feeble sons. In 1750 her American colonies extended from Patagonia to Oregon. The La Plata was too far north for her southern limit, the Columbia too far south for her north-

---

of the Bay," a "bark of thirty tons," launched in 1634. Not far from the spot where her keel was laid, a ship has recently been built, three hundred and ten feet long, and more than six thousand tons burden.

On the 30th September, 1851, there were, if the accounts are reliable, 12,805 miles of railroad in the United States. At present, there are probably about 15,000 miles.

The most important articles of export for five-and-twenty years appear in the following:

Table of the chief articles of Export from 1825 to 1850.

Years.	Cotton.	Breadstuffs and Provisions.	Tobacco.
1825	$36,846,649	$11,634,449	$6,115,623
1830	29,674,883	12,075,430	5,586,365
1835	64,961,302	12,009,399	8,250,577
1840	63,870,307	19,067,535	9,883,957
1845	51,739,643	16,743,421	7,469,819
1850	71,484,616	26,051,373	9,951,023
1852	87,965,732	25,857,177	10,031,283

The greatest amount of cotton was exported in 1852,— 1,093,-230,639 pounds; but the greatest value of cotton was in 1851, amounting to $112,351,317. In 1847, the value of breadstuffs and provisions exported was $68,701,921.

The government revenues for the fiscal year 1852 were $49,-728,386.89; there was a balance in the treasury of $10,911,645.68; making the total means for that year $60,640,032.57. On the 1st January, 1853, the national debt amounted to $65,131,692.

ern bound. The Mississippi and the Amazon were
Spanish rivers, and emptied the waters of a continent
into the lap of America, the Mexique Gulf, which
was also a Spanish sea. But Spain allowed only
eight-and-thirty vessels to ply between the mother
country and the family of American daughters on
both sides of the continent. The empire of Spain,
mother country and colonies, extending from Bar-
celona to Manila, with more sea-coast than the whole
continent of Africa, employed but sixteen thousand
sailors in her commercial marine. Portugal forbade
Brazil to cultivate any of the products of the Indies.

Look at this day at Anglo-Saxon, and then at Spanish America. In 1606 there was not an English settlement in America. In 1627 only two, Jamestown
and Plymouth. But the Spanish colonies date back
to 1493. Compare the history of the basin of the
Amazon with the valley of the Mississippi. The
Amazon, with its affluents, commands seventy thousand miles of internal navigation, draining more ara-
ble land than all Europe contains, the largest, the
most fertile valley in the world. It includes 1,796,-
000 square miles. Everything which finds a home
on earth will flourish in the basin of the Amazon,
between the level of the Atlantic and the top of the
Andes. But the tonnage on the Amazon does not
probably equal the tonnage on Lake Champlain.
Only an Anglo-Saxon steamer ruffles the waters of the
Amazon. Pará, at its mouth, more than three hundred years old, contains less than 20,000 inhabitants.

The Mississippi with its tributaries drains 982,000
square miles, and affords 16,694 miles of steam navigation. In 1851 there were 1,190 steamboats on its
bosom, measuring 249,054 tons, running at an an-

nual cost of $39,774,194; the value of the merchandise carried on the river in 1852 was estimated at $432,651,240, more than double the whole foreign trade of the United States for that year. New Orleans, at the mouth of the Mississippi, was founded in 1719, and in 1850 contained 119,461 inhabitants; in 1810 it had not 18,000!

The Anglo-Saxon colonists brought with them the vigorous bodies and sturdy intellect of their race; the forms of representative and constitutional government; publicity of political transactions; trial by jury; a fondness for local self-government; an aversion to centralization; the Protestant form of religion; the Bible; the right of private judgment; their national administrative power; and that stalwart self-reliance and thrift which mark the Englishman and American wherever they go. New Spain had priests and soldiers; New England, ministers and school-masters. In two centuries, behold what consequences come of such causes!

But America itself is not unitary; there is a Spanish America in the United States. Unity of idea and interest by no means prevails here.

America was settled by two very different classes of men, one animated by moral or religious motives, coming to realize an idea; the other animated by only commercial ideas, pushing forth to make a fortune or to escape from jail. Some men brought religion, others only ambition; the consequence is, two antagonistic ideas, with institutions which correspond, antagonistic institutions.

First there is the democratic idea: that all men are endowed by their Creator with certain natural rights; that these rights are alienable only by the possessor thereof; that they are equal in all men; that government is to organize these natural, inalienable, and equal rights into institutions designed for the good of the governed; and therefore government is to be of all the people, by all the people, and for all the people. Here government is development, not exploitation.

Next there is the oligarchic idea, just the opposite of this; that there is no such thing as natural, inalienable, and equal rights, but accidental, alienable, and unequal powers; that government is to organize the might of all, for the good of the governing party; is to be a government of all, by a part, and for the sake of a part. The governing power may be one man, King Monarch; a few men, King Noble; or the majority, King Many. In all these cases, the motive, the purpose, and the means, are still the same, and government is exploitation of the governed, not the development thereof. So far as the people are developed by the government, it is that they may be thereby exploitered.

Neither the democratic nor the oligarchic idea is perfectly developed as yet: but the first preponderates most at the North, the latter at the South — one in the free, the other in the slave States.

The settlers did not bring to America the democratic idea fully grown. It is the child of time. In all great movements there are three periods — first, that of sentiment — there is only a feeling of the new thing; next of idea — the feeling has become a thought; finally of action — the thought becomes a thing. It is pleasant to trace the growth of the democratic sentiment and idea in the human race, to watch the efforts to make the thought a thing, and found domestic, social, ecclesiastical, and political institutions corresponding thereto. Perhaps it is easier to trace this here than elsewhere. It has sometimes been claimed that the Puritans came to America to found such institutions. But they had no fondness for a democracy; the thought did not enter their heads that the substance of man is superior to the accidents of men, his nature more than his history. New England men on the 4th of July claim the compact on board the Mayflower, as the foundation of democracy in America, and of the Declaration of Independence. But the signers of that famous document had no design to found a democracy. Much of the liberality of the settlers at Plymouth seems to have been acquired by their residence in Holland, where they saw the noblest example of religious toleration then in the world.

The democratic idea has had but a slow and gradual growth, even in New England. The first form of government was a theocracy, an intense tyranny in the name of God. The next world was for the "elect" said Puritan theology; "let us also have this," said the elect. The distinction between clerical and laical was nowhere more prominent than in puritan New England. The road to the ballot-box lay under the pulpit; only church-members could vote, and if a man's politics were not marked with the proper stripe it was not easy for him to become a church-member. The "Lords Brethren" were as tyrannical in the New World as the "Lords Bishops" in the Old.

There was a distinction between "gentlemen," with the title of *Mr.*, and men with only the name, *John, Peter*, and *Bartholomew*, or the title "*Goodman.*"

Slavery was established in the New World; there were two forms of it — absolute bondage of the Africans and the Indians; the conditional bondage of white men, called " servants," slaves for a limited period. Before the Revolution the latter were numerous, even in the North.

The Puritan had little religious objection to the establishment of slavery. But the red man would fight, and would not work. It was not possible to make useful slaves of Indians: the experiment was tried; it failed, and the savage was simply destroyed.

In theocratic and colonial times at the North, the democratic idea contended against the Church; and gradually weakened and overcame the power of the clergy and of all ecclesiastical corporations. At length all churches stand on the same level. The persecuted Quaker has vindicated his right to free inspiration by the Holy Ghost; the Baptist enjoys the natural right to be baptized after the apostolic fashion; the Unitarian to deny the Holy Trinity; the Universalist to affirm the eternal blessedness of all men; and the philosophical critic to examine the claims of Christianity as of all religions, to sweep the whole ocean of religious consciousness, draw his net to land, gather the good into vessels, and cast the bad away.

The spirit of freedom contended against the claims of ancestral gentility. In the woods of New England it was soon found that a pair of arms was worth more than a coat of arms, never so old and horrid with griffins. A man who could outwit the Indians, " whip his weight in wild cats," hew down trees, build ships, make wise laws, and organize a river into a mill, or men into towns and States, was a valuable person; and if born at all was well born. Men of

no family grew up in the new soil, and often over-
topped the twigs cut from some famous tree. In
the humblest callings of life I have found men of
the most eminent European stocks. But it was rare
that men of celebrated families settled in America;
monarchy, nobility, prelacy did not emigrate, it was
the people who came over. And in 1780, the Convention of Massachusetts put this in the first Article
of the Constitution of the State: " All men are born
free and equal, and have certain natural, essential, and
inalienable rights." All distinction of gentle and simple, bond and free, perished out of Massachusetts.
The same thought is repeated in the constitutions of
many Northern States.

This spirit of freedom contended against the
claims of England. Local self-government was the
aim of the colonies. Opposition to centralization of
authority is very old in America. I hope it will be
always young. England was a hard master to her
western children; she left them to fight their own battles against the Indians, against the French; and
this circumstance made all men soldiers. In King
Philip's War every man capable of bearing arms took
the field, first or last. The frontier was a school for
soldiers. The day after the battle of Lexington, a
hundred and fifty men, in a large farming town of
New Hampshire, shouldered their muskets and
marched for Boston, to look after their brethren.

It was long before there was a clear and distinct
expression of the democratic idea in America. The
Old Testament helped it to forms of denunciatory
speech. The works of Milton, Sidney, Locke, and
the writers on the law of nature and of nations, were
of great service. Rousseau came at the right time, and

aided the good cause. Calvin and Rousseau, strange
to say, fought side by side in the battle for freedom.
It was a great thing for America and the world, that
this idea was so clearly set forth in the Declaration
of Independence, announced as a self-evident truth.
A young man's hand came out of the wall, and wrote
words which still make many tremble as they read.

The battle for human freedom yet goes on; its
victory is never complete. But now in the free States
of the North the fight is against all traditional forms
of evil. The domestic question relates to the equal
rights of men and women in the family and out of it;
there is a great social question, — " Shall money
prevail over man, and the rich and crafty exploiter
the poor and the simple? " In the Church, men ask
— " Shall authority — a book or an institution, each
an accident of human history — prevail over reason,
conscience, the affections, and the soul — the human
substance? " In the State, the minority looks for
the eternal principles of right; and will not heed the
bidding of famous men, of conventions, and majorities; appeals to the still, small voice within, which
proclaims the higher law of God. Even in the North
a great contest goes on.

The democratic idea seems likely to triumph in
the North, and build up its appropriate institutions —
a family without a slave, a family of equals; a community without a lord, a community of co-operators;
a Church without a bishop, a Church of brethren;
a State without a king, a State of citizens.

The institutions of the free States are admirably
suited to produce a rapid development of the understanding. The State guarantees the opportunity of
education to all children. The free schools of the

North are her most original institution, quite imperfect as yet.   The attempts to promote the public education of the people have already produced most
gratifying results.

More than half of the newspaper editors in the
United States have received all their academical education in the common school.   Many a Methodist and
Universalist minister, many a member of Congress,
has been graduated at that beneficent institution.
The intelligence and riches of the North are due to
the common schools.   In the free States books are
abundant; newspapers in all hands; skilled labor
abounds.   Body runs to brain, and work to thought.
The head saves the hands.   Under the benignant influence of public education, the children of the Irish
emigrant, poor and despised, grow up to equality with
the descendants of the rich; two generations will ef-
face the difference between them.   I have seen, of a
Sunday afternoon, a thousand young Irish women,
coming out of a Catholic church, all well dressed, with
ribbons and cheap ornaments, to help elevate their
self-respect; and when remembering the condition of
these same women in their native land, barefoot, dirty,
mendicant, perhaps thievish, glad of a place to serve
at two pounds a year, I have begun to see the importance of America to the world; and have felt as John
Adams, when he wrote in his diary, " I always consider the settlement of America with reverence and
wonder, as the opening of a grand scene and design
of Providence, for the illumination of the ignorant,
and the emancipation of the slavish part of mankind, all over the earth."

The educational value of American institutions, in
the free States is seldom appreciated.   The schools

open to all, where all classes of the people freely mingle, and the son of a rude man is brought into contact with the good manners and self-respectful deportment of children from more fortunate homes; the churches, where everybody is welcome (if not black); the business which demands intelligence, and educates the great mass of the people; the public lectures, delivered in all the considerable towns of New England, the winter through; the newspapers abundant, cheap, discussing everything with as little reserve as the summer wind; the various social meetings of incorporated companies to discuss their affairs; the constitution of the towns, with their meetings, two or three times a year, when officers are chosen, and taxes voted, and all municipal affairs abundantly discussed; the public proceedings of the courts of law, so instructive to jurors and spectators; the local legislatures of the States — each consisting of from two to four hundred members, and in session four or five months of the year; the politics of the nation brought home to every voter in the land — all these things form an educational power of immense value, for such a development of the lower intellectual faculties, as men esteem most in these days.

But the oligarchic idea is also at work. You meet this in all parts of the land, diligently seeking to organize itself. It takes no new forms, however, which are peculiar to America. It re-enacts the old statutes which have oppressed mankind in the eastern world; it attempts to revive the institutions that have cursed other lands in darker days. Now the few tyrannize over the many, and devise machinery to oppress their fellow-mortals; then the majority thus tyrannize over the few, over the minority. There are two forms of democracy — the satanic and the celestial: one is selfishness, which knows no higher law; the other philanthropy, that bows to the justice of the Infinite God, with " Thy will be done." In America we find both — the democratic devil and the democratic angel.

The idea of the North is preponderatingly democratic in the better sense of the word; new justice is organized in the laws; government becomes more and more of all, by all, and for all. You trace the progress of humanity, of liberty, equality, and fraternity in the constitution of the free States from Massachusetts to Wisconsin.

But in the Southern States the oligarchic idea prevails to a much greater extent, and becomes more and more apparent and powerful. The South has adopted the institution of slavery, elsewhere discarded, and clings to it with strange tenacity. In South Carolina the possession of slaves is made the condition, *sine quâ non*, of eligibility to certain offices. The constitution provides that a citizen shall not " be eligible to a seat in the House of Representatives, *unless legally seized and possessed in his own right*, of a settled freehold estate of five hundred acres of land, and *ten negroes*." *

The Puritans of New England made no very strong objection to slavery. It was established in all the colonies of the North and South. White servitude continued till the Revolution. As late as 1757, white men were kidnapped, " spirited away," as it was called in Scotland, and sold in the colonies.

Negro slavery began early. Even the gentler

* Art. I, § 6.

Puritans at Plymouth had the Anglo-Saxon antipathy
to the colored race.   The black man must sit aloof from
the whites in the meeting-house, in a negro pew; he
must " not be joined unto them in burial; " a place
was set apart in the graveyard at Plymouth, for
colored people, and still remains as from time imme-
morial.   In 1851, an abolitionist, before his death,
insisted on being buried with the objects of his tender solicitude.   The request was complied with.

After the Revolution, the Northern States gradually abolished slavery, though not without violent
opposition in some places.   In 1788 three colored
persons were kidnapped at Boston and carried to the
West Indies; the crime produced a great excitement,
and led to executive and legislative action.   The same
year, the General Presbyterian Assembly of America
issued a pastoral letter, recommending " the abolition
of slavery, and the instruction of the negroes in letters and religion."   In 1790, Dr. Franklin, president of the " Pennsylvania Society for the Abolition
of Slavery," signed a memorial to Congress, asking
that body " to countenance the restoration of liberty
to the unhappy men who alone in this land of freedom are degraded into perpetual bondage, and who,
amid the general joy of surrounding provinces, are
groaning in servile subjection; that you will devise
means for removing this inconsistency from the character of the American people; that you will permit
mercy and justice towards this distressed race; and
that you will step to the very verge of the power
vested in you for discouraging every species of traffic in the persons of our fellow-men."

The memorial excited a storm of debate.   Slavery
was defended as a measure of political economy, and a

principle of humanity, South Carolina leading in the defense of her favorite institution. Yet many eminent Southern men were profoundly convinced of the injustice of slavery; others saw it was a bad tool to work with.

Since that time the Southern idea of slavery appears to have changed. Formerly, it was granted by the defenders of slavery that it was wrong; but they maintained: 1. That Americans were not responsible for the wrong, as England had imposed it upon the colonies. 2. That it was profitable to the owners of slaves. 3. That it was impossible to get rid of it. Now the ground is taken that slavery is not a wrong to the slave, but that the negro is fit for a slave, and a slave only.

I pass by the arguments of the Southern clergy and the Northern clergy — whose conduct is yet more contemptible — to cite the language of the prominent secular organs of the South. The *Richmond Examiner*, one of the most able journals of the South, declares: —

" When we deprive the negro of that exercise of his will which the white calls liberty, we deprive him of nothing; on the contrary, when we give him the guidance and protection of a master, we confer on him a great blessing."

" To treat two creatures so utterly different as the white man and the negro man on the same system, is an effort to violate elementary laws." " The aphorisms of the Declaration of Independence " are illogical when applied to the negro. " They involve the assumption that the negro is the white man, only a little different in external appearance and education. But this assumption cannot be supported." " A law rendering perpetual the relation between the negro and his master is no wrong, but a right." " Negroes are not men, in the meaning of the Declaration of Independence."

" ' Haven't negroes got souls?' asks some sepulchral voice. ' Have they no souls?' That question we never answer; we know nothing about it. *Non mi ricordo;* they may have souls, for aught we know to the contrary; so may horses and hogs."

" We expect the institution of slavery to exist for ever." " The production of cotton, rice, sugar, coffee, and tobacco, demands that which slavery only can supply. And in all portions of this Union where these staples are produced, it will be retained. And when we get Hayti, Mexico, and Jamaica, common sense will doubtless extend it, or rather, re-establish it there, too." *

I will now quote a little from the Mr. De Bow's large work: —

" No amount of education or training can ever render the negro equal in intellect with the white." " ' You cannot make a silk purse out of a sow's lug,' is an old and homely adage, but not the less true; so you cannot make anything from a negro but negroism, which means barbarism and inferiority." " As God made them so they have been, and so they will be; the white man, the negro, and the jackass; each to his kind, and each to his nature; true to the finger of destiny (which is the finger of God), and undeviatingly pursuing the track which that finger as undeviatingly points out."

" Is the negro made for slavery? God in heaven! what are we, that because we cannot understand the

* Richmond (Va.) *Semi-weekly Examiner,* January 4, 1853.

mystery of this Thy will, we should dare rise in rebellion, and call it wrong, unjust, and evil? The kindness of nature fits each creature to fulfil its destiny. The very virtues of the negro fit him for slavery, and his vices cry aloud for the shackles of bondage!" "It is the destiny of the negro, if by himself, to be a savage; if by the white, to be a serf." "They may be styled human beings, though of an inherently degraded species. To attempt to relieve them from their natural inferiority is idle in itself, and may be mischievous in its results."

"Equality is no thought nor creation of God. Slavery, under one name or another, will exist as long as man exists; and abolition is a dream whose execution is an impossibility. Intellect is the only divine right. The negro cannot be schooled, nor argued, nor driven into a love of freedom."

"Alas for their folly! (the abolitionists.) But woe! woe! a woe of darkness and of death, a woe of hell and perdition to those who, better knowing, goad folly on to such an extreme. This is, indeed, the sin not to be forgiven; the sin against the Holy Ghost, and against the Spirit of God! The beautiful order of creation breathed down from Almighty intelligence, is to be molded and wrought by fanatic intelligence, until dragged down, at last, to negro intelligence!"

Chancellor Harper, of South Carolina, in an address delivered before "The Society for the Advancement of Learning," at Charleston, makes some statements a little remarkable: —

"The institution of slavery is a principle cause of civilization." "It is as much the order of nature that men should enslave each other, as that other animals should prey upon each other." "The savage

can only be tamed by being enslaved or by having
slaves." "The African slave-trade has given and
will give the boon of existence to millions and millions in our country who would otherwise never have
enjoyed it."

He quotes the Bible to justify slavery: —

"'They shall be your bondmen for ever.'"
"Servitude is the condition of civilization. It was
decreed when the command was given, 'Be fruitful
and multiply, and replenish the earth and subdue it;'
and when it was added 'In the sweat of thy face
shalt thou eat bread.'" Slavery was "forced on us
by necessity, and further forced upon us by the superior authority of the mother country. I, for one,
neither deprecate nor resent the gift." "I am by no
means sure that the cause of humanity has been served
by the change in jurisprudence which has placed their
murder on the same footing with that of a freeman."
"The relation of master and slave is naturally one
of kindness." "It is true that the slave is driven to
his labor by stripes; such punishment would be degrading to a freeman, who had the thoughts and aspirations of a freeman. In general, it is not degrading to a slave, nor is it felt to be so."

It is alleged that "the slave is cut off from the
means of intellectual, moral, and religious improvement, and in consequence his moral character becomes
depraved, and he addicted to degrading vices." To
this the Democratic chancellor of South Carolina
replies: —

"The Creator did not intend that every individual
human being should be highly cultivated, morally and
intellectually." "It is better that a part should be
highly cultivated, and the rest utterly ignorant."

" Odium has been cast upon our legislation on account of its forbidding the elements of education to be communicated to slaves. But, in truth, what injury is done them by this? He who works during the day with his hands does not read in intervals of leisure for his amusement, or the improvement of his mind." " Of the many slaves whom I have known capable of reading, I have never known one to read anything but the Bible, and this task they imposed on themselves as matter of duty." " Their minds generally show a strong religious tendency, . . . and perhaps their religious notions are not much more extravagant than those of a large portion of the free population of our country." " It is certainly the master's interest that they should have proper religious sentiments."

" A knowledge of reading, writing, and the elements of arithmetic, is convenient and important to the free laborer . . . but of what use would they be to the slave? " " Would you do a benefit to the horse or the ox by giving him a cultivated understanding or fine feelings? " *

" The law has not provided for making those marriages [of slaves] indissoluble; nor could it do so." " It may perhaps be said, that ' the chastity of wives is not protected by law from the outrages of violence.' " " Who ever heard of such outrages being offered? . . . One reason, doubtless, may be that often there is no disposition to resist, . . . there is little temptation to this violence as there is so large a population of this class of females [slave wives] who set little value on chastity." " It is true that in this respect the morals of this class are very loose, . . .

* De Bow, vol. ii, p. 217, et seq.

and that the passions of the men of the superior caste tempt and find gratification in the easy chastity of the females. This is evil, . . . but evil is incident to every condition of society."

"The female slave [who yields to these temptations] is not a less useful member of society than before. . . . She has done no great injury to herself or any other human being; her offspring is not a burden but an acquisition to her owner; his support is provided for, and he is brought up to usefulness; if the fruit of intercourse with a free man, his condition is perhaps raised somewhat above that of his mother."

" I do not hesitate to say, that the intercourse which takes place with enslaved females is less debasing in its effects [on man] than when it is carried on with females of their own caste, . . . the attraction is less, . . . the intercourse is generally casual, . . . he is less liable to those extraordinary fascinations."

" He [the slave husband] is also liable to be separated from wife or child, . . . but from native character and temperament, the separation is much less severely felt."

" The love of liberty is a noble passion. But, alas! it is one in which we know that a large portion of the human race can never be gratified." " If some superior power should impose on the laborious poor of this, or any other country, this ['a condition which is a very near approach to that of our slaves'] as their undeniable condition, . . . how inappreciable would the boon be thought." "The evils of their situation they [the slaves] but slightly feel, and would hardly feel at all if they were not sedulously instructed into sensibility." " Is it not desirable that

the inferior laboring class should be made up of such
who will conform to their condition without painful
aspirations and vain struggles? "

" I am aware that, however often assumed, it is
likely to be repeated again and again: — How can
that institution be tolerable, by which a large class of
society is cut off from the hope of improvement and
knowledge; to whom blows are not degrading, theft no
more than a fault, falsehood and the want of chastity
almost venial; and in which a husband or parent looks
with comparative indifference on that which to a free
man would be the dishonor of a wife or child? But why
not, if it produce the greatest aggregate of good?
Sin and ignorance are only evils because they lead to
misery."

" The African negro is an inferior variety of the
human race, . . . and his distinguishing characteristics are such as peculiarly mark him out for the
situation which he occupies among us; . . . the
most remarkable is their indifference to personal liberty." " Let me ask if this people do not present the
very material out of which slaves ought to be made? "
" I do not mean to say that there may not be found
among them some of superior capacity to many white
persons. . . . And why should it not be so? We
have many domestic animals — infinite varieties, distinguished by various degrees of sagacity, courage,
strength, swiftness, and other qualities."

" Slavery has done more to elevate a degraded race
in the scale of humanity; to tame the savage, to civ-
ilize the barbarous, to soften the ferocious, to en-
lighten the ignorant, and to spread the blessing of
Christianity among the heathen, than all the missionaries that philanthropy and religion have ever put

forth." "The tendency of slavery is to elevate the character of the master," "to elevate the female character." "There does not now exist a people in a tropical climate, or even approaching to it, where slavery does not exist that is in a state of high civilization. Mexico and the South American republics, having gone through the farce of abolishing slavery, are rapidly degenerating." "Cuba is daily and rapidly advancing in industry and civilization; and it is owing exclusively to her slaves. San Domingo is struck out of the map of civilized existence, and the British West Indies shortly will be so." "Greece is still barbarous, and scantily peopled." "Such is the picture of Italy — nothing has dealt upon it more heavily than the loss of domestic slavery. Is not this evident?" *

A writer in the same work, speaking of the future of the South, refers to the British and French West Indies as follows: —

"The mind of the devout person who contemplates the condition of the *ci-devant* slave-colonies of these two powers, must become impressed with the fact that Providence must have raised up those two examples of human folly for the express purpose of a lesson to these States, to save which from human errors it has, on more than one occasion, manifestly and directly interposed." "England itself . . . is in some sort the slave of Southern blacks."

"The few articles which are most necessary to modern civilization — sugar, coffee, cotton, and tobacco — are products of compulsory black labor." †

Another writer, whom I take to be a clergyman and

* De Bow, vol. ii, pp. 222–229.
† De Bow, vol. iii, pp. 39, 40.

a Jesuit,* goes so far as to forbid all sympathy for the sufferings of slaves: —

"Sympathy for them could do them no good, because a relief from slavery could not elevate them — could do them no good, but an injury. Hence such sympathy is forbidden;" meaning it is forbidden by God, in such passages as this: "Thine eye shall not pity him" (Deut. xix, 13). He maintains that African slavery is a punishment divinely inflicted on the descendants of Ham for his offense. Ham, he thinks, married a descendant of Cain, and his children inherited the "mark" set upon the first murderer!

Let us now look at some facts connected with slavery in America.

No nation has, on the whole, treated its African slaves so gently as the Americans. This is proved by the rapid increase of the slave population. Compare America in this respect with some of the British West Indies.

In seventy-three years, from 1702 to 1775, the increase of the colored population of Jamaica was 158,614; but in that period there were imported and retained in the island, 360,622; so the slave-owners in seventy-three years must have used up and destroyed about 300,000 human beings. This dreadful exploitation continued a long time. From 1775 to 1794, about 113,000 more were imported; but in 1791 there were only 260,000 colored persons in Jamaica. In sixteen years, the loss was more than 47,000 greater than the entire importation. To say it all in a word: in 1702, Jamaica started with 36,000 slaves; up to 1791, she had imported and retained in

* "John Fletcher of Louisiana," in his *Studies on Slavery in*
(119) *Easy Lessons.* Natchez, 1852. 8vo. pp. xiv, and 637.

bondage 473,000 more; making a total of 509,000 souls, and in 1791, she had only 260,000 to show as the result of her traffic in human souls. There was a waste of 249,000 lives!

About 750,000 slaves were imported into Jamaica between 1650 and 1808. If that number seems excessive, diminish it to 700,000, which is certainly below the fact; then add all the children born in the one hundred and eighty-four years which elapsed before the day of emancipation came. Remember that only 311,000 were there to be emancipated in 1834, and it is plain what a dreadful massacre of human life had been going on in that garden of the western world.*

About 1,700,000 slaves have been imported into the British West Indies. Of all this number, and the vast families of children born thereof, in 1834 there were only 780,993 to be emancipated.

Look at the course of things in the United States. In 1714 the number of colored persons was 58,850; in 1850, 3,626,985.

The United States can show ten Africans now living for every one brought into the country, while the

---

* The same thing took place in all the British West Indies. Look at the following:

Table of Slave Population of British Guiana.

Number in 1820	77,376
Number in 1826	71,382
Number in 1832	65,517
Loss in twelve years	11,859

Table of Births and Deaths.

Years.	Registered Births.	Registered Deaths.
1817 to 1820	4868	7140
1820 to 1823	4512	7188
1823 to 1826	4494	7634
1826 to 1829	4684	5731
1829 to 1832	4086	7016

British West Indies, in 1834, could not show one living man for each two brought thither as slaves.*

A Texan newspaper, the *Columbian Planter*, of April 5, 1853, deprecates all discussion of slavery, and thus speaks of the slave code of that State: — " We consider it the duty of the county court to have these local laws compiled and printed in a cheap form, and a copy placed on each plantation in the county.   But

* The above facts, and the authorities for them, are taken from a valuable and readable book, by H. C. Carey, " The Slave Trade, Domestic and Foreign; why it exists, and how it may be extinguished." Philadelphia, 1853. 1 vol. 12mo., pp. 426. Another work, by M. Charles Comte, contains much information relative to slavery, and its effects in ancient and modern times: — *Traité de Législation ou Exposition des Lois Générales suivant lesquelles les Peuples prospèrent, deperissent, ou restent stationaires*, etc. (3me Edition. Bruxelles, 1837.) Livre v.

In De Bow, vol. ii, p. 340, *et seq.*, is a statement of the importation of slaves to Charleston, from 1804 to 1807, whence I construct the following:

Table of South Carolina Slave-Trade 1804–1807.

70 vessels owned in England............brought	19,649	slaves.
3 vessels owned in France..............brought	1,078	slaves.
61 vessels owned in Charleston..........brought	7,723	slaves.
59 vessels owned in Rhode Island.......brought	8,238	slaves.
4 vessels owned in Baltimore...........brought	750	slaves.
3 vessels owned in other Southern Ports.brought	787	slaves.
3 vessels owned in other Northern Ports.brought	650	slaves.
	39,075	slaves.

Of these, 3433 were imported on account of citizens of the slaveholding States, and 35,642 on account of capitalists in countries where slavery was prohibited! Newport, in **Rhode Island**, was famous for the slave-trade, and its prosperity fell with that business. The cost of paving the only street in the town paved with stone was defrayed by a tax of ten dollars on each slave brought into the harbor. So late as 1850, Boston vessels were engaged in the African slave-trade. The domestic slave-trade still employs many northern vessels,— 1033 slaves were shipped at Baltimore, for various southern ports, in 1851.

we cannot, with what we consider the true policy and interest of the South, open the columns of the *Planter* for their publication."

"We regard the institution of domestic slavery as purely a local subject, which should lie at the feet of the Southern press with deathlike silence; for its great importance will not admit of its discussion."

I will mention three cases of cruelty which have lately come to my knowledge. A black free man, in a city of Kentucky, had a wife who was a slave. One evening her master, who had a grudge against the husband, found him in the kitchen with her, and ordered him out of the house. He went, but left the gate of the back yard open as he passed out. The white man ordered him to return and shut it; the black man grumbled and refused; whereupon the white man shot him dead! The murderer was a " class leader " in the church, and attended a meeting shortly after this transaction. He was asked to " comfort the souls of the meeting, and improve his gift " by some words of exhortation. He declined on the ground that he felt dissatisfied with himself, that he himself " needed to be strengthened, and wished for the prayers of the brethren." They appointed a committee to look into the matter, who reported that he had done nothing wrong. The affair was also brought before a magistrate, who dismissed the case!

Here is another, yet more atrocious. A slaveholder in South Carolina had inflicted a brutal and odious mutilation, which cannot be named, on two male slaves for some offense. Last year the master attempted to inflict the same barbarity upon a third slave. He ordered another black man to help bind the victim. The slave, struggling against them both, seized a knife, killed the master, and then took his own life. The neighbors came together, ascertained the facts, and hung up the slave's dead body at the next four corners, as a terror to the colored people of the place! No account of it was published in the newspapers. Slavery "should lie at the feet of the Southern press with deathlike silence!"

While writing this address I receive intelligence of a slave women recently whipped to death in Missouri. An incautious German, who had not been long enough in the country to become converted to American Christianity, and so callous to such things, published an account of the transaction in a German newspaper. The murderers were not punished.*

---

* The following advertisement is taken from a newspaper published in Wilmington (North Carolina), in March, 1853. Nothing in Mrs. Stowe's work is so atrocious; for American fiction halts this side of the American fact: —

225 DOLLARS REWARD.— State of North Carolina, New Hanover County.— Whereas, complaint upon oath has this day been made to us, two of the Justices of the Peace for the State and county aforesaid, by Benjamin Hallett, of the said county, that two certain male slaves belonging to him, named Lott, aged about twenty-two years, five feet four or five inches high, and black, formerly belonging to Lott Williams, of Onslow Co.; and Bob, aged about sixteen years, five feet high, and black, have absented themselves from their said master's service, and supposed to be lurking about this county, committing acts of felony and other misdeeds. These are, therefore, in the name of the State aforesaid, to command the said slaves forthwith to return home to their masters; and we do hereby, by virtue of the Act of the General Assembly in such cases made and provided, intimate and declare, that if the said Lott and Bob do not return home and surrender themselves, any person may kill and destroy the said slaves, by such means as he or they may think of, without accusation or impeachment of any crime or offense for so doing, and without incurring

I will next proceed to show some of the effects of democracy at the North, and despotism at the South.

First notice the effect on the increase of population. In 1790, the entire population of the territory now occupied by the slave States was 1,961,372 exclusive of Indians; that of the free States was 1,968,455.

In 1850, with an addition of immense territories — Florida, Louisiana, Texas, New Mexico — the population of the slave States amounted to 9,719,779; the free States and territories, not including Oregon and California, had 13,348,371 souls. The population of the free States has increased about six hundred per cent., that of the slave only about four hundred per cent.

Let us compare a free and a slave State which lie side by side. In soil and climate Kentucky is superior to Ohio — only the stream separates them. Slavery is on one side, freedom on the other; and what a difference!

Kentucky contains 37,680 square miles. It is well watered with navigable rivers — the Ohio, Cumberland, Kentucky, Green, and Salt. The soil is admirable, producing abundantly; the climate mild and salubrious. It abounds in minerals — coal, iron, lead. The salt springs were famous even with the French and Indians. Rice, cotton, and the sugar-cane grow in Kentucky.

any penalty or forfeiture thereby.

Given under our hands and seals, this 28th day of February, 1853.

W. N. PEDEN, J. P.   [seal.]

W. C. BETTENCOURT, J. P.   [seal.]

225 DOLLARS REWARD.— Two hundred dollars will be given for negro Lott, either dead or alive; and twenty-five dollars for Bob's head, delivered to the subscriber in the town of Wilmington.   BENJAMIN HALLETT.

March 2, 1853.

Ohio contains 39,964 square miles of land, no better watered, with a soil not superior, less favored with mineral riches, yet also abounding in iron and coal; the climate is sterner, the water power less copious.

In 1790, Kentucky had 73,077 inhabitants; Ohio not a white man. In 1800, Kentucky had 220,959; Ohio only 45,365. But in 1850, Kentucky had only 982,405; while Ohio had grown to 1,980,427 souls. To-day, Kentucky has not 775,000 freemen, while Ohio has more than 2,000,000.

In 1810, Louisville, the capital of Kentucky, numbered 4,012 persons; Cincinnati, the chief town of Ohio, contained 9,644. Now Louisville has less than 50,000, and Cincinnati more than 150,000; while Cleveland and Columbus, in the same State, have risen from nothing to cities each containing 20,000 inhabitants.

Look next at the effect of these different institutions on the productive industry of the different sections of the land. In the North, labor is respected. In 1845, there were in Boston 19,037 private families; there were 15,744 who kept no servant, and only 1,069 who had more than one. Is Boston poor? In 1854, the property of her citizens, taxable on the spot, is more than $225,000,000.

In 1847, the real property in Boston was valued at $97,764,500 — $45,271,120 more than the value of all the real estate of South Carolina, with her 24,500 square miles of land. South Carolina owns 384,984 slaves; at $400 a head, they would come to $153,993,600. The actual property of the inhabitants of Boston, in 1854, is sufficient to buy all those slaves, and then leave a balance sufficient to pay the market value of all the houses and land in that proud State.

In 1839, the census value of the annual agricultural products of the entire South was $312,380,151; thât of the free States, $342,007,446. Yet the South had an advantage by nature, and 249,780 more persons engaged in agriculture.

The manufactures of the South for that year were worth $42,178,184; of the North, $197,658,040.

The aggregate earnings of all the South were $403,-429,718, of the North, $658,705,108. The entire earnings of the two Carolinas, Georgia, Alabama, Mississippi, and Louisiana, amounted to $189,321,719; those of New York to $193,806,433.

Omitting the territories and California from the estimate, in 1850, the fifteen slave States contained 190,-297,188 acres of land in farms; the fifteen Northern States only 97,087,778 acres. But the Northern farms were worth $283,023,483, while the Southern were valued at only $253,583,234. The South has 93,000,000 acres the most land, and it is worth $30,-000,000 the least.

The South has invested $95,918,842 in manufacturing establishments which give an annual return of $167,906,350: while the North has $431,290,351 in manufactures, with a yearly earning of $845,430,428.

In 1853 the South had 438,297 tons of shipping; at $40 a ton it was worth $17,331,880. The North had 3,831,047 tons, worth $153,241,880.

On the 1st of September, 1852, the South had 2,144 miles of railroad; the North 9,661 miles. The cost of 1,140 miles of railroad in Massachusetts with its equipment was $56,559,982.

In 1850, the aggregate value of all the property real and personal of the fifteen slave States was $2,-755,411,554; that of fifteen free States — omitting

California — was $3,186,683,924. But in the Southern estimate the value of the working men is included; appraising the 3,200,412 at $400 apiece, they come to $1,280,164,800; deduct this from the gross sum and there remains $1,475,246,754 as the worth of all the material property of all the persons in the fifteen slave States; while the inhabitants of the free States have material property amounting to $3,186,683,924.

The different effects of democracy and despotism appear in the higher forms of industry — the inventions which perform the work of human hands. From 1790 to 1849, there were 16,514 patents granted for inventions made in the free States, and only 2,202 in the slave States. I omit patents granted to citizens of the district of Columbia, and to foreigners. In 1851, 64 patents were granted to citizens of the slave States; 656 to those of the free States. Besides, many of the Southern patents are granted to men born and bred at the North.

It is not too much to say, that the machinery of Pennsylvania, New York, and Massachusetts, driven by water and steam, earns every year more than all the 3,000,000 slaves of the entire South. Even Chancellor Harper confesses that " free labor is cheaper than the labor of slaves." The South kidnaps men, breeds them as cattle, brands them as cattle, beats them as cattle, sells them as cattle — does not know " whether they have a soul or not "; declares them cursed by God, not fit for human sympathy, incapable of development, indifferent to liberty, to chastity, without natural affection; breaks up their marriages, forbids them to be taught reading and writing — behold the practical results!

Look at the effect of these two institutions, the democratic and the despotic, on the intellectual education of the people, in the North and South.

In 1839, there were in the slave States, at schools and colleges, 301,172 pupils; in the free States, 2,212,444 pupils at school and college. New York sends, to school and college, more than twice as many young persons as all the slave States.

At that time there were in Connecticut 163,843 free persons over twenty years of age; of these only 526 were unable to read and write. In South Carolina, there were 111,663 free persons over twenty, and of these 20,615 were reported as unable to write or read. The ignorant men of Connecticut were almost all foreigners, those of South Carolina natives of that soil. A sixth part of the voters of South Carolina are unable to read the ballot they cast.

According to the census of 1850, in the year 1849, the South paid $2,717,771 for public schools; the North $6,834,388. The South had 976,966 children at school; the North, 3,106,961.

The South had 2,867,567 native whites over twenty years of age; of these 532,605 were unable even to read — more than eighteen per cent. In the North there were 6,649,001 native whites over twenty, and only 278,575 thus illiterate — not four and one-fourth per cent.

In 1850, there were in the United States 2,800 newspapers and other periodicals, from the daily to the quarterly, issuing annually about 422,700,000 copies, to about 5,000,000 subscribers. Of these journals, 716 were in the slave States — including those printed in the capital of America — and 2,084 in the free States. The circulation of Southern periodicals, however, is limited: their average is not more

than one-half or two-thirds that of the northern journals.

Almost all who are eminent in science, literature, or
art — naturalists, historians, poets, preachers — are
Northern men. The Southern pulpit produces nothing remarkable but evidences of the divinity of
slavery.

The respective military power of the democratic and
despotic institutions was abundantly tested in the Revolutionary War. From 1775 to 1783, the free population of the slave States was 1,307,549; there were
also 657,527 slaves. New England contained 673,-
215 free persons, and 3,886 slaves. During the nine
years of that war, the slave States furnished the continental army with 58,421 regular soldiers; New England alone furnished 118,380 regulars. The slave
States had also 12,719 militia-men, and New England
46,048 militia-men.

After the battle of Bunker Hill, when the States in
Congress were called on to furnish soldiers, South
Carolina, in consequence of her " peculiar institutions," asked that hers might remain at home. In
1779 (March 29th) a committee of Congress reported
that " the State of South Carolina is unable to make
any effectual effort, with militia, by reason of the
great proportion of the citizens necessary to remain at
home, to prevent insurrection among the negroes, and
prevent the desertion of them to the enemy." From
1775 to 1783, South Carolina contained 166,018 free
persons, Connecticut only 158,760. During the nine
years of the war, South Carolina sent 5,508 soldiers to
the army, and Connecticut 39,831. While the six
slave States could raise only 58,421 soldiers, and 12,-
779 militia-men, Massachusetts alone contributed 67,-

937 soldiers to the continental army, and 15,155 militia-men — in all 83,092!

The demoralizing influence of American despotism is fearfully obvious in the conduct of the general government. It debases the legislative and the executive power; the Supreme Court is its venal prostitute. You remember the inaugural of President Pierce: —

" I believe that involuntary servitude is recognized by the Constitution. I believe that it stands like any other admitted right. I hold that the laws of 1850, commonly called the 'compromise measures,' are strictly constitutional, and to be unhesitatingly carried out." "The laws to enforce these [rights to property in the body and soul of men] should be respected and obeyed, not with a reluctance encouraged by abstract opinions as to their propriety in a different state of society, but cheerfully, and according to the decisions of the tribunal to which their exposition belongs."

The effect of slavery on the morality of the North is painful to reflect upon. Northern merchants engage in the internal slave trade; in the foreign slave trade; they own plantations at the South; they lend money to the South, and take slaves as security. The Northern church is red with the guilt of bondage; most of its eminent preachers are deadly enemies to the freedom of the African. How many clerical defenders has the Fugitive Slave Act found in the North? The court-house furnished kidnappers at Philadelphia, New York, and Boston; the church justified them in the name of God. I know of no church which has ever showed itself more cowardly than the American. Since 1849, the Bible Society dares not distribute the Scriptures to slaves. The American Tract Society adapts its publications to the Southern market, by expunging every word hostile to the patriarchal institution. Mr. Gurney says, " If this love had always prevailed among professing Christians, where would have been the sword of the crusader? *Where the African slave-trade? Where the odious system which permits to man a property in his fellow-man, and converts rational beings into marketable chattels?* " The American Tract Society alters the text, and instead of what I have italicized, it prints: " Where the tortures of the Inquisition? Where every system of oppression and wrong by which he who has the power revels in luxury and ease at the expense of his fellow-men! "

In 1850 and 1851, the most prominent preachers in the North came out in public and justified the kidnapping of men in Philadelphia, New York, and Boston. It is true some noble ministers lifted up their voices against it; but the theological leaders went for man-stealing, and knew no higher law.

Commercial and political journals denounced every minister who applied the Golden Rule of the Gospel to the poor fugitives from slavery. Several clergymen were driven from their parishes in Massachusetts, because they preached against kidnapping. Metropolitan newspapers invited merchants to refuse to trade with towns where the Fugitive Slave Bill was unpopular; lawyers and doctors opposed to slavery must not be employed.

Anti-Slavery sentiments are carefully excluded from school-books: the writers want a Southern market. The principal men in the Northern colleges appear to be on the side of oppression. The political and commercial press of the North is mainly on the side of the slaveholder. While preparing this paper

I find in a Northern newspaper (the *Boston Courier*, of April 26, 1853) an advertisement as follows: —

A RARE CHANCE FOR CAPITALISTS!

FOR SALE.

"The Pulaski House, at Savannah, and Furniture, and a number of PRIME NEGROES, accustomed to hotel business," etc.

The advertisement is dated " Savannah, 19*th April.*"

On that day, 1851, Boston landed at Savannah a man whom she had kidnapped in her own streets; on that day, in 1775, a few miles from Boston, a handful of farmers and mechanics first drew the sword of America against the oppressions of her parent, " in the sacred cause of God and their country." Nemesis is never asleep! If men are to be advertised for sale in a Boston newspaper, it is well that the advertisement should date from the battle of Lexington, or the Declaration of Independence.

Last year the State of Illinois passed " An Act to prevent the immigration of free negroes " into that State. A man who brings a free negro or mulatto into the State is to be fined not less than $100, nor more than $500, and to be imprisoned not more than a year. Every negro thus coming, shall be fined fifty dollars, and, if unable to pay, shall be sold to any person " who will pay said fine and costs, for the shortest time." " Every person who shall have one-fourth negro blood shall be deemed a mulatto." Delaware has just passed a similar law, though with penalties less severe.

In the commercial journals of the free and the slave States, the most scandalous abuse has been poured out upon Mrs. Stowe for her " Uncle Tom's Cabin," and its key. " Priestess of Darkness " is one of the pleas-

ant epithets applied to her. The Duchess of Suther-
land receives, also, a large share of abuse from the
same quarter. When the kidnapper is honored; when
" prime negroes " are advertised for sale; when clergymen recommend man-stealing in the name of Christ
and of God, it is very proper that ladies of genius and
philanthropy should be held up as objects of scorn
and contempt! Men who know no law higher than
the Fugitive Slave Bill, must work after their kind.

It is a strange spectacle which America just now
offers. Exiles flee hither, four hundred thousand in a
year, and are welcome; while Americans born take their
lives in their hand, and fly to Canada, to Nova Scotia,
for an asylum. Unsuccessful " rebels," who have
committed " treason " at home, find a shelter in America, a welcome, and the protection of the democratic
government; while 3,300,000 men, guilty of no crime,
are kept in a bondage worse than Siberian. The
" chief judicial officer " of South Carolina thinks of
all " distinguishing characteristics " of the negroes
" the most remarkable is their indifference to personal
liberty." But democratic Calhoun, with Clay, Webster, and all the leaders of the South, must unite to
make the Fugitive Slave Bill, and hinder those men
who are indifferent to personal liberty from running
away! After all the tumult, fifteen hundred fugitives
got safely out of the slave soil of the United States in
the year 1853. Alas, they must escape to the territories of a monarch! Every foot of monarchic
British soil can change a slave to a free man;
while in all the three million square miles of democratic
America, there is not an inch of land where he can
claim the natural and inalienable right to life, liberty,
and the pursuit of happiness. English is the only

tongue for liberty; it is also the only speech in which kidnapping is justified by the clergy in the name of God. The despots of the European continent point with delight to the American democrats enslaving one another, and declaring there is no higher law.

There can be no lasting peace between the two conflicting ideas I have named above. One wants a democracy, the other a despotism; each is incursive, aggressive, exterminating. Which shall yield? The answer is plain: slavery is to perish out of America; democracy is to triumph. Every census makes the result of the two ideas more apparent. The North increases in numbers, in riches, in the intellectual development of the great mass of its people — out of all proportion to the South. Slavery is a bad tool to work with. In the South, there is little skilled labor, little variety of industry; rude farm labor, rearing corn, coffee, tobacco, sugar, cotton, that is all. At Boston, at New York, on the Kennebec, and the Penobscot, Northern men build ships of oak from Virginia, and hard pine from Georgia; they get the pitch and tar from Carolina, the hemp from Kentucky — that State which has no shipping. Labor is cheap on the fair land of the Carolinas, the best in the world for red wheat; labor is dear in Pennsylvania, but she undersells the Carolinas in the wheat market. Tennessee has rich mines of iron ore — the fine bloomer iron; slave labor is cheap, coal abundant. Work is dear in Pennsylvania; but there free labor makes better iron at cheaper rates. The South is full of water power; within six miles of the President's house there is force enough to turn all the mills of British Manchester; it runs by as idle as a cloud. The Southerner draws water in a Northern bucket, drinks from

a Northern cup; with a Northern fork and spoon he
eats from a Northern dish, set on a Northern table.
He wears Northern shoes made from Southern hides;
Northern coats, hats, shirts; he keeps time with a
Northern watch; his wife wears Northern jewels, plays
on a Northern pianoforte; he sleeps in a Northern bed;
reads (if read he can) a Northern book; and writes
(if writing be not a figure of speech) on Northern
paper, with a pen from the North. The laws of Mississippi must be printed in a Northern town! The
Southerner has no market near at hand, no variety of
labor, little that is educational in toil; industry is dis-
honorable. It is the curse of slavery which makes
it so!

Three forces now work against this institution: political economy, showing that it does not pay; the
public opinion of England, France, Germany, of all
Christendom, heaping shame on the " model republic "—" the first and most enlightened nation in the
world; " the still small voice of conscience in all men.
The political economist scoffs at the absolute right;
the partisan politician mocks at the higher law; the
Pharisee in the pulpit makes mouths at the invisible
Spirit, which silently touches the hearts of women and
of men. But he who knows the world because he
knows man, and man's God, understands very well, that
though Justice has feet of wool, her hands are of iron.
These three forces — it is plain what they will do with
American slavery.

This institution of slavery has brought us into most
deadly peril. A story is told of some Italian youths,
of famous family, in the middle ages. Borgia and
his comrades sat riotously feasting, long past midnight, hot with young blood, giddy with passion,

crazed with fiery wine. In their intemperate laughter they hear the hoarse voice of monks in the street, coming round the corner, chanting the *Miserere* as service for the dying, " Have mercy upon me, O God, according to thy loving-kindness!" " What is that? " cries one. " Oh," answers another, " it is only some poor soul going to hell, and the priests are trying to cheat the devil of his due! Push round the wine." Again comes the chant, " For I acknowledge my transgression, and my sin is ever before me!" " How near it is; under the windows," says a reveler, turning pale. " What if it should be meant for one of us; let me look." He opens the window, the torches flash in from the dark street, and the chant pours on them, " Purge me with hyssop, and I shall be clean: wash me, and I shall be whiter than snow!" They all spring to their feet. " Whom is it for? " they cry out. " Deliver me from blood-guiltiness, O God, thou God of my salvation; and my tongue shall sing aloud of thy righteousness," is the answer. They throw open the door — the mother of Borgia rushes in: " You are all dead men," she cries; " I poisoned the wine myself. Confess, and make your peace with God; here are His ministers." The white-robed priests fill up the room, chanting, " The sacrifices of God are a broken spirit: a broken and a contrite heart, O God, thou wilt not despise!" " But here is an antidote for my son," cries the mother of Borgia. " Take it!" He dashes the cup on the ground — and the gay company lies there, pale-blue, poisoned, and dead! Shall that be the fate of America? Yes; if she cast the cup of healing to the ground! Other admonitions must come, yet more terrible, before we learn for whom the *Miserere* is now wailing forth.

If America were to keep this shameful pest in the land, then ruin is sure to follow,— ruin of all the dear-bought institutions of our fathers. The slaves double in about twenty-five years; so in A. D. 1930, there would be 27,000,000 of slaves! What a thought! The question is not merely, shall we have slavery and freedom, but slavery *or* freedom. The two cannot long continue side by side.

VIII

THE NEW CRIME AGAINST HUMANITY
1854

Since last we came together, there has been a man
stolen in this city of our fathers. It is not the first; it
may not be the last. He is now in the great slave
pen in the city of Boston. He is there against the
law of the Commonwealth, which, if I am rightly informed, in such cases prohibits the use of State edi-
fices as United States jails. I may be mistaken. Any
forcible attempt to take him from that barracoon of
Boston, would be wholly without use. For besides the
holiday soldiers who belong to the city of Boston, and
are ready to shoot down their brothers in a just or an
unjust cause, any day when the city government gives
them its command and its liquor, I understand that
there are one hundred and eighty-four United States
marines lodged in the court-house, every man of them
furnished with a musket and a bayonet, with his side
arms, and twenty-four ball cartridges. They are sta-
tioned also in a very strong building, and where five
men, in a passage-way, about the width of this pulpit,
can defend it against five-and-twenty, or a hundred.
To " keep the peace," the mayor, who, the other day
" regretted the arrest " of our brother, Anthony Burns,
and declared that his sympathies were wholly with the
alleged fugitive — and of course wholly against the
claimant and the marshal — in order to keep the peace
of the city, the mayor must become corporal of the
guard for kidnappers from Virginia. He must keep
the peace of our city, and defend these guests of Bos-

ton over the graves, the unmonumented graves, of John
Hancock and Samuel Adams.

A man has been killed by violence. Some say he
was killed by his own coadjutors: I can easily believe
it; there is evidence enough that they were greatly
frightened. They were not United States soldiers, but
volunteers from the streets of Boston, who, for their
pay, went into the court-house to assist in kidnapping
a brother man. They were so cowardly that they
could not use the simple cutlasses they had in their
hands, but smote right and left, like ignorant and
frightened ruffians as they are. They may have slain
their brother or not — I cannot tell. It is said by
some that they killed him. Another story is, that he
was killed by a hostile hand from without. Some say
by a bullet, some by an ax, and others still by a knife.
As yet nobody knows the facts. But a man has been
killed. He was a volunteer in this service. He liked
the business of enslaving a man, and has gone to render an account to God for his gratuitous wickedness.
Twelve men have been arrested, and are now in jail to
await their examination for wilful murder!

Here, then, is one man butchered, and twelve men
brought in peril of their lives. Why is this? Whose
fault is it?

Some eight years ago, a Boston merchant, by his
mercenaries, kidnapped a man " between Faneuil Hall
and old Quincy," and carried him off to eternal slavery. Boston mechanics, the next day, held up the
half-eagles which they received as pay for stealing a
man. The matter was brought before the grand jury
for the county of Suffolk, and abundant evidence was
presented, as I understand, but they found " no bill."
A wealthy merchant, in the name of trade, had stolen

a black man, who, on board a ship, had come to this
city, had been seized by the mercenaries of this merchant, kept by them for awhile, and then, when he escaped, kidnapped a second time in the city of Boston.
Boston did not punish the deed!

The Fugitive Slave Bill was presented to us, and
Boston rose up to welcome it! The greatest man in
all the North came here, and in this city told Massachusetts she must obey the Fugitive Slave Bill with
alacrity — that we must all conquer our prejudices in
favor of justice and the inalienable rights of man.
Boston did conquer her prejudices in favor of justice
and the inalienable rights of man.

Do you not remember the " Union meeting " which
was held in Faneuil Hall, when a " political soldier of
fortune," sometimes called the " Democratic Prince of
the Devils," howled at the idea that there was a law
of God higher than the Fugitive Slave Bill? He
sneered, and asked, " Will you have the ' higher law of
God,' to rule over you? " and the multitude which occupied the floor, and the multitude that crowded the
galleries, howled down the higher law of God! They
treated the higher law to a laugh and a howl! That
was Tuesday night. It was the Tuesday before
Thanksgiving Day. On that Thanksgiving Day, I told
the congregation that the men who howled down the
higher law of Almighty God, had got Almighty God
to settle with; that they had sown the wind, and would
reap the whirlwind. At that meeting Mr. Choate told
the people —" REMEMBER! REMEMBER! *Remember!* " Then nobody knew what to remember. Now
you know. That is the state of that case.

Then you remember the kidnappers came here to
seize Thomas Sims. Thomas Sims was seized. Nine

days he was on trial for more than his life; and never saw a judge — never saw a jury. He was sent back into bondage from the city of Boston. You remember the chains that were put around the court-house; you remember the judges of Massachusetts stooping, crouching, creeping, crawling under the chain of slavery, in order to get to their own courts. All these things you remember. Boston was non-resistant. She gave her " back to the smiters "— from the South; she " withheld not her cheek "— from the scorn of South Carolina, and welcomed the spitting of kidnappers from Georgia and Virginia. To-day we have our pay for such conduct. You have not forgotten the " fifteen hundred gentlemen of property and standing," who volunteered to conduct Mr. Sims to slavery — Marshal Tukey's " gentlemen." They remember it. They are sorry enough now. Let us forgive — we need not forget. " REMEMBER! REMEMBER! *Remember!* "

The Nebraska Bill has just now been passed. Who passed it? The fifteen hundred " gentlemen of property and standing " in Boston, who, in 1851, volunteered to carry Thomas Sims into slavery by force of arms. They passed the Nebraska Bill. But to every demand of the slave power, Massachusetts has said, " Yes, yes! — we grant it all! " " Agitation must cease! " " Save the Union! "

Southern slavery is an institution which is in earnest. Northern freedom is an institution that is not in earnest. It was in earnest in '76 and '83. It has not been much in earnest since. The compromises are but provisional! Slavery is the only finality! Now, since the Nebraska Bill is passed, an attempt is made to add insult to insult, injury to injury. Last

week, at New York, a brother of the Rev. Dr. Pen-
nington, an established clergyman, of large reputation,
great character, acknowledged learning, who has his
diploma from the University of Heidelberg, in Germany — a more honorable source than that from
which any clergyman in Massachusetts has received
one — his brother and two nephews were kidnapped
in New York, and without any trial, without any defense, were hurried off into bondage. Then, at Boston, you know what was done in the last four days.
Behold the consequences of the doctrine that there is
no higher law. Look at Boston to-day. There are
no chains round your court-house — there are only
ropes round it this time. A hundred and eighty-four
United States soldiers are there. They are, I am told,
mostly foreigners — the scum of the earth — none but
such enter into armies as common soldiers, in a country
like ours. I say it with pity — they are not to blame
for having been born where they were and what they
are. I pity the scum as well as I pity the mass of
men. The soldiers are there, I say, and their trade is
to kill. Why is this so?

You remember the meeting at Faneuil Hall, last
Friday, when even the words of my friend, Wendell
Phillips, the most eloquent words that get spoken in
America in this century, hardly restrained the multitude from going, and by violence storming the court-
house. What stirred them up? It was the spirit of
our fathers — the spirit of justice and liberty in your
heart, and in my heart, and in the heart of us all.
Sometimes it gets the better of a man's prudence, especially on occasions like this; and so excited was that
assembly of four or five thousand men, that even the
words of eloquent Wendell Phillips could hardly re-

strain them from going at once rashly to the court-house, and tearing it to the ground.

Boston is the most peaceful of cities. Why? Because we have commonly had a peace which was worth keeping. No city respects laws so much. Because the laws have been made by the people, for the people, and are laws which respect justice. Here is a law which the people will not keep. It is a law of our Southern masters; a law not fit to keep.

Why is Boston in this confusion to-day? The Fugitive Slave Bill commissioner has just now been sowing the wind, that we may reap the whirlwind. The old Fugitive Slave Bill commissioner stands back; he has gone to look after his " personal popularity." But, when Commissioner Curtis does not dare appear in this matter, another man comes forward, and for the first time seeks to kidnap his man also in the city of Boston. Judge Loring is a man whom I have respected and honored. His private life is mainly blameless, so far as I know. He has been, I think, uniformly beloved. His character has entitled him to the esteem of his fellow-citizens. I have known him somewhat. I never heard a mean word from him — many good words. He was once the law-partner of Horace Mann, and learned humanity of a great teacher. I have respected him a good deal. He is a respectable man — in the Boston sense of that word, and in a much higher sense; at least, I have thought so. He is a kind-hearted, charitable man; a good neighbor; a fast friend — when politics do not interfere; charitable with his purse; an excellent husband; a kind father; a good relative. And I should as soon have expected that venerable man who sits before me, born before your Revolution [Samuel May],— I should as soon have expected him to go and kidnap Robert Morris, or any of the other colored men I see around me, as I should have expected Judge Loring to do this thing. But he has sown the wind, and we are reaping the whirlwind. I need not say what I now think of him. He is to act to-morrow, and may yet act like a man. Let us wait and see. Perhaps there is manhood in him yet. But, my friends, all this confusion is his work. He knew he was stealing a man born with the same inalienable right to " life, liberty, and the pursuit of happiness " as himself. He knew the slaveholders had no more right to Anthony Burns than to his own daughter. He knew the consequences of stealing a man. He knew that there are men in Boston who have not yet conquered their prejudices — men who respect the higher law of God. He knew there would be a meeting at Faneuil Hall — gatherings in the streets. He knew there would be violence.

Edward Greeley Loring, Judge of Probate for the county of Suffolk, in the State of Massachusetts, Fugitive Slave Bill Commissioner of the United States, before these citizens of Boston, on Ascension Sunday, assembled to worship God, I charge you with the death of that man who was killed on last Friday night. He was your fellow-servant in kidnapping. He dies at your hand. You fired the shot which makes his wife a widow, his child an orphan. I charge you with the peril of twelve men, arrested for murder, and on trial for their lives. I charge you with filling the court-house with one hundred and eighty-four hired ruffians of the United States, and alarming not only this city for her liberties that are in peril, but stirring up the whole Commonwealth of Massachusetts with indignation, which no man knows how to stop — which no man can stop. You have done it all!

This is my Lesson for the Day.
My text is

" Then one of the twelve, called Judas Iscariot, went unto
the chief priests, and said unto them, What will ye give me,
and I will deliver him unto you? And they covenanted with
him for thirty pieces of silver. And from that time he sought
opportunity to betray him."— Matt. xxvi. 14–16.

" Then Judas, which had betrayed him, when he saw that he
was condemned, repented himself, and brought again the thirty
pieces of silver to the chief priests and elders, saying, I have
sinned in that I have betrayed the innocent blood. And they
said, What is that to us? see thou to that."— Matt. xxvii. 3, 4.

[The sermon which follows was printed in the *Boston Commonwealth,* on Monday, from the phonographic report of
Messrs. Slack and Yerrinton. They copied out the notes at my
house, and I revised them. We did not complete our labors
till half-past three o'clock Monday morning. It may easily
be imagined that some errors appeared in the print — for the
perishable body weigheth down the mind, and, though the spirit
be willing, the flesh is too weak to work four-and-twenty hours
continuously. Yet the errors were surprisingly few. In this
edition of the sermon some passages have been added which
were omitted in the report, and some also which, though written, were not delivered on Sunday.]

Boston, *June* 10, 1854.

Within the last few days, we have seen some of the
results of despotism in America, which might indeed
easily astonish a stranger; but a citizen of Boston has
no right to be surprised. The condition of this town
from May 24th to June 2nd is the natural and unavoidable result of well-known causes, publicly and deliberately put in action. It is only the first-fruit of
causes which in time will litter the ground with similar
harvests, and with others even worse. Let us pretend
no amazement that the seed sown has borne fruit after
its kind. Let us see what warning or what guidance
we can gather from these events, their cause and consequence. So this morning I ask your attention to

a sermon of the New Crime against Humanity committed in the midst of us, of the last kidnapping which has taken place in Boston.

I know well the responsibility of the place I occupy this morning. To-morrow's sun shall carry my words to all America. They will be read on both sides of the continent. They will cross the ocean. It may astonish the minds of men in Europe to hear of the iniquity committed in the midst of us. Let us be calm and cool, and look the thing fairly in the face.

Of course you will understand, from my connection with what has taken place in part, that I must speak of some things with a good deal of reserve, and others pass by entirely. However, I have only too much to say. I have had but short time for preparation, the deed is so recent. Perhaps I shall trespass a little on your patience this morning, that hand overrunning my customary hour some twenty or thirty minutes. If any of you find your patience exhausted, and standing too wearisome, you can retire; and, if without noise, none will be disturbed, and none offended.

On Wednesday night, the 24th of May, a young man, without property, without friends — I will continue to call his name Anthony Burns — was returning home from his usual lawful and peaceful work in the clothing shop of Deacon Pitts, in Brattle Street. He was assaulted by six ruffians, who charged him with having broken into a jeweller's shop. They seized him, forced him to the court-house, thrust him into an upper chamber therein, where he was surrounded by men, armed, it is said, with bludgeons and revolvers. There he was charged with being a fugitive slave. A man from Virginia, claiming to be his owner, and another man, likewise from Virginia, confronted the poor victim, and extorted from him a confession, as they allege, that he was the claimant's fugitive slave — if, indeed, the confession was not purely an invention of his foes who had made the false charge of burglary; for they who begin with a lie are not to be trusted after that lie has been told. He was kept all night, guarded by ruffians hired for the purpose of kidnapping a man. No friend was permitted to see him; but his deadliest foes, who clutched at what every one of us holds tenfold dearer than life itself, were allowed access. They came and went freely, making their inquisition, extorting or inventing admissions to be used for Mr. Burns's ruin.

At nine o'clock the next morning, Thursday (May 25th), the earliest hour at which the courts of Massachusetts ever open, he was brought to the court-room and arraigned before Edward Greeley Loring, judge of probate, one of the Fugitive Slave Bill commissioners of the city of Boston, and immediately put on trial. Intimidated by the mob about him, and stupefied with terror and fear, he makes no defense. " As a lamb before his shearers is dumb, so he opened not his mouth." How could he dare make a defense, treated as he had been the night before? — confronted as he was by men clutching at his liberty? — in a court-room packed with ruffians, where the slaveholders' counsel brought pistols in their breasts? He had been in duress all night, with inquisitors about him. His claimant was there, with documents manufactured in Alexandria; with a witness brought from Richmond; with two lawyers of Boston to aid them.

What a scene it was for a Massachusetts court! A merchant from Richmond, so Mr. Brent called him-

self; another from Alexandria, who was a sheriff and
member of the Virginia legislature — for such Colonel
Suttle has been — they were there to steal a man!
They had him already in jail; they went out and came
in as they liked, and shut from his presence everybody
who was not one of the minions hired to aid them in
their crime.

Further they had two lawyers of Boston giving them
the benefit of their education and their knowledge of
the law; and, in addition to that, the senior lawyer,
Seth J. Thomas, brought considerable experience, acquired on similar occasions — for he has been the kidnappers' counsel from the beginning. The other lawyer was a young man of good culture and amiable
deportment, I think with no previous stain on his
reputation. This is his first offense. I trust it will
be also his last — that he will not bring shame on his
own and his mother's head. I know not how the kidnappers enticed the young man to do so base a deed;
nor what motive turned him to a course so foul as this.
He is a young man, sorely penitent for this early
treason against humanity. Generous emotions are
commonly powerful in the bosoms of the young. A
young man with only cruel calculation in his heart is a
rare and loathsome spectacle. Let us hope better
things of this lawyer; that a generous nature only
sleeps in him. It is his first offense. I hope he will
bring forth " fruits meet for repentance." Judge of
him as charitably as you can. Of Mr. Thomas I have
only this to add: — that he is chiefly known in the
courts as the associate of Mr. Curtis in attempts like
this; the regular attorney of the stealers of men, and
apparently delighted with his work. He began this
career by endeavoring to seize William and Ellen

Craft. He is a member of the Democratic party who has not yet received his reward.

On the side of the kidnapper there were also the district marshal, the district attorney, the Fugitive Slave Bill commissioner, and sixty-five men whom I counted as the marshal's "guard." When the company was ordered to disperse, and the guard to remain, I tarried late, and counted them. I reckoned sixty-five in the court-room, and five more outside. I may have been mistaken in the count.

On the other side there was a poor, friendless negro, sitting between two bullies, his wrists chained together by stout handcuffs of steel — a prisoner without a crime, chained; on trial for more than life, and yet there was no charge against him, save that his mother had been a slave!

Mr. Burns had no counsel. The kidnapper's lawyers presented their documents from Alexandria, claiming him as a slave of Colonel Suttle, who had escaped from "service." They brought a Virginia merchant to identify the prisoner. He was swiftly sworn, and testified with speed. The claimant's lawyers declared that Mr. Burns had acknowledged already that he was Colonel Suttle's slave, and willing to go back. So they demanded a "certificate"; and at first it seemed likely to be granted at once. Why should a Fugitive Slave Bill commissioner delay? Why does he want evidence? Injustice is swift of foot. You know what was done in New York, the very same week: — three men were seized, carried before a commissioner, and, without even a mock trial, without any defense, hurried to bondage, pitiless and for ever! Only an accident, it seems, saved Boston from that outrage.

But there came forward in the court-room two young lawyers, Richard H. Dana and Charles M. Ellis, noble and honorable men, the pride of the mothers that bore them, and the joy of the fathers who have trained them up to piety and reverence for the law of God. Voluntarily, gratuitously, they offered their services as counsel for Mr. Burns. But it was said by the kidnappers that he did not want counsel; that he would make no defense; that he was "willing to go back." Messrs. Dana and Ellis did not wish to speak with him, or seem to plead that he might be their client. I spoke with him. His fear gave him a sad presentiment of his fate. He feared that he should be forced into slavery. How could he think otherwise? Arrested on a lying charge; kept in secret under severe and strict duress; guarded by armed men; confronted by his claimant; seeing no friends about him; how could he do otherwise than despair? If he went back at all, it was natural that he should "wish to go back easily," fearing that, if he resisted his claimant in Boston, he "must suffer for it in Alexandria." His conqueror, he thought, would take vengeance on him when he got him home, if he resisted his claim. That is the best evidence which I have seen that the man had ever been a slave: he knew the taste and the strength of the slave-driver's whip. That was not brought forward in evidence. If I had been the kidnapper's counsel I should have said, "The man is doubtless a slave; he is afraid to go back!" When I was in the court-room, as I was about to ask poor Burns if he would have counsel, one of the guard said to me, "You will never get him to say he wants a defense." Another more humanely said, "I hope he will; at any rate, it will do no harm to try." I asked him, and he said, "Do as you think best."

But still the counsel felt a delicacy in engaging under such circumstances. For they thought that, if, after all, he was to be sent to bondage, and when in the hands of the slave-master should be tortured the more for the defense they had made for him in Boston court-house, it would surely be better to let the marshal take his victim as soon as he liked, and allow the Fugitive Slave Bill commissioner to earn his " thirty pieces of silver " without delay. They begged for time, however, that the intimidated man might make up his mind, and determine whether he would have a defense or not.

There is no end to human atrocity. The kidnapper's lawyers objected to the delay, and wished the trial to proceed at once " forthwith." They said that the claimant, Colonel Suttle, was here, having come all the way from Alexandria to Boston, at great cost; that the case was clear; that Burns made no defense: and they asked for an instant decision. The Democratic lawyer [Thomas] thought it was not worth while to delay; there was only the liberty of a man at stake — a poor man, with no reputation, no friends, nothing but the " natural, essential, and inalienable rights " wherewith he was " endowed by his Creator " — nothing but that: — let the Virginia colonel have his slave! That is administration democracy in Massachusetts. There are two democracies — the celestial and the satanic. One — it is the democracy of the Beatitudes of the New Testament and of Jesus Christ; that says, " My brother, you are as good as I: come up higher, and let me take you by the hand, and we will help each other." Such democracy is the worship of the great God. The other — it says, " I am as good as you, and, if you don't let me triumph over you, I will smite you to the ground." That is the democracy of Caleb Cushing, the democracy of the administration, and of a great many political men, Democrat and Whig, and neither Whig nor Democrat.

Commissioner Loring asked Mr. Burns if he wanted time to think of the matter, and counsel to aid in his defense. I shall never forget how he looked round that court-room, at the marshal, at the kidnapper's lawyers, at the commissioner, the claimant and his witness! Save the counsel, whom he had never seen before, there was scarce a friendly face that his eye rested on. At length he said timidly, and catching for breath, " Yes." Mr. Loring put off the case until Saturday. The Fugitive Slave Bill commissioner was to lecture at Cambridge on Friday. He is a professor at Harvard College, and he could not conveniently hold court on that day. He is a judge of probate, and looks after widows and orphans; he must be in the probate office on Monday. Saturday was the most convenient day for the commissioner. So, in a matter which was to determine whether the prisoner should be a free man or only a thing which might be sold and beaten as a beast, the court allowed him forty-eight hours' delay! It really gave him time to breathe a little. Let us be grateful to the commissioner! He gave more favor than any Fugitive Slave Bill commissioners have done before, I believe.

You know the rest. He was on trial ten days. He was never in a court; all this time he has not seen a jury; he has not even seen a judge; the process is " summary," not " summary in time," as Mr. Loring declares; but it is " without due form of law." Why do you want a court to make a negro a slave in Boston? Surely, a commissioner is enough in such a

case. Let him proceed as swiftly as he will: — the
kidnapper's lawyers said —" forthwith; " not in a
hurry, but " immediately."

You remember what followed. You have seen the
streets crowded with armed men. You have read the
newspapers, the handbills, and the posters. You remember the Faneuil Hall meeting, when all the influence of the platform scarce kept the multitude from
tearing the court-house that night to the ground. You
remember the attack on the court-house — a man killed
and twelve citizens in jail, charged with crimes of an
atrocious character. You recollect the conventions —
Free-soil and anti-slavery. You call to mind the aspect of Court Square last Monday. Boston never
saw such an Anniversary Week. There were meetings
of theological societies, philanthropic societies, reform-
atory societies, literary societies: and Boston was in
a state of siege — the court-house full of United States
soldiers — marines from the navy yard, troops from
the forts, from New York, from Portsmouth, from
Rhode Island. The courts sat with muskets at their
backs, or swords at their bosoms; drunken soldiers
charged bayonet on the witnesses, on counsel, and on
strangers, who had rights where the soldier had none.
The scene last Friday you will never forget — business suspended, the shops shut, the streets blocked up,
all the " citizen-soldiery " under arms. Ball cartridges were made for the city government on Thursday
afternoon in Dock Square, to be fired into your bosoms
and mine; United States soldiers loaded their pieces
in Court Square, to be discharged into the crowd of
Boston citizens whenever a drunken officer should give
command; a six-pound cannon, furnished with forty
rounds of canister shot, was planted in Court Square,

manned by United States soldiers, foreigners before they enlisted. The town looked Austrian. And, at high change, over the spot where, on the 5th of March, 1770, fell the first victim in the Boston Massacre,— where the negro blood of Crispus Attucks stained the ground,— over that spot Boston authorities carried a citizen of Massachusetts to Alexandria as a slave; "and order reigns in Boston"— or Warsaw, call it which you will.

So much for a brief statement of facts.

Pause with me a moment, and look at the general causes of the fact. Here are two great forces in the nation. One is slavery, freedom is the other. The two are hostile, deadly foes — irreconcilable. They will go on fighting till one kills the other outright. From 1775 to 1788, freedom generally prevailed over slavery. It was the period of revolution, when the nation fell back on its religious feelings, and thence developed the great political ideas of America. But even then slavery was in the midst of us. It came into the Constitution, and, from the adoption of the Federal Constitution to the present time, it has advanced, and freedom declined. It has gone over the Alleghanies, over the Rio del Norte, over the Cordilleras; it extends from the forty-ninth parallel to the thirty-second, from the Atlantic to the Pacific; it has gone into ten new States, into all the territories except Oregon.

Since the annexation of Texas, in 1845, slavery has been the obvious master, freedom the obvious servant. Fidelity to slavery is the *sine quâ non* for office-holders. Slavery is the "peculiar institution" of the industrial democracy of America. Slavery is terribly in earnest, as freedom has never been since the Revolution. It

controls all the politics of the country. It strangles
all our " great men." There is not a great Democrat, nor a great Whig, who dares openly oppose slavery. All the commercial towns are on its side. There
is not an anti-slavery governor of any State in the
Union. The supreme courts of the States are all pro-
slavery, save in Vermont. The leading newspapers are
nearly all on the side of wrong — almost all the commercial, almost all the political newspapers. I know but
few exceptions — of course I do not speak of those devoted to philanthropy — the democratic *Evening
Post*, truly democratic, of New York; and the *New
York Tribune*, which is truly democratic, though it
hoists another banner. Many of the theological journals — Protestant as well as Catholic — are cruelly
devoted to slavery. But proudly above all the religious journals of the land rises the *Independent*, and
bears a noble witness to the humane spirit of Christianity. These are eminent exceptions, which would
do honor to any nation.

The friends of freedom appeal religiously to the
souls and consciences of men: piety and justice demand
that all be free; the appeal immediately touches a few.
They address also the reason and the understanding of
men: Freedom is the great idea of politics; it is
self-evident that " all men are created equal." That
argument touches a few more. But the religious, who
reverence God's higher law, and the intellectual, who
see the great ideas of politics, they are few. Slavery
addresses the vulgar interests of vulgar men. To the
slaveholder it gives political power, pecuniary power,
and here is an argument which the dullest can understand, and the meanest appreciate. Able and cunning men feel this, and avail themselves of slavery to

secure money and political power. These are the objects of most intense desire in America. They are our highest things — marks of our " great men." Office is transient nobility ; money is permanent, heritable nobility. Accordingly, slavery is the leading idea of America — the great American institution. I think history furnishes no instance of one section of a country submitting so meanly to another as we have done in America. The South is weak in numbers and in money — the North strong in both. The South has few schools, no commerce, few newspapers, no large mass of intelligent men, wherein the North abounds. But the most eminent Southern men are devoted to politics, while the Northern turn to trade: and so the South commands the North. I am only translating facts into ideas, and bringing the condition of America to the consciousness of America. Some men knew these things before, but the mass of men know them not.

So much for the general causes.

Now look at some of the special causes. I shall limit myself chiefly to those which Massachusetts has had a share in putting into activity.

In 1826, on the 9th of March, Mr. Edward Everett made a speech in Congress. He was the representative of Middlesex county. Once he was a minister of the church where John Hancock used to worship, and as clergyman officially resided in the house which John Hancock gave to that church. Next, he was a professor in Harvard College, where the Adamses — the three Adamses, Samuel, John, and John Quincy — were educated, and where John Hancock had graduated. He represented Lexington, and Concord, and Bunker Hill, and in his speech he said: —

" Neither am I one of those citizens of the North who would think it immoral and irreligious to join in putting down a servile insurrection at the South. I am no soldier, sir. My habits and education are very unmilitary; but there is no cause in which I would sooner buckle a knapsack to my back, and put a musket to my shoulder, than that." " Domestic slavery . . . is not, in my judgment, to be set down as an immoral or irreligious institution." " Its duties are presupposed by religion." " The New Testament says, ' Slaves, obey your masters.' "

The *Daily Advertiser* defended Mr. Everett, declaring that it was perfectly right in him to justify the continuance of the relation between the master and his slaves, and added (I am now quoting from the *Daily Advertiser* of March 28th, 1826): —" We hold that it is not time, and never will be, that we should be aroused to any efforts for their redemption." That was the answer which the " respectability of Boston " gave to Mr. Everett's speech. True, some journals protested against the iniquitous statement; the *Christian Register* was indignant. But Middlesex county sent him again. Lexington, and Concord, and Bunker Hill returned their apostate representative a second, a third, a fourth, and a fifth time. And, when he was weary of that honor, the State of Massachusetts made him her governor, and he carried to the State House the same proclivities to despotism which he had evinced in his maiden speech.

In 1835, the anti-slavery men and women were mobbed in Boston by an assembly of " respectable gentlemen; " the mayor did not stop the tumult, the destruction of property, and the peril of life! There were no soldiers in the streets then; nobody, I think, was punished.

The next winter, the General Assemblies of several Southern States sent resolutions to the Massachusetts General Court, whereof this is one from South Carolina: —" The formation of abolition societies, and the acts and doings of certain fanatics, calling themselves abolitionists, in the non-slaveholding States of this confederacy, are in direct violation of the obligations of the compact of the Union."

South Carolina requested the government " promptly and effectually to suppress all those associations," and would consider " the abolition of slavery in the District of Columbia as a violation of the rights of citizens, and a usurpation to be at once resited." Georgia asked Massachusetts " to crush the traitorous designs of the abolitionists." Virginia required the non-slaveholding States " to adopt penal enactments, or such other measures as will effectually suppress all associations within their respective limits, purporting to be, or having the character of, abolition societies; " and that they " will make it highly penal to print, publish, or distribute newspapers, pamphlets, or other publications, calculated or having a tendency to incite the slaves of the Southern States to insurrection and revolt." How do you think Massachusetts answered? In solemn resolutions the committee of the Massachusetts legislature declared that the agitation of the question of domestic slavery had " already interrupted the friendly relations between the several States of the Union; " expressed its " entire disapprobation of the doctrines and speeches of such as agitate the question," and advised them " to abstain from all such discussion " as might " tend to disturb and agitate the public mind." That was the voice of a committee appointed by the Massachusetts legislature. True, it was not accepted by the House of Representatives, but the report was only too significant. What followed?

In 1844, one of the most eminent lawyers of this State was sent by Massachusetts to the city of Charleston, to proceed legally and secure the release of Massachusetts colored citizens from the jails of Charleston, where they were held without charge of crime, and contrary to the Constitution of the United States. Mr. Hoar was mobbed out of Charleston by a body of respectable citizens, the high sheriff aiding in driving him out.

Mr. Hoar made his report to the governor of Massachusetts, and said: —

" Has the Constitution of the United States the least practical validity or binding force in South Carolina, excepting when she thinks its operation favorable to her? She prohibits the trial of an action in the tribunals established under the Constitution for determining such cases, in which a citizen of Massachusetts complains that a citizen of South Carolina has done him an injury; saying that she has herself already tried that cause, and decided against the plaintiff."

The evil complained of continues unabated to this day. South Carolina imprisons all the free colored citizens of the North who visit her ports in our ships.

In 1845, Texas was admitted, and annexed as a slave State, with the promise that she might bring in four other slave States.

In 1847 and '48 came the Mexican War, with the annexation of an immense territory as slave soil. Many of the leading men of Massachusetts favored the annexation of Texas. New England might have stopped it; Massachusetts might have stopped it; Boston might have stopped it. But Mr. Webster said she could not be aroused. The politicians of Massachusetts favored the Mexican War. It was a war for slavery. Boston favored it. The newspapers came out in its defense. The governor called out the soldiers, and they came. From the New England pulpit we heard but a thin and feeble voice against the war.

But there were men who doubted that wrong was right, and said, " Beware of this wickedness! " The sober people of the country disliked the war: they said, " No! let us have no such wicked work as this! " Governor Briggs, though before so deservedly popular, could never again get elected by the people. He had violated their conscience by issuing his proclamation calling for volunteers.

In 1850 came the Fugitive Slave Bill. You all remember Mr. Webster's speech on the 7th of March. Before that time he had opposed all the great steps of the slave power — the Missouri Compromise, the annexation of Texas, the Mexican War, the increase of slave territory. He had voted, I think, against the admission of every slave State. He was opposed to the extension of American slavery, " at all times, now and for ever." He claimed the Wilmot Proviso as his " thunder." He could " stand on the Buffalo platform " in 1848. But, in 1850, he proffered his support to the Fugitive Slave Bill, " with all its provisions, to the fullest extent." He volunteered the promise that Massachusetts would " obey," and that " with alacrity." You remember his speech at the Revere House — discussion " must be suppressed, in Congress and out; " Massachusetts must " conquer her prejudices " in favor of the inalienable rights of man, which she had fought the Revolution to secure. You have not forgotten his speeches at Albany, at Syracuse, at Buffalo; nor his denial of the higher law of God at Capon Springs in Virginia —" The North Mountain is very high; the Blue Ridge higher still; the Alleghanies higher than either; yet this ' higher law ' ranges an eagle's flight above the highest peak of the Alleghanies." What was the answer from the crowd? Laughter. The multitude laughed at the higher law. There is no law above the North Mountain, above the Blue Ridge, above the peaks of the Alleghany — is there? The Fugitive Slave Bill reaches up where there is no God!

Men of property and standing all over New England supported the apostacy of Mr. Webster. You remember the letters from Maine, from New Hampshire, and the one from Newburyport. I am sure you have not forgotten the letter of the nine hundred and eighty-seven prominent men in and about Boston, telling him that he had " convinced the understanding and touched the conscience of a nation." Good men, whom I have long known, and tenderly loved, put their names to that letter. Did they think the " Union in danger? " Not one of them. A man of great understanding beguiled them.

You remember the tone of the newspapers, Whig and Democratic. With alacrity they went for kidnapping to the fullest extent. They clasped hands in order to seize the black man. When the time came, Mr. Eliot gave the vote of Boston for the Fugitive Slave Bill. When he returned to his home, some of the most prominent men of the city went and thanked him for his vote. They liked it. I believe no " emi-

nent man " of Boston spoke against it. They
" strained their consciences," as Mr. Walley has just
said, " to aid in the passage of the Fugitive Slave
Act." Boston fired a hundred guns on the Common,
at noon-day, in honor of that event.

I know there was opposition — earnest and fierce
opposition; but it did not come from the citizens of
" eminent gravity," whom Boston and Massachusetts
are accustomed stupidly to follow. You know what
hatred was felt in Boston against all men who taught
that the natural law of God was superior to the Fugitive Slave Bill, and conscience above the Constitution.

You have not forgotten the Union meeting at Faneuil Hall. I never saw so much meanness and so
little manhood on that platform. The Democratic
Herods and the Whig Pilates were made friends that
day that they might kidnap the black man. You
recollect the howl of derision against the higher law
of God, which came from that ignoble stage, and was
echoed by that ignoble crowd above it and below —
speakers fit for fitting theme.

When the Fugitive Slave Bill was proposed, prominent men said, " It cannot pass: the North will reject
it at once; and, even if it were passed, it would be
repealed the next day. We will petition for its repeal." After it was passed, they said: " It cannot be executed, and never will be." But, when asked
to petition for its repeal, the same men refused —
" No, it would irritate the South." I received the petitions which our fellow-citizens sent from more than
three hundred towns in Massachusetts. I took the
smallest of them all, and sent it to the representative
of Boston, Mr. Eliot, with a letter, asking him to

present it to the House. He presented it to — me!
It was not " laid on the table " ; he put it in the post-
office. I sent it back to Washington, to some Southern or Western member, and he presented it in Congress.

The next Congress reaffirmed the Fugitive Slave
Bill.

> " Twice they routed all their foes,
> And twice they slew the slain."

The new representative from Boston, Mr. Apple-
ton, gave the vote of Boston for it. He was never
censured for that act. He was approved, and re-
elected.

You remember the conduct of the Boston newspapers. Almost all of them went for the Fugitive Slave
Bill. They made atheism the first principle in American politics — " There is no higher law." The instinct of commerce is adverse to the natural rights
of labor: so the chief leaders in commerce wish to
have the working man but poorly paid; the larger
gain falls into their hands; their laborer is a mill,
they must run him as cheap as they can. So the
great cities of the North were hostile to the slave —
hostile to freedom. The wealthy capitalists did not
know that in denying the higher law of God they
were destroying the rock on which alone their money
could rest secure. The mass of men in cities, servants of the few, knew not that in chaining the black
man they were also putting fetters on their own feet.
Justice is the common interest of all men! Alas, that
so few know what God writes in letters of fire on the
world's high walls!

You have not forgotten the general tone of the
pulpit — " Conscience and the Constitution," at An-

dover. Mr. Stuart says, " Keep the laws of men, come what may come of the higher law of God." One minister of Boston said, " I would drive the fugitive from my own door." The most eminent doctor of divinity in the Unitarian ranks declared he would send his own mother into slavery. He says he said brother! Give him the benefit of the ethical distinction; he would send back his own brother! What had Andover and New Haven to say, in their collegiate churches? What the churches of commerce in New York, Boston, Philadelphia, Albany, Buffalo? They all went for kidnapping. " Down with God and up with iniquity." That was the shout of the lower-law religion which littered the land. The ecclesiastical teachers did more to strengthen infidelity then, than all the " infidels " that ever taught. What else could you expect from the lower-law divines? All at once this blessed Bible seemed to have become a treatise in favor of man-stealing. Kidnapping arguments were strewn all the way through from Genesis to Revelation. These were the reverend gentlemen who call me " infidel," or " atheist!" Nothing has so weakened the Church in America as this conduct of these " leading ministers " at that time. I mean ministers of churches that are rich in money, which lead the fashion and the opinion of the day. What defenses of kidnapping have I heard from clerical lips! " No matter what the law is — it must be executed. The men who made the Fugitive Slave Bill, and those who seek to execute it, are ' Christian men,' ' very conscientious!' " Turn back and read the newspapers of 1850 and 1851. Nay, read them not — they are too bad to read!

When the Fugitive Slave Bill was before Congress, some of the Northern politicians said to the people,

"Let it pass; it will 'save the Union,' and we will repeal it at the next session of Congress." After it had passed they said, "Do not try to repeal it; that would irritate the South, and 'dissolve the Union'; it will never be executed; it is too bad to be." But when the kidnapper came to Boston, and demanded William and Ellen Craft, the same advisers said, "Of course the *niggers* must be sent back; the law must be enforced because it is law!"

At length the time came to execute the Act. Morton was busy in New York, Kane in Philadelphia, Curtis, the Boston commissioner, was also on his feet. William and Ellen Craft fled off from the stripes of America to the lion of England. Shadrach — he will be remembered as long as Daniel — sang his psalm of deliverance in Canada. Taking him out of the Kidnappers' Court was high treason. It was "levying war." Thomas Sims will not soon be forgotten in Boston. Mayor Bigelow, Commissioner Curtis, and Marshal Tukey, they will also be remembered; they will all three be borne down to posterity, riding on the scourged and bleeding shoulders of Thomas Sims. The government of Boston could do nothing for the fugitive but kidnap him. The officers of the county nothing; they were only cockade and vanity. The Supreme Court could do nothing; the judges crouched and crawled, and went under the chain. The Free-soil governor could do nothing; the Free-soil legislature nothing. The court-house was in chains. Faneuil Hall was shut. The victim was on trial. A thousand able-bodied men sat in Tremont Temple all day in a Free-soil convention, and — went home at night! Most of the newspapers in the city were for kidnapping. The greater part of the clergy were

for returning the fugitive — " Send back our brother."
In Boston wealthy traders entertained the kidnappers
from the South. Merchants and railroad directors
withdrew their advertising from newspapers which opposed the stealing of men. More than one minister
in New England was driven from his pulpit for declaring the Golden Rule superior to the Fugitive
Slave Bill!

When Judge Woodbury decided not to grant the
writ of habeas corpus, and thus at one spurt of his
pen cut off Mr. Sims's last chance for liberty and life,
the court-house rang with plaudits, and the clapping
of hands of " gentlemen " who had assembled there!
Fifteen hundred " gentlemen, of property and standing," volunteered to escort the poor fugitive out of
the State, and convey him to bondage for ever. It
was not necessary. When he stepped from Long
Wharf on board John H. Pearson's brig,— the owner
is sorry for it now, and has repented, and promises to
bring forth fruits meet for repentance; let that be
remembered to his honor,— when Thomas Sims stepped
on board the " Acorn," these were his words: " And
this is Massachusetts liberty ! " There was that great
stone finger pointing from Bunker Hill towards
heaven; and this was Massachusetts liberty! " Order reigned in Warsaw." But it was some comfort
that he could not be sent away till soldiers were bil-
leted in Faneuil Hall; then, only in the darkest hour
of the night!

Boston sent back the first man she ever stole since
the Declaration of Independence. Thomas Sims
reached Savannah on the 19th of April, seventy-six
years after the first battle of the Revolution, fought
on the soil of Lexington. He was sent back on Sat-

urday, and the next Sunday the " leading ministers "
of this city — I call them leading, though they lead
nobody — gave God thanks. They forgot Jesus.
They took Iscariot for their exemplar. " The Fugitive Slave Bill must be kept," they said, " come what
will come to justice, liberty, and love; come what
may come of God."

I know there were noble ministers, noble men in
pulpits, whose hearts bled in them, and who spoke brave
warning words of liberty; some were in the country,
some in town. I know one minister, an " orthodox
man," who in five months helped ninety-and-five fugitives flee from American stripes to the freedom of
Canada! I dare not yet tell his name! Humble
churches in the country towns — Methodist, Baptist,
Unitarian — of all denominations save that of commerce — dropped their two mites of money into the
alms-box for the slave, and gave him their prayers
and their preaching too. But the " famous churches "
went for " law," and stealing men.

Slavery had long been master at Washington: the
" Union meeting " proved that it was master at Boston; proved it by words. The capture and sending
back of Thomas Sims proved it by deeds. No prominent Whig openly opposed the Fugitive Slave Bill
or its execution. No prominent Democrat opposed it. Not a prominent clergyman in Boston
spoke against it. I mean a clergyman of a " rich
and fashionable church "— for in these days the wealth
and social standing of the church make the minister
prominent. Intellectual power, eloquence, piety,—
they do not make a " prominent minister " in these
days.* Not ten of the rich men of Massachusetts gave

* Dr. Charles Lowell, with the humane piety which has beauti-

the weight of their influence against it.　Slavery is master; Massachusetts is one of the inferior counties of Virginia; Boston is only a suburb of Alexandria. Many of our lawyers, ministers, merchants, politicians, were negro-drivers for the South.　They proved it by idea before; then by deed.　Yet there were men in Boston who hated slavery — alas! they had little influence.

Let me not pass by the Baltimore Conventions, and the two platforms.　The Fugitive Slave Bill was the central and topmost plank in them both.　Each confessed slavery to be master; it seemed that there was no North; slave soil all the way from the south of Florida to the north of Maine.　All over the land slavery ruled.

You cannot forget the President's inaugural address, nor the comments of the Boston press thereon. He says the Fugitive Slave Bill is to be " unhesitatingly carried into effect; " " not with reluctance," but " cheerfully and willingly."　The newspapers of Boston welcomed the sentiment; and now Mr. Pierce's organ, the *Washington Union*, says it is very proper this Bill should be enforced at Boston, for " Boston was among the first to approve of this emphatic declaration."　So let the promise be executed here till we have enough of it!

You know the contempt which has been shown towards everybody who opposed slavery here in Massachusetts.　Horace Mann — there is not a man in the State more hated than he by the " prominent politicians," — or more loved by the people — because he opposed slavery with all his might; and it is a great

fied his long and faithful ministry, at that time opposed the Fugitive Slave Bill with manly earnestness.

might. Robert Rantoul, though a politician and a party man, fought against slavery; and when he died, though he was an eminent lawyer, the members of the Suffolk bar, his brother lawyers, took no notice of him. They wore no crape for Robert Rantoul! He had opposed slavery; let him die unnoticed, unhonored, unknown. Massachusetts sent to the Senate a man whose chief constitutional impulse is the instinct of decorum — Mr. Everett, who had been ready to buckle on his knapsack, and shoulder his musket, to put down an insurrection of slaves; a Cambridge professor of Greek, he studied the original tongue of the Bible to learn that the Scripture says " slaves," where the English Bible says only " servants." Fit senator!

Then came the Nebraska Bill. It was at once a measure and a principle. As a measure, it extends the old curse of slavery over half a million square miles of virgin soil, and thus hinders the growth of the territory in population, riches, education, in moral and religious character. It makes a South Carolina of what might else be a Connecticut, and establishes paganism in the place of Christ's piety. As a principle, it is worse still — it makes slavery national and inseparable from the national soil; for the principle which is covertly endorsed by the Nebraska Bill might establish slavery in Massachusetts — and ere long the attempt will be made.

In the House of Representatives, forty-four Northern men voted for the enslavement of Nebraska. They are all Democrats — it is an administration measure. Mr. Everett, the senator from Boston, did " not know exactly what to do." The thing was discussed in committee, of which he was a member; but when it

came up in public, it "took him by surprise." He
wrote, I am told, to eleven prominent Whig gentlemen of Massachusetts, and asked their advice as to
what he should do. With singular unanimity, every
man of them said, "Oppose it with all your might!"
But he did not. Nay, his vote has not been recorded
against it yet. I am told his vote was in favor of
prohibiting aliens from voting in that territory; his
name against the main question has never been recorded yet. Nay, he did not dare to present the
remonstrance which three thousand and fifty of his
fellow-clergymen manfully sent to their clerical
brother, and asked him to lay before the Senate. Did
any one suppose that he would dare do it? None
who knew his antecedents.

There was an anti-Nebraska meeting in Boston at
Faneuil Hall. It was Siberian in its coldness — it
was a meeting of icebergs. The platform was arctic.
There seemed to be no heart in the speeches. It must
have been an encouragement to the men at Washington who advocated the bill. I suppose they understood it so. I am sure I should. The mass of
the people in Massachusetts who think at all, are indignant; but so far as I can learn, the men who
control the politics of Boston, or who have controlled
them until the last week, feel no considerable interest
in the matter. In New York, men of great property
and high standing came together and protested
against this iniquity. New York has been, for once,
and in one particular, morally in advance of Boston.
The platform there was not arctic, not even Siberian.
Such a meeting could not have been held here.

Now, put all these things together, and you see
the causes which bore the fruits of last week — in

general, the triumph of slavery over freedom, and in special, the indifference of Massachusetts, and particularly of Boston, to the efforts which are made for freedom; her zeal to promote slavery and honor its defenders. Men talk of dividing the Union. I never proposed that. Before last week I should not have known where to begin. I should have had to draw the line somewhere north of Boston.

Last week Massachusetts got part of her pay for obeying the Fugitive Slave Bill with alacrity; for suppressing discussion; for conquering her prejudices; pay for putting cowardly, mean men, in the place of brave, honorable men; pay for allowing the laws of Massachusetts to be trodden underfoot, and her court-house of Northern granite to be surrounded by Southern chains. Thomas Sims was scourged on the 19th of April, when he was carried back to Savannah. Boston did not feel it then. She felt it last week — felt it sorely. In September, 1850, we heard the hundred guns fired on Boston Common, in honor of the Fugitive Slave Bill — fired by men of "eminent gravity." Last Friday you saw the cannon! One day you will see it again grown into many cannons. That one was only a devil's grace before a devil's meat! No higher law, is there? Wait a little longer, and you shall find there is a "lower law," a good deal lower than we have yet come to! Sow the wind, shall we? When the whirlwind comes up therefrom, it has a course of its own, and God only can control the law of such storms as those. We have not yet seen the full consequences of sowing atheism with a broad hand among the people of this continent. We have not yet seen the end. These are only the small early apples that first fall to the earth. There is a whole tree full of them. When some autumnal storm shakes the boughs, they will cover the ground — sour and bitter in our mouths, and then poison.

Yet this triumph of slavery does not truly represent the wishes of the Northern people. Not a single pro-slavery measure has ever been popular with the mass of men in New England or Massachusetts. The people disliked the annexation of Texas in that unjust manner: they thought the Mexican War was wicked. They were opposed to the extension of slavery; they hated the Fugitive Slave Bill, and rejoiced at the rescue of Shadrach. The kidnapping of Thomas Sims roused a fierce indignation. Only one town in all New England has ever returned a fugitive — all the rest hide the outcasts, while Boston bewrays him that wandereth. The Nebraska Act is detested by the people.

A few editors have done a manly duty in opposing all these manifold iniquities. A few ministers have been faithful to the spirit of this Bible, and to their own conscience, heedless of law and constitution. Manly preachers of all denominations — save the commercial — protested against kidnapping, against enacting wickedness by statute. From humble pulpits their voices rang out in Boston and elsewhere. But what were they among so many? There were theological journals which stoutly resisted the wickedness of the prominent men, and rebuked the mammon-worship of the churches of commerce. The *Independent* at New York, the *Congregationalist* at Boston, not to mention humbler papers, did most manly service — now with eloquence, now with art, then with satiric scorn — always with manly religion. Even in the cities, there were editors of secular prints who opposed the wicked law and its execution.

No man in New England, within the last few years, has supported slavery without at the same time losing the confidence of the best portion of the people — sober, serious, religious men; who believe there is a law of God writ in the nature of things. Even Mr. Webster quailed before the conscience of the North: the Supreme Court of Massachusetts no longer enjoys the confidence of the people; the most " prominent clergymen " of New England — pastors, I mean, of the richest churches — are not looked up to with the same respect as before.

The popularity of " Uncle Tom's Cabin " showed how deeply the feelings of the world were touched by this great outrage. No one of the encroachments of slavery could have been sustained by a direct popular vote. I think seven out of every ten of all the New England men would have voted against the Fugitive Slave Bill; nine out of ten against kidnapping. But alas! we did not say so — we allowed wicked men to rule over us. Now behold the consequences! Men who will not love God must fear the devil.

Boston is the test and touchstone of political principles and measures. Faneuil Hall is the " Cradle of Liberty," and therein have been rocked the great ideas of America — rocked by noble hands.

Well, if Boston had said, " No Texan annexation in that wicked way! " we might have had Texas on fair conditions. If Boston had opposed the Mexican War, all New England would have done the same — almost all the North. We might have had all the soil we have got, without fighting a battle, or taking or losing a life, at far less cost; and have demoralized

nobody. If, when the Fugitive Slave Bill was before Congress, Boston had spoken against that iniquity, all the people would have risen, and there would
have been no Fugitive Slave Act. If, after that
Bill was passed, she had said, " No kidnapping,"
there would have been none. Then there would have
been no Nebraska Bill, no repeal of the Missouri Compromise, no attempt to seize Cuba and San Domingo.
If the fifteen hundred gentlemen of " property and
standing " in Boston, who volunteered to return Mr.
Sims to bondage, or the nine hundred and eighty-seven
who thanked Mr. Webster for the Fugitive Slave Bill,
had come forward on the side of justice, they might
have made every commissioner swear solemnly that
he would not execute that Act. Thus the " true sons of
liberty," on the 17th of December, 1765, induced
Commissioner Oliver to swear solemnly, at noon-day,
in " presence of a great crowd," and in front of the
Liberty Tree, that he would not issue a single stamp!
Had that been done, there would have been no man
arrested. There are only eight commissioners, and
public opinion would have kept them all down. We
should have had no kidnappers here.

Boston did not do so; Massachusetts did no such
thing. She did just the opposite. In 1828, the legislature of Georgia passed resolutions relative to the
tariff, declaring that the General Government had no
right to protect domestic manufactures, and had been
guilty of a " flagrant usurpation; " she will insist
on her construction of the Constitution, and " will submit to no other." Georgia carried her point. The
tariff of 1828 went to the ground! South Carolina
imprisons our colored citizens; we bear it with a patient shrug,— and pay the cost; Massachusetts is

non-resistant; New England is a Quaker,— when a
blustering little State undertakes to ride over us. Georgia
offers a reward of five thousand dollars for
the head of a non-resistant in Boston,— and Boston
takes special pains to return Ellen Craft to a citizen
of Georgia, who wished to sell her as a harlot for the
brothels of New Orleans! Northern clergymen defended
the character of her " owner " — a man of
" unquestionable piety." You know what denunciations
were uttered in this city against the men and
women who sheltered her! Boston could not allow
the poor woman to remain. Did the churches of commerce
" put up a prayer " for her? " Send back my
own mother!" Not a Northern minister lost his pulpit
or his professional respectability by that form
of practical atheism. Not one! At the South not a
minister dares preach against slavery; at the North
— think of the preaching of so many " eminent divines!"

My friends, we deserve all we have suffered. We
are the scorn and contempt of the South. They are
our masters, and treat us as slaves. It is ourselves
who made the yoke. We offer our back to the slave-
driver's whip. A Western man travels all through
Kentucky — he was in Boston three days ago — and
hears only this rumor: " The Yankees are cowards;
they dare not resist us. We will drive them just where
we like. We will force the Nebraska Bill down their
throats, and then force San Domingo and Cuba after
it." That is public opinion in Kentucky. My
brothers, it is very well deserved.

The North hated the Missouri Compromise. Daniel
Webster fought against it with all his manly might;
and then it was very manly and very mighty. When

he collects his speeches, in 1850, for electioneering purposes — a political pamphlet in six octavos — he leaves out all his speeches and writings against the Missouri Compromise! His friend, Mr. Everett, writes his memoir, and there is nothing about Mr. Webster's opposition to the extension of slavery ; about the Missouri Compromise not one single word.

My friends, the South treat us as we deserve. They make compromises, and then break them. They say we are cowards. Are they mistaken? They put our seamen in jail for no crime but their complexion. We allow it. Then they come to New England, and in Boston steal our fellow-citizens — no! our fellow-subjects, our fellow-slaves. We call out the soldiers to help them! Go into a bear's den, and steal a young cub; and if you take only one, all the full-grown bears in the den will come after you and follow till you die, or they die, or their strength fails, and they must give up the pursuit.

> "O Justice! thou art fled to brutish beasts,
> And men have lost their reason!"

The Nebraska Bill has hardly got back to the Senate again when a Virginian comes here to see how much Boston will bear. He brings letters to eminent citizens of Boston, lodges at the Revere House, and bravely shows himself to the public in the streets. He walks upon the Common, and looks at the eclipse — the eclipse of the sun I mean, not the eclipse of Boston; that he needs no glass to look at, as there is none smoked dark enough to hinder it from dazzling his eyes. He gets two Boston lawyers to help him kidnap a man. He finds a commissioner, a probate officer of Massachusetts, ready to violate the tenure

of his own trust, prepared for the work; a marshal
anxious to prove his democracy by stealing a man;
he finds newspapers ready to sustain him; the governor lets him go unmolested; the mayor lends him
all the police of the city; and then, illegally and without any authority, against the protestations of the
aldermen, calls out all the soldiers among a hundred
and sixty thousand people, in order to send one innocent negro into bondage, and gives them orders, it
is said, to shoot down any citizen who shall attempt
to pass their lines! The soldiers, half drunk, present
their horse-pistols at the heads of women — their
thumb on the hammer! They stab horses, and with
their sabers slash the heads of men!

When Mr. Burns was first seized by the kidnappers,
nearly all the daily newspapers took sides against the
fugitive. The city was full of ministers all the week;
two anti-slavery conventions were held, one of them
two thousand men strong; the Worcester " Freedom
Club " came down here to visit us: they all went home,
and " order reigns in Warsaw." In South Carolina
there is a public opinion stronger than the law. Let
Massachusetts send an honored citizen to Charleston,
to remonstrate against an iniquitous statute, and most
respectable citizens drive him away. Colored citizens
of Massachusetts rot in the jails of Charleston.
Northern merchants pay the costs. Boston merchants
remonstrated years ago, and the Boston senator did
not dare to offer their paper in Congress! Yes, a
Boston senator did not dare present the remonstrances
of Boston merchants! The South despises us. Do
you wonder at the treatment we receive? I wonder
not at all.

Now, let me say another word — it must be a brief

one — of this particular case. When Mr. Burns was kidnapped, a public meeting was called in Faneuil Hall. Who went there? Not one of the men who are accustomed to control public opinion in Boston. If ten of them had appeared on that platform, Mr. Phillips and myself would not have troubled the audience with our speech. We would have yielded the place — to citizens of " eminent gravity " giving their counsel, and there would have been no man carried out of Boston. I could mention ten men, known to every man here, who, if they had been there, would have so made such public opinion, that the Fugitive Slave Bill commissioner never would have found " evidence " or " law " enough to send Anthony Burns back to Alexandria. There was not one of them there. They did not wish to be there. They cared nothing for freedom.

In general, the blame of this wickedness rests on the city of Boston, much of it on Massachusetts, on New England, and on all the North. But here I must single out some of the individuals who are personally responsible for this outrage.

I begin with the commissioner. He was the prime mover.

Now, as a general thing, the commissioners who kidnap men in America have had a proclivity to wickedness. It has been structural, constitutional. Manstealing was in their bones. It was an osteological necessity. A phrenologist, examining their heads, would have said: " Beware of this man. He is ' fit for treason, stratagems, and spoils.' "

It seems natural that Mr. Kane should steal men in Philadelphia. His name is warrant to bear out the deed. In Boston, the former kidnapper lost no

" personal popularity " by the act. His conduct seems alike befitting the disposition he was born with, and the culture he has attained to; and so appears equally natural and characteristic. But I thought Mr. Loring of a different disposition. His is a pleasant face to look at, dignified, kindly — a little weak, yet not without sweetness and a certain elevation. I have seen him sometimes in the probate office, and it seemed to me a face fit to watch over the widow and the fatherless. When a bad man does a wicked thing, it astonishes nobody. When one otherwise noble and generous is overtaken in a fault, we " weep to record, and blush to give it in," and in the spirit of meekness seek to restore such a one. But when a good man deliberately, voluntarily, does such a deed as this, words cannot express the fiery indignation which it ought to stir up in every man's bosom. It destroys confidence in humanity.

The wickedness began with the commissioner. He issued the writ. It was to end with him — he is sheriff, judge, jury. He is paid twice as much for condemning as for acquitting the innocent.

He was not obliged to be a commissioner. He was not forced into that bad eminence. He went there voluntarily fifteen years ago, as United States commissioner, to take affidavits and acknowledgments. Slave-catching was no part of his duty. The soldiers of Nicholas execute their master's tyranny because they are forced into it. The only option with them is to shoot with a musket, or be scourged to death with the knout. If Mr. Loring did not like kidnapping, he need not have kept his office. But he liked it. He wrote three articles, cold and cruel, in the *Daily Advertiser*, defending the Fugitive Slave Bill.

But if he kept the office he is not officially obliged to do the work. The district attorney is not suspected of being so heavily fraught with conscience that he cannot trim his craft to sail with any political wind which offers to carry him to port; but even Mr. Hallett refused to kidnap Ellen Craft. He did not like the business. It was not a part of Mr. Loring's official obligation. A man lets himself to a sea-captain as a mariner to go a general voyage. He is not obliged to go privateering or pirating whenever the captain hoists the black flag. He can leave at the next port. A laborer lets himself to a farmer to do general farm work. By and by his employer says, " I intend to steal sheep." The man is not obliged by his contract to go and steal sheep because his employer will. That would be an illegal act no doubt. But suppose the General Government had made a law, authorizing every farmer to steal all the black sheep he can lay his hands on; nay, commanding the felony. Is this servant, who is hired to do general farm work, obliged in his official capacity to go and steal black sheep? I do not look at it so. I do not think any man does. A lawyer turns off many a client. A constable refuses many a civil job. He does not like the business. The commissioner took this business because he liked to take it. I do not say he was not " conscientious." I know nothing of that. I only speak of the act. Herod was " conscientious," for aught I know, and Iscariot and Benedict Arnold, and Aaron Burr. I do not touch that question. To their own master they stand or fall. The torturers of the Spanish Inquisition may have been " conscientious."

It was entirely voluntary for Mr. Loring to take this case. There was no official obligation, no profes-

sional honor, that required him to do it. He had a
" great precedent," even, in Mr. Hallett, to decline it.

In 1843, Massachusetts enacted a law prohibiting
any State officer from acting as slave-catcher, for
fear of abuse of our own law. Since that, Mr. Loring has become judge of probate. There was a
chance for a good man to show his respect for the
law of the State which gives him office.

Now see how the case was conducted. I am no
lawyer, and shall not undertake to judge the technical
subtleties of the case. But look at the chief things
which require no technical skill to judge.

The commissioner spoke very kindly, and even pa-
ternally, when he consulted Burns. I confess the tear
started to my eye when he looked so fatherly towards
the man, like a judge of probate, and asked him,
" Would you like a little time to prepare to make a
defense? " And when Mr. Burns replied, " Yes," he
honorably gave him some time, forty-eight hours, to
decide whether he would make a defense on Saturday,
May 27. He also honorably gave Mr. Burns and
his counsel a little time to make ready for trial. He
gave them from Saturday until Monday! True, it
was only twenty-four hours; Sunday intervened, and
lawyers, like other laymen, and ministers, are supposed to be at meeting on Sunday. That twenty-
four hours — it was not very much time to allow for
the defense of a man whose liberty was in peril! If
Mr. Burns had been arraigned for murder, he would
have had several months to prepare for his trial, the
purse and the arm of Massachusetts to summon witnesses for his defense. But as he was charged with
no crime, only with being the involuntary slave of one
of our Southern masters — as the Fugitive Slave Act

was not designed to " establish justice," but its opposite, or to " insure the blessings of liberty," but the
curse of bondage — he may have only twenty-four
hours to make ready for his defense: his counsel and
a minister may visit him — others are excluded!

If Mr. Burns had been arraigned for stealing a
horse, for slander, or anything else, not twenty-four
hours, or days, but twenty-four weeks would have been
granted him to make ready for trial. A common
lawsuit, for a thousand dollars, in the Supreme Court
of Suffolk, is not ordinarily tried within a year; and,
if any questions of law are to be settled, not disposed
of within two years. Here, however, a man was on
trial for more than life, and but twenty-four hours
were granted him! I accept that thankfully, and tender Mr. Loring my gratitude for that! It is more
than I looked for from any Fugitive Slave Bill commissioner, except him. I never thought him capable
of executing this wickedness. Honor him for this
with due honor — no more, no less.

When the hearing began, the kidnapper's counsel
urged that the testimony taken at first, when Mr.
Burns was brought up, was in the case. The commissioner held to this monstrous position; and it was
only after the urgent opposition of the prisoner's
counsel that he consented it should be put in *de novo*.

But after the kidnapping lawyers put in their evidence, the counsel for Mr. Burns asked time for conference and consultation, as the most important questions of law and fact came up; they were weary with
long service and exhausting labor — and they begged
the commissioner to adjourn for an hour or two. It
was already almost three o'clock. When hard pressed,
he granted them thirty minutes to get up their law

and their evidence, take refreshment, and come back
to court.   At length he extended it to forty minutes!
Much of that time was lost to one of the counsel by
the troops, who detained him at the door.   But the
next day, after Mr. Burns's counsel had brought in
evidence to show that he was in Boston on the 1st
of March — which nobody expected, for Brent al-
leges that he saw him in Virginia on the 19th of
March, and that he escaped thence on the 24th —
then, after a conference with the marshal, he grants
the kidnapper's lawyers an hour and a quarter to
meet this new and unexpected evidence.   Of course he
knew that in granting them this he really gave them all
night to get up their evidence, prepare their defense,
and come into court the next morning, and rebut what
had been said.   Is that fair?   Consider what a matter there was at stake — a man's liberty for ever and
ever on earth!   Consider that Mr. Loring was judge
and jury — that it was a " court " without appeal;
that no other court could pass upon his verdict, and
reverse it, if afterwards it was shown to be suspicious
or proved to be wrong.   He grants Mr. Burns thirty
minutes, and the other side, at once, an hour and a
quarter, virtually all night!   That is not all.   His
decision was limited to one point, namely, the identity
of the prisoner.   If Mr. Burns answered the description of the fugitive given in the record, the commissioner took it for granted, first, that he was a slave —
there was no proof; second, that he had escaped into
another State — that was not charged in the record,
nor proved by testimony; third, that he owed service
and labor to Colonel Suttle, not to the lessee, who
had a limited fee in his services, nor to the mortgagee,
who had the conditional fee of his person; but to

Colonel Suttle, the reversioner, the original claimant of his body.

Now the statute leaves the party claimant his choice between two processes; one under its sixth section, the other under the tenth.

The sixth section obliges the claimant to prove three points — 1, That the person claimed *owes* service; 2, That he has *escaped;* and, 3, That the party before the court is the *identical one* alleged to be a slave.

The tenth section makes the claimant's certificate conclusive as to the first two points, and only leaves the identity to be proved.

In this case, the claimant, by offering proof of service and escape, made his election to proceed under the sixth section.

Here he failed: failed to prove service; failed to prove escape. Then the commissioner allowed him to swing round and take refuge in the tenth section, leaving identity only to be proved; and this he proved by the prisoner's confession, made under duress and in terror, if at all; wholly denied by him; and proved only by the testimony of a witness of whom we know nothing, but that he was contradicted by several witnesses as to the only point to which he affirmed capable of being tested.

So, then, the commissioner reduced the question precisely to this: Is the prisoner at the bar the same Anthony Burns whom Brent saw in Virginia on the 19th day of March last, and who the claimant swears in his complaint escaped from Virginia on the 24th of March?

One man, calling himself " William Brent, a merchant of Richmond," testified as to the question of

identity — " This is Burns."   He was asked, " When
did you see him in Virginia? " and he answered, " On
the 19th of March last."   But nobody in court knew
Mr. Brent, and Mr. Loring himself confessed that he
stood " under circumstances that would bias the fairest mind."   He had come all the way from Richmond
to Boston to make out the case.   Doubtless he expected his reward — perhaps in money, perhaps in
honor; for it is an honor in Virginia to support the
institutions of that State.   But on the other side,
many witnesses testified that Burns was here in Boston on the 1st of March, and worked several days at
the Mattapan Iron Works, at South Boston.   Several
men, well known in Boston — persons of unimpeached
integrity — testified to the fact.   No evidence
rebutted their testimony.   Nothing was urged to im-
pugn their veracity.   The commissioner says their
" integrity is admitted," and " no imputation of bias
could be attached " to them.   So, to decide between
these two, Mr. Loring takes the admissions of the
fugitive, alleged to have been made under duress, in
the presence of his " master," made in jail; when he
was surrounded by armed ruffians; when he was " intimidated " by fear — admissions which Mr. Burns
denied to the last, even after the decision.   This was
the proof of identity!

The record called Burns a man with " dark complexion."   The prisoner is a full-blooded negro.   His
complexion is black almost as my coat.   The record
spoke of Burns as having a scar on his right hand.
The right hand of this man had been broken; it was
so badly injured that when it was opened he could
only shut it by grasping it with his left.   The bone
stuck out prominent.   The kidnapper's witness tes-

tified that Burns was in Virginia on the 19th of March.
Several witnesses — I know not how many — testified
that he was in Boston nineteen days before!

Mr. Brent stated nothing to show that he had ever
had any particular knowledge of Mr. Burns, or particularly observed his person. Some of the witnesses
for the prisoner did not testify merely from general
observation of his form or features, but they stated
that they had noted especially the scar on his cheek,
and his broken hand, and they knew him to be the man.
Besides, this testimony is of multiplied force, not
being that of so many to one fact; that of each
stands by itself. There was a cloud of witnesses to
prove that Mr. Burns was in Boston from the 1st of
March. If their evidence could be invalidated, it was
not attacked in court. Their fairness was admitted.

Not many years ago, a woman was on trial in Boston for the murder of her own child. At first she
pleaded guilty, and, weeping, stated the motives which
led to the unnatural crime. But the court interfered,
induced her to retract the plea, and to make a defense. And in spite of her voluntary admissions made
in court, she was acquitted — for there was not evidence to warrant a legal conviction.

Mr. Loring seemed to regard slavery as a *crimen
exceptum;* and when a man is charged with it he is
presupposed to be guilty, and must be denied the usual
means of defense. So out of the victim's own mouth
he extorts the proof that this is the man named in
the record.

A man not known to anybody in court brings a paper
from Alexandria claiming Anthony Burns as his slave;
the paper was drawn up five hundred miles off; in the
absence of Mr. Burns; by his enemies, who sought for

his liberty and more than his life. He brought one witness to testify to the identity of the man, who says that, in his fear, Burns said, " I am the man." But seven witnesses, whose veracity was not impeached in the court, testify that the prisoner *was in Boston* in the early part of March; and therefore it appears that he is not the Burns who *was in Virginia* on the 19th of March, and thence escaped on the 24th. To decide between the two testimonies — that of one Virginian under circumstances that would bias the fairest mind, and seven Bostonians free from all bias — the commissioner takes the words put into the mouth of Mr. Burns.

Now, the Fugitive Slave Bill provides that the testimony of the fugitive shall not be received as evidence in the case. Mr. Loring avoids that difficulty. He does not call it " testimony " or " evidence " He calls it " admissions "; accepts it to prove the " identity," and decides the case against him. But who proves that Mr. Burns made the admissions? There are two witnesses: 1. A man hired to kidnap him, one of the marshal's " guard," a spy, a hired informer, set to watch the prisoner and make inquisition. Of what value was his testimony? 2. Mr. Brent, who had come five hundred miles to assist in catching a runaway slave, and claimed Mr. Burns as the slave. This was the only valuable witness to prove the admission. So the admission is proved by the admission of Mr. Brent, and the testimony of Mr. Brent is proved by the admission! Excellent Fugitive Slave Bill " evidence " ! Brent confirms Brent! There is, I think, a well-known axiom of the common law, that " admissions shall go in entire " — all that the prisoner said. Now, Mr. Loring rules in just what serves the interest of the claimant, and rules out everything that serves Mr. Burns's interest. And is that Massachusetts justice?

Remember, too, that Commissioner Loring is the whole court — a " judge " not known to the Constitution; a " jury " only known in the inquisition! There is no appeal from his decision. The witness came from Virginia to swear away the freedom of a citizen of Massachusetts, charged with no crime. When the marshal, and the men hired to kidnap, are about the poor black man, it is said he makes an admission that he is the fugitive; and on that " evidence " Mr. Loring decides that he is to go into bondage for ever. It was conduct worthy of the Inquisition of Spain!* Let doubts weigh for the prisoner, is a rule as old as legal attempts at justice. Here, they weigh against him. The case is full of doubts — doubts on every side. He rides over them all. He takes the special words he wants, and therewith strikes down the prisoner's claim to liberty.

Suppose, in the present instance, the fugitive had been described as a man of light complexion, blue eyes, and golden hair: then, suppose some white man, you or I, answered the description, and some ruffian swore to the identity. By that form of law, any man, any woman, in the city of Boston, might have been taken and carried off into bondage straightway, irredeemable bondage, bondage for ever.

Commissioner Loring had no better ground for tak-

---

* Tacitus thinks it a piece of good fortune that Agricola died before such " admissions " were made evidence to ruin a man, as in Domitian's time *quum suspiria nostra subscriberentur!* — Agricola, c. xlv.

ing away the liberty of Anthony Burns than in the case I have just supposed.

Suppose Colonel Suttle had claimed the mayor and aldermen of Boston as his slaves; had brought a "record" from Alexandria reciting their names, and setting forth the fact of their owing service, and their escape from it; had them kidnapped and brought before Mr. Loring. According to his own ruling, the only question he has to determine is this: "the identity of the persons." A witness testifies that the mayor and aldermen of Boston are the parties named in the record as owing service and having escaped therefrom. The Commissioner says "the facts to be proved by the claimant are three.

"1. That the parties charged owed him service in Virginia.

"2. That they escaped from that service.

"These facts he has proved by the record which the statute (sec. 10) declares 'shall be held, and taken to be full and conclusive evidence of the fact of escape, and that the service or labor of the person escaping is due to the party in such record mentioned.'

"Thus these two facts are removed entirely and absolutely from my jurisdiction, and I am entirely and absolutely precluded from applying evidence to them; if, therefore, there is in the case evidence capable of such application, I cannot make it.

"3. The third fact is the identity of the parties before me with the parties mentioned in the record.

"This identity is the only question I have a right to consider. To this, and to this alone, I am to apply the evidence.

"And then, on the whole testimony, my mind is satisfied beyond a reasonable doubt of the identity of the respondents with the parties named in the record.

"On the law and facts of the case, I consider the claimant entitled to the certificate from me which he claims."

The mayor and aldermen go into bondage for ever. The liberty of all this audience might be thus sworn away by a commissioner and another kidnapper.

But the "ruling" is not the worst thing in the case. The commissioner had prejudged it all. He had prejudged it entirely before he had even begun this mock trial; before he heard the defense; before the prisoner had any counsel to make a defense. Here is my proof. On Friday (May 26), Wendell Phillips went to Cambridge to see Mr. Loring. He is a professor of law in Harvard College, teaching law and justice to the young men who go up thither to learn law and justice! Mr. Phillips went there to get permission to visit Mr. Burns, and see if he would make a defense and have counsel. Mr. Loring advised Mr. Phillips to make no defense. He said: "Mr. Phillips, I think the case is so clear that you would not be justified in placing any obstructions in the way of the man's going back, as he probably will."

So, as the matter was decided beforehand, it was to be only a mock trial, and might just as well have been dispensed with. It keeps up some hollow semblance to the form of the Fugitive Slave Bill; but it was all prejudged before Mr. Burns had selected his counsel or determined to have any. Place no "obstructions in the way of the man's going back, *as he probably will!*"

Nor is that all. Before any defense had been made, on Saturday night, Mr. Loring drew up a bill of sale of Anthony Burns. Here it is, in his own handwriting : —

" Know all men in these Presents — That I, Charles F. Suttle, of Alexandria, in Virginia, in consideration of twelve hundred dollars, to me paid, do hereby release and discharge, quitclaim and convey to Antony Byrnes, his liberty; and I hereby manumit and release him from all claims and services to me for ever, hereby giving him his liberty to all intents and effects for ever.

" In testimony whereof, I have hereto set my hand and seal, this twenty-seventh day of May, in the year of our Lord, eighteen hundred and fifty-four."

What should you say of a judge of the Supreme Court of Massachusetts who should undertake to negotiate a note of hand which was a matter of litigation before him in court? What if the chief justice, before he had heard a word of the case of the last man tried for murder — before the prisoner had any counsel — had told some humane man taking an interest in the matter, " You would not be justified in placing any obstructions in the way of the man's being hanged as he probably will "? Add this, also: here Commissioner Loring is justice to draw the writ, judge, jury, all in one! Do the annals of judicial tyranny show a clearer case of judgment without a hearing?

This is not yet the end of the wickedness. Last Wednesday night the Kidnapper's Court adjourned till Friday morning at nine o'clock. Then the " decision " was to be made. But the kidnapper and his assistants, the marshal, etc., knew it on Thursday night. How long before, I know not. The men who hired Mr. Loring to steal a man, with the Fugitive Slave Bill

for his instrument, they knew the decision at least fourteen hours before it was announced in court — I think
twenty hours before.

First, he judged the case before he heard it; second,
he judged it against evidence when he heard it; third,
he clandestinely communicated the decision to one of
the parties half a day before he declared it openly in
court. Could Kane or Curtis do worse? I do not
find that they have ever done so bad. Does Boston
teem with Epsoms and Dudleys, the vermin of the law?
Does New England spawn Jeffreyses and Scroggses,
whom we supposed impossible — fictitious characters
too bad to be?

Look at the marshal's conduct. Of his previous
character I say nothing. But his agents arrested Mr.
Burns on a false charge; threatened violence if he
should cry out; they kept him in secret. Nobody
came nigh unto him.

The trial was unfairly conducted on the marshal's
part. The public was excluded from the court-house.
His servants lined the stairways, insulting the people.
Southerners were freely admitted, but Northern gentlemen kept out. Rude, coarse, and insolent fellows
found no check. Clergymen and lawyers were turned
back, and Southern students of law let in. Two gentlemen were refused admission; but when one declared
he was from Virginia, the other from South Carolina,
they were both admitted on the instant. The whole
court-house seemed to be the property of the slave
power.

He crowded the court-house with soldiers. Some of
them were drunk, and charged bayonet upon the counsel and witnesses for Burns, and thrust them away.
He employed base men for his guard. I never saw

such a motley crew as this kidnapper's gang collected together, save in the darkest places of London and Paris, whither I went to see how low humanity might go down, and yet bear the semblance of man.   He raked the kennels of Boston.   He dispossessed the stews, bawding the courts with unwonted infamy.   He gathered the spoils of brothels; prodigals not peni- tent, who upon harlots had wasted their substance in riotous living; pimps, gamblers, the *succubus* of slav- ery; men which the gorged jails had cast out into the streets scarred with infamy; fighters, drunkards, pub- lic brawlers; convicts that had served out their time, waiting for a second conviction; men whom the subtlety of counsel, or the charity of the gallows, had left un- hanged.   " No eye hath seen such scarecrows."   The youngest of the police judges found ten of his constit- uents there.*   Jailer Andrews, it is said, recognized forty of his customers among them.   It is said that Albert J. Tirrell was invited to move in that leprous gang, and declined! †   " The wicked walk on every side when the vilest men are exalted! "   The publican who fed those locusts of Southern tyranny, said that out of the sixty-five, there was but one respectable man, and he kept aloof from all the rest.   I have seen courts of justice in England, Holland, Belgium, Germany, France, Italy, and Switzerland, and I have seen just such men.   But they were always in the dock, not the servants of the court.   The marshal was right; " the statute is so cruel and wicked that it should not be executed by good men."   He chose fit tools for fitting

---

* Thomas Russell.
† While these sheets are passing through the press I learn that three of the marshal's guard have been arrested for crimes of violence committed *within twenty-four hours after the rendi- tion. Set a thief to serve a thief.*

XIII—20

work. I do not think Herod sent the guardian of orphans to massacre the innocents of Bethlehem. I
doubt that Pontius Pilate employed a judge of probate to crucify Jesus between two thieves!

There was an unfairness about the offer to sell Mr.
Burns. I do not know whose fault that was. His
claimant pretended that he would sell; but when
the money was tendered, his agents delayed, equivo-
cated, wore out the time, till it was Sunday; and the
deed could not legally be done. It was the man, and
not the money they wanted. He offered to sell the
man for twelve hundred dollars. The price was exorbitant, he would not bring eight hundred at Alexandria.

There was another trick. At one time it was
thought the evidence would compel the reluctant commissioner to free his victim. Then it was proposed
that he should be seized in the court, and either sum-
marily declared a slave by some other commissioner,
or else carried off with no further mock trial. I think
it would have been done; but Commissioner Loring was
ready to do the work demanded of him, and earn his
twofold pay.

The conduct of the governor requires same expla-
nation. The law of Massachusetts was cloven down
by the sword of the marshal; no officer could be found
to serve the writ of personal replevin, designed by
the Massachusetts legislature to meet exactly such
cases, and bring Mr. Burns before a Massachusetts
court. The governor could not be induced to attend
to it: Monday he was at the meeting of the Bible Society; Thursday at the meeting of the Sunday Schools.
If the United States marshal had invaded the sovereignty of South Carolina, where do you think her
governor would have been?

The conduct of the mayor of Boston deserves to be remembered. He had the police of the city in Court Square, aiding the kidnapper. It was not their fault. They served against their will. Captain Hayes, of the police, that day magnanimously resigned his charge.* The mayor called out the soldiers at great cost, to some one. He did this on his own responsibility. Five aldermen have publicly protested against the breach of honor and justice. After the wicked deed was over, he attended a meeting of Sunday School children in Faneuil Hall. When he was introduced to the audience, " out of the mouth of babes and sucklings " came a hiss! At night, the " citizen soldiery " had a festival. The mayor was at the supper, and toasted the military — eating and drinking and making merry. What did they care, or he, that an innocent citizen of Boston was sent into bondage for ever, and by their hands! The agony of Mr. Burns only flavored their cup.

Thus, on the 2nd of June, Boston sent into bondage the second victim. It ought to have been fifteen

---

* Here is the note of Mr. Hayes to the city authorities; one day his children will deem it a noble trophy: —

" Boston, June 2, 1854.

" To His Honor the Mayor and the Aldermen of the City of Boston: —

" Through all the excitement attendant upon the arrest and trial of the fugitive by the United States Government, I have not received an order which I have conceived inconsistent with my duties as an officer of the police until this day, at which time I have received an order which, if performed, would implicate me in the execution of that infamous " Fugitive Slave Bill."

" I therefore resign the office which I now hold as a Captain of the Watch and Police from this hour, 11 A. M.

Most respectfully yours,

JOSEPH K. HAYES."

days later — the 17th of June. What a spectacle it was! The day was brilliant; there was not a cloud; all about Boston there was a ring of happy summer loveliness; the green beauty of June; the grass, the trees, the heaven, the light; and Boston itself was the theater of incipient civil war!

What a day for Boston! Citizens applauding that a man was to be carried into bondage! Drunken soldiers, hardly able to stand in the street, sung their ribald song — " Oh, carry me back to old Virginia ! " *

* I copy this from one of the newspapers: —

" The Pay of the Boston Military for their Aid in the Rendition of Anthony Burns.

"We write with an 'iron pen' for the benefit of some future historian, that in the 'year of our Lord eighteen hundred and fifty-four, in the city of Boston, there was received for their aid in consigning to the bondage of American chattel slavery one Anthony Burns,— by the grace of God and his own efforts a freeman,— by the independent volunteer militia of said city, the following sums: —

" National Lancers, Capt. Wilmarth	$ 820.00
Boston Light Dragoons, Capt. Wright	1,128.00
Fifth Regiment of Artillery, by Col. Cowdin, for himself, staff, and regiment	3,946.00
Boston Light Infantry, Capt. Rogers	460.00
New England Guards, Capt. Henshaw	432.00
Pulaski Guards, Capt. Wright	328.00
Boston Light Guard, Capt. Follett	500.00
Boston City Guard, Capt. French	488.00
(of which $190 was paid by order to George Young for 'refreshments.')	
Boston Independent Fusileers, Capt. Cooley	320.00
Washington Light Infantry, Capt. Upton	536.00
Mechanic Infantry, Capt. Adams	428.00
National Guard, Lieut. Harlow commanding	416.00
Union Guard, Capt. Brown	476.00
Sarsfield Guard, Capt. Hogan	308.00
Boston Independent Cadets, Capt. Amory	1,136.00
Boston Light Artillery, Capt. Cobb	168.00
Major-General Edmands and staff	715.00

Daniel Webster lies buried at Marshfield; but his dead hand put the chain on Anthony Burns. Last winter it was proposed to build him a monument. He needs it not. Hancock has none; Samuel Adams sleeps in a nameless grave; John Adams has not a stone. We are their monuments; the homage of the people is their epitaph. Daniel Webster also had his monument last Friday. It was the court-house crowded with two hundred and twenty United States soldiers and flanked with a cannon. His monument reached all the way from John Hancock's house in Court Street to the T

Major Pierce and staff of the First Battalion Light Dragoons	$ 146.00
Colonel Holbrook and staff of the first Regiment of Light Infantry	26.00
Brigadier-General Andrews and staff of the First Brigade	107.50
Major Burbank and staff of the Third Battalion of Light Infantry	76.00
William Read, hardware and sporting apparatus dealer, for ammunition	155.28

Total........$13,115.78 "

The sum paid to the *civil officers* of Boston for their services has not yet been made public.

Mr. Burns was subsequently sold to David McDaniel, of Nash county, N. C., on condition that he should *"never be sold to go North."* A most piteous letter was received from him in January, 1855, full of pious gratitude to all who sought to preserve for him the inalienable right to life, liberty, and the pursuit of happiness.

Presently, after Commissioner Loring had accomplished his "legal" kidnapping, he tried to purchase a piece of meat of a noble-hearted butcher in Boylston Market. "I will take that pig," said the Commissioner. "You can't have it," replied the butcher. "What, is it sold?" "No, sir! But you can't buy your meat of me. I want none of your blood-money. It would *burn my pocket!"*

Rev. Nehemiah Adams, D.D., subsequently sent to the Commissioner a presentation copy of his "South Side View of Slavery," with the author's regards!

Wharf; nay, it went far out to sea in the revenue cutter, and is borne seaward or shoreward. Conquer your prejudices! No higher law! On the brass cannon you could read, I STILL LIVE.

Mr. Burns was seized on that day which the Christian Church has consecrated to two of the martyrs, Saints Donatian and Rogatian. They seem to have been put to death by Rictius Varus, the commissioner of Belgic and Celtic Gaul. They suffered death at Nantes. They were impeached for professing themselves Christians. Simple death was not torment enough for being a Christian in the year 287. They were put to the rack first. Their bodies, still held in great veneration, now sleep their dusty slumber in the great cathedral of the town. The antiquarian traveler wonders at the statues of those two martyrs still standing at the corner of the Money-Changers' Street, and telling the tale of times when the Christians only suffered persecution. St. Rogatian's day was not an unfitting time for puritanic Boston to steal a man!

The day on which Mr. Burns was sent from Boston into Alexandrian bondage is still more marked in the Christian Church. It is consecrated to a noble army of martyrs who tasted death at Vienna, in Gaul,— now Vienne, in the south of France — in the year 178 after Christ. I shall never forget the little town, once famous and eminent, where the dreadful event took place. A letter written, it is said, by St. Irenæus himself details the saddening history. It begins, " We the servants of Christ [Mr. Everett might translate it ' *slaves* '], dwelling at Vienna and Lyons in Gaul, to the brethren in Asia and Phrygia who have the same faith and hope with us. Peace, and Grace, and Glory from God the Father, and from our Lord Jesus

Christ." The whole letter is a most touching memorial of the faithful piety of the Christians in days when it cost life to be religious. Anybody may read what remains of it in Eusebius. Here is the story in short: —

A law was passed forbidding Christians to be out of their own houses " in any place whatsoever." The most cruel punishments were denounced against all persons who professed the Christian religion.

The governor, who was also a commissioner appointed for persecuting and murdering the Christians, had the most prominent members of the Church arrested and brought before him. In the " examination " they were treated with such cruelty that Vettius Epagathus, a Christian of distinguished family, undertook their defense, a man so exactly virtuous, that, though young, he won the honor of old Zacharias —" walking in all the commandments and ordinances of the Lord blameless." The commissioner asked him: " Art thou also a Christian? " Epagathus made his " admission " in a loud voice, and shared the fate of the martyrs. The Christians called him the Comforter of Christians,—" for he had the Comforter, the Spirit, in him, more than Zacharias himself; " a title as hateful then as Friend of the Slave now is in the Court or the Church of Kidnappers in Boston.

Sanctus, the deacon; Maturus, a new convert; Attalus, from Asia Minor, one of the pillars of the Church; Blandina, a female slave; Pothinus, ninety years old, and Bishop of Lyons, hard by, were put to the most cruel tortures. Four of them were exposed to the wild beasts in the amphitheatre to divert the spectators! Blandina was fastened to a post to be eaten up by the beasts, and when they left her untouched, the marshal haled her to prison again. "But, last of all, St. Blandina, like a well-born mother who has nursed her children and sent them victorious to the king, hastened after them, rejoicing and leaping for joy at her departure; thrown, indeed, to the wild beasts, she went as if invited to a bridal feast; and after the scourging, after the exposure to wild beasts, after the chair of fire, she was wrapped in a net and tossed by a bull — and at last killed." Others fell with them: Ponticus, a boy of fifteen; Alexander the Phrygian, and many more. They were tortured with cudgels, with whips, with wild beasts, and red-hot plates of iron; at last they died, one by one. The tormentors threw their dead bodies to the dogs: some raged and gnashed their teeth over the dead, seeking to take yet more abundant vengeance thereon; others laughed and made mockery thereof. And others, more gentle, seeming to sympathize as much as they dared, made grievous reproaches, and said, "Where is now their God, and of what profit is their piety, which they loved better even than their own life! Now we shall see if they will ever rise from the dead, and if their God can help and deliver them out of our hands!"

So things went at Allobrogian Vienna on the 2nd of June, sixteen hundred and seventy-six years ago last Friday. The murder of those Christians was just as "legal" as the rendition of Anthony Burns. It would be curious to know what the "respectable" men of the town said thereupon: to see the list of fifteen hundred citizens volunteering their aid; to read the letter of nine hundred and eighty-seven men thanking the commissioner for touching their conscience. The preaching of the priests must have been edifying: —

" I would drive a Christian away from my own door!
I would murder my own mother!"

Doubtless some men said, " The statute which commands the torturous murder of men, women, and children, for no crime but piety, if constitutional, is
wicked and cruel." And doubtless some heathen
" Chief Justice Parker" choked down the rising conscience of mankind, and answered, " Whether the statute is a harsh one or not, it is not for us to determine." * No! it is not for the bloodhound to ask
whether the victim he rends to quivering fragments is
a sinner or a saint; the bloodhound is to bite, and not
consider; he has teeth, not conscience. The Fugitive
Slave Bill commissioner is not to do justly, and love
mercy, and walk humbly with his God; he is to kidnap
men in Boston at ten dollars a head! The pagan
murder of Christians at Vienna under Aurelian, did not
differ much from the Christian kidnapping of Mr.
Burns in Boston under Pierce. But, alas for these
times — it is not recorded of the Romans that any
heathen judge of probate came forward and volunteered to butcher the widows and orphans of the early
Church! Then the tormenter worshiped Mars and
Bellona; now he sits in the Church of Jesus Christ.

Boston chose a fit day to consummate her second
kidnapping. St. Pothinus was a Christian preacher,
so was Anthony Burns —" a minister of the Baptist
denomination," " regularly ordained!" Commissioner Loring could not have done better than select
this time to execute his " decision." On St. Pothinus's
day, let Anthony Burns be led to a martyrdom more

* Reference is here made to the words used by Commissioner
Loring in his " decision," citing the words of the late Chief
Justice Parker.

atrocious! The African churches of Boston may write a letter to-day, which three or four thousand years hence will sound as strange as now the epistle of St. Irenæus. Sixteen hundred and seventy-six years hence, it may be thought the marshal's " guard " is a fair match for the bullies who tortured Blandina. In the next world the district marshal may shake hands with the heathen murderer who put the boy Ponticus to cruel death. I make no doubt there were men at the corners of the streets who clapped hands, as one by one the lions in the public square rent the Christian maidens limb from limb, and strewed the ground with human flesh yet palpitating in its severed agony. Boston can furnish mates for them. But the judge of probate, the teacher of a Sunday School, the member of a church of Christ,— he may wander through all Hades, peopled thick with Roman tormentors, nor never meet with a heathen guardian of orphans who can be his match. Let him pass by. Declamation can add nothing to his deed.

> " To guild refined gold, to paint the lily,
> To throw a perfume on the violet,
> To smooth the ice, or add another hue
> Unto the rainbow, or with taper light
> To seek the beauteous eye of heaven to garnish,
> Is wasteful and ridiculous excess."

No doubt the commissioner for murdering the Christians at Vienna reasoned as " legally " and astutely in the second century as the Fugitive Slave Bill commissioner at Boston in the nineteenth. Perhaps the " argument " was after this wise: — *

" This statute has been decided to be constitutional by the unanimous opinion of the judges of the Su-

* See the commissioner's " decision."

preme Court of the Province of Gaul, after the fullest
argument and the maturest deliberation, to be the law
of this province, as well as and because it is a constitutional law of the Roman Empire; and the wise
words of our revered chief-justice * may well be repeated now, and remembered always. The chief justice says: —

" ' The torture, persecution, and murder of Christians was not created, established, or perpetuated by
the constitution; it existed before; it would have existed if the constitution had not been made. The
framers of the constitution could not abrogate the custom of persecuting, torturing, and murdering Christians, or the rights claimed under it. They took it as
they found it, and regulated it to a limited extent.
The constitution, therefore, is not responsible for the
origin or continuance of this custom of persecuting,
torturing, and murdering Christians — the provision it
contains was the best adjustment which could be made
of conflicting rights and claims to persecute, torture,
and murder, and was absolutely necessary to effect
what may now be considered as the general pacification
by which harmony and peace should take the place of
violence and war. These were the circumstances, and
this the spirit in which the constitution was made —
the regulation of persecution, torture, and murder of
Christians, so far as to prohibit provinces by law from
harboring fugitive Christians, was an essential element
in its formation; and the union intended to be established by it was essentially necessary to the peace and
happiness and highest prosperity of all the provinces

* Hon. Lemuel Shaw. See his "opinion" on the constitu-
tionality of the Fugitive Slave Bill, in 7 Cushing's Reports,
p. 285, et seq.

and towns.   In this spirit, and with these views stead-
ily in prospect, it seems to be the duty of all judges
and magistrates to expound and apply these provisions in the constitution and laws of the Roman Empire, and in this spirit it behooves all persons bound
to obey the laws of the Roman Empire to consider and
regard them.'

"Therefore *Christianos ad Leones* — Let the Christians be torn to pieces by the wild beasts."

Wednesday, the 24th of May, the city was all calm
and still.   The poor black man was at work with one
of his own nation, earning an honest livelihood.   A
judge of probate, Boston born and Boston bred, a
man in easy circumstances, a professor in Harvard
College, was sitting in his office, and with a single
spurt of his pen he dashes off the liberty of a man —
a citizen of Massachusetts.   He kidnaps a man endowed by his Creator with the inalienable right to
life, liberty, and the pursuit of happiness.   He leaves
the writ with the marshal, and goes home to his family,
caresses his children, and enjoys his cigar.   The frivolous smoke curls round his frivolous head, and at
length he lays him down to sleep, and, I suppose, such
dreams as haunt such heads.   But when he wakes next
morn, all the winds of indignation, wrath, and honest
scorn, are let loose.   Before night, they are blowing
all over this Commonwealth — aye, before another
night they have gone to the Mississippi, and wherever
the lightning messenger can tell the tale.   So have I
read in an old medieval legend, that one summer afternoon there came up a "shape, all hot from Tartarus,"
from hell below, but garmented and garbed to represent
a civil-suited man, masked with humanity.   He walked
quiet and decorous through Milan's stately streets, and

scattered from his hand an invisible dust.   It touched
the walls; it lay on the streets; it ascended to the cross
on the minister's utmost top.   It went down to the
beggar's den.   Peacefully he walked through the
streets, vanished and went home.   But the next morning, the pestilence was in Milan, and ere a week had
sped half her population were in their graves; and
half the other half, crying that hell was clutching at
their hearts, fled from the reeking City of the Plague!

Why did the commissioner do all this?   He knew
the consequences that must follow.   He knew what
Boston was.   We have no monument to Hancock and
Adams; but still we keep their graves; and Boston,
the dear old mother that bore them, yet in her bosom
hides the honored bones of men whom armies could
not terrify, nor England bribe.   Their spirit only
sleeps.   Tread roughly, tread roughly on the spot —
their spirit rises from the ground!   He knew that here
were men who never will be silent when wrong is done.
He knew Massachusetts; he knew Boston; he knew that
the Fugitive Slave Bill had only raked the ashes over
fires which were burning still, and that a breath might
scatter those ashes to the winds of heaven, and bid the
slumbering embers flame.   Had he determined already
what should happen to Anthony Burns?   He knew
what had befallen Thomas Sims.   Did he wish another
inhabitant of Boston whipped to death?

I have studied the records of crime — it is a part of
my ministry.   I do not find that any college professor has ever been hanged for murder in all the Anglo-
Saxon family of men, till Harvard College had that
solitary shame.   Is not that enough?   Now she is the
first to have a professor that kidnaps men.   " The
Athens of America " furnished both.

I can understand how a man commits a crime of passion, or covetousness, or rage,— nay, of revenge, or of ambition. But for a man in Boston, with no passion, no covetousness, no rage, with no ambition nor revenge, to steal a poor negro, to send him into bondage,— I cannot comprehend the fact. I can understand the consciousness of a lion, not a kidnapper's heart. Once Mr. Loring defined a lawyer to be " a human agent for effecting a human purpose by human means." Here, and now, the commissioner seems an inhuman agent for effecting an inhuman purpose by inhuman means.

I belong to a school that reverences the infinite perfection of God,— if, indeed, there be such a school. I believe, also, in the nobleness of man; but last week my faith was somewhat sorely tried. As I looked at that miscreant crew, the kidnapper's body-guard, and read in their faces the record and the prophecy of many a crime,

> " Felons by the hand of nature marked,
>   Quoted and signed to do a deed of shame,"

I could explain and not despair. They were tools, not agents. But as I looked into the commissioner's face, mild and amiable, a face I have respected, not without seeming cause; as I remembered his breeding and his culture, his social position, his membership of a Christian church, and then thought of the crime he was committing against humanity, with no temptation, I asked myself, can this be true? Is man thus noble, made in the dear image of the Father, God? Is my philosophy a dream: or are these facts a lie?

But there is another court. The Empsons and the Dudleys have been summoned there before; Jeffreys and Scroggs, the Kanes, and the Curtises, and the Lorings, must one day travel the same unwelcome road. Imagine the scene after man's mythologic way. "Edward, where is thy brother Anthony?" "I know not; am I my brother's keeper, Lord?" "Edward, where is thy brother Anthony?" "Oh, Lord, he was friendless, and so I smote him; he was poor, and I starved him of more than life. He owned nothing but his African body. I took that away from him, and gave it to another man!"

Then listen to the voice of the Crucified —" Did I not tell thee, when on earth, ' Thou shalt love the Lord thy God with all thy understanding and thy heart?'" " But I thought thy kingdom was not of this world."

" Did I not tell thee that thou shouldst love thy neighbor as thyself? Where is Anthony, thy brother? I was a stranger, and you sought my life; naked, and you rent away my skin; in prison, and you delivered me to the tormentors — fate far worse than death. Inasmuch as you did it to Anthony Burns, you did it unto me."

The liberty of America was never in greater peril than now. Hessian bayonets were not half so dangerous as the gold of the national treasury in the hands of this administration. Which shall conquer, slavery or freedom? That is the question. The two cannot long exist side by side. Think of the peril; remember the rapacity of this administration; its reckless leaders: think of Douglas, Cushing, and the rest. They aimed at the enslavement of Nebraska. The Northern majority in Congress yielded that.

Now they aim at Hayti and Cuba. Shall they carry that point? Surely, unless we do our duty. Shall slavery be established at the North, at the West,

and the East; in all the free States? Mr. Toombs
told Mr. Hale —"Before long the master will sit
down at the foot of Bunker Hill monument with his
slaves." Will do it? He has done it already, and
not an officer in the State of Massachusetts made the
least resistance. Our laws were trod down by insolent
officials, and Boston ordered out her soldiers to help the
disgraceful deed. Strange that we should be asked to
make the fetters which are to chain us. Mr. Suttle
is only a feeler. Soon there will be other Suttles in
Boston. Let them come!

It is not only wicked; it is costly. The kidnapping
of Mr. Burns must have cost in all at least one hundred thousand dollars, including the loss of time and
traveling expenses of our friends from the country.
The publican's bill for feeding the marshal's crew is already more than six thousand dollars!

Consider the demoralization of the people produced
by such a deed. Mr. Dana was knocked down in the
street by one of the marshal's posse — as it is abundantly proved.* The blow might easily have been
fatal. It is long since a bully had attacked a respectable citizen in Boston before. Hereafter I fear
it will be more common. You cannot employ such a
body-guard as the marshal had about him in such
business without greatly endangering the safety of
the persons and the property of the town. We shall
hear from them again. What a spectacle it was; the
army of the United States, the soldiers of Boston,
sending an innocent man into slavery! What a lesson

---

* The culprit was held in trifling bail by the court, one of
the marshal's gang became his surety. But the ruffian ab-
sconded, was subsequently arrested at New Orleans, and sent to
the House of Correction for a year and a half.

to the children in the Sunday Schools — to the vagrant
children in the streets, who have no school but the
sights of the city! What a lesson of civilization to
the Irish population of Boston! Men begin to understand this. There never was so much anti-slavery
feeling in Boston before — never so much indignation
in my day. If a law aims at justice, though it fail of
the mark we will respect the law — not openly resist
it or with violence: wait a little, and amend it or repeal
it. But when the law aims at injustice, open, manifest, palpable wickedness, why, we must be cowards
and fools too, if we submit.

Massachusetts has never felt so humiliated before.
Soldiers of the government enforcing a law in peaceful
Boston, the most orderly of Christian cities! We have
had no such thing since the Declaration of Independence! The rendition of Mr. Burns fills New England with sorrow and bitter indignation. The people
tolled the bells at Plymouth. The bones of the forefathers gave that response to the kidnappers in Boston.
At Manchester and several other towns they did the
same. To-day, ministers are preaching as never before. What will it all come to? Men came to Boston peacefully last week. Will they always come
" with only the arms God gave? " One day in the
seventeenth century five thousand country gentlemen
rode into London with a " petition to the king "—
with only the arms God gave them. Not long after
they went thither with Oliver Cromwell at their head
and other " arms " which God also had given. May
such times never return in New England! *

* While this sermon is passing through the press, I find the
following paragraph in a newspaper: —
" One of the Fourth of July celebrations at Columbus, Ga.,
XIII—21

We want no rashness, but calm, considerate action, deliberate, prudent far-seeing. The Fugitive Slave Bill is a long wedge, thin at one end, wide at the other; it is entered between the bottom planks of our Ship of State; a few blows thereon will " enforce " more than the South thinks of. A little more,— and we shall go to pieces. Men talk wildly just now, and I do not credit what cool men say in this heat. But I see what may come — what must come, if a few more blows be struck in that quarter. It was only Mr. Webster's power to manufacture public opinion by his giant will and immense eloquence, which made the North submit at all to the Fugitive Slave Bill. He strained his power to the utmost — and died! Now there is no Webster or Clay; not even a Calhoun; not a first-rate man in the pro-slavery party, North or South. Slavery is not well manned — many hands, dirty, cunning, stealthy,— not a single great, able head.

The cowardice of Mr. Everett has excited the clergy of New England; of all the North. They are stung

was the sale of ninety or a hundred men, women, and boys, by the order of Robert Toombs, United States senator. Here is the advertisement: —

" ' ADMINISTRATOR'S SALE.— Will be sold on the first Tuesday in July next, at the court-house door of Stewart county, within the usual hours of sale, between ninety and one hundred negroes, consisting of men, women, boys, etc. These negroes are all very likely, and between forty and fifty of the number are men and boys. Sold as the property of Henry J. Pope, deceased, in pursuance of an order of the Court of Ordinary of Stewart county, for the benefit of heirs and creditors. Terms of sale, a credit (with interest) until 25th December next.

" ' ROBERT TOOMBS,
" ' Adm'r of Henry J. Pope, deceased.'

" ' Men, women, and boys,' bought on the Fourth of July,— paid for on Christmas! "

with the reproach of the people, and ashamed of their
own past neglect. The Nebraska Bill opens men's
eyes. Agitation was never so violent as at this day.
The prospect of a war with Spain is not inviting to
men who own ships, and want a clear sea and open
market. Pirates, privateers,— Algerine, Greek, Spanish, Portuguese, West Indian,— are not welcome to the
thoughts of men. The restoration of the slave trade
is not quite agreeable to the farmers and mechanics
of the North. This attempt to seize a man in Boston;
the display of force; the insolence of the officials; the
character of the men concerned in this iniquity — all is
offensive. Then there was insult, open and intentional.
Boston merchants feel as they never did before. All
Massachusetts is incensed. The wrath of Massachusetts is slow, but she has wrath, has courage, " perse-
verance of the saints."

Let us do nothing rashly. What is done hastily
must be done over again — it is not well done. This is
what I would recommend:

1. A convention of all Massachusetts, without distinction of party, to take measures to preserve the
rights of Massachusetts. For this we want some new
and stringent laws for the defense of personal liberty,
for punishing all who invade it on our soil. We want
powerful men as officers to execute these laws.

2. A general convention of all the States to organize
for mutual protection against this new master.

It is not speeches that we want — but action; not
rash, crazy action, but calm, deliberate, systematic
action — organization for the defense of personal liberty and the State rights of the North. Now is a good
time; let us act with cool energy. By all means let
us do something, else the liberties of America go to

ruin — then what curses shall mankind heap upon us!

" And deep, and more deep — as the iron is driven,—
    Base slaves, will the whet of our agony be,
When we think — as the damned haply think of the heaven
    They had once in their reach — that we might have been free."

But, my friends, out of all this dreadful evil we can bring relief. The remedy is in our hearts and hands. God works no miracles. There is power in human nature to end this wickedness. God appointed the purpose, provided the means — a divine purpose, human means. Only be faithful, and in due time we shall triumph over the destroyer. Every noble quality of man works with us; each attribute of God. We are His instruments. Let us faithfully do the appointed work! Darkness is about us! Journey forward; light is before us!

" O God, who in Thy dear still heaven
    Dost sit and wait to see
The errors, sufferings, and crimes
    Of our humanity;
How deep must be Thy causal love,
    How whole Thy final care,
Since Thou who rulest all above
    Canst see, and yet canst bear!"

APPENDIX

I

My friend, the Rev. Dr. Edward Beecher, thinks I have been unjust to the ministers,— judging from the sermon as reported in the *Commonwealth*. So he published an article in that paper on Friday, June 9. It comes from a powerful and noble man. I wish he had made out a stronger case against me.

" THEODORE PARKER AND THE MINISTRY.

" *Mr. Editor,*— In his sermon, last Sabbath, Mr. Parker seems to charge the clergy of the country with a general, if not uni-

versal, delinquency in the cause of freedom with respect to the
Fugitive Slave Law.

*   *   *   *   *   *   *

" Now, if Mr. Parker were to be represented, on both continents, as an advocate of kidnapping, and of the Fugitive
Slave Law, he would probably regard it as unjust. But he
does not seem to be sufficiently alive to the idea, that it is
unjust to convey the idea that this is true of clergymen who
have from the first opposed these measures as earnestly and
decidedly as he himself. He seems to be fully convinced that
to rob even one slave of his liberty is a crime. He does not
seem as deeply to feel that it is a crime to rob even our ministers of that reputation which in his own case he prizes so
highly. Even if the cases of fidelity were few, for that very
reason they should receive from a lover of the cause the more
careful and particular notice and praise. In cases like these,
if ever, discriminations and truthful statements of facts are a
sacred duty. Let those be censured who deserve censure, and
let those be commended who deserve praise.

" Allow me, then, to state some of the facts of the case chiefly
concerning the Orthodox Congregational pastors and churches,
leaving to other denominations, if they see fit, to state similar
facts, more at large, in their own case. From my own knowledge, I am assured that it would not be difficult to multiply
them, especially if a full account were to be given of all the
unpublished sermons of the times.

" It is not true, as Mr. P.'s statements imply, that Mr.
Parker was the only one who preached and wrote and prayed
against the Fugitive Slave Law.

" The *Congregationalist,* then edited by the Rev. H. M. Dexter, Rev. Mr. Storrs, and myself, devoted all its energies to
a conflict with the Fugitive Slave Bill, and a vindication of
the claim of the higher law. Some of its articles were considered of such importance as to be honored with special attention and censure by Mr. Choate, at the Boston Union Saving
meeting. Our articles, if collected, would make a large volume.

" The law was also most earnestly opposed from the pulpit
by many ministers, Mr. Stone, Mr. Dexter, and myself among
the number. The same thing was true of a large number of
the clergymen of New England and the Middle States. I have
before me published sermons or other addresses to this effect
from Storrs and Spear, of Brooklyn, N. Y.; Beecher, of Newark,
N. J.; Thompson and Cheever, of New York; Bacon, of New
Haven, Conn.; Colver, of Boston; Wallcott, now of Providence;
Leavitt, then of Newton; Withington, of Newbury, Mass.;

Whitcomb, of Stoneham; Thayer, of Ashland; Arvine, of West Boylston, and others. Nothing can be more able and eloquent than their defense of God's law, as opposed to the infamous Slave Bill. Others also were published which I have not on file, and I know of several very able discourses against the law which were not published. If a true report could be made of all the sermons then preached, and of the influence then exerted in other ways by the ministry of the North, there is reason to believe that a very large majority would be found to have set themselves decidedly against the law, and to have advocated its entire disobedience.

"The fact is, that undue importance has been given to those of the ministry who favored obedience to that law, and they have been made to overshadow its more numerous opponents.

"In relation to Andover, the facts are these: — Professor Stuart, who for some years had ceased to act as professor in the Seminary, published his views, greatly to the regret of a large portion of his brethren. That the body of the professors of the institution did not sympathize in these views, is evident from the fact that when a paper approving the compromise was circulated there, Professors Park, Phelps, and Edwards refused to sign. Only one acting professor did sign, much to his own subsequent regret. This does not justify the sweeping affirmation, 'Andover went for kidnapping.' Mr. Parker ought to be more careful, and less free in the use of such wholesale charges. Moreover, the positions of Professor Stuart were thoroughly exposed by members of his own denomination.

"The Rev. Rufus Clark, now of East Boston, published in the columns of the *Atlas* a thorough refutation of his pamphlet in a series of very able articles, which were subsequently republished in a pamphlet form.

"Rev. George Perkins, of Connecticut, performed a similar service in that State. Rev. Mr. Dexter, of Boston, exposed himself to an excited retort from Professor Stuart, for his keen and able exposure of his course on the Compromises.

"That there was a sad failure on the part of too many of the clergy of Boston and other commercial cities, cannot be denied; nor do I desire to avert from them merited censure. But ought the labors of such men as the clerical editors and contributors of the *Independent* to be passed by in silence in speaking of the prominent clergy of the city of New York?

"As to the other cities named, if there were but one exception in each, it ought to have been prominently named and honored. I do not doubt that there were more.

"As to the country churches and pastors of New England,

I have already stated my opinion that the vast majority were opposed to the Fugitive Slave Law. It is not just to regard the Nebraska protest as a virtual confession and reparation of past neglect, but rather as a development of the real feeling of the clergy of New England. Charity thinketh no evil, and there is no gain at this time in depreciating the merits of any earnest opponents of the aggressions of slavery.

"As Mr. Parker expects to be read in all parts of this nation and on both sides of the Atlantic, I will not doubt that his strongly avowed appreciation of what is just and honorable in action will induce him to revise and correct his statement of facts, and instead of such sweeping and indiscriminate censure, to give honor where honor is due.

EDWARD BEECHER."

I have repeatedly and in the most public manner done honor to the ministers who have opposed this great iniquity, and did not suppose that any one would misunderstand the expressions which Dr. Beecher considers as "sweeping." When he reads in the Bible that *"Jerusalem and all Judea went out,"* I suppose he thinks that some persons stayed at home. But I am sorry he could not make out a stronger case for his side. I know nothing of what was said *privately,* or of sermons which never get spoken of out of the little parish where they are written. He mentions *sixteen Orthodox ministers* who published matter in opposition to the Fugitive Slave Bill. It is not a very large number for all the churches in New Jersey, New York, Connecticut, Rhode Island, and Massachusetts to furnish. I can mention more.

These are the facts in respect to Andover: Professor Stuart, the most distinguished clergyman in all New England, wrote an elaborate defense of the Fugitive Slave Bill, and of Mr. Webster's conduct in defending it. He was induced to do this by Mr. Webster himself. The work is well known — *Conscience and the Constitution* — and it is weak and doting as it is wicked. Professor Stuart and two other Andover professors — Rev. Ralph Emerson, D.D., and Rev. Leonard Woods, D.D. — signed the letter to Mr. Webster expressing their "deep obligations for what this speech has done and is doing;" thanking him "for recalling us to our duties under the Constitution, and for the broad, national, and patriotic views" it inculcates, and desiring to "express to you our entire concurrence in the sentiments of your speech." It seems three other professors — Messrs. Park, Phelps, and Edwards — did not sign it, and one of the signers — Dr. Woods or Dr. Emerson — did it much to his own subsequent regret. But did he make his regret public?

Did Andover in public say anything against the conduct of the signers?

At the Annual Conference of Unitarian Ministers, in May, 1851, long and public defenses of kidnapping were made by "the most eminent men in the denomination." One doctor of divinity vindicated the attempt of his parishioners to kidnap mine, whom I took to my house for shelter. Dr. Dewey's promise to send back his own mother or brother got the heartiest commendation from more than one "prominent minister." Dr. Dewey was compared with "faithful Abraham;" his declaration was "imputed to him for righteousness." Many of the country ministers were of a different opinion. Some of them declared his conduct "atrocious." Of course there were noble men in the Unitarian denomination, who were faithful to the great principles of Christianity. I have often spoken in their praise, and need not now mention their names, too well known to require honor from me.

But I am sorry to say that I can retract nothing from what I have said in general respecting the conduct of the clergy of all denominations at that time. At a large public meeting in Boston a Vigilance Committee was appointed to look after the fugitives and furnish them aid. The Committee sent a circular to every church in Massachusetts, asking for the fugitives donations of money and clothes; and received replies from *eighty-seven churches,* which gave us $1484.56!

Here is my letter in reply to Dr. Beecher, from the *Commonwealth* of June 10, 1854: —

"Dr. Edward Beecher and Theodore Parker.

"*Rev. Edward Beecher, D.D.,*— My dear Sir, I have just read your letter in the *Commonwealth* of this morning, in which you maintain that the statements in my last sermon respecting the delinquency of the Northern clergy were too sweeping, and that I did injustice to the ministers who stoutly resisted the Fugitive Slave Bill and its execution. Perhaps the language of the sermon would seem to warrant your opinion. But I have so many times, and in so public a manner, expressed my respect and veneration for those noble men who have been found faithful in times of peril, that I cannot think I am in general obnoxious to the charge you make against me.

In respect to the special sermon of last Sunday, I beg leave to inform you that the *whole* was neither printed nor preached; the entire sermon is now in press, and when you see it, I think you will find that I do no injustice to the men you speak of. As I spoke on Sunday, I did not suppose any one would misunderstand my words, or think I wished to be regarded as the only one found faithful. Certainly I have many times done honor to the gentlemen you mention, and to the journals you refer to — with others you do not name. And allow me to say, the conduct of yourself and all your family has not only been a strong personal encouragement to me, but a theme of public congratulation which I have often brought forward in lectures, and sermons, and speeches. I am a little surprised that you should suppose that by the *churches of commerce* in New York, Boston, etc., I mean *all the churches* of these towns. I still think that from 1850 to 1852 the general voice of the New England churches, so far as it was heard through the press, was in favor of the Fugitive Slave Bill and its execution. This was especially true of the rich and fashionable churches in the great commercial towns. Surely you cannot forget the numerous clerical eulogies on the late Mr. Webster, which sought to justify all his political conduct. I do not think you have made out a very strong case for Andover.

"I am sorry to have given pain to a man whose life is so noble and his character so high; but believe me,

Respectfully and truly yours,

THEODORE PARKER.

II

"Mr. Attorney Hallett's Interference with the Purchase of the Fugitive.

Boston, Saturday, June 3, 1854.

"*To the Editors of the Atlas:* — You have called my attention to an article in your paper this morning signed " L.," and to a contradiction of its statement in the *Journal* of this evening, by authority of the United States district attorney. I know nothing of the origin of either of these articles, but will, at your request, give you a narrative of my own connection with the recent negotiation for the freedom of " Byrnes," believing that such a narrative will be altogether pertinent to the fact which you seek to establish, namely, the interference of the United States district attorney in the negotiation above referred to.

"On Saturday afternoon last, the Rev. Mr. Grimes called upon me and said that the owner of Byrnes had offered to sell him for twelve hundred dollars, and that he (Grimes) was anxious to raise the money at once. He desired my advice and assistance in the matter, and requested me to draw up a suitable subscription paper for that purpose, which I did in these words: —

Boston, May 27, 1854.

" We, the undersigned, agree to pay to Anthony Byrnes, or order, the sum set against our respective names, for the purpose of enabling him to obtain his freedom from the United States Government, in the hands of whose officers he is now held as a slave.

" This paper will be presented by the Rev. L. A. Grimes, pastor of the 12th Baptist Church.

" Upon this paper Mr. Grimes obtained signatures for six hundred and sixty-five dollars, and with the aid of Colonel Suttle's counsel, Messrs. Parker and Thomas, who interested themselves in this matter, four hundred dollars more were got in a check, conditionally, and held by Mr. Parker. It was agreed by me that I should be near at hand on Saturday night, to assist and advance the money, which was accordingly done; and my check for eight hundred dollars, early in the night, was placed in the hands of the United States marshal for this purpose. About eleven o'clock, all parties being represented, we met at Mr. Commissioner Loring's office. This gentleman, with commendable alacrity, prepared necessary papers.

" At this juncture the actual money was insisted on, which threatened for a time the completion of the negotiation; but anticipating this contingency, which, under all circumstances, was not an unreasonable demand, we adjourned to the marshal's office, and I prepared myself with the needful tender. The United States attorney, Mr. Hallett, was in attendance, and the respective parties immediately discussed the mode of procedure. The hour of twelve was rapidly approaching, after which no action could be taken. Mr. Grimes was prepared to receive Byrnes, and anxious to take him as he might peacefully. The matter lingered, and official action ceased.

" I am not disposed to charge any one with designedly defeating the desired end on that occasion. The business was new, the questions raised novel. But when we had proceeded thus far, and were ready in good faith to make good the sum requisite on Monday, in view also of the friendly understanding had after midnight with all parties in interest, we had a right to expect Byrnes's liberation on Monday. When that day came, the owner refused to treat. Learning from rumor only that four thousand dollars had been named as the sum then asked for, I on Monday addressed Colonel Suttle, then in court, a respectful note, reminding him of the position of things on Saturday night, and urging that Mr. Grimes had the right to expect the original agreement to be carried out, but further asking him if any additional sum was required; to which he replied, that the " case is before the Court, and must await its decision."

" Tuesday morning, I had an interview with Colonel Suttle in the U. S. marshal's office. He seemed disposed to listen to me, and met the subject in a manly way. He said he wished to take the boy back, after which he would sell him. He wanted to see the result of the trial, at any rate. I stated to him that we considered his claim to Byrnes clear enough, and that he would be delivered over to him, urging particularly upon him that the boy's liberation was not sought for except with his free consent, and his claim being fully satisfied. I urged upon him no consideration of the fear of a rescue, or possible unfavorable result of the trial to him, but offered distinctly, if he chose, to have the trial proceed, and whatever might be the result, still to satisfy his claim.

" I stated to him that the negotiation was not sustained by any society or association whatsoever, but that it was done by some of our most respectable citizens, who were desirous not to obstruct the operation of the law, but in a peaceable and honorable manner sought an adjustment of this unpleasant case; assuring him that this feeling was general among the people. I read to him a letter, addressed to me by a highly-esteemed citizen, urging me to renew my efforts to accomplish this, and placing at my disposal any amount of money that I might think proper for the purpose.

" Colonel Suttle replied that he appreciated our motives, and that he felt disposed to meet us. He then stated what he would do. I accepted his proposal at once; it was not entirely satisfactory to me, but yet, in view of his position, as he declared to me, I was content. At my request, he was about to commit our agreement to writing, when Mr. B. F. Hallett entered the office, and they two engaged in conversation apart from me. Presently Colonel Suttle returned to me, and said: " I must withdraw what I have done with you." We both immediately approached Mr. Hallett, who said, pointing to the spot where Mr. Batchelder fell, in sight of which we stood, ' That blood must be avenged.' I made some pertinent reply, rebuking so extraordinary a speech, and left the room.

" On Friday, soon after the decision had been rendered, finding Colonel Suttle had gone on board the cutter at an early hour, I waited upon his counsel, Messrs. Thomas and Parker, at the court-house, and there renewed my proposition. Both these gentlemen promptly interested themselves in my purpose, which was to tender the claimant full satisfaction, and receive the surrender of Byrnes from him, either there, in State Street,

or on board the cutter, at his own option. It was arranged
between us that Mr. Parker should go at once on board the
cutter, and make an arrangement, if possible, with the Colonel.

"I provided ample funds, and returned immediately to the
court-house, when I found that there would be difficulty in getting on board the cutter. Application was made by me to the
marshal; he interposed no objection, and I offered to place Mr.
Parker alongside the vessel. Presently Mr. Parker took me aside
and said these words: "Colonel Suttle has pledged himself to
Mr. Hallett that he will not sell his boy until he gets him
home." Thus the matter ended.

"In considering, Mr. Editor, whose interference was potent in
thus defeating the courteous endeavors of citizens of Boston,
peacefully and with due respect to the laws of the land, to put
to rest the painful scenes of the past week, it must be borne
in mind that the United States marshal, who, throughout this
unfortunate negotiation, has conducted himself towards us with
great consideration, consented individually to hold the funds,
as a party not in interest, thus early acquiescing in the success
of our plan; the owner himself was willing to release his claim;
his counsel, Messrs. Thomas and Parker, volunteered their aid
in raising the money, urged it, and interested themselves in its
speedy accomplishment — even in the latest moment when it
could be effected, with commendable alacrity, they offered their
assistance; the United States commissioner himself consented to
be at his post until midnight of Saturday, to give his official
service for the object — I repeat, in view of all these consid-
erations, the conclusion must come home irresistibly to every
candid mind, that there was one personage who, officially or
individually, in this connection either did do, or left undone,
something whereby his interference became essential to a less
painful termination of this case.

Respectfully,

HAMILTON WILLIS."

IX

THE RIGHTS OF MAN IN AMERICA
1854

And he gave them their request; but sent leanness into their
soul. — PSALM cvi. 15.

Next Tuesday will be the seventy-eighth anniversary of American Independence. The day suggests
a national subject as theme for meditation this morning. The condition of America makes it a dark and
a sad meditation. I ask your attention, therefore, to
a sermon of the Dangers which threaten the Rights of
Man in America.

The human race is permanent as the Mississippi, and
like that is fed from springs which never dry; but the
several nations are as fleeting as its waves. In the
great tide of humanity, States come up, one after the
other, a wave or a bubble; each lasts its moment, then
dies — passed off, forgot:

> " Or like the snow-falls in the river,
> A moment white — then melts forever,"

while the great stream of humanity rolls ever forward,
from time to eternity: — not a wave needless; not a
snow flake, no drop of rain or dew, no ephemeral bubble, but has its function to perform in that vast, unmeasured, never-ending stream.

How powerless appears a single man! He is one
of a thousand million men; the infinitesimal of a vulgar fraction; one leaf on a particular tree in the forest.
A single nation, like America, is a considerable part
of mankind now living; but when compared with the

human race of all time, past and to come, it seems as nothing; it is but one bough in the woods. Nay, the population of the earth, to-day, is but one tree in the wide primeval forest of mankind, which covers the earth and outlasts the ages. The leaf may fall and not be missed from the bough; the branch may be rudely broken off, and its absence not marked; the tree will die and be succeeded by other trees in the forest, green with summer beauty, or foodful and prophetic with autumnal seed. Tree by tree, the woods will pass away, and, unobserved, another forest take its place,— arising, also, tree by tree.

How various the duration of States or men — dying at birth, or lasting long periods of time! For more than three thousand years, Egypt stood the queen of the world's young civilization, invincible as her own pyramids, which yet time and the nations alike respect. From Romulus, the first half-mythologic king of the seven-hilled city, to Augustulus, her last historic emperor, it is more than twelve centuries. At this day the Austrian, the Spanish, the French and German sovereigns sit each on a long-descended throne. Victoria is " daughter of a hundred kings." Pope Pius the Ninth claims two hundred and fifty-six predecessors, canonical and infallible. His chair is reckoned more than eighteen hundred years old; and it rests on an Etrurian platform yet ten centuries more ancient. The Turkish throne has been firmly fixed at Constantinople for four hundred years. Individual tyrants, like summer flies, are short-lived; but tyranny is old and lasting. The family of ephemera, permanent amid the fleeting, is yet as old as that of elephants, and will last as long.

But free governments have commonly been brief.

If the Hebrew people had well-nigh a thousand years of independent national life, their commonwealth lasted but about three centuries; the flower of their literature and religion was but little longer.   The historic period of Greece begins 776 B. C.; her independence was all over in six hundred and thirty years. The Roman deluge had swallowed it up.   No Deucalion and Pyrrha could re-people the land with men. Her little states — how brief was their hour of freedom for the people!   From the first annual archon of Athens to her conquest by Philip, and the death of her liberty, it was only two hundred and forty-five years! Her tree of freedom grew in a narrow field of time and briefly bore its age-outlasting fruit of science, literature, and art.   Now the tree is dead; its fragments are only curious Athenian stone.   The Grecian colonies in the East, Ætolian, Dorian, Ionian — how fair they flourished in the despotic waste of Asia! how soon those liberal blossoms died!   Even her colonies in the advancing West had no long independent life. Cyrene, Syracusa, Agrigentum, Crotona, Massilia, Saguntum,— how soon they died! — flowers which the savage winter swiftly nipped.

The Roman commonwealth could not endure five hundred years.   Her theocratic Tarquin the Proud must be succeeded by a more despotic dictator, with the style of democrat; and Rome, abhorring still the name of king, must see all her liberties laid low.   The red sea of despotism opened to let pass one noble troop — the elder Brutus at the head, the younger bringing up the rear — then closed again and swallowed up that worse than Egyptian host, clamoring only for " bread and games! "

The republics of Italy in the middle ages were no

more fortunate. The half-Grecian commonwealths, Naples, Amalfi, Gaeta,— what promise they once held forth; and what a warning fate! They were only born to die. A similar destiny befell the towns of more northern Italy, where freedom later found a home,— Milan, Padua, Genoa, Verona, Venice, Bologna, Florence, Pisa. Nay, in the midnight of the dark ages, seven hundred years ago, in the very city of the Popes and Cæsars, in the center of that red Roman sea of despotism, there was a momentary spot of dry free land; and Arnaldo da Brescia eloquently spoke of " Roman Liberty." The " Roman Republic " and " Roman Senate " became once more familiar words. Italian liberty, Lombard republics,— how soon they all went down! No city — not even Florence — kept the people's freedom safe three hundred years. Silently the wealthy nobles and despotic priests sapped the walls. Party spirit blinded the else clear eyes: " the State may perish; let the faction thrive." The Republicans sought to crush the adjacent feeble States. They forgot justice, the higher law of God: unworthy of liberty, they fell and died! Let the tyrant swallow up the Italian towns; they were unfit for freedom. " A generous disdain of one man's will is to republics what chastity is to woman; " they spurned this austere virtue. Let them serve their despots. " Liberty withdrew from a people who disgraced her name." Let Dante burn his poetic brand of infamy into the forehead of his countrymen. But while freedom lasted, how fair was her blossom, how rich and sweet her fruit! What riches, what beauty, what science, letters, art, came of that noble stock! Italy was the world's wonder — for a day; its sorrow ever since. So the cactus flowers into one gorgeous ecstasy of bloom; then the excessive blossom, with withering collapse, swoons and dies of its voluptuous and tropical delight.

Liberty wanders from the North, through Italy, the fairest of all earthly lands; then sits sadly down on the tallest of the Alps, and once more reviews those famous towns; the jewels that adorn the purple robe of history — all tarnished, shattered, spoiled. Slowly she turns her face northward and longs for hope. But even the Teutonic towns, where freedom ever wore a sober dress, were only spots of sunshine in a day of wintry storm. Swiss, German, Dutch, they were brief as fair. In Novogorod and in Poland, how soon was Slavonian freedom lost!

So in a winter day in the country have I seen a little frame of glass screening from the northern snow and ice a nicely sheltered spot, where careful hands tended little delicate plants, for beauty and for use. How fair the winter garden seemed amid the wildering snow, and else all-conquering frost! The little roses lifted up their face and kissed the glass which sheltered from the storm. But anon, some rude hand broke the frail barrier down, and in an hour the plants were frozen, stiff and dead; and the little garden was all filled with snow and ice; — a garden now no more!

How often do you see in a great city a man perish in his youth, bowed down by lusts of the body. The graves of such stand thick along the highway of our mortal life,— numberless, nameless, or all too conspicuously marked. Other men we see early bowed down by their ambition, and they live a life far worse than merely sensual death — themselves the ghastliest monuments, beacons of ruin! And so, along the highway that mankind treads, there are the open

sepulchers of nations, which perished of their sin;
or else transformed to stone, the gloomy sphinxes
sit there by the wayside — a hard, dread, awful lesson to the nations that pass by. Let America,

"The heir of all the ages! and the youngest born of time!"

gather up every jewel which the prodigal scattered
from his hand, look down into his grave, and then
confront these gloomy, awful sphinxes, and learn what
lessons of guidance they have; or of warning, if it
alone is to be found! Ever the sphinx has a riddle
which we needs must learn, or else perish.

The greater part of a nation's life is not delight;
it is discipline. A famous political philosopher, who
has survived two revolutionary storms in France, has
just now written, " God has made the condition of
all men more severe than they are willing to believe.
He causes them at all times to purchase the success
of their labors and the progress of their destiny
at a dearer price than they had anticipated."

The merchant knows how difficult it is to acquire
a great estate; the scholar, youthful and impatient,
well understands that the way of science or of letters
is steep and hard to climb; the farmer, knowing the
stern climate of New England, her niggard soil, rises
early and retires late, and is never off his guard.
These men all thrive. But, alas! the people of America do not know on what severe conditions alone national welfare is to be won. Human nature is yet
only a New England soil and climate for freedom to
grow in.

Nations may come to an end through the decay
of the family they belong to; and thus they may
die out of old age,— for there is an infancy, man-

hood, and old age to a nation as well as to a man.
Then the nation comes to a natural end, and like
a shock of corn fully ripe, in its season, it is gathered to its people.   But I do not find that any State
has thus lived out its destiny, and died a natural
death.

Again, States may perish by outward violence, military conquest,— for as the lion in the wilderness
eateth up the wild ass, so the strong nations devour
the weak.   But this happened most often in ancient
times, when men and States were more rapacious even
than now.

Thirdly, States may perish through their own vice,
moral or political.   Their national institutions may
be a defective machine which works badly, and fails
of producing national welfare of body or spirit.   It
may not secure national unity of action — there being no national gravitation of the great masses which
fly asunder; or it may fail of individual variety of
action — having no personal freedom; excessive national gravitation destroys individual cohesion, and
pulls the people flat; the men are slaves; they cannot reach the moral and spiritual welfare necessary
for a nation's continuous life.   In both these cases
the vice is political; the machinery is defective, made
after false ideas.   Or when the institutions are good
and capable of accommodating the nation's increase and
growth, the vice may be moral, lying deeper in the
character of the people.   They may have a false and
unimprovable form of religion, which suits not the
nature of man or of God, and which consequently
produces a false system of morals, and so corrupts the
nation's heart.   They may become selfish, gross, cowardly, atheistic, and so decay inwardly and perish.

If left all alone, such a people will rot down and die of internal corruption. Mexico is in a perishing condition to-day; so is Spain; so are some of the young nations of South America, and some of the old of Asia and Europe. Nothing can ever save Turkey,— not all the arms of all the allied West; and though Protestant and Catholic join hands, Christendom cannot propagate Mahometanism, nor keep it from going down.

Leave these nations to their fate and they will die. But commonly, they are not left to themselves; other people rush in and conquer. The wild individual man is rapacious by instinct. The present nations are rapacious also by calculation; they prey on feeble States. The hooded crow of Europe watches for the sickly sheep. In America the wolves prowl round the herd of buffaloes and seize the sickly, the wounded, and the old. And so there are scavengers of the nations,— filibusters, the flesh-flies and carrion-vultures of the world, who have also their function to perform. Wealth and power are never left without occupants. Rome was corrupt, her institutions bad, her religion worn out, her morals desperate; northern nations came upon her. " Wheresoever the body is, thither the eagles will be gathered together."

In Europe there are nations in this state of decay, from moral or political vice. All the Italo-Greek populations, most of the Celto-Roman, all the Celtic, all the old Asiatic populations — the Hungarians and Turks. The Teutonic and Slavic families alone seem to prosper, full of vigorous, new life, capable of making new improvements, to suit the altered phases of the world.

In America there is only one family in a condition of advance, of hardy health. Spanish America is in a state of decay; she has a bad form of religion, and bad morals; her republics only " guarantee the right of assassination; " an empire is her freest state. But in the north of North America the Anglo-Saxon British colonies rapidly advance in material and spiritual development, and one day doubtless they will separate from the parent stem and become an indedependent tree. The roots of England run under the ocean; they come up in Africa, India, Australia, America, in many an island of all the seas. Great fresh, living trunks grow up therefrom. One day these offshoots will become self-supporting, with new and independent roots, and ere long will separate from the parent stem; then there will be a great Anglo-Saxon trunk in Australia, another in India, another in Africa, another in the north of our own continent, and yet others scattered over the manifold islands of the sea, an Anglo-Saxon forest of civilization.

But in the center of the North American continent, the same Anglo-Saxons have passed from their first condition of scattered and dependent colonies, and become a united and independent nation, five-and-twenty millions strong. Our fellow-countrymen here in America compose one-fortieth part of all the inhabitants of the globe. We are now making the greatest political experiment which the sun ever looked down upon.

First, we are seeking to found a State on industry, and not war. All the prizes of America are rewards of toil, not fighting. We are ruled by the constable, not by the soldier. It is only in exceptional cases, when the liberal institutions of America are to be trodden under foot, that the constable disappears, and the red arm of the soldier clutches at the people's throat. That is the first part of our scheme — we are aiming to found an industrial State.

Next, the national theory of the government is a democracy — the government of all, by all, for all, All officers depend on election, none are foreordained. There are to be no special privileges, only natural, universal rights.

It would be a fair spectacle,— a great industrial commonwealth, spread over half the continent, and folding in its bosom one-fortieth of God's whole family! It is a lovely dream; not Athenian Plato, nor English Thomas More, nor Bacon, nor Harrington, ever dared to write on paper so fair an ideal as our fathers and we have essayed to put into men. I once thought this dream of America would one day become a blessed fact! We have many elements of national success. Our territory for quantity and quality is all we could ask; our origin is of the Caucasian's best. No nation had ever so fair a beginning as we. The Anglo-Saxon is a good hardy stock for national welfare to grow on. To my American eye, it seems that human nature had never anything so good for popular liberty to be grafted into. We are already strong, and fear nothing from any foreign power. The violent cannot take us by force. No nation is our enemy.

But the question now comes, Is America to live or to die? If we live, what life shall it be? Shall we fall into the sepulcher of departed States — a new debauchee of the nations? Shall we live petrified to stone, a despotism many-headed, sitting — another sphinx — by the wayside of history, to scare young

nations in their march and impede their progress?   Or
shall we pursue the journey — a great, noble-hearted
commonwealth, a nation possessing the continent, full
of riches, full of justice, full of wisdom, full of piety,
and full of peace?   It depends on ourselves.   It is
for America, for this generation of Americans, to say
which of the three shall happen.   No fate holds us up.
Our character is our destiny.

I am not a timid man; I am no excessive praiser of
times passed by; I seldom take counsel of my fears,
often of my hopes; — but now I must say that since
'76 our success was never so doubtful as at this time.
England is in peril; the despots on the Continent hate
her free Parliament, which makes laws for the people
— just laws; they hate her free speech, which tells
every grievance at home or abroad; they hate her
free soil, which offers a home to every exile, republican
or despotic.   England is in peril, for every tyrant
hates her.   Russia is in danger, for the two strongest
powers of Christendom have just clasped hands, and
sworn an oath to fight against that great marauding
empire of the East.   Their armies threaten her cities;
her sovereign deserts his capital; her treasure is carried a thousand miles inward; the western fleets block-
ade her ports and sweep her navies from the sea.   But
Russia has no peril like ours; England has no danger
so great as that which threatens us this day.   In the
darkest periods of the American Revolution, when
Washington's army, without blankets, without coats,
without shoes, fled through the Jerseys, when they
marked the ice of the Delaware, and left revolutionary
tracks in frozen blood, we were not in such peril as
to-day.   When General Gage had the throat of Boston in his hand, and perfidiously disarmed the people,

we were not in such danger. Yea, when four hundred houses in yonder town went up in one great cloud of smoke towards heaven, the liberties of America were not in such peril as they are to-day. Then we were called to fight with swords — and when that work was to be done, was America ever found wanting? Then our adversary was the other side of the sea, and wicked statutes were enacted against us in Westminster Hall. Now our enemy is at home; and something far costlier than swords is to be called into service.

Look at some of these dangers. I shall pass by all that are trifling. I find four great perils. Here they are: —

I. There comes the danger from our exclusive devotion to riches.

II. The danger from the Roman Catholic Church, established in the midst of us.

III. The danger from the idea that there is no higher law above the statutes which men make.

IV. The danger from the institution of slavery, which is based on that atheistic idea last named.

I. OF THE DANGER WHICH COMES FROM OUR EXCLUSIVE DEVOTION TO RICHES.

Power is never left without a possessor: when it fell from the theocratic and military classes, from the priest, the noble, and the king, it passed to the hands of the capitalists. In America, ecclesiastical office is not power; noble or royal birth is of small value. If Madison or Jefferson had left any sons but mulattoes, their distinguished birth would avail them nothing. The son of Patrick Henry lived a strolling schoolmaster, and a pauper's funeral was asked for his body. Money is power; the only permanent and transmissible power; it goes by device. Money " can ennoble sots and slaves and cowards."

It gives rank in the Church. The millionaire is always a saint. The priests of commerce will think twice before damning a man who enhances their salary and gives them dinners. In one thing the American heaven resembles the New Jerusalem: — its pavement is " of fine gold." The capitalist has the chief seat in our Christian synagogue. It is a rare minister who dares assail a vice which has riches on its side. Is there a clergyman at the South who speaks against the profitable wickedness which chains three million American men? How few at the North! European gentility is ancient power; American is new money hot from the stamping.

In society, money is genteel; it is always respectable. The high places of society do not belong to ecclesiastical men, as in Rome; to military men, as in St. Petersburg; to men of famous family, as in England and Spain; to men of science and literature, men of genius, as in Berlin; but to rich men.

Money gives distinction in literature, so far as the literary class can control the public judgment. The colleges revere a rich man's son; they name professorships after such as endow them with money, not mind. Critics respect a rich man's book; if he has not brains, he has brass, which is better. The capitalist is admitted a member of the Academies of Arts and Sciences, of collegiate societies; if he cannot write dissertations, he can give suppers, and there must be a material basis for science. At anniversaries, he receives the honorary degree. " 'Tis easier to weigh

purses, sure, than brains." A dull scholar is expelled
from college for idleness, and twenty years later returns
to New England with half a million of money, and
gets his degree. As he puzzles at the Latin diploma,
he asks, "If I had come home poor, I wonder how
long it would have taken the 'Alma Mater' to find
out that I was ever a 'good scholar,' and now 'merited
an honorary degree'— facts which I never knew before!"

In politics, money has more influence here than in
Turkey, Austria, Russia, England, or Spain. For
in our politics the interest of property is preferred
before all others. National legislation almost invaria-
bly favors capital, and not the laboring hand. The
Federalists feared that riches would not be safe in
America — the many would plunder the wealthy few.
It was a groundless fear. In an industrial commonwealth, property is sure of popular protection.
Where all own hayricks no one scatters firebrands.
Nowhere in the world is property so secure or so
much respected; for it rests on a more natural basis
than elsewhere. Nowhere is wealth so powerful, in
Church, society, and State. In Kentucky and elsewhere, it can take the murderer's neck out of the halter. It can make the foolish "wise;" the dull man
"eloquent;" the mean man "honorable, one of our
most prominent citizens;" the heretic "sound orthodox;" the ugly "fair;" the old man a "desirable
young bridegroom." Nay, vice itself becomes virtue,
and man-stealing is Christianity!

Here, nothing but the voter's naked ballot holds
money in check: there are no great families with their
historic tradition, as in all Europe; no bodies of literary or scientific men to oppose their genius to mere

material gold. The Church is no barrier, only its servant, for when the minister depends on the wealth of his parish for support, you know the common consequence. Lying rides on obligation's back. The minister respects the hand that feeds him: " the ox knoweth his owner, and the ass his master's crib." Yet now and then a minister looks starvation in the face, and continues his unpopular service of God. No political institutions check the authority of wealth; it can bribe and buy the venal; the brave it sometimes can intimidate and starve. Money can often carry a bill through the legislature — State or national. The majority is hardly strong enough to check this pecuniary sway.

In the " most democratic " States, gold is most powerful. Thus, in fifteen States of America, three hundred thousand proprietors own thirteen hundred millions of money invested in men. In virtue thereof they control the legislation of their own States, making their institutions despotic, and not republican; they keep the poor white man from political power, from comfort, from the natural means of education and religion; they destroy his self-respect, and leave him nothing but his body; from the poorest of the poor, they take away his body itself. Next they control the legislation of America; they make the President, they appoint the Supreme Court, they control the Senate, the Representatives; they determine the domestic and foreign policy of the nation. Finally, they affect the laws of all the other sixteen States — the Southern hand coloring the local institutions of New Haven and Boston.

That is only one example — one of many. Russia is governed by a long-descended czar; England by a queen, nobles, and gentry,— men of ancient family, with culture and riches. America is ruled by a troop of men with nothing but new money and what it brings — three hundred thousand slaveholders and their servants, North and South. Boston is under their thumb; at their command the mayor spits in the face of Massachusetts law, and plants a thousand bayonets at the people's throat. They make ball-cartridges under the eaves of Faneuil Hall.

Accordingly, money is the great object of desire and pursuit. There are material reasons why this is so in many lands: — in America there are also social, political, and ecclesiastical reasons for it. " To be rich is to be blessed: poverty is damnation: " that is the popular creed.

The public looks superficially at the immediate effect of this opinion, at this exceeding and exclusive desire for riches; they see its effect on Israel and John Jacob, on Stephen, Peter, and Robert: it makes them rich, and their children respectable and famous. Few ask, What effect will this have on the nation? They foresee not the future evil it threatens. Nay, they do not consider how it debauches the institutions of America — ecclesiastical, academic, social, political; how it corrupts the hearts of the people, making them prize money as the end of life, and manhood as only the means thereto, making money master, and human nature its tool or servant, but no more.

The political effect of this unnatural esteem for riches is not at all well understood. History but too plainly tells of the dangerous power of priests or nobles consolidated into a class, and their united forces directed by a single able head. The power of allied kings, concentrating whole realms of men and money

on a single point; the effect of armies and navies collected together and marshaled by a single will; is all
too boldly written in the ruin of many a State. We
have often been warned against the peril from forts,
and castles, and standing armies. But the power of
consolidated riches, the peril which accumulated property may bring upon the liberties of an industrial
commonwealth, though formidably near, as yet is all
unknown, all unconsidered too. Already the consolidated property of one-eightieth part of the population controls all the rest.

Two special causes, both exceptional and fleeting,
just now stimulate the acquisitiveness of America almost to madness.

One is the rapid development of the art of manufacturing the raw materials gathered from the bosom
or the surface of the earth. The invention of printing
made education and freedom possible on a large scale;
one of the immediate results thereof is this — the head
briefly performs the else long-protracted labor of the
hand. Wind, water, fire, steam, lightning, have become pliant forces to manufacture wood, flax, cotton,
wool, and all the metals. This result is nowhere so
noticeable as in New England, where education is almost universal. The New England school-house is
the machine-shop of America. What the State invests in slates and teachers pays dividends in hard
coin. This new power over the material world, the
first and unexpected commercial result of the public
education of the people, gives a great and perhaps
lasting stimulus to the pursuit of wealth. It affects the
most undisciplined portions of the world,— for the educated man leaves much rough labor for the ignorant,
and enhances the demand for the results of their toil.

The thinking head raises the wages of all mere hands. Hence arises the increased value of slaves at the South, and the rapid immigration of the most ignorant Irishmen to the North. They are to the thoughtful projector what the Merrimac is to the cotton-spinner — a rude force pliant before his will. Dr. Faustus is the unconscious pioneer of many a pilgrimage.

The other cause is the discovery of gold in California and then in Australia. This doubles or trebles the pecuniary momentum of America. Its stimulating influence on our covetousness, accumulation, and luxury, is obvious. What further and ultimate effects it will produce I shall not now pause to inquire. When a whirlwind rises, all men can see that dust is mounting to the sky.

Besides, the form of American industry is changed. Once New England and all the North were chiefly agricultural; manufactures and commerce were conducted on a small scale; and therein each man wrought on his own account. There was a great deal of individual activity, individuality of character. Few men worked for wages. Now New England is mainly manufacturing and commercial, Vermont is the only farming State. Mechanics, men and women, work for wages; many in the employment of a single man; thousands in the pay of one company, organized by superior ability. The workman loses his independence, and is not only paid but governed also by his employer's money. His opinions and character are formed after the prescribed pattern, by the mill he works in. The old military organizations for defense or aggression brought freedom of body distinctly in peril: the new industrial organizations jeopardize spiritual individuality, all freedom of mind and conscience. New England is a monumental proof thereof.

Another change also follows: the military habits of the North are all gone. Once New England had more firelocks than householders; every man was a soldier and a marksman. Now the people have lost their taste for military discipline, and neither keep nor bear arms. Of course a few holiday soldiers, called out by a doctor, and commanded by an apothecary, can overawe the town.

The Northern, and especially the Eastern and Middle States, are the great center of this industrial development. Here, and especially in New England the desire for riches has become so powerful that a very large proportion of our men of the greatest practical intellect have almost exclusively turned their attention to purely productive business, to commerce and manufactures. They rarely engage in the work of politics — unprofitable and distasteful to the individual, and, at first sight, merely preservative and defensive to the community. This they shun or neglect, as the mass of men avoid military discipline.

The statutes must be made and administered by politicians. Here they are not able men. Of the forty-one New England delegates in Congress, of the six governors, of the many other professional leaders in politics, how many first-rate men are there? how many middle-sized second-rate men? The control of the national affairs passes out of the fingers of the North — which has yet three-fifths of the population, and more than four-fifths of the speculative and practical intelligence and material wealth. The nation is controlled by the South, whose ablest men almost exclusively attend to politics. Besides, the State politics

of the North fall into the hands of men quite inadequate to such a weighty trust. This mistake is as
fatal as it would be in time of war to send all the able-
bodied men to the plough, and the women and children
to the camp. We are mismanaged at home, and dis-
honorably routed in the Federal capital. In the present state of the world I think no nation would be
justified in turning non-resistant, tearing down its
forts, disbanding its armies, melting up its guns and
swords; and I am sure the North suffers sadly from
devoting so large a part of its masterly, practical men
to the productive work of commerce and manufactures.
Her politicians are not strong enough for her own defense. In American politics the great battle of ideas
and principles, yea, of measures, is to be fought.
Shall we keep our Washingtons surveying land?

The national effect of this estimate and accumulation of riches is to produce a great and rapid development of the practical understanding; a great love for
vulgar finery which pleases the palate or the eye; great
luxury of dress, ornament, furniture. You see this
in the hotels and public carriages on land and sea, in
the costume of the nation, at public and private tables.
Along with this there comes a certain refinement of the
public taste.

But there is no proportionate culture of the higher
intellectual faculties — of the reason and imagination;
still less of yet nobler powers — moral, affectional,
and religious. From the common school to the college, the chief things taught are arithmetic and elocu-
tion; not the art to reason and create, but the trade to
calculate and express. Everything is measured by
the money standard. "The protection of property
is the great object of government." The politician

must suit the pecuniary interest of his constituency, though at the cost of justice; the writer, author, or editor, the pecuniary interest of his readers, though at the sacrifice of truth; the minister, the pecuniary interest of his audience, though piety and morality both come to the ground. Mammon is a profitable god to worship — he gives dinners.

I think it must be confessed in the last eighty years the general moral and religious tone of the people in the free States has improved. This change comes from the natural forward tendency of mankind, the instinct of development quickened by our free institutions. But, at the same time, it is quite plain to me that the moral and religious tone of American politicians, writers, and preachers, has proportionately and absolutely gone down. You see this in the great towns: if Boston were once the " Athens of America," she is now only the " Corinth." Athens has retreated to some inland Salamis.

But, in general, this peril from the excessive pursuit of riches comes unavoidably from our position in time and space, and our consequent political institutions. It belongs to the period of transition from the old form of vicarious rule by theocratic, military, and aristocratic governments, to the personal administration of an industrial commonwealth. I do not much fear this peril, nor apprehend lasting evil from it. One of the great things which mankind now most needs is power over the material world as the basis for the higher development of our spiritual faculties. Wealth is indispensable; it is the material pulp around the spiritual seed. No nation was ever too rich, too well fed, clad, housed, and comforted. The human race still suffers from poverty, the great obstacle to our

progress. Doubtless we shall make many errors in
our national attempt to organize the productive forces
into an industrial State, as our fathers — thousands of
years ago — in organizing their destructive powers
into a military state. Once, man cut his fingers with
iron; he now poisons them with gold. All Christendom shares this peril, though America feels it most.
She is now like a thriving man who gets rich fast, and
thinks more than he ought of his money, and less of
his manhood. Some misfortune, the ruin of a prodigal son perishing in quicksands of gold, will, by and
by, convince him that riches is not the only thing in
life.

II. OF THE DANGER WHICH COMES FROM THE ROMAN
CATHOLIC CHURCH.

The Roman Catholic Church claims infallibility for
itself, and denies spiritual freedom, liberty of mind
or conscience, to its members. It is therefore the foe
to all progress; it is deadly hostile to democracy. To
mankind this is its first command — Submit to an external authority; subordinate your human nature to
an element foreign and abhorrent thereto! It aims
at absolute domination over the body and the spirit of
man. The Catholic Church can never escape from the
consequences of her first principle. She is the natural ally of tyrants, and the irreconcilable enemy of
freedom. Individual Catholics in America, as elsewhere, are inconsistent, and favor the progress of
mankind. Alas! such are exceptional; the Catholic
Church has an iron logic, and consistently hates liberty in all its forms — free thought, free speech.

I quote the words of her own authors in America,
recently uttered by the press. " Protestantism

. . has not and never can have any rights where Catholicity is triumphant." " We lose all the breath we expend in declaiming against bigotry and intolerance, and in favor of religious liberty." " Religious liberty [in America] is merely endured until the opposite can be carried into execution without peril to the Catholic world." " Catholicity will one day rule in America, and then religious liberty is at an end." " The very name of Liberty . . . ought to be banished from the very domain of religion." " No man has a right to choose his religion." " Catholicism is the most intolerant of creeds. It is intolerance itself, for it is the truth itself." *

The Catholic population is not great in numbers. In 1853, there were in America 1,712 churches, 1,574 priests, 396 theological students, 32 bishops, 7 archbishops, church-property worth about $10,000,000, and 1,728,000 Catholics. But most of them are of the Celtic stock, which has never much favored Protestantism or individual liberty in religion; and in this respect is widely distinguished from the Teutonic population, who have the strongest ethnological instinct for personal freedom.

Besides, the Catholics are governed with absolute rigor by their clergy, who are celibate priests, a social caste by themselves, not sympathizing with mankind, but emasculated of the natural humanities of our race. There are exceptional men amongst them, but such seems to be the rule with the class of Catholic priests in America. They are united into one compact body,

* The above, and many more similar declarations, may be found in a little pamphlet —" Familiar Letters to John B. Fitzpatrick, the Catholic Bishop of Boston, by an Independent Irishman." Boston, 1854.

with complete corporate unity of action, and ruled despotically by their bishops, archbishops, and pope. The Catholic worshiper is not to think, but to believe and obey; the priest not to reason and consider, but to proclaim and command; the voter is not to inquire and examine, but to deposit his ballot as the ecclesiastical authority directs. The better religious orders do not visit America; the Jesuits, the most subtle enemies of humanity, come in abundance; some are known, others stealthily prowl about the land, all the more dangerous for their disguise. They all act under the direction of a single head. One shrewd Protestant minister may be equal to one Jesuit, but no ten or forty Protestant ministers is a match for a combination of ten Jesuits, bred to the business of deception, knowing no allegiance to truth or justice, consciously disregarding the higher law of God, with the notorious maxim that " the end justifies the means," bound to their order by the most stringent oath, and devoted to the worst purposes of the Catholic Church.

All these priests owe allegiance to a foreign head. It is not an American Church; it is Roman, not free, individual, but despotic; nay, in its designs not so much human as merely papal.

The Catholic Church opposes everything which favors democracy and the natural rights of man. It hates our free churches, free press, and, above all, our free schools. No owl more shuns the light. It hates the rule of majorities, the voice of the people; it loves violence, force, and blood.

The Catholic clergy are on the side of slavery. They find it is the dominant power, and pay court thereto that they may rise by its help. They love slavery itself; it is an institution thoroughly congenial to them, consistent with the first principles of their Church. Their Jesuit leaders think it is " an ulcer which will eat up the Republic," and so stimulate and foster it for the ruin of democracy, the deadliest foe of the Roman hierarchy.

Besides, most of the Catholics are the victims of oppression,— poor, illiterate, oppressed, and often vicious. Their circumstances have ground the humanity out of them. No sect furnishes half so many criminals — victims of society before they become its foes; no sect has so little philanthropy; none is so greedy to oppress. All this is natural. The lower you go down the coarser and more cruel do you find the human being.

I am told there is not in all America a single Catholic newspaper hostile to slavery; not one opposed to tyranny in general; not one that takes sides with the oppressed in Europe. There is not in America a man born and bred in the Catholic Church, who is eminent for philosophy, science, literature, or art; none distinguished for philanthropy! The water tastes of the fountain.

Catholic votes are in the market; the bishops can dispose of them — politicians will make their bid. Shall it be the sacrifice of the free schools? of other noble institutions? In some States it seems not unlikely.

I do not think our leading men see all this danger. But the baneful influence of the Church of the dark ages begins to show itself in the press, in the schools, and still more in the politics of America. Yet I am glad the Catholics come here. Let America be an asylum for the poor and the downtrodden of all lands; let the Irish ships, reeking with misery, land their hu-

man burdens in our harbors.   The continent is wide
enough for all.   I rejoice that in America there is no
national form of religion ; — let the Jew, the Chinese
Buddhist, the savage Indian, the Mormon, the Protestant, and the Catholic have free opportunity to be
faithful each to his own conscience.   Let the American
Catholic have his bishops, his archbishops, and his
pope, his Jesuits, his convents, his nunneries, his celibate priesthood of hard drinkers, if he will.   Let him
oppose the public education of the people ; oppose the
press, the meeting-house, and the ballot-box ; nay, oppose temperance and religion, if he likes.   If, with
truth and justice on our side, the few Catholics can
overcome the many Protestants, we deserve defeat.
We should be false to the first principles of democratic
theory, if we did not grant them their inalienable
rights.   Let there be no tyranny ; let us pay the Catholics good for ill; and cast out Satan by the finger
of God, not by the Prince of Devils.   This peril is
easily mastered.   The Catholic Church has still many
lessons to offer the Protestants.

III. OF THE DANGER FROM THE IDEA THAT THERE
IS NO HIGHER LAW ABOVE THE STATUTES OF MEN.

Of late years, it has been industriously taught in
America that there is no law of nature superior to the
statutes which men enact; that politics are not amenable to conscience or to God.   Accordingly, the American Congress knows no check in legislation but the
Constitution of the United States and the will of the
majority ; none in the Constitution of the Universe and
the will of God.   The atheistic idea of the Jesuits,
that the end justifies the means, is made the first principle in American politics.   Hence it has been repeat-

edly declared by " prominent clergymen " that politics should not be treated of in the pulpit; they are
not amenable to religion; Christianity has nothing to
do with making or administering the laws.   When
the Pharisees and Sadducees have silenced the prophet
and the apostle, it is not difficult to make men believe
that Machiavelli is a great saint, and Jesuitism the
revealed religion of politics!   Let the legislators make
what wicked laws they will against the rights of man;
the priest of commerce is to say nothing.   Nay, the
legislators themselves are never to refer to justice and
the eternal right, only to the expediency of the hour.

Then when the statute is made, the magistrate is not
to ask if it be just, he is only to execute it; the people are to obey and help enforce the wicked enactment,
never asking if it be right.   The highest virtue in the
people is —" unquestioning submission to the Constitution; " or, when the statute violates their conscience,
to do " a disagreeable duty! "   Thus the political action of the people is exempted from the jurisdiction
of God and His natural moral law!   " Christianity
has nothing to do with politics! "

Within a few years this doctrine has been taught
in a great variety of forms.   At first it came in with
evil laws, simply as the occasional support of a measure; at length it is announced as a principle.   It has
taken a deep hold on the educated classes of the community; for our " superior education " is almost
wholly of the intellect, and of only its humbler powers.   It appears among the lawyers, the politicians,
the editors, and the ministers.   Some deny the natural
distinction between right and wrong.   " Justice," is a
matter of convention; things are not " true," but
" agreed upon; " not " right," only " assented to."

There is no "moral obligation." Government rests on a compact, having its ultimate foundation on the caprice of men, not in their moral nature. What are called natural rights are only certain conveniences agreed upon amongst men; legal fictions — their recognition is their essence, they are the creatures of a compact. Property has no foundation in the nature of things; it may consist of whatever the legislature determines — land, cattle, food, clothing; or of men, women, and children. Dives may own Lazarus as well as the dogs who serve him at the gate. There is no political morality, only political economy.

This conclusion arises from the philosophy of Hobbes and Filmer; yes, from the first principles of Locke and Rousseau. It is one of the worst results of materialism and practical atheism. It takes different forms in different nations. In a monarchy it has for its axiom, " The king can do no wrong; he is the norm of law — *Vox Regis vox Dei.*" In a democracy, " The majority can do no wrong; they are the norm of law — *Vox Populi vox Dei.*" So the statute becomes an idol; loyalty takes the place of religion, and despotism becomes enthroned on the necks of the people.

It is not surprising that this doctrine should be taught from the pulpit in Catholic countries — it is conformable to the general conduct of the Roman Church. It belongs also with the sensational philosophy which has yet done so much to break to pieces the theology of the dark ages; — and does not astonish one in the sects which build thereon. But at first sight it seems amazing that American Christians of the puritanic stock, with a philosophy that transcends sensationalism, should prove false to the only principle which at once justifies the conduct of Jesus, of Luther, and the Puritans themselves. For certainly if obedience to the established law be the highest virtue, then the patriots and Pilgrims of New England, the reformers of the Church, the glorious company of the apostles, the goodly fellowship of the prophets, and the noble army of martyrs,— nay, Jesus himself,— were only criminals and traitors. To appreciate this denial of the first principle of all religion, it would be necessary to go deep into the theology of Christendom, and touch the fatal error of all the three parties just referred to. For that there is now no time.

One of the consequences of this atheistic denial of the natural foundation of human laws is the preponderance of parties. An opinion before it becomes a law, while it is yet a tendency, becomes organized into a faction, or party. Members of the party feel the same loyalty thereto which narrow patriots feel for their nation, or bigots for their sect; they give up their mind and conscience to their party. So fidelity to their party, right or wrong, is deemed a great political virtue; the individual member is bound by the party opinion. Thus is the private conscience still further debauched by the second act in this atheistic popular tragedy.

Thus both national and party politics are taken out of the jurisdiction of morals, declared not amenable to conscience: in other words, are left to the control of political Jesuits. An American may read the natural result of such principles in the downfall of the Grecian and Italian Republics, or wait to behold it in his own land.

IV. OF THE DANGERS FROM THE INSTITUTION OF SLAVERY WHICH RESTS ON THIS FALSE IDEA.

Slavery is the child of violence and atheism. Brute material force is its father: the atheistic idea that there is no law of God above the passions of men — that is the mother of it. I have lately spoken so long, so often, and with such publicity, both of speech and print, respecting the extent of slavery in America, and its constant advance since 1788, that I shall pass over all that theme, and speak more directly of the present danger it brings upon our freedom.

There can be no national welfare without national unity of action. That cannot take place unless there is national unity of idea in fundamentals. Without this a nation is a " house divided against itself ; " of course it cannot stand. It is what mechanics call a figure without equilibrium; the different parts thereof do not balance.

Now, in the American State there are two distinct ideas — freedom and slavery.

The idea of freedom first got a national expression seventy-eight years ago next Tuesday. Here it is. I put it in a philosophic form. There are five points to it.

First. All men are endowed by their Creator with certain natural rights, amongst which is the right to life, liberty, and the pursuit of happiness.

Second. These rights are inalienable; they can be alienated and forfeited only by the possessor thereof; the father cannot alienate them for the son, nor the son for the father; nor the husband for the wife, nor the wife for the husband; nor the strong for the weak, nor the weak for the strong; nor the few for the many, nor the many for the few; and so on.

Third. In respect to these all men are equal; the rich man has not more, and the poor less; the strong man has not more, and the weak man less: — all are exactly equal in these rights, however unequal in their powers.

Fourth. It is the function of government to secure these natural, inalienable, and equal rights to every man.

Fifth. Government derives all its divine right from its conformity with these ideas, all its human sanction from the consent of the governed.

That is the idea of freedom. I used to call it " the American idea;" it was when I was younger than I am to-day. It is derived from human nature; it rests on the immutable laws of God; it is part of the natural religion of mankind. It demands a government after natural justice, which is the point common between the conscience of God and the conscience of mankind, the point common also between the interests of one man and of all men.

Now this government, just in its substance, in its form must be democratic: that is to say, the government of all, by all, and for all. You see what consequences must follow from such an idea, and the attempt to re-enact the law of God into political institutions. There will follow the freedom of the people, respect for every natural right of all men, the rights of their body, and of their spirit — the rights of mind and conscience, heart and soul. There must be some restraint — as of children by their parents, as of bad men by good men; but it will be restraint for the joint good of all parties concerned; not restraint for the exclusive benefit of the restrainer. The ultimate consequence of this will be the material and spiritual welfare of all — riches, comfort, noble manhood, all desirable things.

That is the idea of freedom. It appears in the Declaration of Independence; it reappears in the Preamble to the American Constitution, which aims " to establish justice, insure domestic tranquillity, provide for the common defense, promote the general welfare, and secure the blessings of liberty." That is a religious idea; and when men pray for the " reign of justice " and the " kingdom of heaven," to come on earth politically, I suppose they mean that there may be a commonwealth where every man has his natural rights of mind, body, and estate.

Next is the idea of slavery. Here it is. I put it also in a philosophic form. There are three points which I make.

First. There are no natural, inalienable, and equal rights, wherewith men are endowed by their Creator; no natural, inalienable, and equal right to life, liberty, and the pursuit of happiness.

Second. There is a great diversity of powers, and in virtue thereof the strong man may rule and oppress, enslave and ruin the weak, for his interest and against theirs.

Third. There is no natural law of God to forbid the strong to oppress the weak, and enslave and ruin the weak.

That is the idea of slavery. It has never got a national expression in America; it has never been laid down as a principle in any act of the American people, nor in any single State, so far as I know. All profess the opposite; but it is involved in the measures of both State and nation. This idea is founded in the selfishness of man; it is atheistic.

The idea must lead to a corresponding government; that will be unjust in its substance — for it will depend not on natural right, but on personal force; not on the constitution of the universe, but on the compact of men. It is the abnegation of God in the universe and of conscience in man. Its form will be despotism — the government of all by a part, for the sake of a part. It may be a single-headed despotism, or a despotism of many heads; but whether a Cyclops or a Hydra, it is alike " the abomination which maketh desolate." Its ultimate consequence is plain to foresee — poverty to a nation, misery, ruin.

At first slavery came as a measure; nothing was said about it as a principle. But in a country full of schoolmasters, legislatures, newspapers, talking men — a measure without a principle to bear it up is like a single twig of willow cast out on a wooden floor; there is nothing for it to grow by; it will die. So of late the principle has been boldly avowed. Mr. Calhoun denied the self-evident truths of the Declaration of Independence; denied the natural, inalienable, and equal rights of man. Many since have done the same — political, literary, and mercantile men, and, of course, ecclesiastical men; there are enough of them always in the market. All parts of the idea of slavery have been affirmed by prominent men at the North and the South. It has been acted on in the formation of the constitution of every slave State, and in the passage of many of its laws. It lies at the basis of a great deal of national legislation.

Hear the opinions of some of our Southern patriots: " Slavery is coeval with society: " " It was commended by God's chosen theocracy, and sanctioned by His apostles in the Christian Church." All ancient

literature is " the literature of slaveholders; " " Rome
and Greece owed their literary and national greatness
exclusively to the institution of slavery; " " Slavery
is as necessary for the welfare of the Southern States
as sunshine is for the flowers of the prairies; " " A
noble and necessary institution of God's creation." *
" Nature is the mother and protector of slavery; "
" Domestic slavery is not only *natural* and *necessary*,
but a great blessing." " Free society is a sad and
signal failure; " " It does well enough in a new country." " Free society has become diseased by abolishing slavery. It can only be restored to pristine health,
happiness, and prosperity by re-instituting slavery."
" Slavery may be administered under a new name."
" Free society is a monstrosity. Like all monsters it
will be short-lived. We dare and do vindicate slavery
in the abstract." The negro " needs a master to protect and govern him; so do the ignorant poor in old
countries." †

" There is no moral wrong in slavery; " it " is the
normal condition of human society." " The benefits
and advantages which so far have resulted from this
institution we take as lights to guide us to the brighter
truths of its future history." " We belong to that
society of which slavery is the distinguishing element,
and we are not ashamed of it. We find it marked by
every evidence of Divine approval." ‡

These two ideas are now fairly on foot. They are
hostile; they are both mutually invasive and destructive. They are in exact opposition to each other, and
the nation which embodies these two is not a figure

* *Richmond Examiner* for June 30, 1854.
† *Richmond Examiner,* June 23, 1854.
‡ *Charleston Standard* (S.C.), June 21, 1854.

of equilibrium.   As both are active forces in the minds
of men, and as each idea tends to become a fact — a
universal and exclusive fact — as men with these ideas
organize into parties as a means to make their idea
into a fact, it follows that there must not only be
strife amongst philosophical men about these antagonistic principles and ideas, but a strife of practical
men about corresponding facts and measures.   So the
quarrel, if not otherwise ended, will pass from words
to what seems more serious ; and one will overcome the
other.

So long as these two ideas exist in the nation as
two political forces there is no national unity of idea,
of course, no unity of action.   For there is no center
of gravity common to freedom and slavery.   They
will not compose an equilibrious figure.   You may cry,
" Peace ! peace ! " but so long as these two antagonistic
ideas remain, each seeking to organize itself and get
exclusive power, there is no peace ; there can be none.

The question before the nation to-day is, Which
shall prevail — the idea and fact of freedom, or the
idea and the fact of slavery ; freedom, exclusive and
universal, or slavery, exclusive and universal?   The
question is not merely, Shall the African be bond or
free? but, Shall America be a democracy or a despotism?   For nothing is so remorseless as an idea, and no
logic is so strong as the historical development of a national idea by millions of men.   A measure is nothing
without its principle.   The idea which allows slavery in
South Carolina will establish it also in New England.
The bondage of a black man in Alexandria imperils
every white woman's daughter in Boston.   You cannot escape the consequences of a first principle more
than you can " take the leap of Niagara and stop

when half-way down." The principle which recognises slavery in the Constitution of the United States would make all America a despotism; while the principle which made John Quincy Adams a free man would extirpate slavery from Louisiana and Texas. It is plain America cannot long hold these two contradictions in the national consciousness. Equilibrium must come.

Now there are three possible ways of settling the quarrel between these two ideas; only three. The categories are exhaustive.

This is the first: The discord may rend the nation asunder and the two elements separate and become distinct nations — a despotism with the idea of slavery, a democracy with the idea of freedom. Then each will be an equilibrious figure. The Anglo-Saxon despotism may go to ruin on its own account, while the Anglo-Saxon democracy marches on to national welfare. That is the first hypothesis.

Or, second: The idea of freedom may destroy slavery, with all its accidents — attendant and consequent. Then the nation may have unity of idea, and so a unity of action, and become a harmonious whole, a unit of freedom, a great industrial democracy, reenacting the laws of God, and pursuing its way, continually attaining greater degrees of freedom and prosperity. That is the second hypothesis.

Here is the third: The idea of slavery may destroy freedom, with all its accidents — attendant and consequent. Then the nation will become an integer; only it will be a unit of despotism. This involves, of course, the destructive revolution of all our liberal institutions, State as well as national. Democracy must go down; the free press go down; the free church go down; the free school go down.   There must be an industrial despotism, which will soon become a military despotism.   Popular legislation must end; the Federal Congress will be a club of officials, like Nero's Senate, which voted his horse first consul.   The State legislature will be a knot of commissioners, tide-waiters, postmasters, district attorneys, deputy-marshals.   The town-meeting will be a gang of government officers, like the " Marshal's Guard," revolvers in their pockets, soldiers at their back.   The habeas corpus will be at an end; trial by jury never heard of, and open courts as common in America as in Spain or Rome. Commissioners Curtis, Loring, and Kane will not be exceptional men; there will be no other " judges; " all courts, courts of the kidnapper; all process summary; all cases decided by the will of the government; arbitrary force the only rule.   The constable will disappear, the soldier come forth.   All newspapers will be like the " Satanic press " of Boston and New York, like the journal of St. Petersburg, or the *Diario Romano*, which tell lies when the ruler commands, or tell truth when he insists upon it.   Then the wicked will walk on every side, for the vilest of men will be exalted, and America, become the mock and scorn and hissing of the nations, will go down to worse shame than was ever heaped upon Sodom; for with her lust for wealth, land, and power, she will also have committed the crime against nature.   Then America will be another Italy, Greece, Asia Minor, yea, like Gomorrah — for the Dead Sea will have settled down upon us with nothing living in its breast, and the rulers will proclaim peace where they have made solitude.

Which of these three hypotheses shall we take?

I. Will there be a separation of the two elements,

and a formation of two distinct States,— freedom with democracy, and slavery with a tendency to despotism? That may save one half the nation, and leave the other to voluntary ruin.   Certainly it is better to enter into life halt or maimed, rather than having two hands and two feet to be cast into everlasting fire.

Now, I do not suppose it is possible for the Anglo-Saxons of America to remain as one nation for a great many years.   Suppose we become harmonious and prosper abundantly: when there are a hundred millions on the Atlantic slope, another hundred millions in the Mississippi Valley, a third hundred millions on the Pacific slope, and a fourth hundred millions in South America,— it is not likely that all these will hold together.   We shall be too wide spread.   And, besides, it is not according to the disposition of the Teutonic family to aggregate into one great State any very large body of men; division, not conglomeration, is after the ethnologic instinct and the historical custom of the Teutonic family, and especially of its Anglo-Saxon tribe.   We do not like centralization of power, but have such strong individuality that we prefer local self-government; we are social, not gregarious like the Celtic family.   I, therefore, do not look on the union of the States as a thing that is likely to last a great length of time, under any circumstances.   I doubt if any part of the nation will desire it a hundred years hence.

True, there are causes which tend to keep us united: community of ethnologic origin — fifteen millions are Anglo-Saxon; — unity of language, literature, religion; historic and legal traditions, and commercial interest.   But all these may easily be overcome, and doubtless will be.   So a dissolution of the great Anglo-

Saxon State seems likely to take place, when the territory is spread so wide that there is a practical inconvenience in balancing the nation on a single governmental point; when the numbers are so great that we require many centers of legislative and administrative action in order to secure individual freedom of the parts, as well as national unity of the whole; or when the Federal Government shall become so corrupt that the trunk will not sustain the limbs. Then the branches which make up this great American banyan-tree will separate from the rotten primeval trunk, draw their support from their own local roots, and spread into great and independent trees. All this may take place without fighting. Massachusetts and Maine were once a single State; now friendly sisters.

But I do not think this " dissolution of the Union " will take place immediately, or very soon. For America is not now ruled — as it is commonly thought — either by the mass of men who follow their national, ethnological, and human instincts; or by a few far-sighted men of genius for politics, who consciously obey the law of God made clear in their own masterly mind and conscience, and make statutes in advance of the calculation or even the instincts of the people, and so manage the Ship of State that every occasional tack is on a great circle of the universe, a right line of justice, and therefore the shortest way to welfare; but by two very different classes of men; — by mercantile men, who covet money, actual or expectant capitalists; and by political men, who want power, actual or expectant office-holders. These appear diverse; but there is a strong unanimity between the two; — for the mercantile men want money as a means of power, and the political men power as a means of money. There are noble men in both classes, exceptional, not instantial, men with great riches even, and great office. But as a class, these men are not above the average morality of the people, often below it: they have no deep, religious faith, which leads them to trust the higher law of God. They do not look for principles that are right, conformable to the constitution of the universe, and so creative of the nation's permanent welfare; but only for expedient measures, productive to themselves of selfish money or selfish power. In general, they have the character of adventurers, the aims of adventurers, the morals of adventurers; they begin poor, and of course obscure, and are then " democratic," and hurrah for the people: " Down with the powerful and the rich " is the private maxim of their heart. If they are successful, and become rich, famous, attaining high office, they commonly despise the people: " Down with the people! " is the axiom of their heart — only they dare not say it; for there are so many others with the same selfishness, who have not yet achieved their end, and raise the opposite cry. The line of the nation's course is a resultant of the compound selfishness of these two classes.

From these two, with their mercantile and political selfishness, we are to expect no comprehensive morality which will secure the rights of mankind; no comprehensive policy, which will secure expedient measures for a long time. Both will unite in what serves their apparent interest, brings money to the trader, power to the politician,— whatever be the consequence to the country.

As things now are, the Union favors the schemes of both of these classes of men; thereby the politician gets power, the trader makes money.

If the Union were to be dissolved and a great Northern commonwealth were to be organized, with the idea of freedom, three quarters of the politicians, Federal and State, would pass into contempt and oblivion; all that class of Northern demagogues who scoff at God's law, such as filled the offices of the late Whig administration in its day of power, or as fill the offices of the Democratic administration to-day — they would drop down so deep that no plummet would ever reach them; you would never hear of them again.

Gratitude is not a very common virtue; but gratitude to the hand of slavery, which feeds these creatures, is their sole and single moral excellence; they have that form of gratitude. When the hand of slavery is cut off, that class of men will perish just as caterpillars die when, some day in May, the farmer cuts off from the old tree a great branch to graft in a better fruit. The caterpillars will not vote for the grafting. That class of men will go for the Union while it serves them.

Look at the other class. Property is safe in America: and why? Because we have aimed to establish a government on natural rights, and property is a natural right; say oligarchic Blackstone and socialistic Proudhon what they may, property is not the mere creature of compact, or the child of robbery; it is founded in the nature of man. It has a very great and important function to perform. Nowhere in the world is it so much respected as here.

But there is one kind of property which is not safe just now: — property in men. It is the only kind of property which is purely the creature of violence and law; it has no root in itself.

Now, the Union protects that " property." There

are three hundred thousand slaveholders, owning thirteen hundred millions of dollars invested in men. Their wealth depends on the Union; destroy that, and their unnatural property will take to itself legs and run off, seeking liberty by flight, or else stay at home and, like an Anglo-Saxon, take to itself firebrands and swords, and burn down the master's house and cut the master's throat. So the slaveholder wants the Union; he makes money by it. Slavery is unprofitable to the nation. No three millions earn so little as the three million slaves. It is costly to every State. But it enriches the owner of the slaves. The South is agricultural; that is all. She raises cotton, sugar, and corn; she has no commerce, no manufactures, no mining. The North has mills, ships, mines, manufactures; buys and sells for the South, and makes money by what impoverishes the South. So all the great commercial centers of the North are in favor of Union, in favor of slavery. The instinct of American trade just now is hostile to American freedom. The money power and the slave power go hand in hand. Of course such editors and ministers as are only the tools of the money power, or the slave power, will be fond of " Union at all hazards." They will sell their mothers to keep it. Now these are the controlling classes of men; these ministers and editors are the mouthpieces of these controlling classes of men; and as these classes make money and power out of the Union, for the present I think the Union will hold together. Yet I know very well that there are causes now at work which embitter the minds of men, and which, if much enforced, will so exasperate the North that we shall rend the Union asunder at a blow. That I think not likely to take place, for the South sees the peril and its own ruin.

II. The next hypothesis is, freedom may triumph over slavery. That was the expectation once, at the time of the Declaration of Independence; nay, at the formation of the Constitution. But only two national steps have been taken against slavery since then — one the Ordinance of 1787, the other the abolition of the African slave-trade; really that was done in 1788, formally twenty years after. In the individual States, the white man's freedom enlarges every year; but the Federal Government becomes more and more addicted to slavery. This hypothesis does not seem very likely to be adopted.

III. Shall slavery destroy freedom? It looks very much like it. Here are nine great steps, openly taken since '87, in favor of slavery. First, America put slavery into the Constitution. Second, out of old soil she made four new slave States. Third, America, in 1793, adopted slavery as a Federal institution, and guaranteed her protection for that kind of property as for no other. Fourth, America bought the Louisiana territory in 1803, and put slavery into it. Fifth, she thence made Louisiana, Missouri, and then Arkansas slave States. Sixth, she made slavery perpetual in Florida. Seventh, she annexed Texas. Eighth, she fought the Mexican War, and plundered a feeble sister republic of California, Utah, and New Mexico, to get more slave soil. Ninth, America gave ten millions of money to Texas to support slavery, passed the Fugitive Slave Bill, and has since kidnapped men in New England, New York, New Jersey, Pennsylvania, Ohio, Michigan, Wisconsin, Illinois, Indiana, in all the East, in all the West, in all the Middle States. All the great cities have kidnapped their own citizens. Professional slave-hunters are members of New England churches;

kidnappers sit down at the Lord's table in the city of Cotton, Chauncy, and Mayhew. In this very year, before it is half through, America has taken two more steps for the destruction of freedom. The repeal of the Missouri Compromise and the enslavement of Nebraska: that is the tenth step. Here is the eleventh: The Mexican treaty, giving away ten millions of dollars and buying a little strip of worthless land, solely that it may serve the cause of slavery.

Here are eleven great steps openly taken towards the ruin of liberty in America. Are these the worst? Very far from it! Yet more dangerous things have been done in secret.

I. Slavery has corrupted the mercantile class. Almost all the leading merchants of the North are proslavery men. They hate freedom, hate your freedom and mine! This is the only Christian country in which commerce is hostile to freedom.

II. See the corruption of the political class. There are forty thousand officers of the Federal Government. Look at them in Boston — their character is as well known as this hall. Read their journals in this city — do you catch a whisper of freedom in them? Slavery has sought its menial servants — men basely born and basely bred: it has corrupted them still further, and put them in office. America, like Russia, is the country for mean men to thrive in. Give him time and mire enough, a worm can crawl as high as an eagle flies. State rights are sacrificed at the North; centralization goes on with rapid strides; State laws are trodden under foot.* The Northern President is all for slavery.

* While this volume is passing through the press, another example of this same corruption appears. The Senate passes a bill to protect United States officers engaged in kidnapping

The Northern members of the Cabinet are for slavery; in the Senate, fourteen Northern Democrats were for the enslavement of Nebraska; in the House of Representatives, forty-four Northern Democrats voted for the bill,— fourteen in the Senate, forty-four in the House, fifty-eight Northern men voted against the conscience of the North and the law of God. Only eight men out of all the South could be found friendly to justice and false to their own local idea of injustice. The present administration, with its supple tools of tyranny, came into office while the cry of " No higher law " was echoing through the land!

III. Slavery has debauched the press. How many leading journals of commerce and politics in the great cities do you know that are friendly to freedom and opposed to slavery?   Out of the five large daily commercial papers in Boston, Whig or Democratic, I know of only one that has spoken a word for freedom this great while. The American newspapers are poor defenders of American liberty. Listen to one of them, speaking of the last kidnapping in Boston: " We shall need to employ the same measures of coercion as are necessary in monarchical countries." There is always some one ready to do the basest deeds. Yet there are some noble journals — political and commercial; such as the *New York Tribune* and *Evening Post*.

IV. Then our colleges and schools are corrupted by slavery. I do not know of five colleges in all the North which publicly appear on the side of freedom. What the hearts of the presidents and professors are, God knows, not I. The great crime against humanity, practical atheism, found ready support in Northern

citizens of the free States, from the justice of the people. Such kidnappers are to be tried in the Kidnappers' Court.

colleges, in 1850 and 1851. Once, the common reading books of our schools were full of noble words. Read the school-books now made by Yankee peddlers of literature, and what liberal ideas do you find there? They are meant for the Southern market. Slavery must not be offended!

V. Slavery has corrupted the churches! There are twenty-eight thousand Protestant clergymen in the United States. There are noble hearts, true and just men among them, who have fearlessly borne witness to the truth. I need not mention their names. Alas! they are not very numerous; I should not have to go over my fingers many times to count them all. I honor these exceptional men. Some of them are old, far older than I am; older than my father need have been; some of them are far younger than I; nay, some of them younger than my children might be: and I honor these men for the fearless testimony which they have borne — the old, the middle-aged, and the young. But they are very exceptional men. Is there a minister in the South who preaches against slavery? How few in all the North!

Look and see the condition of the Sunday Schools. In 1853, the Episcopal Methodists had 9,438 Sunday Schools; 102,732 Sunday School teachers; 525,008 scholars. There is not an anti-slavery Sunday School in the compass of the Methodist Episcopal Church. Last year, in New York, they issued, on an average, two thousand bound volumes every day in the year, not a line against slavery in them. They printed also two thousand pamphlets every day; there is not a line in them all against slavery; they printed more than two hundred and forty million pages of Sunday School books, not a line against slavery in them all; not a

line showing that it is wicked to buy and sell a man,
for whom, according to the Methodist Episcopal
Church, Christ died!

The Orthodox Sunday School Union spent last year
$248,201; not a cent against slavery, our great na-
tional sin. They print books by the million. Only one
of them contains a word against slavery; that is Cowper's *Task*, which contains these words — my mother
taught them to me when I was a little boy, and sat in
her lap: —

> " I would not have a slave to till my ground,
>   To carry me, to fan me when I sleep,
>   And tremble when I wake, for all the wealth
>   That sinews, bought and sold, have ever earned!"

You all know it: if you do not, you had better learn
and teach it to your children. That is the only anti-
slavery work they print. Once they published a book
written by Mr. Gallaudet, which related the story, I
think, of the selling of Joseph: at any rate, it showed
that Egyptian slavery was wrong. A little girl in a
Sunday School in one of the Southern States one day
said to her teacher, " If it was wrong to make Joseph
a slave, why is it not wrong to make Dinah, and Sambo,
and Chloe slaves? " The Sunday School teacher and
the church took alarm, and complained of the Sunday
School Union: " You are poisoning the South with
your religion, telling the children that slavery is
wicked." It was a serious thing, " dissolution of the
Union," " levying war," or at least, " misdemeanor,"
for aught I know, " obstructing an officer of the United
States." What do you think the Sunday School Union
did? It suppressed the book! It printed one Sunday
School book which had a line against Egyptian slavery

and then suppressed it! and it cannot be had to-day. Amid all their million books, there is not a line against slavery, save what Cowper sung. There are five million Sunday School scholars in the United States, and there is not a Sunday School manual which has got a word against slavery in it.

You all know the American Tract Society. Last year the American Tract Society in Boston spent $79,-983.46; it visited more than fourteen thousand families; it distributed 3,334,920 tracts — not a word against slavery in them all. The American Tract Society in New York last year visited 568,000 families, containing three million persons; it spent for home purposes $406,707; for foreign purposes $422,294; it distributed tracts in English, French, German, Dutch, Danish, Swedish, Norwegian, Italian, Hungarian, and Welsh — and it did not print one single line, nor whisper a single word against this great national sin of slavery! Nay, worse: — if it finds English books which suit its general purpose, but containing matter adverse to slavery, it strikes out all the anti-slavery matter, then prints and circulates the book. Is the Tract Society also managed by Jesuits from the Roman Church?

At this day, 600,000 slaves are directly and personally owned by men who are called " professing Christians," " members in good fellowship " of the churches of this land; 80,000 owned by Presbyterians, 225,000 by Baptists, 250,000 owned by Methodists: — 600,000 slaves in this land owned by men who profess themselves Christians, and in churches sit down to take the Lord's Supper, in the name of Christ and God! There are ministers who own their fellow-men — " bought with a price."

Does not this look as if slavery were to triumph over freedom?

VI. Slavery corrupts the judicial class. In America, especially in New England, no class of men has been so much respected as the judges; and for this reason: we have had wise, learned, excellent men for our judges; men who reverenced the higher law of God, and sought by human statutes to execute justice. You all know their venerable names, and how reverentially we have looked up to them. Many of them are dead; some are still living, and their hoary hairs are a crown of glory on a judicial life, without judicial blot. But of late slavery has put a different class of men on the benches of the Federal courts — mere tools of the government; creatures which get their appointment as pay for past political service, and as pay in advance for iniquity not yet accomplished. You see the consequences. Note the zeal of the Federal judges to execute iniquity by statute and destroy liberty. See how ready they are to support the Fugitive Slave Bill, which tramples on the spirit of the Constitution, and its letter too; which outrages justice and violates the most sacred principles and precepts of Christianity. Not a United States judge, circuit or district, has uttered one word against that " bill of abominations." Nay, how greedy they are to get victims under it! No wolf loves better to rend a lamb into fragments than these judges to kidnap a fugitive slave, and punish any man who dares to speak against it. You know what has happened in Fugitive Slave Bill courts. You remember the " miraculous " rescue of Shadrach; the peaceable snatching of a man from the hands of a cowardly kidnapper was " high treason; " it was " levying war." You remember the " trial " of the

rescuers! Judge Sprague's charge to the grand jury,
that, if they thought the question was which they ought
to obey, the law of man or the law of God, then they
must "obey both!" serve God and mammon, Christ
and the devil, in the same act! You remember the
"trial," the "ruling" of the Bench, the swearing on
the stand, the witness coming back to alter and "en-
large his testimony" and have another gird at the
prisoner! You have not forgotten the trials before
Judge Kane at Philadelphia, and Judge Grier at
Christiana and Wilkesbarre.

These are natural results of causes well known. You
cannot escape a principle. Enslave a negro, will you?
— you doom to bondage your own sons and daughters,
by your own act.

Do you forget the Union meeting in Faneuil Hall,
November 26th, 1850, the Tuesday before Thanksgiv-
ing Day? It was called to indorse the Fugitive Slave
Bill — a meeting to promote the stealing of men in
Boston, of your fellow-worshipers and my parishioners.
Do you remember the Democratic Herods and Whig
Pilates, who were made friends that day, melted into
one unity of despotism, in order that they might en-
slave men? They had unity of idea and unity of ac-
tion, that day. Do you remember the speeches of Mr.
Curtis and Mr. Hallett; their yelp against the inaliena-
ble rights of men; their howl at God's higher law?
The worser half of that platform is now the United
States court; — the Fugitive Slave Bill judge, the
United States attorney. They got their offices for
their political services past and for their character —
very fitting reward to very fitting men! A man pro-
fesses a fondness for kidnapping, hurrahs for it in
Faneuil Hall: — give him the United States judgeship;

make him United States attorney — fit to fit! When slavery dispenses offices, every service rendered to despotism is well paid. Men with foreheads of brass, with iron elbows, with consciences of gum elastic, whose chief commandment of their law, their prophets, and their gospel, is to

"—— crook the pregnant hinges of the knee,
Where thrift may follow fawning;"

verily they shall have their reward! They shall become Fugitive Slave Bill judges; yea, attorneys of the United States!

In 1836, a poor slave girl named Med, who had been brought from Louisiana to Boston by her master, sued for her freedom in the courts of Massachusetts. Mr. Benjamin R. Curtis appeared as the slave-hunter's counsel, long, and stoutly, and learnedly contending that she should not receive her freedom by the laws, Constitution, and usages of this Commonwealth, but should be sent back to eternal bondage.* On the 7th of March, 1850, Mr. Webster made his speech against freedom, so fatal to himself; but soon after found such a fire in his rear that he must return to Massachusetts

* The girl was set free, and the principle laid down that slaves coming to a free State with the consent of their masters, secured their freedom. An account of the case was published in the *Boston Daily Advertiser* of August 29, 1836, and introduced with the following editorial comment: —" In some of the States there is, we believe, legislative provision for cases of this sort [namely, allowing the master to bring and keep slaves in bondage], and it would seem that some such provision is necessary in this State, unless we would prohibit citizens of the slaveholding States from traveling in this State with their families, and unless we would permit such of them as wish to emancipate their slaves, to throw them at their pleasure upon the people of this State."

to rescue his own popularity — then apparently in great peril. On the 29th of April, the same Mr. Curtis, faithful to his proclivities towards slavery, made a public address to the apostate senator, at the Revere House, and expressed his " abounding gratitude for the ability and fidelity " which Mr. Webster had " brought to the defense of the Constitution and the Union; " praising him as " eminently vigilant, wise, and faithful to our country, without shadow of turning." At the Union meeting in Faneuil Hall (Nov. 26th), Mr. Curtis declared the fugitive slaves " a class of foreigners," " with whose rights Massachusetts has nothing to do. It is enough for us that they have no right to be *here*." Other services, similar or analogous, which he has rendered to the cause of inhumanity, I here pass by.

This is a world in which " men do nothing for nothing; " the workman is worthy of his hire; in due time Mr. Curtis received his reward.

He has lately (June 7th) " charged " the grand jury of the circuit court of the United States, pointing out their duty in respect to recent events in Boston. A Federal enactment of 1790 provides that, if any person shall wilfully obstruct, resist, or oppose any officer of the United States in executing any legal writ or process thereof, he shall be imprisoned not more than twelve months, and fined not more than three hundred dollars. Mr. Curtis charges that the offense is " a misdemeanor: " to constitute the crime, it is " not necessary to prove the accused used or even threatened active violence." " If a multitude of persons should assemble, even in a public highway, with the design to stand together, and thus prevent the officer from passing freely along the way, ... this would of

itself, and without any active violence, be such an ob-
struction as is contemplated by this law."

So much for what constitutes the crime. Now see
who are criminals: " All who are present and actually
obstruct, resist, or oppose, are of course guilty. So
are all who are present, leagued in the common design,
and so situated as to be able, in case of need, to afford
assistance to those actually engaged, though they do
not actually obstruct, resist, or oppose." That is, they
are guilty of a misdemeanor, because they are in the
neighborhood of such as oppose a constable of the
United States, and are " able " " to afford assistance."
" If they are present for the purpose of affording assistance, though no overt act is done by them, they
are still guilty under this law." They are guilty of
a misdemeanor, not merely as accessory before the fact,
but as principals, for " in misdemeanors all are principals."

" Not only those who are present, but those who,
though absent when the offense was committed, did
procure, counsel, command, or abet others to commit
the offense, are indictable as principals." But what
amounts to such counseling as constitutes a misdemeanor? " Evincing an express liking, approbation,
or assent to another's criminal design." It need not
appear that the precise time, or place, or means advised, were used." So all who evinced " an express
liking, approbation, or assent " to the rescue of Mr.
Burns are guilty of a misdemeanor; if they evinced
" an express liking " that he should be rescued by a
miracle wrought by Almighty God,— and some did
express " approbation " of that " means,"— they are
indictable, guilty of a misdemeanor; " " it need not
appear that the precise time, or place, or means ad-

vised, were used!" If any colored woman, during the wicked week — which was ten days long — prayed that God would deliver Anthony, as it is said his angel delivered Peter, or said "Amen" to such a prayer, she was "guilty of a misdemeanor:" to be indicted as a "principal."

So every man in Boston who, on that bad Friday, stood in the streets of Boston between Court Square and T Wharf, was "guilty of a misdemeanor," liable to a fine of three hundred dollars, and to jailing for twelve months. All who at Faneuil Hall stirred up the minds of the people in opposition to the Fugitive Slave Bill; all who shouted, who clapped their hands at the words or the countenance of their favorites, or who expressed "approbation" by a whisper of "assent," are "guilty of misdemeanor." The very women who stood for four days at the street corners, and hissed the infamous slave-hunters and their coadjutors, they, too, ought to be punished by fine of three hundred dollars and imprisonment for a year! Well, there were fifteen thousand persons "assembled" "in the highway" of the city of Boston that day opposed to kidnapping; half the newspapers in the country towns of Massachusetts "evinced an express liking" for freedom, and opposed the kidnapping; they are all "guilty of a misdemeanor;" they are "principals." Nay, the few ministers all over the State, who preached that kidnapping was a sin; those who read brave words out of the Old Testament or the New; those who prayed that the victim might escape: they, likewise, were "guilty of a misdemeanor," liable to be fined three hundred dollars and jailed for twelve months. Excellent Fugitive Slave Bill judge! Mr. Webster did wisely in making that appointment! He

chose an appropriate tool. The charge was worthy
of the worst days of Jeffreys and the second James!

We all know against whom this judicial iniquity
was directed — against men who at Faneuil Hall, under
the pictured and sculptured eyes of John Hancock
and the three Adamses, appealed to the spirit of humanity, not yet crushed out of your heart and mine,
and lifted up their voices in favor of freedom and the
eternal law of God. If he had called us by our names
he could not have made the thing plainer. You know
the zeal of the United States attorney, you have heard
of the swearing before the grand jury and at the grand
jury. Did the judge's lightning only glow with judicial ardor and zeal for the Fugitive Slave Bill? — or
was it also red with personal malignity and family
spleen? Judge you!

But, alas! there was a grand jury, and the Sal-
monean thunder of the Fugitive Slave Bill judge fell
harmless — quenched, conquered, disgraced, and brutal
— to the ground. Poor Fugitive Slave Bill court! it
can only gnash its teeth against freedom of speech in
Faneuil Hall; only bark and yelp against the inalienable rights of man, and howl against the higher law of
God! it cannot bite! Poor imbecile, malignant court!
What a pity that the Fugitive Slave Bill judge was not
himself the grand jury, to order the indictment! what a
shame that the attorney was not a petty jury to convict! Then New England, like Old, might have had
her " bloody assizes," and Boston streets might have
streamed with the heart's gore of noble men and women ;
and human heads might have decked the pinnacles all
round the town; and Judge Curtis and Attorney Hallett might have had their place with Judge Jeffreys
and John Boilman of old. What a pity that we have

a grand jury and a traverse jury to stand between
the malignant arm of the slave-hunter and the heart
of you and me! Perhaps the court will try again,
and find a more pliant grand jury, easier to intimidate.
Let me suggest to the court, that the next time it should
pack its jurors from the marshal's " guard." Then
there will be unity of idea; of action, too — the court a
figure of equilibrium.*

At a Fugitive Slave Bill meeting in Faneuil Hall, it
is easy to ask a minister a question designed to be insulting, and not dare listen to the proffered reply; easy
to bark at justice, and howl at the inalienable rights
of man; easy to yelp out the vengeance of a corrupt
administration of slave-hunters upon all who love the
higher law of God; but He himself has so fashioned the
hearts of men that we instinctively hate all tyranny, all
oppression, all wrong; and the hand of history brands
ineffaceable disgrace on the brass foreheads of all such
as enact iniquity by statute, and execute wickedness as
law. The memory of the wicked shall rot. Scroggs
and Jeffreys also got their appointment as pay for
their service and their character — fitting bloodhounds for a fitting king. For near two hundred years
their names have been a stench in the face of the Anglo-
Saxon tribe. Others as unscrupulous may take warning by their fate.

Thus has slavery debauched the Federal courts.

VII. Alas me! Slavery has not ended yet its long
career of sin. Its corruption is sevenfold. It debauches the elected offices of our city, and even our
State. In the Sims time of 1851, the laws of Mas-

* The experiment was made; the brother-in-law of the Fugitive Slave Bill judge was put on the jury, and indictments
were found in October and November.

sachusetts were violated nine days running, and the Free-soil governor sat in the State House as idle as a feather in his chair. In the wicked week of 1854, the Whig governor sat in the seat of his predecessor; Massachusetts was one of the inferior counties of Virginia, and a slave-hunter had eminent domain over the birthplace of Franklin and the burial-place of Hancock! Nay, against our own laws the Free-soil mayor put the neck of Boston in the hands of a " train-band captain " — the people " wondering much to see how he did ride! " Boston was a suburb of Alexandria; the mayor a slave-catcher for our masters at the South! You and I were only fellow-slaves!

All this looks as if slavery was to triumph over freedom. But even this is not the end. Slavery has privately emptied her seven vials of wrath upon the nation — committing seven debaucheries of human safeguards of our natural rights. That is not enough — there are other seven to come. This apocalyptic dragon, grown black with long-continued deeds of shame and death, now meditates five further steps of crime. Here is the programme of the next attempt — a new political tragedy in five acts.

I. The acquisition of Dominica — and then all Hayti — as new slave territory.

II. The acquisition of Cuba, by purchase, or else by private filibustering and public war,— as new slave territory.

III. The re-establishment of slavery in all the free States, by judicial " decision " or legislative enactment. Then the master of the North may " sit down with his slaves at the foot of Bunker Hill monument! "

IV. The restoration of the African slave-trade, which is already seriously proposed and defended in the Southern journals. Nay, the Senate Committee on Foreign Relations recommend the first step towards it — the withdrawal of our fleet from the coast of Africa. You cannot escape the consequence of your first principle: if slavery is right, then the slave-trade is right; the traffic between Guinea and New Orleans is no worse than between Virginia and New Orleans; it is no worse to kidnap in Timbuctoo than in Boston.

V. A yet further quarrel must be sought with Mexico, and more slave territory be stolen from her.

Who shall oppose this fivefold wickedness? The Fugitive Slave Bill party; — the Nebraska enslavement party? Northern servility has hitherto been ready to grant more than Southern arrogance dared to demand!

All this looks as if the third hypothesis would be fulfilled, and slavery triumph over freedom; as if the nation would expunge the Declaration of Independence from the scroll of Time, and, instead of honoring Hancock and the Adamses and Washington, do homage to Kane and Grier and Curtis and Hallett and Loring. Then the Preamble to our Constitution might read — " to establish injustice, insure domestic strife, hinder the common defense, disturb the general welfare, and inflict the curse of bondage on ourselves and our posterity." Then we shall honor the Puritans no more, but their prelatical tormentors; nor reverence the great reformers, only the inquisitors of Rome. Yea, we may tear the name of Jesus out of the American Bible; yes, God's name; worship the Devil at our Lord's table, Iscariot for Redeemer!

See the steady triumph of despotism! Ten years more, like the ten years past, and it will be all over with the liberties of America. Everything must go

down, and the heel of the tyrant will be on our neck.
It will be all over with the rights of man in America,
and you and I must go to Austria, to Italy, or to Si-
beria for our freedom; or perish with the liberty which
our fathers fought for and secured to themselves —
not to their faithless sons! Shall America thus miserably perish? Such is the aspect of things to-day!

But are the people alarmed? No, they fear nothing — only the tightness in the money-market! Next
Tuesday at sunrise every bell in Boston will ring joy-
ously; every cannon will belch sulphurous welcome
from its brazen throat. There will be processions,—
the mayor and the aldermen and the marshal and the
naval officer, and, I suppose, the " marshal's guard,"
very appropriately taking their places. There is a
chain on the Common to-day — it is the same chain that
was around the court-house in 1851 — it is the chain
that bound Sims; now it is a festal chain. There are
mottoes about the Common —" They mutually pledged
to each other their lives, their fortunes, and their sacred
honor." I suppose it means that the mayor and the
kidnappers did this. " The spirit of '76 still lives."
Lives, I suppose, in the Supreme Court of Fugitive
Slave Bill judges. " Washington, Jefferson, and their
compatriots! — their names are sacred in the heart of
every American." That, I suppose, is the opinion of
Thomas Sims and of Anthony Burns. And opposite
the great Park Street Church, where a noble man is
this day, I trust, discoursing noble words, for he has
never yet been found false to freedom —" Liberty and
independence, our father's legacy! — God forbid that
we their sons should prove recreant to the trust!"
It ought to read, " God forgive us that we their sons
have proved so recreant to the trust!" So they will

celebrate the 4th of July, and call it "Independence Day!" The foolish press of France, bought and beaten and trodden on by Napoleon the Crafty, is full of talk about the welfare of the "Great Nation!" Philip of Macedon was conquering the Athenian allies town by town; he destroyed and swept off two and thirty cities, selling their children as slaves. All the Cassandrian eloquence of Demosthenes could not rouse degenerate Athens from her idle sleep. She also fell — the fairest of all free States; corrupted first — forgetful of God's higher law. Shall America thus perish, all immature!

So was it in the days of old: they ate, they drank, they planted, they builded, they married, they were given in marriage, until the day that Noah entered into the ark, and the flood came and devoured them all!

Well, is this to be the end? Was it for this the Pilgrims came over the sea? Does Forefathers' Rock assent to it? Was it for this that the New England clergy prayed, and their prayers became the law of the land for a hundred years? Was it for this that Cotton planted in Boston a little branch of the Lord's vine, and Roger Williams and Higginson — he still lives in an unregenerate son — did the same in the city which they called of peace, Salem? Was it for this that Eliot carried the Gospel to the Indians? that Chauncy, and Edwards, and Hopkins, and Mayhew, and Channing, and Ware labored and prayed? for this that our fathers fought — the Adamses, Washington, Hancock? for this that there was an eight years' war, and a thousand battle-fields? for this the little monument at Acton, Concord, Lexington, West Cambridge, Danvers, and the great one over there on the spot which our fathers' blood made so red? Shall America become Asia Minor? New England, Italy? Boston such as Athens — dead and rotten? Yes! if we do not mend, and speedily mend. Ten years more, and the liberty of America is all gone. We shall fall, the laugh, the byword, the proverb, the scorn, the mock of the nations, who shall cry against us. Hell from beneath shall be moved to meet us at our coming, and in derision shall it welcome us: —

"The heir of all the ages, and the youngest born of time!"

We shall lie down with the unrepentant prodigals of old time, damned to everlasting infamy and shame.

Would you have it so? Shall it be?

To-day, America is a debauched young man, of good blood, fortune, and family, but the companion of gamesters and brawlers; reeking with wine; wasting his substance in riotous living; in the lap of harlots squandering the life which his mother gave him. Shall he return? Shall he perish? One day may determine.

Shall America thus die? I look to the past,— Asia, Africa, Europe, and they answer, " Yes! " Where is the Hebrew Commonwealth; the Roman Republic; where is liberal Greece,— Athens, and many a far-famed Ionian town; where are the commonwealths of medieval Italy; the Teutonic free cities — German, Dutch, or Swiss? They have all perished. Not one of them is left. Parian statues of liberty, sorely mutilated, still remain; but the Parian rock whence Liberty once hewed her sculptures out — it is all gone. Shall America thus perish? Greece and Italy both answer, " Yes! " I question the last fifty years of American history, and it says, " Yes." I look to the American pulpit, I ask the five million Sunday School scholars, and they say, " Yes." I ask the Federal court, the Democratic party, and the Whig, and the answer is still the same.

But I close my eyes on the eleven past missteps we have taken for slavery; on that sevenfold clandestine corruption; I forget the Whig party; I forget the present administration; I forget the judges of the courts; — I remember the few noblest men that there are in society, Church and State; I remember the grave of my father, the lessons of my mother's life; I look to the spirit of this age — it is the nineteenth century, not the ninth; — I look to the history of the Anglo-Saxons in America, and the history of mankind; I remember the story and the song of Italian and German patriots; I recall the dear words of those great-minded Greeks — Ionian, Dorian, Ætolian; I remember the Romans who spoke, and sang, and fought for truth and right; I recollect those old Hebrew prophets, earth's nobler sons, poets and saints; I call to mind the greatest, noblest, purest soul that ever blossomed in this dusty world; — and I say, " No! " Truth shall triumph, justice shall be law! And, if America fail, though she is one fortieth of God's family, and it is a great loss, there are other nations behind us; our truth shall not perish, even if we go down.

But we shall not fail! I look into your eyes — young men and women, thousands of you, and men and women far enough from young! I look into the eyes of fifty thousand other men and women, whom, in the last eight months, I have spoken to, face to face, and they say, " No! America shall not fail! "

I remember the women who were never found faithless when a sacrifice was to be offered to great principles; I look up to my God, and I look into my own heart, and I say, " We shall not fail! We shall not fail! "

This, at my side, it is the willow; * it is the symbol of weeping: — but its leaves are deciduous; the autumn wind will strew them on the ground; and beneath, here is a perennial plant; it is green all the year through. When this willow branch is leafless, the other is green with hope, and its buds are in its bosom; its buds will blossom. So it is with America.

Did our fathers live? are we dead? Even in our ashes live their holy fires! Boston only sleeps; one day she will wake! Massachusetts will stir again! New England will rise and walk! the vanished North be found once more queenly and majestic! Then it will be seen that slavery is weak and powerless in itself, only a phantom of the night.

Slavery is a " finality,"— is it? There shall be no " agitation,"— not the least,— shall there? There is a Hispaniola in the South, and the South knows it. She sits on a powder magazine, and then plays with fire, while humanity shoots rockets all round the world. To mutilate, to torture, to burn to death revolted Africans whom outrage has stung to crime — that is only to light the torches of San Domingo. This black bondage will be red freedom one day: nay, lust, vengeance, redder yet. I would not wait till that flood comes and devours all.

When the North stands up, manfully, united, we can tear down slavery in a single twelvemonth; and, when we do unite, it must be not only to destroy slavery in the territories, but to uproot every weed of slavery throughout this whole wide land. Then leanness will

* Referring to the floral ornaments that day on the desk.

depart from our souls; then the blessing of God will come upon us; we shall have a commonwealth based on righteousness, which is the strength of any people, and shall stand longer than Egypt,— national fidelity to God our age-outlasting pyramid!

How feeble seems a single nation; how powerless a solitary man! But one of a family of forty, we can do much. How much is Italy, Rome, Greece, Palestine, Egypt to the world? The solitary man — a Luther, a Paul, a Jesus — he outweighs millions of coward souls! Each one of you take heed that the Republic receive no harm!

X

THE PRESENT ASPECT OF THE ANTI-SLAVERY ENTERPRISE

1856

MR. PRESIDENT, LADIES AND GENTLEMEN: — After that Trinitarian introduction,* in which I am presented before you as one anti-slavery nature in three persons,— a fanatic, an infidel, and a traitor,— I am sure a Unitarian minister will bring his welcome along with him. And yet I come under great disadvantages: for I follow one whose color is more than the logic, which his cause did not need (alluding to Mr. Remond); and another whose sex is more eloquent than the philosophy of noblest men (referring to Mrs. Blackwell), whose word has in it the wild witchery which takes captive your heart. I am neither an African nor a woman. I shall speak, therefore, somewhat in the way of logic, which the one rejected; something also, perhaps, of philosophy, which the other likewise passed by.

Allow me to say, however, still further, by way of introduction, that I should not weary your ears at all this morning, were it not that another man, your friend and mine, Mr. Phillips, lies sick at home. Re-

---

* The President, Mr. Garrison, thus introduced Mr. Parker to the audience at New York: —

"Ladies and Gentlemen,— The fanaticism and infidelity and treason which are hateful to the traffickers in slaves and the souls of men must be well-pleasing to God, and are indications of true loyalty to the cause of liberty. I have the pleasure of introducing to you a very excellent fanatic, a very good infidel, and a first-rate traitor, in the person of Theodore Parker, of Boston."

member the threefold misfortune of my position: I come after an African, after a woman, and in the place of Wendell Phillips.

I shall ask your attention to some Thoughts on the Present Aspect of the Anti-slavery Enterprise, and the Forces which work therefor.

In all great movements of mankind, there are three special works to be done, so many periods of work, and the same number of classes of persons therein engaged.

First is the period of sentiment. The business is to produce the right feeling,— a sense of lack, and a fore-feeling of desire for the special thing required. The aim is to produce a sense of need, and also a feeling of want. That is the first thing.

The next period is that of ideas, where the work is to furnish the thought of what is wanted,— a distinct, precise, adequate idea. The sentiment must precede the thought: for the primitive element in all human conduct is a feeling; everything begins in a spontaneous emotion.

The third is the period of action, when the business is to make the thought a thing, to organize it into institutions. The idea must precede the action, else man begins to build and is not able to finish: he runs before he is sent, and knows not where he is going, or the way thither.

Now these three special works go on in the anti-slavery movement; there are these three periods observable, and three classes of persons engaged in the various works. The first effort is to excite the anti-slavery feeling; the next, to furnish the anti-slavery idea; and the third is to make that thought a thing,— to organize the idea into institutions which shall be as wide as the idea, and fully adequate to express the feeling itself.

I. The primitive thing has been, and still is, to arouse a sense of humanity in the whites, which should lead us to abolish this wickedness.

Another way would be to arouse a sense of indignation in the person who has suffered the wrong,— in the slave,— and to urge him, of himself, to put a stop to bearing the wickedness.

Two things there were which hindered this from being attempted. First, some of the anti-slavery leaders were non-resistant; they said it is wrong for the black man to break the arm of the oppressor, and we will only pray God to break it: the slaves must go free without breaking it themselves. That was one reason why the appeal was not made to the slave. The leaders were non-resistants; some of them covered with a Quaker's hat, some of them (pointing to Mr. Garrison, who was bald) not by any covering at all.

The other reason was, the slaves themselves were Africans,— men not very good at the sword. If the case had been otherwise,— if it had been three and a half millions of Anglo-Saxons,— the chief anti-slavery appeal would not have been to the oppressor to leave off oppressing, but to the victim to leave off bearing the oppression. For, while the African is not very good with the sword, the Anglo-Saxon is something of a master with that ugly weapon; at any rate, he knows how to use it. If the Anglo-Saxon had not been a better fighter than the African, slave-ships would fill this side of Sandy Hook and Boston Bay; they would not take pains to go to the Gulf of Guinea. The only constitution which slave-hunters respect is writ on the parchment of a drum-head. If the three and a half millions of slaves had been white men, with this dreadful Anglo-Saxon blood in their bosoms, do you suppose the affair at Cincinnati would have turned out after that sort? Do you believe Governor Chase would have said, " No slavery outside of the slave States; but, inside of the slave States, just as much en- slavement of Anglo-Saxon men as you please "? Why, his head would not have been on his shoulders twenty-four hours after he had said it. In the State of Ohio, when Margaret Garner was surrendered up, there were four hundred thousand able-bodied men between the ages of eighteen and forty-five; there were half a million of firelocks in that State; and, if that woman had been the representative of three and a half millions of white persons held as slaves, every one of those muskets would have started into life, and four hundred thousand men would have come forth, each with a firelock on his shoulder; and then one hundred thousand women would have followed, bringing the rest of the muskets. That would have been the state of things if she had been a white Caucasian woman, and not a black African. We should not then have asked Quakers to lead in the greatest enterprise in the world: the leaders would have been soldiers; I mean such men as our fathers, who did not content them- selves with asking Great Britain to leave off oppres- sing them. They asked that first; and when Great Britain said, " Please God, we never will! " what did the Saxon say? " Please God, I will make you! " And he kept his word.

> "Gods!" (we should have said,)
>   "Can a Saxon people long debate
> Which of the two to choose,— slavery, or death?
> No: let us rise at once, gird on our swords,
> . . . Attack the foe, break through the thick array
> Of his thronged legions, and charge home upon him!"

That would have been the talk. Meetings would have been opened with prayer by men who trusted in God, and likewise kept their powder dry.

But in this case it was otherwise. The work has not been to arouse the indignation of the enslaved, but to stir the humanity of the oppressor, to touch his conscience, his affection, his religious sentiment; or to show that his political and pecuniary interests required the freedom of all men in America.

And it has been very fortunate for us that this great enterprise fell into the hands of just such men as these,— that it was not soldiers who chiefly engaged in it, but men of peace. By and by I will show you why.

The attempt was made at first, and by that gentleman too (pointing to Mr. Garrison), with others, to arouse the anti-slavery feeling in the actual slaveholders at the South. You know what followed. He and every one who tried it there were driven over the border. Then the attempt was made at the North; and there it has been continued. It is exceedingly important to get a right anti-slavery feeling at the North: for two-thirds of the population are at the North; three-fourths of the property, four-fifths of the education are here, and I suppose six-sevenths of the Christianity; and one of these days it may be found out that seven-eighths of the courage are at the North also. I do not say it is so; but it may turn out so. So much for the matter of sentiment.

II. Now look at the next point. If the sentiment be right, then the mind is to furnish the idea. But a statement of the idea before the sentiment is fixed helps to excite the feeling; and so a great deal has been done to spread abroad the anti-slavery idea, even amongst persons who had not the anti-slavery feeling; for, though the heart helps the head, the head likewise pays back the debt by helping the heart. If Mr. Garrison has a clear idea of freedom, he will go to men who have no very strong sentiment of freedom, and will awake the soul of liberty underneath those ribs of death. The womanhood of Lucy Stone Blackwell will do it; the complexion of Mr. Remond will do it.

In spreading this idea of freedom, a good deal has been done, chiefly at the North, but something also at the South. Attempts have been made to diffuse the anti-slavery idea in this way: Men go before merchants, and say, "Slavery is bad economy; it don't pay: the slave can't raise so much tobacco and cotton as the freeman." That is an argument which Mr. May's mercantile friend could have understood; and a political economist might have shown him, that, although there were millions of dollars invested "on account of slavery," there were tens of millions invested on account of freedom; and that latter investment would pay much larger dividends when it got fairly to its work.

Then, too, the attempt has been made to show that it was bad policy: bondage would not breed a stalwart, noble set of men; for the slave contaminated the master, and the master's neighbor not the less.

It has been shown, likewise, that slavery injured education; and while, in Massachusetts, out of four hundred native white men, there is but one who cannot read the Bible, in Virginia, out of nine white native adults born of "the first families" (they having none others except "black people"), there is always one who cannot read his own name.

All kinds of schemes, too, have been proposed to

end this wickedness of slavery. There has been a most multifarious discussion of the idea; for, after we have the right sentiment, it is difficult to get the intellectual work done, done well, in the best way. It takes a large-minded man, with great experience, to cipher out all this intellectual work, and show how we can get rid of slavery, and what is to take its place, and how the thing is to be done. Accordingly, very various schemes are proposed.

Now, the idea which has been attained to, the anti-slavery idea reached by the ablest men, is embodied in these two propositions: first, NO SLAVERY ANYWHERE IN AMERICA; second, NO SLAVERY ANYWHERE ON EARTH. That is the topmost idea.

There has been an opposite work going on. First, an attempt " to crush out " the sentiment of humanity from all mankind. That was the idea of a very distinguished son of Massachusetts. He said, " It must be crushed out." Second, to put down the idea of freedom. That has been attempted, not only by political officers, but also by a great many other men. It is not to be denied that, throughout the South, in the controlling classes of society, the sentiment and idea of freedom are much less widely spread than twenty years ago. The South has grown despotic, while the North becomes more humane.

III. The third thing is to do the deed. After the sentiment is right, and the idea right, organization must be attended to. But the greatest and most difficult work is to get the heart right and the head right; for, when these are in a proper condition, the hand obeys the two, and accomplishes its work. Still it is a difficult matter to organize freedom. It will require great talent and experience; for, as it takes a master mind to organize thought into matter, and to make a Sharp's rifle or a sewing-machine, so it requires a great deal more mind to organize an idea into political institutions, and establish a State where the anti-slavery sentiment shall blossom into an idea, and the idea grow into a national fact, a State where law and order secure to each man his natural and inalienable rights.

In the individual Northern States a good deal has been done in five-and-twenty years to organize the idea of freedom for white men, a little also for colored men; for the feeling and thought must lead to action. But in the Federal Government the movement has been continually the other way. Two things are plain in the conduct of Congress: (1) Acts to spread and strengthen African slavery; (2) Subsidiary acts to oppress the several Northern States which love freedom, and to " crush out " individual men who love freedom. Slavery centralizes power, and destroys local self-government.

Something has been done in the Northern States in respect to awakening the sentiment and communicating the idea; but there has nothing been done as yet in the Federal Congress towards accomplishing the work. I mean to say, for the last seventy years, Congress has not taken one single step towards abolishing slavery, or making the anti-slavery idea an American fact. So even now all these three operations must needs go on. Much elementary work still requires to be done, producing the sentiment and the idea, before the nation is ready for the act.

Now look at the special forces which are engaged in this enterprise. I divide them into two great parties.

The first party consists of the political reformers,—

men who wish to act by political machinery, and are in government offices, legislative, judicial, and executive.

The second party is the non-political reformers, who are not, and do not wish to be, in government offices, legislative, judicial, or executive.

Look a moment at the general functions of each party, and then at the particular parties themselves,—at the business, and then at the business men.

The business of the political man, legislative, judicial, and executive, is confined to the third part of the anti-slavery work; namely, to organizing the idea, and making the anti-slavery thought a thing. The political reformer, as such, is not expected to kindle the sentiment or create the idea, only to take what he finds ready, and put it into form. The political legislature is to make laws and institutions which organize the idea. The political judiciary is to expound the laws, and is limited thereby. The political executive is to administer the institution, and is limited to that: he cannot go beyond it. So the judiciary and the executive are limited by the laws and institutions. The legislature is chosen by the people to represent the people; that is, it is chosen to represent and to organize the ideas, and to express the sentiments, of the people; not to organize sentiments which are in advance of the people, or which are behind the people. The political legislator is restricted by the ideas of the people: if he wants what they do not want, then they do not want him. If Senator Wilson had a million of men and women in Massachusetts who entertained the sentiments and ideas of Mr. Garrison, why he would represent the sentiments and ideas of Mr. Garrison, would express them in Congress, and would go to work to organize those ideas.

In hoisting the anchor of a ship, two sets of men are at work, two machines. One, I think, is called the windlass. Many powerful men put their levers to that, and hoist the anchor up out from the deep. Behind them is the capstan, whose business it is to haul in the rope. Now, the function of the non-political reformer is to hoist the anchor up from the bottom: he is the windlass. But the business of Chase, Hale, Sumner, and Wilson, and other political reformers, is to haul in the slack, and see that what the windlass has raised up is held on to, and that the anchor does not drop back again to the bottom. The men at the windlass need not call out to the men at the capstan, "Haul in more slack!" when there is no more to haul in. This is the misfortune of the position of the men at the capstan,— they cannot turn any faster than the windlass gives them slack rope to wind up. That ought to be remembered. Every political man, before he takes his post, ought to understand that; and the non-political men, when they criticize him never so sharply, ought to remember that the men at the capstan cannot turn any faster than the men at the windlass.

If the politician is to keep in office, he must accommodate himself to the ideas of the people; for the people are sovereign, and reign, while the politicians only govern with delegated power, but do not reign: they are agents, trustees, holding by a special power of attorney, which authorizes them to do certain things, for doing which they are responsible to the people. In order to carry his point, the politician must have a majority on his side: he cannot wait for it to grow, but must have it now, else he loses his post. He takes the wolf by the ears; and, if he lets go, the wolf eats him up: he must therefore lay hold where he can clinch fast and continue. If Mr. Sumner, in his place in the Senate, says what Massachusetts does not indorse, out goes Mr. Sumner. It is the same with the rest. All politicians are well aware of that fact. I have sometimes thought they forgot a great many other things; they very seldom forget that.

See the proof of what I say. If you will go into any political meeting of Whigs or Democrats, you shall find the ablest men of the party on the platform, — the great Whigs, the great Democrats; " the rest of mankind " will be on the floor. Now, watch the speeches. They do not propose an idea, or appeal to a sentiment that is in advance of the people. But, when you go into an anti-slavery meeting, you find that the platform is a great ways higher than the pews, uniformly so. Accordingly, when an African speaks (who is commonly supposed to be lower than the rest of mankind) and says a very generous thing, there is a storm of hisses all round this hall. What does it show? That the anti-slavery platform which the African stands on is somewhat higher than the general level of the floor, even in the city of New York. The politician on his platform often speaks to the bottom of the floor, and not to the top of the ceiling.

So much for the political reformers: I am not speaking of political hunkers. Now a word of the non-political reformers. Their business is, first, to produce the sentiment; next, the idea; and, thirdly, to suggest the mode of action. The anti-slavery non-political reformer is to raise the cotton, to spin it into thread, to weave it into web, to prescribe the pattern after which the dress is to be made; and then he is to pass over the cloth and the pattern to the political reformer, and say, "Now, sir, take your shears, and cut it out, and make it up." You see how very inferior the business of the political reformer is, after all. The non-political reformer is not restricted by any law, any constitution, any man, nor by the people, because he is not to deal with institutions; he is to make the institutions better. If he does not like the Union, he is to say so; and, just as soon as he has gathered an audience inside of the Union that is a little too large for its limits, the Union will be taken down without much noise, and piled up,— just as this partition (alluding to the partition dividing the hall) has been taken down this morning,— and there will be a larger place. The non-political reformer can say, "Down with the Constitution!" but the political reformer has sworn to keep the Constitution. He is foreclosed from saying that to-day: by and by he can recant his oath, and say it when he gets ready. The non-political reformer is not restricted by fear of losing office. Wendell Phillips can say just what he pleases anywhere: if men will not hear him in Faneuil Hall, they will, perhaps, in the Old South Meeting-house. If they will not hear him there, he can speak on the Common; at any rate, in some little school-house.

The political reformer must have a majority with him, else he cannot do anything; he has not carried his point or accomplished his end. But the non-political reformer has accomplished part of his end, if he has convinced one man out of a million; for that one man will work to convince another, and by and by the whole will be convinced. A political reformer must get a majority; a non-political reformer has done something if he has the very smallest minority, even if

it is a minority of one. The politician needs bread:
he goes, therefore, to the baker; and bread must be
had to-day. He says, " I am starving: I can't wait."
The baker says, " Go and raise the corn." " Why,
bless you," he replies, " it will take a year to do that;
and I can't wait." The non-political reformer does
not depend on the baker. The baker says, " I have
not much flour." " Very well," he says, " I am going
to procure it for you." So he puts in the seed, and
raises the harvest. Sometimes he must take the land
wild, and even cut down the forest, and scare off the
wild beasts. After he has done that preliminary work,
he has to put in the anti-slavery seed, raise the anti-
slavery corn, and then get the public baker to make
the bread with which to feed the foremost of the political reformers,— men like Seward, Hale, Sumner,
and Wilson. They do all that is possible in their present position, with such a constituency behind them:
they will do more and better soon as the people command; nay, they will not wait for orders,— soon as
the people allow them. These men are not likely to
prove false to their trust. They urge the people forward.

So much for the business. Now look at the business
men.

I. Look first at the political part of the anti-slavery
forces.

1. There is the Republican party. That is a direct
force for anti-slavery; but, as the anti-slavery idea
and sentiment are not very wide-spread, the ablest
members of the Republican party are forced to leave
their special business as politicians, and go into the
elementary work of the non-political reformers. Accordingly, Mr. Wilson stumped all Massachusetts last

year,— yes, all the North; not working for a purpose purely political, but for a purpose purely anti-slavery, — to excite the anti-slavery sentiment, to produce an anti-slavery idea. And Mr. Sumner has had to do that work, even in our city of Boston. Yet New England is further advanced in anti-slavery than any other part of America. The superiority of the Puritan stock shows itself everywhere; I mean its moral superiority. Look at this platform: how many persons here are of New England origin? If an anti-slavery meeting was held at San Francisco or New Orleans, it would be still the same; the platform would be Yankee. It is the foot of New England which stands on that platform. It is to tread slavery down. But, notwithstanding New England is the most anti-slavery portion of the whole land, these political men, whose business ought to be only to organize the anti-slavery ideas, and give expression to anti-slavery sentiments in the Senate, or House of Representatives, are forced to abandon that work from time to time, to go about amongst the people, and produce the anti-slavery sentiment and idea itself. Let us not be very harsh in criticising these men, remembering that they are not so well supported behind as we could all wish they were.

This Republican party has some exceedingly able men. As a Massachusetts man, in another State, I am not expected to say anything in praise of Mr. Sumner, or Mr. Wilson, or Mr. Banks. It would be hardly decorous for a Massachusetts man, out of his own State, to speak in praise of those men. And they need no praise from my lips. And, as a New England man, I think it is not necessary for me to praise Mr. Hale or Mr. Foote, Mr. Collamer, Mr. Fessenden, or any other eminent political men of New England. But, as a New Englander and a Massachusetts man, you will allow me to say a word in praise of one who has no drop of Puritan blood in his veins; who was never in New England but twice,— the first time to attend a cattle-show, and the last to stand on Plymouth Rock, on Forefathers' Day, and, in the bosom of the sons and daughters of the Puritans, to awaken the anti-slavery sentiment and kindle the anti-slavery idea. I am speaking of your own Senator Seward. As I cannot be accused of State pride or of sectional vanity in praising him, let me say, that, in all the United States, there is not at this day a politician so able, so far-sighted, so cautious, so wise, so discriminating, and apparently so gifted with power to organize ideas into men, and administer that organization, as William Henry Seward. I know the other men; I detract nothing from them. It is a great thing to be second where Seward is first.

Of course, this party, as such, will make mistakes; individual Republicans will do wrong things. It has been declared here that Mr. Hale says, in his place in the Senate, that he would not disturb slavery nor the slaveholders. I doubt that he ever said so in public; I am sure it is not his private opinion. I know not what he said that has been so misunderstood. His sentiment is as strongly anti-slavery as our friend Garrison's; but he is just now in what they call a "tight place," he wants to do one thing at a time. The same is true of Henry Wilson and of Charles Sumner: they want to do one thing at a time. I do not find fault with their wishing to do that. The Constitution is the power of attorney which tells them how to act as official agents of the people; how to govern for the sovereign people, whose vicegerents they are. But there are Republican politicians who limit their work to one special thing, and say, " To-day will we do this, and then strike work for ever. We do not intend to do anything to-morrow." They say, " Please God, we will pull up these weeds to-day." The South says, " You shan't! " And these men say, " Let us pull up these: we will never touch those which grow just the other side of the path." They hate those other weeds just as much; they mean to pull them up: but I am sorry to hear them say they do not intend to: and I am glad to hear severe censure passed upon them for promising never to do that particular thing,— not for taking one step at a time. If we only find fault with real offenders, we shall still have work enough to do.

I say this party has great names and powerful men. It will gain others from the Democrats and from the Whigs alike. See what it has gathered from the Democrats! Look at that high-toned and noble newspaper, the *Evening Post*, and its editor, not only gifted with the genius of poetry, which is a great thing, but with the genius of humanity, which is tenfold greater. See likewise such a man as Francis P. Blair coming into this movement! Governor Chase is another that it has gathered from that party. There are various other men whom I might mention from both the old political parties. Then see what service is rendered to the cause of humanity by a newspaper, which, a few years ago, seemed sworn for ever to Henry Clay. I speak of the only paper in the world which counts its readers by the million,— the *New York Tribune*. The Republican party gathers the best hearts and the noblest heads out of the Whig and the Democratic parties. If faithful, it will do more in this way for the future than in the past. The Democratic party continues to exist by these two causes: (1) Its admirable organization; (2) The tradition of noble ideas and sentiments. In this respect, it is to the Americans what the Catholic Church is to Europe; the leaders of the two about equally corrupt, the rank and file about equally deceived, hoodwinked, and abused. Which is the better,— to be politician-ridden, or priest-ridden? Good men will become weary of such service, and leave the party for a better, soon as they are sure that it is better.

2. Look next at the American party, so called: it is anti-American in some particulars. This is an indirect anti-slavery force, as the Republican party is a direct anti-slavery force. I suppose you know what its professed principle is,— " No foreign influence in our politics." Now, that principle comes partly from a national instinct, whose function is this: first, to prevent the excess of foreign blood in our veins; and, secondly, the excess of foreign ideas in the American consciousness. Well, it was necessary there should be that party. It has a very important function; because it is possible for a people to take so much foreign blood in its veins, and so many foreign ideas to its consciousness, that its nationality perishes.

In part, this principle comes from the national instinct; and that is always stronger in the great mass of the people than it is in any class of men with " superior education: " for the superior education consists almost wholly in development of the understanding,— the thinking part,— not in culture of the conscience, the affections, and the religious element. Therefore, for the national instinct, I never look to lawyers, ministers, doctors, literary and scientific men, or, in short, to the class of men who have what is called the "best education:" I look to the great mass of the people. It seems to me that the national instinct of the Saxon had something to do in making this principle of the American party so popular.

However, I do not think the chief devotion to this principle comes from that source, but from one very much corrupter than that,— a source a great deal lower than the uneducated mass of the Northern people. It comes from political partisans,— men who want office. There are two ways of getting into high office. One is to fly there: that is a very good way for an animal furnished with wings. The other is to crawl there: that is the only way left for such as have no wings, and no legs, and no arms. Well, there was a class of men at the North who could not fly into office; and when the way which led up to the office was perpendicular, and went up straight, they could not crawl; they were so slippery, that they fell off: there was not strength enough in their natural gluten to hold up their natural weight. Such men could not fly there; they could not crawl there, so long as the road went straight up; so they took the Know-nothing plank, which sloped up pretty gradually; and on it Mr. Gardner crawled into the governorship of Massachusetts. A good many men, in various other States, wormed up on that gently sloping inclined plane, who else never would have been within sight of any considerable office. Now it is this class of men, who caught sight of that principle demanded by the national instinct, which fears an excess of foreign blood in our veins, and of foreign ideas in our consciousness; and they said, "Let us make use of that as a

plank upon which we can crawl up into office." They
have got in there; but before long they will fall out
of their lofty hole, or, if they stay in, will be shriv-
eled up, dried clear through, and by and by be blown
off so far that no particle of them will ever be found
again. The American party just now, throughout
all the United States, I fear, has fallen into the hands
of this class of men. It does not any longer, I think,
represent the instinct of the less-educated people, or
the consciousness of the more thoughtful people, but
the designs of artful, crafty, and rather low-minded
persons.

But let no injustice be done. In the party are still
noble men, who entered it full of this national instinct,
with these three negations on their banner,— No
Priestcraft, No Liquor, No New Slave States. Some
of them still adhere to the worst of the leaders of
their party. Loyalty is as strong in the Saxon as in
the Russian or Spaniard; as often attaches itself to a
mean man. It is now painful to see such faithful
worshipers of such false " gods." " An idol is nothing," says St. Paul: it may also be a Know-nothing.

This party, notwithstanding its origin and character, has done two good works — one negative, one
positive.

First, it helped destroy the Whig and Democratic
party. That was very essential. The anti-slavery
man, the non-political reformer, wanted to sow his seed
in the national soil. It was dreadfully cumbered with
weeds of two kinds — Whig-weed and Democrat-
weed. The Know-nothings lent their hands to destroy
these weeds; and they have pulled up the Whig-weed
pretty thoroughly: they have torn it up by the roots,
shaken the soil from it, and it lies there partly drying

and partly rotting, but, at any rate, pretty thoroughly dead. They laid hold of the Democrat-weed. That was a little too rank, and strongly rooted in the ground, for them to pull up. Nevertheless, they loosened its roots; they gave it a twist in the trunk; they broke off some branches, and stripped off some of its leaves, and it does not look quite so flourishing as it did several years ago.

Now this negative work is very important; for, if we could get both these kinds of weed out of the soil, it would not be a very difficult matter to sow the seed and raise a harvest of anti-slavery.

Next for the positive work. It calls out men who hitherto have never taken the initiative in politics, but have voted just as they were bid. I will speak of Massachusetts, of Boston. We had there a large class of excellent men, who always went, a week or two before the election, to the Whigs and Democrats, and said, " Whom are we to vote for? " The great Whigs said, " We have not yet taken counsel of the Lord; we shall do so to-morrow, and then we will tell you." So these men went home, and bowed their knees, and waited in silent submission; and the next day their masters said, " You are to vote for John Smith or John Brown," or whosoever it chanced to be. And the people said, " Hurrah for the great John Smith!" " Hurrah for the great John Brown!" " Did you ever hear of him before? " asked some one. " No: but he is the greatest man alive." " Who told you so? " " Oh! our masters told us so." Now, the Know-nothings went to that class of men, and said, " You have been fooled long enough." " So we have," said the people, " and no mistake! and we will not bear it any longer." They would not be fooled any longer by the Whigs, and some of them no longer by the Democrats; but they were fooled by the Know-nothings. Nevertheless, it was an important thing for this class of people to take the initiative in political matters. If they stumbled as they tried to go alone, it is what all children have done. "Up and take another," is good advice. So the Know-nothings not only pulled up the Whig-weed, and left it to rot, but they stirred the land; they ploughed it deep with a subsoil plough, turning up a whole stratum of people which had never been brought up to the surface of the political garden before. That was another very important matter; and yet, allow me to say, with all this subsoiling, they have not turned up one single man who proves powerful in politics, and at the same time new. Mr. Wilson owes his place in the Senate to the Know-nothings: he was known to be a powerful man before. Mr. Banks owes his place to this party; he also was a powerful man before. I do not find, anywhere in the United States, that the Americans have brought one single able man before the people, who was not known to the people just as well before. You shall determine what that fact means. I shall not say just now.

At the South, this party has done greater service than at the North; for, among the non-slaveholders at the South, there is a class of men with very little money, less education, and no social standing whatsoever. That class have been deprived of their political power by the rich, educated, and respectable slaveholders; for the slaveholders make the laws, fill the offices, and monopolize all the government of the South. Those " poor whites " are nothing but the dogs of the slaveholder. Whenever he says, " Seize him, Dirt-eater! " away goes this whole pack of pro-slavery dogs, catching hold of whomsoever their master set them upon. This class of men, having no money and no education, and no means of getting any, deprived of political influence, felt that they were crushed down; but they were too ignorant to know what hurt them. They had no newspapers, no means of concerted action. Northern men have undertaken to help those men. Mr. Vaughan established his newspaper at Cleveland chiefly for the purpose of reaching them. Cassius M. Clay, in Kentucky, said, " Let us speak to that class of men." Once in a while, you hear of their holding a meeting somewhere in Virginia, and uttering some kind of anti-slavery sentiment or idea. Very soon they are put down. Now, the Know-nothings went among the " poor whites " in the South, and organized American lodges. The whole thing was done in secret; so that the organization was established, and set on its legs, before the slaveholders knew anything about it: it was strong, and had grown up to be a great boy before they knew the child was born. Of course, the Southern Know-nothing party, at first, does not know exactly what to do; so it takes the old ideas of persons that are about it, and becomes intensely pro-slavery. That is not quite all. The Whigs at the South have always been feeble. They saw that their party was going to pieces; and, with the instinct of that other animal which flees out of the house which is likely to fall, they sought shelter under some safer roof: they fled to the Know-nothing organization. The leading Whigs got control of the party at the South, and made that still more pro-slavery in the

South which was already sufficiently despotic at the North. Nevertheless, there has now risen up, at the South, a body of men who, when they come to complete consciousness of themselves, will see that they are in the same boat with the black man, and that what now curses the black man will also ruin the " poor white " at last. At present, they are too ignorant to understand that; for the bulk of the American party at the South consists of Know-nothings, who were such before they ever went into a lodge — natural Know-nothings, who need no initiation. Nevertheless, they are human; and the truth, driven with the slave-holder's hammer, will force itself even into such heads.

Such men are not hopeless. One day, we shall see a great deal of good come from them. At present, they are in the same condition with the Irish at Boston — first, ignorant; and next, controlled by their priests; for, as the Irish Catholic in Boston and New York is roughly ridden by that heavy ecclesiastical rider, the priest, so the Know-nothings at the South are still more roughly ridden by this desperate political rider mounted upon their backs. One day, both the Irish and the Know-nothing master will be unhorsed, and there will be no more such riding.

So much for these two anti-slavery forces — one direct, and the other indirect.

This, let me say in general, is the sin of the politician — he seeks office for his own personal gain, and, when he is in it, refuses to organize the anti-slavery ideas which he was put in office to develop and represent. After the windlass has lifted the anchor, he refuses to haul in the slack cable. That was the case with Webster; it caused him his death. It was

the case with Everett; it brought him to private life
and political ruin. Many are elected as anti-slavery
men, who prove false to their professions. New England is rich in traitors. The British executive
bought Benedict Arnold with money; the American
executive has since bought many an Arnold. Look
at the present national administration. In 1852,
had he published his programme of principles and
measures, do you think Mr. Pierce would have had
the vote of a single Northern State? Not an elec-
toral vote would have been given by the North for
robbing the people of a million square miles of land,
and bestowing it on three hundred and fifty thousand
slaveholders! He is an official swindler. He got
his place by false pretenses — the juggling trick of
the thimble-rigger. Mr. Hale says, "For every
doughfaced representative, there is a doughfaced
constituency." It is true; but the constituency is
not always quite so soft as the delegate; it is at least
slack-baked, and does not pretend to be what it knows
it is not.

Here, too, let me say, it is a great misfortune
that the North has not sent more strong men to the
political work. In time of war, you take the ablest
men you can find, and put them to do the military
work of the people. The North commonly sends her
ablest men to science, literature, productive industry,
trade, and manufactures; the South, hers to politics;
and so she outwits and beats us from one fifty years
to another. But, in such a terrible battle as this
before us now, rest assured the North cannot afford
to send her strong men to callings directly productive
of pecuniary value: we must have them in politics —
men of great mind, able to see far behind and be-

fore; of great experience, to organize and administer.
Above all must our statesmen be men of great justice
and humanity, such as reverence the higher law of
God. Integrity is the first thing needed in a statesman.
The time may come when the men of largest human
power may go to the shop, the counting-room, the
farm, the ship, to science, or preaching: just now we
cannot afford to make a land-surveyor out of a Washington, or turn our Franklins into tallowchandlers.
When we can afford such expenditure, I shall not object: now we are not rich enough to allow Moses to
tend sheep, asses, and young camels, or to keep Paul
at tent-making.

Here are the anti-slavery forces which are not political. They are various.

At first, the anti-slavery men looked to the American
Church, and said: " That will be our great bulwark
and defender." Instead of being a help, it has been a
hindrance. If the American Church, twenty years
ago, could have dropped through the continent, and
disappeared altogether, the anti-slavery cause would
have been further on than it is at this day. If, remaining above ground, every minister in the United
States had sealed his lips, and said, " Before God,
I will say no word for freedom or against it, in behalf of the slaveholder or of his victim," the anti-
slavery enterprise would have been further on than it
is at this day. I say that, notwithstanding the majestic memory of William Ellery Channing, a mag-
nanimous man, whose voice rang like a trumpet
through the continent, following that other clearer,
higher, more widely sounding voice, still spared to
us on earth (Mr. Garrison's); notwithstanding the
eloquent words which do honor to the name of Beecher

and the heart of humanity; notwithstanding the presence of this dear good soul (referring to Samuel J. May), whose presence in the anti-slavery cause has been like the month whose name he bears, and has brought a whole lapful of the sweetest flowers,— the Church has hindered more than it has helped. For the tallest heads in the great sects were lifted up to blaspheme the God of Righteousness, and commit the sin which Mr. Remond says is second only to atheism,— the denial of humanity. While the atheist openly denied God, many a minister openly denied man. I think the minister committed the worst sin; for he sinned in the name of God, and hypocritically: he wrought his blasphemy that he might gain his daily bread, while the atheist periled his bread and his reputation when he stood up, and said, " I think there is no God." I have no respect for atheism; but when a man in the pulpit blasphemes the divinity of God by treading the humanity of man under his anointed foot, I say I would take my chance in the next world with him who speaks out of his own heart, in his blindness, and says, " There is no God," rather than share the lot of that man who, in the name of Jesus and of the Father, treads down humanity, and declares there is no higher law.

There are a great many direct anti-slavery forces.

1. The conduct of the slaveholders in the South, and their allies, has awakened the indignation of the North. The Fugitive Slave Bill was an anti-slavery measure. We said so six years ago; now we know it. Kidnapping is anti-slavery; it makes anti-slavery men. The repeal of the Missouri Compromise stirred anti-slavery sentiment in Northern hearts. The conduct of affairs in Kansas, Judge Kane's wickedness,

and the horrible outrage at Cincinnati,— all these turn out anti-slavery measures. Mr. Douglas stands in his place in the Senate, and turns his face north, and says, " We mean to subdue you." The mass at the North says, " We are not going to be subdued." It is an anti-slavery resolution. The South repudiates Democracy: the *Charleston Mercury* and the *Richmond Examiner* say that the Declaration of Independence is a great mistake when it says all men are by nature equal in their right to life, liberty, and the pursuit of happiness,— that there is no greater lie in the world. When the North understands that, it says, " I am anti-slavery at once." The North has not heard it yet thoroughly. One day it will.

2. Then there are the general effects of education: it enlightens men, so that they can see that slavery is a bad speculation, bad economy.

3. Then there is the progressive moralization of the North. The North is getting better, more and more Christian and humane. It was never so temperate as to-day, never so just, never so moral, never so humane and philanthropic. To be sure, even now we greatly overlook our black brother: it is because he is not an Anglo-Saxon. But he has human blood in his veins: by and by we shall see our black brother also.

4. Then the better portion of the Northern press is on our side. Consider what quantities of books have been written within the last ten years full of anti-slavery sentiment, and running over with anti-slavery ideas. Think of " Uncle Tom's Cabin " and the host of books, only inferior to that, which have been published. Then look at the newspapers. I just spoke of the *Evening Post*, and *Tribune:* look

at the *New York Independent,* with twenty thousand subscribers, with so much anti-slavery in it. It does not go the length that I wish it did, and sometimes it does very mean things; for it is not unitary. See what powerful anti-slavery agents are the *Evening Post,* the *Independent,* the *New York Times,* and the *New York Tribune,* and that whole army of newspapers, some of them in every Northern city; not to forget the *National Era,* at Washington. Besides these, there are the anti-slavery newspapers proper, the *Liberator,* the *Standard,* and divers others, only second where it is praise to be inferior.

5. Then there is the anti-slavery party proper, with its men, its money, and its immense force in the country. What power of religion it has! I know it has been called anti-religious, anti-Christian, infidel. Was not Jesus of Nazareth nailed to the cross, between two thieves, on the charge that he blasphemed God? How rich is this party in its morals, how mighty in its eloquence! I am sorry its most persuasive lips are not here to-day to speak for themselves and for you, and instead of me. Here is a woman also in the anti-slavery ranks. I need say nothing of her: her own sweet music just now awoke the tune of humanity in your hearts, and I saw the anti-slavery sentiment spring in tears out of your eyes. One day, from such watering, it will blossom into an anti-slavery idea, and fruiten into anti-slavery acts.

(1.) Here is the merit of this anti-slavery party. It appeals to the very widest and deepest humanity. It knows no restriction of State or Church. If the State is wrong, the anti-slavery party says, " Away with the State!" if the Church is mistaken, " Down with the Church!" If the people are wrong, then it says, "Woe unto you, O ye people! you are sinning against God, and your sin will find you out." It does not appeal to the politician, the priest, the editor alone; it goes to the people, face to face, eye to eye, heart to heart, and speaks to them, and with immense power. It knows no man after the flesh. Let me suppose an impossibility — that Mr. May should become as Everett, and Mr. Garrison as Webster: would their sin be forgiven by the abolitionists? No: those who sit behind them now would stand, not on this platform, but on this table, and denounce them for their short-coming and wrong-doing. They spare no man; they forgive no sin against the idea of freedom.

They are not selfish; for they ask nothing except an opportunity to do their duty. And they have had nothing except a " chance " to do that; always in ill report until now, when you shall judge how much there is of good report awaiting them.

They are untiring. I wish they would sink through the platform, so that I could say what would now put them to the blush before so large an audience.

They appeal to the high standard of absolute right. This is their merit. The nation owes them a great debt, which will not be paid in this life. Their reward is in the nobleness which does such deeds and lives such life: thus they will take with them " an inheritance incorruptible, undefiled, and which fadeth not away."

(2.) Here, I think, is their defect. They forget, sometimes, that there must be political workmen. This comes from the fact, that, to so great an extent,

they are non-voters, even " non-resistants." If they
were the opposite, they would have appealed to violence: being Quakers and non-resistants, they have not
done quite justice always, it seems to me, to those who
work in the political way.

This has been charged against them: that they
quarrel among themselves; two against three, and
three against two; Douglass against Garrison, and
Garrison against Douglass; the liberty-party men
against the old anti-slavery men; and all that. That
is perfectly true. But remember why it is so. You
can bring together a Democratic body, draw your line,
and they all touch the mark: it is so with the Whigs.
They have long been drilled into it. But, whenever
a body of men with new ideas comes to organize, there
are as many opinions as persons. Pilate and Herod,
bitter enemies of each other, were made friends by
a common hostility to Jesus; but, when the twelve
disciples came together, they fell out: Paul resisted
Peter; James differed from John; and so on. It is
always so on every platform of new ideas, and will
always be so — at least for a long time. We must
bear with one another the best we can.

I think that the anti-slavery party has not always
done quite justice to the political men. See why. It
is easy for Mr. Garrison and Mr. Phillips or me to
say all of our thought. I am responsible to nobody,
and nobody to me. But it is not easy for Mr. Sumner, Mr. Seward, and Mr. Chase to say all of their
thought; because they have a position to maintain,
and they must keep in that position. The political
reformer is hired to manage a mill owned by the people, turned by the popular stream — to grind into
anti-slavery meal such corn as the people bring him

for that purpose, and other grain also into different meal. He is not principal and owner, only attorney and hired man. He must do his work so as to suit his employers, else they say, " Thou mayest be no longer miller." The non-political reformer owns his own mill, which is turned by the stream drawn from his private pond: he put up the dam, and may do what he will with his own — run it all night, on Sunday, and the 4th of July; may grind just as he likes, for it is his own corn. He sells his meal to such as will buy. He is in no danger of being turned out of his office; for he has no master — is not hired man to any one.

The anti-slavery non-political reformer is to excite the sentiment, and give the idea: he may tell his whole scheme all at once, if he will. But the political reformer, who, for immediate action, is to organize the sentiment and idea he finds ready for him, cannot do or propose all things at once: he must do one thing at a time, tell one thing at a time. He is to cleave slavery off from the government; and so must put the thin part of his wedge in first, and that where it will go the easiest. If he takes a glut as thick as an anti-slavery platform, and puts it in anywhere, head foremost, let him strike never so hard, he will not rend off a splinter from the tough log; nay, will only waste his strength, and split the head of his own beetle!

Still, this non-political, anti-slavery party — averse to fighting, hostile to voters under present, if not all possible, circumstances — has been of most immense value to mankind. It has been a perpetual critic on politicians; and now it has become so powerful that every political man in the North is afraid of it; and, when he makes a speech, he asks not only, What will the Whigs or the Democrats think of it? but, What will the anti-slavery men say; what will the *Liberator* and the *Standard* say of it?   And, when a candidate is to be presented for the office of President, the men who make the nomination go to the Quakers of Pennsylvania, and say, " Whom do you want? "   They go to the non-resistants of Massachusetts — men that never vote or take office — and ask if it will do to nominate this, that, or the other man.   A true Church is to criticize the world by a higher standard.   The non-political anti-slavery party is the Church of America to criticize the politics of America.   It has been of immense service; it is now a great force.

6. Besides that, there is the spirit of the Anglo-Saxon tribe, which hates oppression, which loves justice and liberty, and will at last have freedom for all.   Look at its history for three hundred years — from 1556, when the three millions of Old England were ruled by the bloody Mary, to 1856, when the three millions of New England govern themselves!   Do you fear for the next three hundred years?   That historic momentum will not be lost.

7. Then there is the spirit of the age we live in. Only see what has been done in a century!   A hundred years ago there were slaves in every corner of the land. There are men on this platform, whose fathers, within fourscore years, have not only owned black, but red and white slaves also.   See what a steady march there has been of freedom in New England, and throughout the North — likewise on the continent of Europe! Christendom repudiates bondage.   Think of British and French emancipation, of Dutch and Danish. Slavery is only at home in three places in Christendom,

— Russia, Brazil, and the south of the United States.
A hundred years ago there was not a spot in all Europe where there was not slavery in one form or another,— men put up at auction.   It is only ninety-eight years ago since men were kidnapped in Glasgow, Scotland, and sold into bondage for ever in the City of Brotherly Love, at Philadelphia.   That thing took place in 1758.   See what an odds there is!

It is plain that American slavery is to end ultimately. It cannot stand.   The question before us is, " Shall it ruin America before it stops? "   I think it will not. The next question is, " Shall it end peaceably, as the Quakers wish, and as all anti-slavery men wish, or shall it end in blood? "   On that point I shall not now give my opinion.

XI

THE PRESENT CRISIS IN AMERICAN AFFAIRS

1856

"Oh! ill for him, who, bettering not with time,
  Corrupts the strength of Heaven-descended will,
And ever weaker grows through acted crime,
Or seeming-genial venial fault,—
  Recurring and suggesting still!
He seems as one whose footsteps halt,—
  Toiling in immeasurable sand,
  And o'er a weary, sultry land;
Far beneath a blazing vault,
  Sown in a wrinkle of the monstrous hill,
The city sparkles like a grain of salt."

America has now come to such a pass, that a small misstep may plunge us into lasting misery. Any other and older nation would be timidly conscious of the peril; but we, both so confident of destined triumph and so wonted to success, forecast only victory, and so heed none of all this danger. Who knows what is before us? By way of warning for the future, look at the events in the last six years.

1. In the spring of 1850, came the discussions on the Fugitive Slave Bill, and the programme of practical atheism; for it was taught, as well in the Senate as the pulpits, that the American Government was amenable to no natural laws of God, but its own momentary caprice might take the place of the eternal reason. "The Union is in danger" was the affected cry. Violent speeches filled the land, and officers of the government uttered such threats against the people of the North as only Austrian and Russian ears were

430

wont to hear. Even " discussion was to cease." That year, the principle was sown whence measures have since sprung forth, an evil blade from evil seed.

2. The next spring, 1851, kidnapping went on in all the North. Kane ruled in Philadelphia, Rynders in New York. Boston opened her arms to the stealers of men, who barked in her streets, and howled about the " Cradle of Liberty,"— the hiding-place of her ancient power. All the municipal authority of the town was delivered up to the kidnappers. Faneuil Hall was crammed with citizen-soldiers, volunteers in men-stealing, eager for their —

" Glorious first essay in war."

Visible chains of iron were proudly stretched round the court-house. The supreme judges of Massachusetts crouched their loins beneath that yoke of bondage, and went under to their own place, wherein they broke down the several laws they were sworn and paid to keep. They gave up Thomas Sims to his tormentors. On the 19th of April, the seventy-sixth anniversary of the first battle of the Revolution, the city of Hancock and Adams thrust one of her innocent citizens into a slave-prison at Savannah; giving his back to the scourge, and his neck to the everlasting yoke.

3. In the spring of 1854, came the discussions on the Kansas-Nebraska Bill; the attempt to extend bondage into the new territory just opening its arms to the industrious North; the legislative effort to rob the Northern laborer thereof, and give the spoils to Southern slaveholders. Then came the second kidnapping at Boston: a judge of probate stole a defenseless man, and made him a slave. The old volunteer soldiers put on their regimentals again to steal another victim. But

they were not quite strong enough alone; so the United States troops of the line were called out to aid the work of protecting the orphan.   It was the first time I ever saw soldiers enforcing the decisions of a New England judge of probate; the first time I ever saw the United States soldiers in any service.   This was characteristic work for a democratic army!   Hireling soldiers, mostly Irishmen,— sober that day, at least till noon,— in the public square loaded their cannon, charged their muskets, fixed their bayonets, and made ready to butcher the citizens soon as a slaveholder should bid them strike a Northern neck.   The spectacle was prophetic.

4. Now, in 1856, New England men migrate to Kansas, taking their wives, their babies, and their cradles. The old Bible goes also on that pilgrimage,— it never fails the sons of the Puritans.   But the fathers are not yet dead; —

" E'en in our ashes live their wonted fires."

Sharp's rifle goes as missionary in that same troop; an indispensable missionary — an apostle to the Gentiles — whose bodily presence is not weak, nor his speech contemptible, in Missouri.   All the parties go armed. Like the father, the Pilgrim son is also a Puritan, and both trusts in God and keeps his powder dry.

A company went from Boston a few days ago, a few of my own friends and parishioners among them. There were some five-and-forty persons, part women and children.   Twenty Sharp's rifles answered to their names, not to speak of other weapons.   The ablest minister in the United States stirs up the " Plymouth Church " to contribute firearms to this new mission; and a spirit, noble as Davenport's and Hooker's, pushes off from New England, again to found a New Haven in the

wilderness.   The bones of the regicide sleep in Connecticut; but the revolutionary soul of fire flames forth
in new processions of the Holy Ghost.

In 1656, when Boston sent out her colonists, they
took matchlocks and snaphances to fend off the red
savage of the wilderness; in 1756, they needed weapons
against the French enemy; but, in 1856, the dreadful
tools of war are to protect their children from the white
border-ruffians, whom the President of the United States
invites to burn the new settlements, to scalp and kill.

In 1850, we heard only the threat of arms; in 1851,
we saw the volunteer muskets in the kidnapper's hand;
in 1854, he put the United States cannon in battery;
in 1856, he arms the savage Missourians.   But now,
also, there are tools of death in the people's hand.   It
is high time.   When the people are sheep, the government is always a wolf.   What will the next step be?
Mr. Cushing says, " I know what is requisite; but it is
means that I cannot suggest! "   Who knows what *coup
d'état* is getting ready?   Surely affairs cannot remain
long in this condition.

To understand this present emergency, you must go
a long ways back, and look a little carefully at what
lies deep down in the foundation of States.

The welfare of a nation consists in these three things;
namely: first, possession of material comfort, things of
use and beauty; second, enjoyment of all the natural
rights of body and spirit; and, third, the development
of the natural faculties of body and spirit in their harmonious order, securing the possession of freedom, intelligence, morality, philanthropy, and piety.   It ought
to be the aim of a nation to obtain these three things
in the highest possible degree, and to extend them to
all persons therein.   That nation has the most welfare

which is the furthest advanced in the possession of these three things.

Next, the progress of a nation consists in two things : first, in the increasing development of the natural faculties of body and spirit,— intellectual, moral, affectional, and religious,— with the consequent increasing enjoyment thereof ; and, second, in the increasing acquisition of power over the material world, making it yield use and beauty, an increase of material comfort and elegance.   Progress is increase of human welfare for each and for all.   That is the most progressive nation which advances fastest in this development of human faculties, and the consequent acquisition of material power.   There is no limit to this progress.

That is the superior nation, which, by nature, has the greatest amount of bodily and spiritual faculties, and, by education, has developed them to the highest degree of human culture, and, consequently, is capacious of the greatest amount of power over the material world, to turn it into use and beauty, and so of the greatest amount of universal welfare for all and each.   The superior nation is capable of most rapid progress ; for the advance of man goes on with accelerated velocity ; the further he has gone, the faster he goes.

The disposition in mankind to acquire this increase of human development and material power, I will call the instinct of progress.   It exists in different degrees in various nations and races : some are easily content with a small amount thereof, and so advance but slowly ; others desire the most of both, and press continually forward.

Of all races, the Caucasian has hitherto shown the most of this instinct of progress, and, though perhaps the youngest of all, has advanced furthest in the devel-

opment of the human faculties, and in the acquisition
of power over the material world; it has already won
the most welfare, and now makes the swiftest progress.

Of the various families of the Caucasian race, the
Teutonic, embracing all the Germanic people kindred
to our own, is now the most remarkable for this instinct
of progress. Accordingly, in the last four hundred
years, all the great new steps of peaceful Caucasian
development have been first taken by the Teutonic people, who now bear the same relation to the world's
progress that the Greeks did a thousand years before
Christ, the Romans eight hundred years later, and the
Romanized Celts of France at a day yet more recent.

Of the Teutons, the Anglo-Saxons, or that portion
thereof settled in the Northern States of America, have
got the furthest forward in certain important forms of
welfare, and now advance the most rapidly in their general progress. With no class of capitalists or scholars
equal to the men of great estates and great learning in
Europe, the whole mass of the people have yet attained
the greatest material comfort, enjoyment of natural
rights, and development of the human faculties. They
feel most powerfully the general instinct of progress,
and advance swiftest to future welfare and development. Here the bulk of the population is Anglo-
Saxon; but this powerful blood has been enriched by
additions from divers other sources,— Teutonic and
Celtic.

The great forces which in the last four hundred
years have most powerfully and obviously helped this
welfare and progress, may be reduced to two marked
tendencies, which I will sum up in the form of ideas,
and name the one Christianity and the other Democracy.

By Christianity I mean that form of religion which consists of piety — the love of God, and morality — the keeping of His laws. That is not the Christianity of the Christian Church, nor of any sect; it is the ideal religion which the human race has been groping after, if haply we might find it. It is yet only an ideal, actual in no society.

By Democracy I mean government over all the people by all the people, and for the sake of all. Of course, it is government according to the natural law of God, by justice, the point common to each man and all men, to each nation and all mankind, to the human race and to God. In a democracy, the people reign with sovereign power; their elected servants govern with delegated trust. There is national unity of action, represented by law; this makes the nation one, a whole; it is the centripetal force of society. But there is also individual variety of action, represented by the personal freedom of the people who ultimately make the laws; this makes John John, and not James, the individual, a free person, discrete from all other men; this is the centrifugal force of society, which counteracts the excessive solidification that would else go on. Thus, by justice, the one and the many are balanced together, as the centripetal and centrifugal forces in the solar system.

This is not the democracy of the parties, but it is that ideal government, the reign of righteousness, the kingdom of justice, which all noble hearts long for, and labor to produce, the ideal whereunto mankind slowly draws near. No nation has yet come so close to it as the people of some of the Northern States, who are yet far beneath ideals of government now known, that are yet themselves vastly inferior to others which mankind shall one day voyage after, discover, and annex to human possession.

In this democracy, and the tendency towards it, two things come to all; namely, labor and government.

Labor for material comfort, the means of use and beauty, is the duty of all, and not less the right, and practically the lot, of all; so there is no privilege for any, where each has his whole natural right.   Accordingly, there is no permanent and vicariously idle class, born merely to enjoy and not create, who live by the unpurchased toil of others; and, accordingly, there is no permanent and vicariously working-class, born merely to create and not enjoy, who toil only for others.   There is mutuality of earning and enjoying: none is compelled to work vicariously for another, none allowed to rob others of the natural fruit of their toil.   Of course, each works at such calling as his nature demands: on the *mare liberum*, the open sea of human industry, every personal bark sails whither it may, and with such freight and swiftness as it will or can.

Government, in social and political affairs, is the right of all, not less their duty, and practically the lot of each.   So there is no privilege in politics, no lordly class born to command and not obey, no slavish class born to serve and not command: there is mutuality of command and obedience.   And as there is no compulsory vicarious work, but each takes part in the labor of all, and has his share in the enjoyment thereof; so there is no vicarious government, but each takes part in the making of laws and in obedience thereunto.

Such is the ideal democracy, nowhere made actual.

Practically, labor and government are the two great forces in the education of mankind.   These take the youth where schools and colleges leave him, and carry him further up to another seminary, where he studies for what honors he will, and graduates into such degrees as he can attain to.

This sharing of labor and government is the indispensable condition for human development; for, if any class of men permanently withdraws itself from labor, first it parts from its human sympathy; next it becomes debauched in its several powers; and presently it loses its masculine vigor and its feminine delicacy; and dies, at last, a hideous ruin. Do you doubt what I say? Look then at the Roman aristocracy from two centuries before Christ to four centuries after — at the French aristocracy from Louis XIII. to Louis XVI.

If any class of men is withheld from government — from its share in organizing the people into social, political, and ecclesiastical forms, from making and executing the laws — then that class loses its manhood and womanhood, dwindles into meanness and insignificance, and also must perish. For example, look at the populace of Rome from the second century before Christ to the fourth after; look at the miserable people of Naples and Spain, too far gone ever to be raised out of the grave where they are buried now; look at the inhabitants of Ireland, whose only salvation consists in flight to a new soil, where they may have a share in political government, as well as in economic labor.

So much for the definition of terms frequently to be used, and the statement of the great principles which lie at the foundation of human progress and welfare.

Now, in the history of a nation, there are always two operating forces,— one positive, the other negative. One I will call the progressive force. It is that instinct of progress just named, with the sum total of all the excellencies of the people, their hopefulness, human sympathy, virtue, religion, piety. This is the power to advance. The other I will call the regressive force; that is, the *vis inertiæ*, the sluggishness of the people, the sum total of all the people's laziness and despair, all the selfishness of a class, all the vice and anti-religion. This is power to retard. I do not speak of the conservative force which would keep, or the destructive force which would wastefully consume, but only of those named. The destructive force in America is now small; the conservative, or preservative, exceeding great.

Every nation has somewhat of the progressive force, each likewise something of the regressive. Let me illustrate this regressive force a little further. You sometimes in the country find a thriving, hardy family, industrious, temperate, saving, thrifty, up early and down late. By some unaccountable misfortune, there is born into the family, and grows up there, a lazy boy. He is weak in the knees, drooping in the neck, limber in the loins, and sluggish all over. He rises late in the morning, after he has been called many times, and, in the dog-days, comes down whilst his mother is getting breakfast, and hangs over the fire. Most of you have doubtless seen such; I have, to my sorrow. That is one form of the regressive force. He is what the Bible calls a heaviness to his mother, and a grief to his father. There is a worse retarding force than this, to wit: sometimes a bad boy is born into the family with head enough, but with a devilish heart; he is a malformation in respect to all the higher faculties,— a destructive form of the regressive force. Now, a nation may have that regressive force in these two forms,— the lazy retardative, the wicked destructive.

Sometimes this progressive force seems limited to a small class of persons,— men of genius, like the Hebrew prophets, the Socratic philosophers, the German reformers of the sixteenth century, or the French *savants* of the eighteenth. But it is not likely it is really thus limited; for these men of genius are merely trees of the common kind, rooted into the public soil, but grown to taller stature than the rest.

In the Northern States of America, and also in England and Scotland, it is plain this progressive force is widely spread among the great mass of the people, who are not only instinctively, but of set purpose, eager for progress; that is, for the increasing development of faculties, and for the consequent increasing power over the material world, transforming it to use and beauty. New England is a monument attesting this fact. But still this force arrives to its highest form in men of genius. Here, in the North, you may find men of money, men of education, literary culture, and scientific skill; men of talent, able to learn readily what can now be taught — who do not share this progressive instinct, whose will is regressive; but these are exceptional men — some maimed by accident, others impotent from their mother's womb; whom no Peter and John could make otherwise than halt and lame. But all the men of genius — aboriginal power of sight, ability to create, to know and teach what none learned before — are on the side of this progressive force. In all the Northern States, I know but one exception among the men of politics, science, art, letters, or religion. Even in his cradle, the Northern genius strangles the regressive snakes of fogydom. Still, these men of genius are not the cause of the progressive force, only expressions of it; not its exclusive

depositaries. They are the thunder and lightning, perhaps the rain, out of the cloud, sparks from the elec-
tric charge: they are not the cloud; they did not make
it. Of course, where the cloud is fullest of the fire
of heaven, there is the reddest lightning, the heaviest
thunder, and the most abounding rain. Still, the men
of genius did not make the progressive spirit of the
North; they but express and help to educate that
force.

In the North, those two educational factors, labor
and government, are widely diffused: more persons partake of each than anywhere else in the world. So there
is no exclusive, permanent servile class — none that
does all the work, and enjoys none of the results: there
is no exclusive and permanent ruling class; all are masters, all servants; all command, and all obey.

So much for the progressive force.

The regressive force may consist in the general
sluggishness of the whole mass of the people: then it
will be either an ethnological misfortune, which belongs to the constitution of the race — and I am sorry
to say that the Africans share that in the largest degree, and, accordingly, have advanced the least of any
of the races — or else an historic accident entailed on
them by oppression; and that is the case also with a
large portion of the Africans in America, who have a
double misfortune — that of ethnologic nature and historic position. But among the Caucasians, especially
among the Teutons, this regressive force is chiefly
lodged in certain classes of men, who are exceptional
to the mass of the people, by an accidental position
separated therefrom, and possessed of power thereover,
which they use for their own selfish advantage, and
against the interest of the people. They commonly

aim at two things — to shun all the labor, and to possess all the government.

This exceptional position was either the accidental attainment of the individual, or else a trust thereto delegated from the people; but the occupiers of the trust considered it at length as their natural, personal right, and so held to it as a finality, and asked mankind to stop the human march in order that they might rejoice in their special occupation.   Thus the fletchers of the fourteenth century, who got their bread by making bows and arrows, opposed the use of gunpowder and cannon; thus the scribes of the fifteenth century opposed printing, and said Dr. Faustus was " possessed by the devil."   In England, two hundred years ago, every top-sawyer resisted the use of saw-mills to cut logs into boards, and wanted to draw off the water from the ponds.   Forty years ago, the hand-weaver of England opposed power-looms.   In 1840, the worshipful company of ass-drivers in Italy begged the pope of Rome not to allow a single railroad in his territory, because it would injure their property invested in packsaddles and jackasses.   The pope consented, and no steam-engine dared to scream and whistle in the papal States.   In Boston, twenty years ago, the Irishmen objected to steam pile-drivers, and broke them to pieces; just now, the stevedores of Boston insist that ships shall not be unladen by horses or steam-power, but that a man, who yet has a head, shall live only by the great muscles in his arms; that all merchandise shall be taken out of ships by an Irishman hanging at the end of a rope.   All these men consider that their exceptional position and accidental business is a finality of human history, a natural right, which the top-sawyer, the scribe, and the others have to stop

mankind.   The stevedore and hand-loom weaver must
have no competitors in the labor-market; the steam-
engine must be shoved off the track, in order that the
donkey may have the whole country wherein to bray
and wheeze.

In Europe, at this day, the regressive force is lodged
chiefly in the twofold aristocracy which exists there,
ecclesiastical and political.   In the sixteenth century,
mankind, and especially the Teutonic family, longed
to have more Christianity: the priestly class, with the
pope at their head, refused, hewed the people to pieces,
burnt them to ashes at Madrid and Oxford.   The
priest stood between the people and the Bible, and said,
" The word of God belongs to us: it is for the priests
only, not for you, you infidels; down with you!"   He
counted his stand as the stopping-place of mankind:
the human race must not go an inch further — he
would kill all that tried.   The result attained was a
finality.   So the thinker must be burned alive, that
the ass-driver might have the whole world to snap his
fingers in and cough to his donkey!   Even now the
same class of men repeat the old experiment; and, in
Italy, Spain, and Spanish America, the regressive
power carries the day.

In this century, when the people of Europe wished
to move on a little nearer to democracy than before,
the political class of aristocrats refused to suffer it;
they put men of political genius in jail, or hung them.
Kossuth and Mazzini were lucky men to escape to a
foreign land; thousands fled to America.   In Europe,
at present, and especially on the continent, this regressive power carries the day, and the progressive force
is held down.   For priests, kings, and nobles, inherit-
ing a position which was once the highest that man-

kind had attained to, and then taking it as a trust, now count it a right of their own, a finality of the human race, the end of man's progress.

When a nation permanently consents to this triumph of the regressive over the progressive force, allows one class to do all the government and shun all the labor, it is presently all over with that nation. Look at Italy, with Rome and Naples; at Spain, which is too far gone ever to be galvanized into life. See what already takes place in France, where the son of the nephew has just been born, and the little baby is recognized as emperor. Look at an election-day in Massachusetts, where the people choose one of themselves to be their temporary governor, responsible to them, swearing him on their statute-book: compare that with the preparation which Napoleon the Little made to anticipate the birth of Napoleon the Least! Why, the garments got ready for this equivocal baby have already cost more than the clothes of all our Presidents since " a young buckskin taught a British general the art of fighting." Eighty thousand dollars is decreed to pay for baptizing this imperial bantling. If twice that sum could christen the father, it might not be ill spent, if thereto decreed. Look at New England, and then at Spain, to see the odds between a people that has the progressive force uppermost, and a nation where the regressive force has trod the people down, and become, as it must, destructive. The Romanic nations of Italy and Spain, and the Romanized Celts of France, consent to a despotism which puts all the labor on the people, and takes all the government from them: they easily enough accept the rule of the political and ecclesiastical aristocracy. But the Teutons, especially the Saxon Teutons, and, above all others, those in the Northern States of America, with their immense love of individual liberty, hate despotism, either political or ecclesiastical. They perpetually demand more Christianity and democracy; that each shall do his own work, and rejoice in its result; that each shall have his share in the government of all. The women, long excluded from this latter right, now claim, and will at length, little by little, gain it. When all thus share the burdens and the joys of life, there is no class of men compelled by their position to hate society: so law and order prevail with ease; each keeps step with all, nor wishes to stay the march; property is secure, the government popular. But when one class does all the ruling, and forces all the toil on another class, nothing is certain but trouble and violence. Thus, in San Domingo, red rebellion scoured black despotism out of the land, but with blood. If a government, like a pyramid, be wide at the bottom, it takes little to hold it up.

So much for the regressive force.

In the United States we have two peoples in one nation, similar in origin, united in their history, but for the last two generations so diverse in their institutions, their mode of life, their social and political aims, that now they have become exceedingly unlike, even alien and hostile; for, though both the stems grow out from the same ethnologic root, one of them has caught such a mildew from the ground it hangs over, and the other trees it mixes its boughs among, that its fruit has become " peculiar," and not like the native produce of the sister trunk.   One of these I will call the Northern States, the other the Southern States.   At present, there is a governmental bond put round both, which holds them together; but no moral union makes the two one. There is no unity of idea between them. A word of each.

In the Northern States we have a population fifteen millions strong, mainly of Anglo-Saxon origin, but early crossed with other Teutonic blood — Dutch, German, Scandinavian — which bettered the stock. Of late, numerous Celts have been added to the mixture, but so recently that no considerable influence yet appears in the collective character, ideas, or institutions of the North. A hundred years hence, the ethnologic fruits of this other seed will show themselves.

These Northern Saxons, moreover, are mainly descended from men who fled from Europe because they had ideas, at least sentiments, of Christianity and democracy which could not be carried out at home. They are born of Puritan pilgrims, who were the most progressive portion of the most progressive people, of the most progressive stock, in all Christendom. They came to America, not for ease, honor, money, or love of adventure, but for conscience' sake, for the sake of their Christianity and their democracy. Such men founded the chief Northern colonies and institutions, and have controlled the doctrines and the development thereof to a great degree.

We see the result of such parentage: more than all other nations of the earth, the North has cut loose from the evil of the past, and set its face towards the future. At one extreme, it has no lordly class, ecclesiastical or political, exclusively and permanently to shun labor and monopolize government, vicariously to enjoy the result of work, vicariously to rule; and, at the other extreme, there is no class slavishly and unwillingly to do the work, and have none of its rewards; to suffer all the obedience, and enjoy none of the command.

No class is permanent, highest or lowest. The Northern States are progressively Christian, also progressively democratic, in the sense just given of Christianity and democracy. No people on earth has such material comfort, such enjoyment of natural rights of body and spirit already possessed, such general development of the human faculties. But the attainment does not satisfy us; for we share this instinct of progress to such a degree, that no achievement will content us. Be the present harvest never so rich, our song is —

"To-morrow to fresh woods and pastures new.

No nation has such love of liberty, such individual variety of action, or such national unity of action; nowhere is such respect for law; nowhere is property so secure, life so safe, and the individual so little disturbed. And, with all this, we are not at all destructive, but eager to create, and patient to preserve. The first thing which a Northern man lays hold of is a working-tool, an ax, or a plough; the last thing he takes in hand is a fighting-tool, a bowie-knife, a rifle: he never touches that till he is driven to the last extremity. He loves to organize productive industry, not war.

So much for the nation North.

Next, there are the Southern States ten millions in population. There also the original germ was Anglo-Saxon, to which additions were made from other stocks, Teutonic and Celtic, though in a smaller degree: France and Spain added more largely to the mixture. But what has most affected the ethnological character of the South is the African element. There are three and a half millions of men in the Southern States, of

African origin, whereof half a million are (acknowledged) mulattoes, African Caucasians; but those monumental half-breeds are much more numerous than the census dares confess.

This is not the only human difference between the North and the South. While the Saxons, who originally came to the North, and have since controlled its institutions and ideas, were mainly pilgrims, who, driven by persecution, fled hither for the sake of establishing democracy and Christianity — the foremost people in an age of movement, when revolution shook the whole Teutonic world, bringing the most Christian and democratic institutions and ideas of their age, and developing them to forms still more human and progressive — the settlers of the South were adventurers, who came to America to mend their fortunes, for the sake of money, ease, honor, love of change. Whilst, subsequently, emigrants came from Europe to the North of their own accord, shared the Northern labor and government, partook of its Christianity and democracy, partook of its best influences, and soon mingled their blood in the great stream of Northern population: many persons from Africa were forced to emigrate to the South, and, by legal violence, compelled to more than their share of labor, driven from all share in the government, branded as inferior, and mingled with the Caucasian population only in illicit lust — which bastardized its own sons and daughters — and were made subordinate to the owners' lash. While the North, from 1620 to 1856, has aimed to spread education over all the land, and facilitate the acquisition of property by the individual, and prevent its entailment in families, or its excessive accumulation by transient corporations, the South has always en-

deavored to limit education, making it the exclusive
monopoly of the few — who yet learned not much —
and now makes it a State prison offense to teach the
laboring class to read and write: it aims to condense
money into large sums, permanently held, if not in
families, at least in a class.   Thus, at one extreme, the
South had formed a permanently idle and lordly class,
who shun labor and monopolize government.

The South culminates in Virginia and South Carolina, which bear the same relation to the slave States
that New England does to the free States; that is,
they are the mother-city of population, ideas, institutions, and character.   As I just said, Christendom
cannot boast a population in any other country where
there are fifteen millions of men so nobly developed as
the fifteen millions of the North; so far advanced in
Christianity and democracy; with so much material
comfort, enjoyment of natural rights, and development of natural powers.   Compare New England with
Old England, Scotland, France, Saxony, Belgium,
Prussia, any of the foremost nations of Europe, and
you see that it is so.   But take the ten millions of the
South, and see what they are: nowhere in Europe, north
of Turkey and west of Russia, can you find ten millions of contiguous men who have so low a development, intellectual, moral, affectional, and religious, as
the ten millions of the slave States; nowhere can you
find Caucasians or any other people in Western Europe
so slightly advanced above the savage.   Three and a
quarter millions are actual slaves.   Take the States of
Virginia and South Carolina, in which the South comes
to its flower: there are 1,170,000 whites, 920,000 colored, whereof 860,000 are slaves; that is to say, out
of two millions, more than one-third are only human

property, not counted as human persons. In South Carolina, out of a hundred native whites over twenty years of age, there are seven who cannot read the name PIERCE, the political lord they worship; in Virginia, out of a hundred native whites over twenty years, there are nine who cannot write the word SLAVE, nor spell it after it is written all over their State; whereas, in Massachusetts, out of four hundred persons over twenty, there is only one man who cannot write, with his own hand, LIBERTY FOR ALL MEN NOW AND FOR EVER!

Take the two million population of Virginia and South Carolina: there is no people in Western Europe so little advanced as they; and, in all Christendom, there are only two nations or collections of men who stand on the same level — the Russian Empire and Spanish America. Behold the reason for the phenomenon which struck many with surprise,— that South Carolina and Virginia, in their politics, have recently sympathized with Russia and Brazil. Birds of a feather flock together, like consorting with like.

Here, then, are these two nations, alike in their ethnological origin, joint in their history, now utterly diverse and antagonistic in disposition and aim. The North has organized freedom, and seeks to extend it; the South, bondage, and aims to spread that. The North is progressively Christian and democratic; while the South is progressively anti-Christian and undemocratic. First, only the Southern *measures* were anti-Christian and undemocratic; now also its *principles*. It lays down anti-Christianity and anti-democracy as the only theory of religion and politics. In New England, man is put before property, the human substance above the material accident; in Virginia and South

Carolina, property is put before man, the material accident before the human substance itself; and, of all property that which is most valued and most carefully preserved, though most "aristocratic" and sacred, is property in the bodies of men.

That is the odds between the North and the South.

Now, the progressive power of America is lodged chiefly in the North, where it is diffused almost universally amongst the people, but most conspicuously comes to light in the men of genius. Accordingly, every man of poetic or scientific genius in the North is an anti-slavery man; every preacher with any spark of Christian genius in him ·is a progressive man and hostile to slavery.

The regressive power is lodged chiefly at the South, where it is considerably diffused among the people. That wide diffusion comes partly from the ethnologic sluggishness of the African element mixed in with the population, but still more from the degradation incident to a people who have long sat under tyrannical masters. It is this which has debased the Caucasian of Virginia, Tennessee, North and South Carolina.

But as the progressive force of the North comes clearest to light in the men of genius, so the regressive force at the South is most shown in the men of eminent ability, ecclesiastical and political, of whom not a single man is publicly progressive in Christianity or democracy. Compare the spirit of the great newspapers of the South, the *Richmond Examiner*, the *Charleston Mercury*, with those of the North, the *New York Tribune*, the *Evening Post*; compare the Southern politicians, the Masons and Toombses, with the Sewards and Chases of the North. See the odds between the mass of the people at the North and the

South; between the eminent genius, all of which at the North is progressive, but all of which at the South turns its back on human progress, and would leave humanity behind. There is the difference.

This regressive force accepts slavery as the Dagon of its idolatry, its " peculiar institution; " and slavery is to the South what the book of Mormon or the car of Juggernaut is to its worshipers. This institution is so iniquitous and base, that in Christian Europe, all the Teutonic nations have swept it away; and all the Celtic, all the Romanic nations, even the inhabitants of Spain, have trodden bondage under their feet. Yes, the Ugrians have driven out such slavery from Hungary, from Livonia, from Lapland itself; and, of all parts of Europe, Russia and Turkey alone still keep the unclean thing; but even there it is progressively diminishing. As a measure, it is felt to be exceptional, and publicly denounced; as a principle, no man defends it: it is there as a fact without a theory. Only two tribes in Christendom yet hold to the theory of this unholy thing,— Spanish America and the slave part of Saxon America, the two Barbary States of the New World.

All the regressive power of Christendom gathers about American slavery, which is the stone of stumbling, the rock of offense in the world's progress.

Slavery is the great obstacle to the present welfare and future progress of the South itself. It prevents the mass of the Southern people from the possession of material comfort, use and beauty; from the enjoyment of their natural rights; and also, for the future, it hinders them from the increasing development of their natural faculties, and the consequent increasing acquisition of power over the material world. It hinders Christianity and Democracy, which it would destroy, or else itself must thereby be brought to the ground. It shuts the mass of the people from their share of the government of society, forces many to unnatural and vicarious labor, and robs them of the fruit of their toil. Thus it is the great obstacle alike to present welfare and future development.

The headquarters of this regressive force are at the South, where its avowed organization and its institutions may be found. At the North it has three classes of allies. Here they are: —

1. The first class is of *base* men, such as are somewhat inhuman by birth; men organized for cruelty, as fools for folly, idiotic in their conscience and heart and soul. If there had been no " inherited sin " up to last night, these men would have " originated " it the first thing this morning; if Adam had had no " fall," and the ground did not incline downward anywhere, they would dig a pit on their own account, and leap down headlong of their own accord. These men are aboriginal kidnappers, and grow up amid the filth of great towns, sweltering in the gutters of the metropolitan pavement at Cincinnati, Philadelphia, New York. Nay, you find them even at Boston, lurking in some office, prowling about the court-house, sneaking into alleys, barking in the newspapers, to let their masters know their whereabouts, turning up their noses in the streets, snuffing after some victim as the wind blows from Virginia or Georgia, and generally seeking whom they may devour. There are " earthly, sensual, devilish." For the honor of humanity, this class of men is exceedingly small, and, like other poisonous vermin, commonly bears its warning on its face.

2. The next class is of *mean* men, of large acquisitiveness, or else a great love of approbation, little conscience, little affection, and only just religion enough to swear by. These men you can buy with office, honor, money, or with a red coat and a fife and drum. There are a great many such persons; you find them in many places; and, for the disgrace of my own profession, I am sorry to say they are sometimes in the pulpit, taking a South-side view of all manner of tyranny, volunteering to send their mothers into bondage, and denying the higher law of God.

3. The third class is of *ignorant* men, who know no better, but may be instructed.

At the South, this regressive force is thus distributed: — (1) There are three hundred and fifty thousand slaveholders, who, with their families, make up a population of a million and three-quarters; (2) There are four and three-quarter millions of non-slaveholders; and (3) Three and a half millions of slaves. A word of each.

1. First, of the slaveholders. Slavery makes them rich: they own the greater part of the land, and all the slaves, and control the greater part of the colored or white laboring population. Slavery is a peculiar curse to the South in general, but a peculiar comfort to the slaveholders. They monopolize the education, own the wealth, have all the political power of the South — are the " aristocracy." But, since the American Revolution, I think this class has not born and bred a single man who has made any valuable contribution to the art, science, literature, morals, or religion of the American people. Marshall's " Life of Washington " is the only great literary work of the South; its hero was born in 1732, its author in 1755; and both Washington the

hero, and Marshall the writer, at their death, abjured the " peculiar institution " of the South.

The Southern " aristocracy " rears two things — negro slaves, of which it is often the father, and regressive politicians, who make the institutions to keep the slaves in bondage for ever, shutting them out from Christianity and democracy. Behold the " aristocracy " of the South! By their fruits ye shall know them. Of the general morals of this class I need not speak: " the dark places of the earth are full of the habitations of cruelty." Since the 1st of January, they have burned four negroes alive, as a joyous spectacle and " act of faith; " a sort of profession of Christianity, like the more ceremonious *autos-da-fé* of their Spanish prototypes. Yet among the slaveholders are noble men; some who, but for their surroundings, would have stood with those eminent in talent, station, and in service, too, the forerunners of human progress. Blame them for their wrong, pity them for the misfortune which they suffer. Yet let me do the South no injustice. Her three hundred and fifty thousand slaveholders have ruled the nation for sixty years; her politicians have beat the North in all great battles.

Now, we commonly judge the South by the slaveholders. This is wrong: it is like measuring England by her gentry, France and Germany by their men of science and letters, Italy by her priests. You shall judge what the whole mass of the people are when the " aristocracy," the picked men, are of that stamp.

2. Next are the non-slaveholders, four and three-quarter millions of men. Some of these are noble men, with property in land and goods, with some intelligence; but, as a class, they are both necessitous and

illiterate, with small political power. They are cursed by slavery, which they yet defend; for it makes labor a disgrace, and, if poor, puts them on the same level with the slave himself. Slavery hinders their development in respect to property, intellectual culture, and manly character; yet, as a whole, they are too ignorant to understand the cause which keeps them down. The morals of this class are exceedingly low: it abounds in murders, and is full of cruelty towards its victims. Nay, where else in Christendom, save Spanish America, is the Caucasian found to take delight in burning his brother with a slow fire, for his own sport, and to please a licentious mob?

3. The third class consists of the slaves themselves, of whom I need say only this — that public opinion and the law, which is only the thunder from that cloud, keep them at labor and from government, from Christianity and democracy, from all the welfare and development of the age, and seek to crush out the instinct of progress from the very nature of the victims. The slave has no personal rights, ecclesiastical, political, social, economical, individual; no right to property — a human accident; none to his body or soul — the substance of humanity itself.

But I fear you do not yet quite understand the difference between the regressive force of slavery at the South, and the progressive force of freedom at the North. Therefore, to see in noonday light the effect of each on the present welfare and the future progress of a people, compare an old typical slave State with an old typical free State, and then compare a new slave State with a new free State.

1. South Carolina contains 29,385 square miles of land; Connecticut, 4,674. In 1850, South Carolina

had 668,507 inhabitants, whereof 283,523 were free, and 384,984 slaves; while Connecticut had 370,792 inhabitants, all free.

The government value of all the land in South Carolina was $5.08 an acre; in Connecticut it was $30.50 the acre. All the farms in South Carolina contained 16,217,700 acres, and were worth $82,431,684; while the farms of Connecticut were worth $72,726,422, though they contained only 2,383,879 acres. Thus slavery and freedom affect the *value of land* in the old States.

In 1850, South Carolina had 340 miles of railroad; and Connecticut 547, on a territory not equal to one-sixth of South Carolina. In 1855, South Carolina had $11,500,000 in railroads; Connecticut had then $20,000,000.

The shipping of South Carolina amounts to 36,000 tons; in Connecticut, to 125,000, though she is not advantageously situated for navigation.

The value of the real and personal property in South Carolina, in 1850, was estimated by the Federal Government at $288,257,694. This includes the value of all the slaves, who, at $400 apiece, amount to $153,993,600. Subtracting this sum, which is neither property in *land* nor *things*, but wholly *unreal* and fictitious, there remains $134,264,094 as the entire property of the great slave State; while the total valuation of the land and things in Connecticut, in 1850, was $155,707,980. In other words, in South Carolina, 670,000 persons, with 30,000 square miles of land, are worth $134,000,000; while in Connecticut, 370,000 men, with only 4,600 square miles of land, are worth $156,000,000. Thus do slavery and freedom affect the *general wealth* of the people in the old States.

In 1850, South Carolina had 365,026 persons under twenty years of age; her whole number of pupils, at schools, academies, and colleges, was 40,373. Connecticut had only 157,146 persons of that age, but 83,697 at school and college. Will you say it is of no consequence whether the *colored child* is educated or not? Then remember that South Carolina had 149,322 white children, and only sent 40,373 of them to school at all in that year; while, out of 153,862 white children, Connecticut gave 82,433 a permanent place in her noble schools.

In South Carolina, there are but 129,350 free persons over twenty years of age; and, of these, 16,564 are unable to read the word heaven. So, in all that great and democratic State, there are only 112,786 persons over twenty who know their A B C's; while in Connecticut there are 213,662 persons over twenty; and, of all that number, only 5,306 are illiterate, and of them 4,013 are foreigners. But, of all the 16,564 ignoramuses of South Carolina only 104 were born out of that State!

Out of 365,026 persons over twenty, South Carolina has only 112,786 who can read their primer; while, out of 213,662, Connecticut has 208,356 who can read and write. South Carolina can boast more than 250,000 native adults who cannot write or read the name of their God — a noble army of martyrs, a cloud of witnesses to its peculiar institution; while poor Connecticut has only 1,293 native adults unable to read their Holy Bible.

Such is the effect of slavery and freedom on *education* in the old States. The Southern politician was right: " Free society is a failure! "

2. Now compare two new States of about the same

age. Arkansas was admitted into the Union in 1836, Michigan in 1837.

Arkansas contains 52,198 square miles, and 209,-807 inhabitants, of whom 151,746 are free, and 58,-161 are slaves. Michigan contains 56,243 square miles, and was entered for settlement later than her sister, but contains 397,654 persons, all free.

In Arkansas, the land is valued at $5.88 the acre; and in Michigan at $11.83. The slave State has 781,531 acres of improved land; and Michigan, 1,929,110. The farms of Arkansas are worth $15,-265,245; and those of Michigan, $51,872,446. Thus slavery and freedom affect the *value of land* in the new States.

Michigan had, in 1855, 699 miles of railroad, which had cost $19,000,000; Arkansas had paid nothing for railroads. The total valuation of Arkansas, in 1850, was $39,871,025: the value of the slaves, $23,264,400, was included. Deducting that, there remains but $16,576,625, as the entire worth of Arkansas; while Michigan has property to the amount of $59,787,255. Thus slavery and freedom affect the *value of property* in the new States.

In 1850, Arkansas had 115,023 children under twenty, whereof 11,050 were in schools, academies, or colleges; while Michigan had 211,969, of whom 112,-382, were at school, academy, or college. Or, to omit the colored population, Arkansas had 97,402 white persons under twenty, and only 11,050 attending school; while, of 210,831 whites of that age in Michigan, 112,175 were at school or college. Last year, Michigan had 132,234 scholars in her public common schools. In 1850, Arkansas contained 64,787 whites over twenty — but 16,935 of these were unable to read and write; while out of 184,240 of that age in Michigan, only 8,281 were thus ignorant — of these, 3,009 were foreigners; while of the 16,935 illiterate persons of Arkansas, only 37 were born out of that State. The slave State had only 47,852 persons over twenty who could read a word; while the free State had 175,959. Michigan had 107,943 volumes in " libraries other than private," and Arkansas 420 volumes. Thus slavery and freedom affect *the education of the people* in the new States.

Now see the effect of slavery and freedom on property and education in their respective neighborhoods. I take examples from the States of Missouri and Virginia, kindly furnished by an ingenious and noble-hearted man.

1. In the twelve counties of Missouri, which border on slaveholding Arkansas, there are 20,982 free white persons, occupying 75,360 acres of improved land, valued at $13 an acre, or $989,932: while in the ten counties of Missouri bordering on Iowa, a free State, though less attractive in soil and situation, there are 26,890 free white persons, with 123,030 acres of improved land, worth $19 an acre, or $2,379,765. Thus the *neighborhood of slavery retards the development of property.*

In those ten Northern counties bordering on freedom, there were 2,329 scholars in the public schools; while in the twelve Southern, bordering on Arkansas, there were only 339. Thus *the neighborhood of slavery affects the development of education.*

2. Compare the Northern with the Southern counties of Virginia, and you find the same results. Monongahela and Preston counties, in Virginia, bordering on free Pennsylvania, contain 122,444 acres

of improved land, valued at $21 an acre, or $2,784,137 in all; are occupied by 24,095 persons, whereof 263 only are slaves; and there are 1,747 children in the public schools: while the corresponding counties of Patrick and Henry, touching on North Carolina, contain but 99,731 acres of improved land, worth only $15 an acre, or $1,554,841 in all; are occupied by 18,481 inhabitants, 5,664 of them slaves; and have only 961 children at school. But cross the borders, and note the change: the adjacent counties of North Carolina, Rockingham, and Stokes, contain 103,784 acres of improved land, worth $14 an acre, or $1,517,-520; 23,701 persons, of whom 7,122 are slaves; and have only 2,050 pupils at school or college: while Fayette and Green counties, in Pennsylvania, adjacent to the part of Virginia above spoken of, contain 297,005 acres of improved land, valued at $49 an acre, or $7,618,919; 61,248 persons, all free; and 12,998 pupils at the common schools.

The South has numerous natural advantages over the North,— a better soil, a more genial climate, the privilege of producing those tropical plants now deemed indispensable to civilization. Of $193,000,000 of exports last year, $93,000,000 were of Southern cotton and tobacco. Yet such is her foolish and wicked system, that, while the North continually increases in riches, the South becomes continually poorer and poorer in comparison. Boston alone could buy up two States like South Carolina, and still have thirteen millions of dollars to spare. Three hundred years ago, Spain monopolized this continent; she exploitered Mexico, Peru, the islands of the Gulf; all the gold of the New World came to her hand. Where is it now? Spain is poorer than Italy. Is here no lesson for South Carolina and Virginia?

In civilized society, there must be an organization
of things and of persons, of labor and of government;
and so slavery is to be looked at, not only in its economical relations, as affecting labor and wealth, power
over matter, but also in its political relations, as affecting government, which is power over men.

There are 350,000 slaveholders in the United
States, with their families, making a population of
1,750,000 persons. Now slavery is a political institution which puts the government of all the people
of the slave States into the hands of those few men:
the majority are the servants of this minority.

1. The 350,000 slaveholders control the 3,250,000
slaves; owning their bodies, and, by direct legislation,
purposely preventing their development.

2. They control the 4,750,000 non-slaveholders,
cutting them off from their share of government, and
hindering them alike in their labor and their education, and *purposely preventing their development.*

3. They control the Federal politics, and thereby
affect the organization of things and persons, of labor
and government, throughout the whole nation, and
*purposely prevent the development of the whole peo-
ple.*

In all these three forms of political action, they
have selfishly sought their own immediate interest, and
wrought to the lasting damage of the slaves, the non-
slaveholders, and the whole people. But neither the
slaves nor the non-slaveholders have made any powerful opposition to this injury: the chief hostility has
been shown by the North, or rather by the few persons
therein who either had mind enough to see this manifold mischief clearly, or else such moral and religious
instinct as made them at once revolt from this wick-

edness. But, ever since the Declaration of Independence, there has been a strife, open or hidden, between the South and this portion of the Northern people; and though the battle has been often joined, yet, since 1788, the North has been beaten in every conflict, pitched battle or skirmish, until last January; then, after much fighting, the House of Representatives chose for Speaker a man hostile to slavery. Always before, the South conquered the North; that is, the minority conquered the majority. The party with the smallest numbers, the least money, the meanest intelligence, the wickedest cause, yet beat the larger, richer, more intelligent party, which had also justice on its side. There is now no time to explain this political paradox.

Between 1787 and 1851, the regressive power, Slavery, took nine great steps towards absolute rule over the United States. These I have spoken of before. It now lifts its foot to take a tenth step,— to stamp bondage on all the territories of this Union, and then organize them into slave States. Look at the facts.

We have now one million four hundred thousand square miles of territory not organized into States (1,400,934). Of this, Kansas, Nebraska, New Mexico, and Utah make nine hundred and twenty-six thousand (926,857). Now, *the South aims to make it all slave territory*, to deliver it over to this regressive force, and establish therein such institutions that a few men shall at first own all the land; next, own the bulk of the working people; and, thirdly, shall control the rest of the whites; then themselves monopolize education, and yet get very little of it; repress freedom of speech, and enact laws for the advantage of the vulgarest of all oligarchies,— a band of men-stealers.

Let me suppose that there is no immediate danger that slavery will go to Oregon or Washington territory,— rather a gratuitous admission: there are still *nine hundred and twenty-six thousand square miles* of land to plant it on; that is, about one-third of all the country which the United States own! the South is endeavoring to establish it there. Within three years the great battle is to be fought; for, before the 4th of March, 1859, all that territory of fourteen hundred thousand square miles will be either free territory or else slave territory.

The battle is first for Kansas. Shall it be free, as the majority of its own inhabitants have voted; or slave, as the Federal Government and the slave power — the general regressive force of America — have determined by violence to make it? This is the question, *Shall the nine hundred and twenty-six thousand miles of territory belong to three hundred and fifty thousand slaveholders, or to the whole people of the United States?* This is a question which directly concerns the material interest of every working man in the nation, and especially every Northern working man. Before the 1st of January, 1858, perhaps before next January, Kansas, with its 114,790 square miles, will be a free State or a slave State. See what follows, immediately or ultimately, if we let the slaveholders have their way, and make *Kansas a slave State.*

Look, first, at the effect on the welfare and progress of individuals.

1. A privileged class, an oligarchy of slaveholders, will be founded there, such as exists in the present

slave States. They will own all the land, almost all the laborers; will make laws for the advantage of the slaveholder against the interest of the slave and the non-slaveholder. That is the effect on the Southern man.

2. Next see the effect on the working men of the North who emigrate to that quarter. They must go as slaveholders or as non-slaveholders.

Some will go as slaveholders, such as take a South-side view of human wickedness in general. You know what the effect will be on them. Compare the condition, the intellectual and moral character, of New England men who have settled in Georgia, and become slaveholders, with others of the same families — their brothers and cousins — who have remained at home, and engaged in agriculture, commerce, and manufactures.

But not many Northern men will go there and become slaveholders. Some will go as non-slaveholders; and you will see under what disadvantage they must labor.

1. They must live by their work, and in a place where industry is not honored, as in Connecticut, but is despised, as in South Carolina and Arkansas. The working white man must stand on a level with the slave. He belongs to a despised caste. He will have but little self-respect, and soon will sink down to the character and condition of the " poor whites " in the old slave States. A scientific friend of mine, who travels extensively in both hemispheres, says that he has not found the Caucasian people anywhere so degraded as in Tennessee and the Carolinas.

2. Next, there will be no miscellaneous mechanical industry, as in New England and all the free States.

Agriculture will be the chief business, almost the only business; and that will be confined to the great staples — corn, wheat, rice, tobacco, cotton; the aim will be only to produce the raw material. Agriculture will be poor, land will be low in price, and continually getting run out by unskilful culture. The slave's foot burns the soil and spoils the land; that is the master's fault. Twenty years hence, land will not be worth $16 an acre, as in sterile New Hampshire, but $4, as in fertile Georgia. There will be no rapid development of wealth; and, as the Northern man values riches, I think he should look to this, and see that the land is not taken from under his foot, and the power of creating wealth from his head and hand.

3. Then there will be no good and abundant roads, as in New England, but only a few, as in Carolina and Virginia, and those miserably poor. In Kansas twenty years hence, there will not be 1,964 miles of railroad, as in Illinois, but 231 miles, as in Missouri.

4. There will be no abundance of beneficent free schools, as in New England, but a few, and of the worst sort. Education will be the monopoly of the rich, who will not get much thereof. Laws will forbid the education of the slave, and discourage the culture of the mass of the people.

5. There will be no lyceums, no courses of lectures; but, in their place, there will be horse-races, occasionally the lynching of an abolitionist, or the burning of a black man at a slow fire! Yet, now and then, a Northern man will be invited thither by the slaveholders; some unapostolical fisherman will take the majestic memory of Washington, disembowel it of all its most generous humanity, skilfully arrange it as bait; and then, with bob and sinker, hook and line,

this " political Micawber," " looking for something
to turn up," will go angling along the shore, praying
for at least a presidential bite, and possibly obtain a
conventional nibble.

6. There will be no " libraries other than private,"
with their one hundred and eight thousand volumes,
as in Michigan; only four hundred and twenty volumes, as in Arkansas. But a noble army of ignoramuses, twenty-five men out of each hundred adult
white men, will attest the value of the " peculiar institution."

7. There will be no multiplicity of valuable newspapers, with an annual circulation of 3,324,000 copies, as in Michigan; but a few political journals, scat-
tering 377,000 dingy sheets, as in Arkansas.

8. There will be no abundant and convenient meeting-houses, as in the North; not one hundred and
twenty thousand comfortable pew-seats in neat and
decorous churches, as in Michigan; but only sixty
thousand benches in barns and log-huts, as in Arkansas. No army of well-educated ministers will help,
instruct, and moralize the community, but ignorant
ranters or calculating hypocrites will stalk through
the Christian year, perverting the Bible to a Fugitive
Slave Bill, and denying the higher law which God
writes in man.

9. There will be no laws favoring all men; but
statutes putting the neck of labor into the claws of
capital, by which the strong will crush the weak, and
enslave the feeblest of all; constitutions like those of
South Carolina, which provide that nobody shall sit
in the popular house of the legislature, unless, in his
own right, he own " ten negro slaves."

10. There will be no universal suffrage, as in Mas-

sachusetts; but a man's political rights will be determined by the color of his skin, and the amount of his estate. One permanent class will monopolize government, money, education, honor, and ease; the other permanent class will be forced to bondage, ignorance, poverty, and shame. This is the prospect which the Northern man will find before him if slavery prevails in the new territory.

11. That is not all: his property and person will not be safe, as in Michigan; border-ruffians will permanently have gone over the border, and a new Arkansas be established in Kansas.

Under such circumstances, Northern men will not go there; and *so Kansas, and then all the other territory, is stolen from the North, as effectually as if ceded to Russia or annexed to the Spanish domain.* Yes, more completely lost; for, if it did belong to Spain, we might reclaim it by filibustering; and the American Government would not disturb, but help us.

Then, if a Northern man wishes to migrate, he has only the poorer land of Washington and Oregon before him, and is shut out from the most valuable territory of the United States.

If the city government of Boston were, next month, to establish a piggery on Boston Common, with fifty thousand swine, and set up an immense slaughterhouse of the savagest and filthiest character in the Granary Burying-ground, on Copp's Hill, and in each of the public squares; were to give all vacant land to the gamblers, thieves, pimps, kidnappers, and murderers — they would not commit a worse injustice, and they would not do a greater proportional damage to the real estate, and more mischief to the health of the inhabitants of the city, than the American Government would do the working people of the South and North by creating this nuisance of slavery on the free soil of Kansas.

So much for the effect of this on the individual interests of the working people of America. I have only taken the lowest possible view of the subject.

See its effects on American politics — on the welfare and progress of the nation. If Kansas is made a slave State, we shall either keep united, or else dissolve the Union and separate.

I. Suppose we keep united: what follows?

First, New Mexico will be a slave State, then Utah.

California is only half for freedom now, and will soon split into two; Lower California will be slave.

Then Texas will peel off into new States; Western Texas will soon be made a new slave State.

The Mesilla Valley, bigger than Virginia, will be a slave territory.

Then we shall dismember Mexico — make slave territory there.

We shall re-annex the Mosquito territory: the government wants it, and lets all manner of filibusters go there now.

We shall seize Cuba, to make that soil red with the white man's blood, which is now black with African bondage.

San Domingo must next fall a prey to American lust for land.

Then we shall carry out the Fugitive Slave Bill in the North as never before. In 1836, Mr. Curtis asked the Supreme Court of Massachusetts to decree that a slaveholder from Louisiana might take his bondman to Boston as a slave, hold him as a slave, sell him as a slave, or, as a slave, carry him back. In

1855, Mr. Kane decreed that a slaveholder might bring his slave into a free State, and keep him there as long as he would *in transitu*. Then we must have laws to enforce these demands: Congress will *legislate*, and the Supreme Court will *rule* to put slavery into every Northern State. In the beginning of June, 1854, this same Mr. Curtis, then become a judge, gave a " charge," in which he made it appear that, to make a speech in Faneuil Hall against kidnapping was " a misdemeanor." Yes, if a Massachusetts minister sees his parishioners kidnapped, and makes a speech in Faneuil Hall against that iniquity, and tells the people that they are slaves of Southern masters, Mr. Justice Curtis says that that man has committed a crime, to be punished by imprisonment for twelve months, and a fine of three hundred dollars! By and by, that charge will be " good common law: " *all* lawyers will be slave-hunters; *all* judges of the Scroggs family; *all* court-houses girt with chains; *all* the news-papers administration and satanic; *all* the Trinitarian doctors of divinity will take a South-side view of wickedness in high places; *all* the Nothingarian doctors of divinity will send back their mothers — for a consideration! And then what becomes of freedom of speech, freedom to worship God? What of inalienable rights to life, liberty, and the pursuit of happiness? They all perish; and the mocking of tyrants rings round the land: " We meant to subdue you," scoffs one; " I said, ' We will crush out humanity,' " laughs forth another. Where, then, is America? It goes where Korah, and Dathan, and Abiram are said to have gone long ago. The earth will open her mouth and swallow us up; the justice of God will visit us — our crime greater than that of Sodom and Go-

morrah — for we shall have committed high treason
against the dearest rights of man! He will rain on
us worse than fire and brimstone; our name shall
rot in the Dead Sea of infamy, and the curses of mankind hang over our memory for ever and ever, world
without end!

II. Suppose we separate. The North may at
length feel some little manhood; become angry at this
continual insult, and be roused by fear of actual ruin;
calculate the value of the Union, and find it not worth
while any longer to be tied to this offensive partner.
See what may follow in the attempt at dissolution.
Look at the comparative military power — the men
and money — of the North and South.

Omitting California and the territories, the North
has fifteen million freeman, or three million men able to
do military duty; and also thirty-two hundred million
dollars ($3,200,000,000); while the South has fifteen
hundred million dollars ($1,500,000,000), six million
five hundred thousand freeman, and three million five
hundred thousand slaves. But the latter are a negative
quantity to be subtracted from the whole. So the
effective population is three millions, or six hundred
thousand men able to bear arms. Such is the comparative personal and material force of the two. I
will not speak of the odds in the quality of Northern
and Southern men, looking now only at the obvious
quantitative difference.

The contest could not be doubtful or long. The
North could dictate the terms of separation, and would
probably take two-thirds of the naval and military
property of the nation, and all of the territories.
Then would come the question, Where shall be the line
of demarcation between freedom and slavery? I

think the North might fix the Potomac and Ohio as the northern, and the Mississippi as the western limit of slavery. Depend upon it, we shall not leave more land than these boundaries indicate to the cause of bondage. Then the ten Barbary States of America might found a new empire, with despotism for their central idea; take the name of Braggadocia, Servilia, Violentia, Thrasonia, or, in plainer Saxon title, Bullydom; and become as famous in future history as the " Five Cities of the Plain " were in the past. But would Virginia, Kentucky, Tennessee, Louisiana, consent to be border States, with no Fugitive Slave Bill to fetter their bondmen?

I do not propose disunion — at present. I would never leave the black men in bondage, or the whites subject to the slaveholding oligarchy which rules them. The Constitution itself guarantees " a republican form of government " to each State in the Union: no slave State has had it yet. Perhaps the North will one day respect the other half of " the compromises of the Constitution." Certainly there must be national unity of idea, either of freedom or of slavery, or else we separate before long.

This regressive force, which retards the progress and diminishes the welfare of the South, and yet controls the politics of America, is determined to conquer the progressive force, to put liberty down, to spread bondage over all the North, to organize it in all the wild land of the continent. The ablest champions of this iniquity are Northern men. The same North which bore Seward and Giddings, Sumner and Hale, not to mention others equally able, is mother also to Cushing and Douglas; and one of these would " crush out " all opposition to slavery, all love of welfare and progress;

the other is reported to have said to the North, in the Senate, " We mean to subdue you." Mark the words —" *We mean to subdue you!* " That is the aim of the administration, to make progress, regress; welfare, illfare; to make Democracy and Christianity, Despotism and anti-Christianity; that is the purpose of the oligarchy of slaveholders, to be executed with those triple Northern tools already named — *base* men, *mean* men, *ignorant* men.

The first great measure is to put slavery into Kansas and Nebraska, into four hundred and fifty thousand six hundred and eighty miles of wild land.

To accomplish that, five steps were necessary. Here they are: —

I. The first was to pass a pro-slavery Act to organize the Kansas and Nebraska territory. That accomplished two things: —

1. It repealed the Missouri Compromise, and laid the territory open to the slaveholder.

2. It established squatter sovereignty, and allowed the settlers to make laws for slavery or freedom, as they saw fit. The South intended that it should be a slave State.

You know how this first step was taken in 1854; what was done by Congress, by the President; you have not forgotten the conduct of Mr. Douglas of Illinois. Massachusetts yet remembers the behavior of Mr. Everett. It is rather difficult to find all the facts concerning this Kansas business; lies have been woven over the whole matter, and I know of no transaction in human history which has been covered up with such abundant lying, from the death of Ananias and Sapphira down to the first nomination of Governor Gardner. Still the main facts appear through this garment of lies.

II. The second step was to give the new territory a slave government, which would take pains to organize slavery into the land, and freedom out of it. So the executive appointed persons supposed to be competent for that work, and, amongst others, Mr. Reeder, of Easton, in Pennsylvania, who was thought to be fit for that business. But it turned out otherwise: he became conscientious, and refused to execute the infamous and unlawful commands of the executive. Finding it was so, the President — I have it on good authority — tried to bribe him to resign, offering him the highest office then vacant — the ministry to China. Governor Reeder refused the bribe, and then was discharged from his office on the pretense of some pecuniary unfaithfulness. Mr. Shannon was thrust into his place, for which he seems to the manner born; for — I have this also on good authority — his habitual drunkenness seems to be one of the smallest of his public vices.

III. The third step was to establish slavery by squatter sovereignty. For this, two things were indispensable: (1.) To elect a legislature friendly to slavery; and (2.) To get laws made by that legislature to secure the desired end.

1. This must be done by actual settlers; and then, for the first time in this career of wickedness, a difficulty was found. The people were to be consulted; and no *coup d'état* of the government could do the work. There was an unexpected difficulty; for, soon as Kansas was open, great bodies went there from the North to settle and secure it to freedom. It soon became plain that they were numerous enough to bring squatter sovereignty itself over to the side of humanity, and, by their votes, exclude bondage for ever.

That must be prevented by the regressive force.   Mr. Atchison, Mr. Stringfellow, and others were appointed to take the matter in hand.   Citizens of Missouri organized themselves into companies, and in military order, with pistols and bowie-knives, and in one instance with cannon, went over the border into Kansas to determine the elections by excluding the legal voters, and themselves casting the ballot.   In ten months, they made four general invasions of Kansas, if I am rightly informed; namely, (1.) On the 29th of July, 1854; (2.) 29th of November, 1854; (3.) 30th March, 1855, and (4.) 22nd May, 1855.   The third was the *great invasion*, made to elect the legislators who were to enact the territorial laws.   It appears that four thousand men marched bodily from Missouri to Kansas, some of them penetrating two hundred miles into the interior, and delivered their votes, electing men who would put slavery into the land.   The fourth was a smaller and local invasion, to fill vacancies in the legislature.

I cannot dwell on these things, nor stop to speak of the violence and murder repeatedly committed by these border ruffians, under the eyes, and with the consent, and by the encouragement, of the American executive.   You can read those things in the newspapers, at least in the *New York Tribune* and *Evening Post.* But, suffice it to say, the legislature thus chosen was wholly illegal.   If Jersey City were to order a municipal election, and New York were to go there, and choose aldermen and common councilmen, and the new officers were to act in that capacity, we should have a parallel of what took place in Kansas.

Thus the slave power which controls the Federal Government secured the first requisite,— a slave legislature.

2. They must next proceed to make the appropriate laws. The legislature came together on the 2nd July, 1855, at the place legally fixed by Governor Reeder: they passed an illegal Act, fixing the seat of government at Shawneetown, on the borders of Missouri, and adjourned thither. The governor vetoed the Act, and repudiated the legislature, illegally chosen at first, illegally acting afterwards. But they continued in session there from July 15th to August 31st, and made a huge statute-book of more than a thousand great pages. It contains substantially the laws of Missouri; but, in some instances, they were made worse. Take this for example: —

" No person who shall have been convicted of any violation of any of the provisions of an Act of Congress " (the Fugitive Slave Bills of 1793 and 1850), " whether such conviction was by criminal proceeding or by civil action, in any courts of the United States, or of any State or territory, shall be entitled to vote at any election, or to hold any office in this territory." " If any person offering to vote shall be challenged and required to take an oath or affirmation that he will sustain the provisions of the above-recited Acts of Congress " (the Fugitive Slave Bills), " and shall refuse to take such oath or affirmation, the vote of such person shall be rejected."— Ch. lxvi. § 11, p. 332.

There is no similar provision depriving a man of his vote if he violate any other statute: but a deed of common humanity disfranchises a man for ever; nay, performing an act of kindness to a brother perpetually deprives a man of his share in the government!

Look at this statute: —

SECT. 11.—" If any person print, write, introduce into, publish, or circulate, or cause to be brought into, printed, written, published, or circulated, or shall knowingly aid or assist in bringing into, printing, publishing, or circulating, within this territory, any book, paper, pamphlet, magazine, handbill, or circular, containing any statements, arguments, opinions, sentiments, doctrines, advice, or inuendo, calculated to promote a disorderly, dangerous, or rebellious disaffection among the slaves in this territory, or to induce such slaves to escape from the service of their masters, or to resist their authority, he shall be guilty of a felony, and be punished by imprisonment and hard labor for a term not less than five years."

But stealing a free child under twelve is punished with imprisonment for not more than five years, or confinement in the county jail not less than six months, or a fine of $500 (Ch. xlviii. Sec. 43).

CHAP. xv. SECT. 13.—" No person who is conscientiously opposed to holding slaves, or who does not admit the right to hold slaves in this territory, shall sit as a juror on the trial of any prosecutions for any violation of any of the sections of this Act."

That law excludes the New Testament and the Old Testament, as well as the Declaration of Independence, and the works of Franklin, Jefferson, and Madison: it shuts humanity from the jury-box.

IV. The next step was to get a pro-slavery delegate from Kansas into the House of Representatives at Washington. So, on the 1st of October, 1855, the day appointed by the border-ruffian legislature to elect a delegate, a fifth invasion was made by outsiders from Missouri, who, as before, took possession of the polls, and chose Hon. J. W. Whitfield to that office. Mr. Shannon, the new and appropriate governor of the territory, gave him a certificate of lawful election. He is now at Washington in that capacity. But the House of Representatives has the matter under advisement; a committee has gone to Kansas to investigate the matter; and the country waits, anxious for the results.

V. The only remaining step is to enforce their slave-law, and then Kansas becomes a slave State. But this is a difficult matter: for the people of the territory, indignant at this invasion of their rights, long since repudiated the legislature of ruffians; held a convention at Topeka; formed a constitution, which was submitted to the people, and accepted by them. They have chosen their own legislature, State officers, senators, and representatives, and applied for admission into the Union as a free State. But men who have already five times invaded the territory, threaten to go there again and enforce the laws which they have already made.

I need only refer to the conduct of the President, and his masters in the Cabinet, and say that he has been uniformly on the side of this illegal violence. You remember his message last winter, his proclamation at a later day, his conduct all the time. He encourages the violence of these tools of the slave power, who have sought to tread the people down. Hence it becomes indispensable for the Northern emigrants to take arms. It is instructive to see the old Puritan spirit coming out in the sons of the North, even those who went on theological errands. Excepting the Quakers, the Unitarians are the most unmilitary of sects; in Boston, their most conspicuous ministers have been — some of them still are — notorious supporters of the worst iniquities of American slavery. Surely you will not forget the ecclesiastical defenses of the Fugitive Slave Bill, the apologies for kidnapping. But a noble-hearted Unitarian minister, Rev. Mr. Nute, " felt drawn to Kansas." Of course he carried his Bible: he knew it also by heart. His friends gave him a " repeating rifle " and a " revolver." These also " felt drawn to Kansas." This " minister at large "— very much at large, too, his nearest denominational brother, on one side five hundred miles off, on the other fifteen hundred — trusts in God, and keeps his powder dry. Listen to this, written December 3rd, 1855: —

"I have just been summoned to be in the village with my repeating rifle. I shall go, and use my utmost efforts to prevent bloodshed. But, if it comes to a fight, in which we shall be forced to defend our homes and lives against the assault of these border savages (and by the way, the Indians are being enlisted on both sides), I shall do my best to keep them off."

On the 10th, he writes: —

"Our citizens have been shot at, and, in two instances, murdered; our houses invaded; hay-ricks burnt; corn and other provisions plundered; cattle driven off; all communication cut off between us and the States; wagons on the way to us with provisions stopped and plundered, and the drivers taken prisoners; and we in hourly expectation of an attack. Nearly every man has been in arms in the village. Fortifications have been thrown up by incessant labor night and day. The sound of the drum, and the tramp of armed men resounded through our streets; families fleeing with their household goods for safety. Day before yesterday the report of cannon was heard at our house from the direction of Lecompton. Last Thursday, one of our neighbors — one of the most peaceable and excellent of men, from Ohio — on his way home, was set upon by a gang of twelve men on horseback, and shot down. Several of the ruffians pursued him some distance after he was shot; and one was seen to push him from his horse, and heard to shout to his companions that he was dead. A neighbor reached him just before he breathed his last. I was present when his family came in to see the corpse, for the first time, at the Free-State Hotel,— a wife, a sister, a brother, and an aged mother. It was the most exciting and the most distressing scene that I ever witnessed. Hundreds of our men were in tears, as the shrieks and groans of the bereaved women were heard all over the building, now used for military barracks. Over eight hundred men are gathered under arms at Lawrence. As yet, no act of violence has been perpetrated by those on our side; no blood of retaliation stains our hands. We stand, and are ready to act, purely in the defense of our homes and lives. I am enrolled in the cavalry, though I have not yet appeared in the

ranks; but, should there be an attack, *I shall be there.* I have
had some hesitation about the propriety of this course; but
some one has said: "In questions of duty, the first thought
is generally the right one." On that principle, I find strong
justification. I could feel no self-respect until I had offered my
services.

"Day before yesterday we received the timely reinforcement
of a twelve pounder howitzer, with ammunition therefor, including grape and canister, with forty bomb-shells. It was
sent from New York (made at Chicopee). By a deed of successful daring and cunning, it was brought through the country
invested by the enemy, a distance of fifty miles, from Kansas
City, by an unfrequented route, boxed up as merchandise.

"*Sunday Morning,* Dec. 9.— The governor has pledged himself to do all he can to make peace; and we are told that the
invaders are beginning to retreat; but we know not what to
believe. Our men are to be kept under arms for twenty-four
hours longer, at least. No religious meetings for the last three
weeks. No work done, of course. Some of the logs to be
sawed for our church were pressed into service to build a fort,
of which we have no less than five, and of no mean dimensions
or strength. For a time, it seemed probable that the founda-
tion-stones for the church would be wet by the blood of the
martyrs for liberty. They were piled up on the ground, and
with the earth thrown out of the excavation, made quite a fort
on the hillside just outside of the line of intrenchments."

That is the report of a Unitarian missionary. You
know what the Trinitarians have done: the conduct of
that valiant man, Henry Ward Beecher,— the most
powerful and popular minister in the United States,—
and his "Plymouth Church," and other "religious
bodies" at New Haven and elsewhere, need not be
spoken of.

One effect of this warlike spirit is curious; "pious"
newspapers are very much troubled at the talk of rifles,
pistols, and cannon. In 1847, they rated me roundly
for preaching against the Mexican War,— a war for
plundering a feeble nation, that we might blacken her
soil with slavery: it was "desecrating the Sabbath."
They liked the Sims brigade, the Burns division; they

did homage to the cannon which men-stealers loaded in
Boston, therewith to shoot the friends of humanity
on the graves of Hancock and Adams! Now, the
mean men and the *base* men are brought over to " peace
principles: " a rifle is " not of the Lord; " a cannon
is " a carnal weapon; " a sword is " of the devil." All
the South thinks gunpowder is " unchristian." Such
a " change of heart " has not been heard of since the
conversion of St. Ananias and Sapphira.

I have no fondness for fighting; not the average
" instinct of destruction." I should suffer a great while
before I struck a blow. But there are times when I
would take down the dreadful weapon of war: this is
one of them for the men in Kansas.

It is not easy for the border ruffians alone to put
down Kansas; not possible for them to break up the
popular organization, destroy the new Constitution,
and hang the officers. Will the President send the
United States soldiers to do this? No doubt his heart
is good enough for that work. We remember what he
did with United States soldiers at Boston, in 1854: the
only service they ever rendered in that town for more
than forty years was to kidnap Anthony Burns. But
the President falters: there is a North; all last winter
there was a North,— Northern ice in the Mississippi;
Banks, of the North, at Washington, in the Speaker's
chair.

Kansas and Nebraska are the " Children in the
Wood." They had a fair inheritance; but the parents,
dying, left them to a guardian uncle,— the President.
I heard the Northern mother say to him,—

> " You must be father and mother both,
>   And uncle, all in one."
> " You are the man must bring our babes
>   To wealth or misery."

> And, if you keep them carefully,
> Then God will you reward;
> But, if you otherwise should deal,
> God will your deeds regard."

It is still the old story: the Executive uncle promises well enough: yet —

> " He had not kept these pretty babes
> But twelve months and a day,
> Before he did devise
> To make them both away.
> He bargained with two ruffians strong

[That is, *Straightwhig* and *Democrat*,]

> Which were of furious mood,
> That they should take these children young,
> And slay them in a wood."

It is still the old story.   One of the ruffians kills the other; but, in this case, Democrat, the strong ruffian, killed Straightwhig,— a weak ruffian, who had no " backbone,"— and now seeks to kill the babes.   He is not content to let them starve,—

> " Their pretty lips with blackberries
> So all besmeared and dyed; "

he " *would make them both away.*"   But that is not quite so easy.   Kansas, the elder, turns out a very male child, a thrifty boy: *he will not die;* he refuses to be killed, but, with such weapons as he has, shows what blood he came of.   His relations hear of the matter, and make a noise about it.   The uncle becomes the town talk.   Even the ghost of Straightwhig is disquieted, and " walks " in obscure places, by graveyards, " haunting " some houses.   Nay, the Northern mother rises from the grave: perhaps the Northern father is not dead, but only sleeping, like Barbarossa in that other fable, with his Sharp's rifle for a pillow. Who knows but he, too, will " rise," and execute his own will? The history may yet end after the old sort: —

> " And now the heavy wrath of God
>   Upon the uncle fell;
> Yea, fearful fiends did haunt his house;
>   His conscience felt a hell.
> His barns were fired, his goods consumed,
>   His lands were barren made;
> Conventions failed to nominate;
>   No office with him staid."

Kansas applies for admission as a free State, with a constitution made in due form and by the people. The regressive force is determined that she shall be a slave State; and so all the 926,000 miles of territory become the spoil of the slaveholder. See the state of things.

The majority of the Senate is pro-slavery, of the satanic democracy. For once, the House inclines the other way,— leans towards freedom. A bill for making Kansas a slave State will pass the Senate; will be resisted in the House: then comes the tug of war. The North has a majority in the House, but it is divided. If all will unite, they make Kansas a free State before the 4th of next July. They can force the administration to this act of justice, simply by refusing to vote a dollar of money until Kansas is free. If the House will determine on that course, the two executives — the presidential and the senatorial — will soon come to terms. This is no new expedient: it was often enough resorted to by our fathers in old England, under the Tudors and Stuarts; nay, even the Dutch used it against Philip II.

But perhaps there is not virtue enough in the House to do this; then let the State legislatures which are now in session send instructions, the people — who are always in session — petitions, to that effect.

But perhaps the people themselves are not quite ready for this measure; and the House and Senate cannot agree. Then the question goes over to the next presidential election, where it will be the most important element. There will be three candidates, perhaps four; for the straight Whigs may put up some invertebrate politician, hoping to catch whatever shall " turn up." It is possible there shall be no choice by the people; then the election goes to the present House of Representatives, where the choice is by States. In either case, if the matter be managed well, the progressive force of America may get into the presidential chair. I mean to say, we can choose an *anti-slavery President next autumn,*— some one who loves man and God, not merely money, loaves and fishes,— who will counsel and work for the present welfare and future progress of America, and so promote that Christianity and democracy spoken of before. I shall not pretend to say who the man is: it must be some one who reverences JUSTICE,— the higher law of God. He must be a strong man, a just man, a man *sure for the right.* Let there be no humbug this time, no doubtful man.

If we once put an anti-slavery man, never so moderate, into the Presidency, then see what follows immediately or at length: —

1. The Executive holds 40,000 offices in his right hand, and 70,000,000 annual dollars in his left hand: both will be dispensed so as to promote the welfare and the prosperity of the people. All the great offices, executive, judicial, diplomatic, commercial, will be con-

trolled by the progressive force; the administration will be celestial-democratic, not satanic merely, and seek by natural justice to organize things and persons so that all may have a share in labor and government. Then, when freedom has money and office to bestow, she will become respectable in the South, where noble men, slaveholders and non-slaveholders, will come out of their hiding-places to bless their land which others have cursed so heavily and so long. There are anti-slavery elements at the South: " One swallow makes no summer; " but one presidential summer of freedom will bring many swallows out from their wintry sleep, fabulous or real. Nay, the *ignorant* men of the North will be instructed; her *mean* men will be attracted by the smell of dinner; and her *base* men, left alone in their rot, will engage in other crime, but not in kidnapping men.

2. Kansas becomes a free State before the 1st of January, 1858. Nebraska, Oregon, Washington, Utah, New Mexico, all will be free States. When Texas sends down a pendulous branch, which takes independent root, a tree of freedom will grow up therefrom. Western Texas will ere long be a free State; she is half ready now. Freedom will be organized in the Mesilla Valley. If we acquire new territory from Mexico, it will be honestly got, and democracy and Christianity spread thither. If Central America, Nicaragua, or other new soil, become ours, it will be all consecrated to freedom, and the inalienable rights of man. Slavery will be abolished in the District of Columbia.

3. There will be no more national attempts to destroy freedom in the North, but continual efforts to restrict slavery. The democratic parts of the Consti-

tution, long left a dead letter therein, will be developed, and the despotic clauses, exceptionable there, and clearly hostile to its purpose and its spirit, will be overruled, and forced out of sight, like odious features of the British common law. There will be a Pacific railroad, perhaps more than one; and national attempts will be made to develop the national resources of the continent by free labor. The South will share with the North in this better organization of things and persons, this development of industry and education.

4. And what will be the future of Kansas? Her 114,000 square miles will soon fill up with educated and industrious men, each sharing the labor and the government of society, helping forward the welfare and the progress of all, aiding the organization of Christianity and democracy. What a development there will be of agriculture, mining, manufactures, commerce! What farms and shops! What canals and railroads! What schools, newspapers, libraries, meeting-houses! Yes, what families of rich, educated, happy, and religious men and women! In the year 1900, there will be 2,000,000 men in Kansas, with cities like Providence, Worcester, perhaps like Chicago and Cincinnati. She will have more miles of railroad than Maryland, Virginia, and both the Carolinas can now boast. Her land will be worth $20 an acre, and her total wealth will be $500,000,000 of money; 600,-000 children will learn in her schools.

5. There will be a ring of freedom all round the slave States, and in them slavery itself will decline. The theory of bondage will be given up, like the theory of theocracy and monarchy; and attempts will be made to get rid of the fact. Then the North will help the

Southern States in that noble work. There will never be another slave State nor another slave President; no more kidnapping in the North; no more chains round the court-house in Boston; no more preaching against the first principles of all humanity.

Three hundred years ago, our fathers in Europe were contending for liberty. Then it was freedom of conscience which the progressive force of the people demanded. Julius the Third had just been pope, who gave the cardinalship, vacated at his election, to the keeper of his monkeys; and Paul IV. sat in his stead in St. Peter's chair, and represented in general for all Europe the regressive power; while Bloody Mary and bloodier Philip sat on England's throne, and, incited thereto by the pontiff, smote at the rights of man.

Two hundred years ago, our fathers in the two Englands — old and new — did grim battle against monarchic despotism: one Charles slept in his bloody grave, another wandered through the elegant debaucheries of the Continent; while Cromwell and Milton made liberal England abidingly famous and happy.

One hundred years ago, other great battling for the rights of man was getting begun. Ah me! the long-continued strife is not ended. The question laid over by our fathers is adjourned to us for settlement. It is the old question between the substance of man and his accidents, labor and capital, the people and a caste.

Shall the 350,000 slaveholders own all the 1,400,000 square miles of territory not yet made States, and drive all Northern men away from it, or shall it belong to the people; shall this vast area be like Arkansas and South Carolina, or like Michigan and Connecticut? That is the *immediate* question.

Shall slavery spread over all the United States, and root out freedom from the land? or shall freedom spread wide her blessed boughs till the whole continent is fed by her fruit, and lodged beneath her arms — her very leaves for the healing of the nations? That is the *ultimate* question.

Now is the time for America to choose between these two alternatives, and choose quick. For America? No, for the North. You and I are to decide this mighty question. I take it, the Anglo-Saxon will not forego his ethnological instinct for freedom; will not now break the historic habit of two thousand years; he will progressively tend to Christianity and democracy; will put slavery down, peaceably if he can, forcibly if he must.

We may now end this crime against humanity by ballots; wait a little, and only with swords and with blood can this deep and widening blot of shame be scoured out from the continent. No election, since that first and unopposed of Washington, has been so important to America as this now before us. Once the nation chose between Aaron Burr and Thomas Jefferson. When the choice is between slavery and freedom, will the North choose wrong? Any railroad company may, by accident, elect a knave for President; but when he has been convicted of squandering their substance on himself, and blowing up their engines, nay, destroying their sons and daughters, will the stockholders choose a swindler for ever?

I think we shall put slavery down; I have small doubt of that. But shall we do it now and without tumult, or by and by with a dreadful revolution, San Domingo massacres, and the ghastly work of war?

Shall America decide for wickedness,— extend the

dark places of the earth, filled up yet fuller with the habitations of cruelty? Then our ruin is certain,— is also just. The power of self-rule, which we were not fit for, will pass from our hands, and the halter of vengeance will gripe our neck, and America shall lie there on the shore of the sea, one other victim who died as the fool dieth. What a ruin it would be! Come away! I cannot look, even in fancy, on so foul a sight.

If we decide for the inalienable rights of man; for present welfare, future progress; for Christianity and democracy; and so organize things and men that all may share the labor and government of society — then what a prospect is before us! How populous, how rich, will the land become! Ere long her borders wide will embrace the hemisphere — how full of men! If we are faithful to our duty, one day, America, youngest of nations, shall sit on the Cordilleras, the youthful mother of the continent of States. Behind her are the Northern lakes, the Northern forest bounded by Arctic ice and snow; on her left hand swells the Atlantic, the Pacific on her right — both beautiful with the white lilies of commerce, giving fragrance all round the world; while before her spreads out the Southern land, from terra firma to the isles of fire, blessed with the Saxon mind and conscience, heart and soul; and underneath her eye, into the lap of the hemisphere, the Amazon and the Mississippi — classic rivers of freedom — pour the riches of either continent; and behind her, before her, on either hand, all round, and underneath her eye, extends the new world of humanity, the commonwealth of the people, justice, the law thereof, and infinite perfection, God; a Church without a bishop, a State without a king, a community without a lord, a family with no holder of slaves; with welfare for the present, and progress for the future, she will show the nations how divine a thing a people can be made.

> " Oh, well for him whose will is strong!
> He suffers, but he will not suffer long;
> He suffers, but he cannot suffer wrong:
> For him nor moves the loud world's random mock,
> Nor all calamity's hugest waves confound,
> Who seems a promontory of rock,
> That, compassed round with turbulent sound,
> In middle ocean meets the surging shock,
> Tempest-buffeted, citadel-crown'd."